The 70's

The Hits and the Trivia

by

Ted Yates

CG Publishing Inc

We acknowledge the financial support of the Government of Canada through the Book Publishing Industry Development Program for our publishing activities.
Published by Collector's Guide Publishing Inc., Box 62034, Burlington, Ontario, Canada, L7R 4K2
Printed and bound in Canada
The 70's The Hits and the Trivia / Ted Yates © 2011 CG Publishing Inc/Ted Yates ISBN 9781-926592-24-4

The 70's

The Hits and the Trivia

by

Ted Yates

Acknowledgements

First of all, I would like to thank my family and friends.

I would like to thank my mother Patricia for encouraging me through the years and allowing me to play the 60's and 70's music as loud as I wanted, downstairs in the Rec room which my late father John W. built during my teen years.

My sons Ted Jr. and James will hopefully enjoy this music of another era and will appreciate what the 70's gave us musically. My brother Mike and sisters Pat and Jackie were there when we grew up as one happy family growing up in Toronto with the hits of the 60's and 70's playing on our radios and record players.

I would like to acknowledge my friends who share the love of the music of the 70's including Rob Muir, Sheldon Frymerman, Burt Thombs, Roger Ashby, Peter Murray, Jeff Paul, Nevin Grant, Douglas Roy, Don Hetherington, Wayne Mahoney, Janet James Penfold, Jack Peets , Peter Grodde, Phil Warnell and Wolf Schimanski and the many others, including the ones I work with on a daily basis.

Thank you to all the great singers, songwriters and producers of the hits from this exciting decade.Please search and purchase your favorite hits of the 70's now that you'll know what you're looking for. Thanks to all the Record Companies/labels including Capitol, Atlantic, London, Atco, Laurie, MGM, Epic, RCA, Fantasy, Bang, Decca, Uni, Motown, Apple, Columbia, Dot, Electra, Philips, Polydor, Mercury, Dunhill, Monument, Pye, ABC, Date, United Artists, Kama Sutra, Roulette, Stax, A & M, Deram, Fontana, Buddah, Reprise, Liberty, Parrot, Smash, Soul City, Imperial, Cadet, Sceptor and all the others.

I would like to thank Robert Godwin of CG Publishing for all his advice and answers to my many questions and to Ric Connors who is great at what he does with marketing and promotion.

Also, thanks to everyone who buys this book and my book 'The 60's The Hits and The Trivia'.

Contents

Page Chart For Lists By Year

Charts	1970	1971	1972	1973	1974	1975	1976	1977	1978	1979
Top 17 Albums	34	80	113	144	177	219	250	280	316	344
Top Country Hits	35	81	114	145	178	220	251	281	317	345
Top Soul & R&B Hits	36	83	115	146	-	-	-	-	-	-
Top Disco Hits	-	-	-	-	179	221	252	282	318	346
Top One Hit Wonders	37	82	116	147	180	222	253	283	319	347
Top Rock Hits	38	84	117	148	181	223	254	284	320	348
Top Lost 45's	39	85	118	149	182	224	255	285	321	349

INTRODUCTION By Ted Yates

For me, 70's music was an extension of the 60's. During the early 70's, I was still living in Toronto, where I spent the first 21 years of my life. Like the 60's, the 70's was also a very exciting decade musically, with many sounds and changes. We began the first year of the decade with the break up of the most successful group of all time, The Beatles. We ended the decade with the death of disco music. In between, we had it all. There was so much variety and so many genres of music popular during the decade.

Think about it. We had Pop Rock with music artists which included Elton John, Paul McCartney and Wings, the Eagles, Doobie Brothers, Chicago, Billy Joel, and 3 Dog Night. We had Hard Rock with new music from Led Zeppelin, Deep Purple, The Who, Rolling Stones and Grand Funk. Soft Rock flourished from America, The Carpenters, Linda Ronstadt, Olivia Newton-John, Bread, Carole King, James Taylor, Jim Croce and Barry Manilow. Motown gave us many hits from the Jackson Five, Marvin Gaye, Diana Ross, Stevie Wonder and The Temptations. We also had great Soul/R & B from Aretha Franklin, Al Green, The Spinners, The O'Jays, Gladys Knight & The Pips and others. How about Glam Rock? Leaders in that genre included David Bowie, Queen, Kiss, Alice Cooper and Rod Stewart. Pop Country was at its peak during the 70's with mega hits from artists like Kenny Rogers, John Denver, Dolly Parton, Glen Campbell and Charlie Rich. We also had Southern Rock with Lynyrd Skynyrd, the Allman Brothers and the Atlanta Rhythm Section. And then of course, Disco, which many think of when you mention the 70's...the Bee Gees, Donna Summer, Village People, K.C. & The Sunshine Band. Could we possibly have more variety in music than what we had in the 70's? There were many surprises during the 70's and lots of One Hit Wonders and Novelty Hits too.

In the 70's The Beach Boys, Four Seasons, Elvis Presley and Rick Nelson still managed to chart hits after their 60's heyday.

It's all here in one incredible book with almost 2,000 hits with trivia and fascinating facts. Between every incredible and memorable year, you will see unique features and lists about the hits and artists of the 70's.

Like 'The 60's The Hits and The Trivia', I wrote a book that a music lover like me would want to read. You can pick it up and start at any page. It's filled with fun and entertaining information that will take you back.

We connect the music with the good times. The emotional attachment with the music we grew up with, will usually last a lifetime. In a world where the only constant is change, (and it's not always for the better) it is nice to know that you can return to the comfort zone whenever you wish. As you read through this book, you will see many great songs you remember, and some you may have forgotten about. It's a great source to find and rediscover the songs you'll want to acquire again

The 70's… bring it on…it's all here in one book and it's yours for a lifetime!

I have compiled the 70's lists from various sources and influences. The ranking of the 70's lists is based on a combination of chart success on Billboard Pop Charts, RPM (Canada) charts and U.K. charts. The ranking of the 70's hit lists is also influenced by the hits appeal, sales and exposure (sometimes in later years) on radio airplay, films, TV shows and various other media outlets.

♫ This was the Beatles final hit, although only 2 were present on the recording of this chart topper.

♫ The writer of this number one hit by 3 Dog Night later went on to write songs for dozens of successful movies.

♫ This hit by the Hollies featured a then-unknown Elton John on piano.

♫ This studio group from Britain had 4 hits in 1970 all under different names

♫ The 2 main members of this British band both committed suicide

♫ This hit song was about a 'she' that turned out to be a 'he'.

FIND OUT THAT… AND MUCH MORE INSIDE…1971!

The Top 170 Hits of 1970

1. Bridge Over Troubled Water by Simon and Garfunkel was written by Paul Simon in the summer of '69. When Paul Simon asked Art Garfunkel if he would like to sing lead on it, although hesitant at first, Art agreed. Apparently Paul Simon later regretted not singing lead on what would become a Grammy Award Winning Song, and their biggest hit of all time.

2. My Sweet Lord by George Harrison was not only his first solo hit, but the first single from his triple album "All Things Must Pass". 'My Sweet Lord', which was primarily about Hindu God Krishna, was originally intended for his musical friend and buddy to the Beatles, Billy Preston. Following the song's release, musical similarities between 'My Sweet Lord' and the Chiffons' hit 'He's So Fine' led to a lengthy legal battle. George Harrison was found to have unintentionally copied the earlier song. The 'B' side of the single in North America was 'Isn't It A Pity'.

3. I'll Be There by The Jackson 5 was the 4th consecutive number one hit from their debut year, 1970. 'I'll Be There', the biggest of all four of their million sellers from 1970, was also their first ballad. This multi-week number one hit was produced and co-written by Hal Davis.

4. Close To You by The Carpenters was the very first hit for the brother and sister duo consisting of Karen and Richard Carpenter. Karen was not only the lead singer, but also the drummer for this soft rock 70's duo. This number one million seller was written by Burt Bacharach and Hal David and was originally intended for Herb Alpert, the co-founder of A & M Records, the Carpenters' record label

5. Let It Be by The Beatles was written by Paul McCartney for his late mother Mary, although many have interpreted the 'Mother Mary' in the song in a religious light. This single featured Paul on lead vocals and piano, John on Bass and Billy Preston on organ.

6. American Woman was the most successful hit ever from the Guess Who, a Canadian Rock Band from Winnipeg, Manitoba which featured Burton Cummings on lead vocals. The song originated as something that was improvised to 'liven up' the crowd during a concert. Burton Cummings made up the lyrics as he was going along. The flip side of this double-sided hit single was 'No Sugar Tonight'.

7. Raindrops Keep Fallin' on My Head by B. J. Thomas was an Academy Award Winning Song written by Burt Bacharach and Hal David. The song was featured in the film 'Butch Cassidy and the Sundance Kid' which starred Paul Newman and Robert Redford.

8. I Think I Love You by The Partridge Family was the first and biggest hit for the TV family act which featured David Cassidy and his real-life stepmother, Shirley Jones. This hit reached number one in the fall when The Partridge Family made its debut on prime time television.

9. Ain't No Mountain High Enough was the first solo number one hit for Diana Ross, the lead singer of the most successful girl group in pop music history, the Supremes. Her remake of the 1967 hit by Marvin Gaye and Tammi Terrell was a slower version complete with a spoken word introduction. The album version of this hit was over 6 minutes long, while the single version checked in at a little over 3 minutes.

10.   War by Edwin Starr was a powerful social comment Motown hit written by Barrett Strong and Norman Whitfield and was originally a Temptations album cut. When it was released as a single by Edwin Starr, it got immediate response and climbed quickly to the number one spot on the charts. He won a Grammy Award for Best Male, R & B vocal performance for 'War'.

11. The Long and Winding Road by The Beatles was produced by Phil Spector. It was the Beatles 20th and final number one hit. Only two Beatles were present in the studio for the recording of this song. Paul wrote and sang a solo vocal and John played bass. Much to Paul's disappointment, Spector later added strings and a choir, without McCartney's approval. The 'B' side of this single was 'For You Blue' which featured George on lead vocals and acoustic guitar. John Lennon was featured on steel guitar while Paul played piano.

12. I Want You Back by The Jackson 5 became their claim to fame and first number one hit. An 11-year old Michael Jackson was the lead singer on this million seller. Motown boss Berry Gordy Jr. signed this family act from Gary, Indiana at the suggestion of superstar Diana Ross. Originally this song was titled 'I Wanna Be Free' and was intended for Gladys Knight & The Pips. Co-writer/producer Deke Richards suggested to Berry Gordy that Diana Ross should record it, but Gordy wanted his new act instead, and with the new title 'I Want You Back'.

13.   The Tears of a Clown by Smokey Robinson & The Miracles was actually the first official number one hit for this legendary Motown group, 10 years after they peaked at number 2 with 'Shop Around'. Stevie Wonder co-wrote this hit which featured the sound of a calliope in the instrumentation of the song. This reminded Smokey Robinson of Pagliacci the clown and he wrote new lyrics based on the theme.

14.   **Cracklin' Rosie** by Neil Diamond was not a song about a girl. The song was inspired by a story Neil Diamond heard while visiting Canada. He met a medical missionary who related the tale about men who could not find a woman to be with for the night. They would buy a bottle of Rose wine and the bottle of wine would be their companion for the evening.

15.   **Venus** by The Shocking Blue reached the top of the charts for this one hit wonder group from Holland. What's amazing is the fact that lead singer Mariska Veras could not speak a word of English, therefore she learned how to sing this million selling number one hit phonetically!

16.   **Thank You (Falettinme Be Mice Elf Agin)** by Sly & the Family Stone was a progressive, psychedelic soul hit which featured the double-sided hit ballad 'Everybody Is a Star' on the 'B' side.

17.   **Everything Is Beautiful** by Ray Stevens was something completely different for the master of wild and wacky novelty hits. To underscore the optimism of 'Everything Is Beautiful', Ray Stevens took a portable tape recorder to his daughter's school. His youngest daughter was in kindergarten, and she was excused to join her sister's second grade class in the school auditorium where the children sang the chorus. It topped the charts in the spring of 1970.

18.   **Make It With You** by Bread was the first and biggest hit for this soft rock group fronted by singer/ songwriter David Gates. Although this was his first hit as a singer, he was successful as a songwriter in the 60's; particularly with writing the top ten hit 'Popsicles and Icicles' for The Murmaids.

19.   **ABC** by The Jackson 5 proved that they were no one hit wonders as their second consecutive single release rose quickly to the number one position. This bubblegum Motown hit was co-written and co-produced (along with Berry Gordy Jr. and two others) by Freddie Perren, a former school teacher who knew about the A B C's. This million seller replaced the Beatles 'Let It Be' at number one, and many years later, Michael Jackson would own the rights to their music.

20.   **Mama Told Me (Not to Come)** by 3 Dog Night was written by Randy Newman, who later went on to write dozens of successful movie scores. This was the first of 3 official number one hits for 3 Dog Night.

21.   **We've Only Just Begun** by The Carpenters was the very successful follow up to their first and biggest hit, (They Long To Be) 'Close To You'. Although this Paul Williams-penned hit peaked at only number two, it became a standard as the first song at weddings for many years to come.

22.   **Which Way You Going Billy** was a hit by The Poppy Family, a Canadian duo consisting of the husband and wife team of Susan and Terry Jacks. This was the first of a string of hits for The Poppy Family, before they each went their own way personally and professionally. Terry Jacks later had a multi-million seller in 1974 with 'Seasons in the Sun'.

23.   **Lookin' Out My Back Door** by C.C.R. was written by John Fogerty for his young son Josh. It was inspired by the parade in the book 'To Think I Saw It on Mulberry Hill' which Fogerty read as a child. The 'B' side of this single was the popular ballad 'Long as I Can See the Light'.

24.   Spirit in the Sky by Norman Greenbaum sold about 2 million copies and continues to be heard everyday on Oldies stations everywhere. Some called Spirit in the Sky 'psychedelic Jesus Rock'. After his music career slowed down, he went into the dairy business and with several dozen goats, marketed the 'Velvet Acres Goat Milk' business in Health Stores in California with his wife.

25.   Band of Gold was a million seller for Freda Payne, a soul singer from Detroit. Motown session player Dennis Coffey supplied the distinctive sounding guitar on this catchy hit. Coffey had an instrumental hit of his own the following year with 'Scorpio'.

26.   One Less Bell to Answer by the 5th Dimension was written by Burt Bacharach and Hal David and featured Marilyn McCoo on lead vocals. It was popular the year after she married Billy Davis Junior of the 5th Dimension.

27.   Travelin' Band/Who'll Stop the Rain by C.C.R. was another double-sided hit single for the legendary group which failed to have an official number one hit, despite huge success. 'Travelin' Band' was a lightning-fast hit delivered by John Fogerty which also caught the ear of the owners of the copyright of Little Richard's 'Good Golly Miss Molly' who claimed the group had stolen the song. A lawsuit was filed and Fantasy Records settled it by buying the song from Venice Music. The 'B' side of this single was the equally popular 'Who'll Stop the Rain'.

28.   Hey There Lonely Girl by Eddie Holman was the only hit for this falsetto-voiced singer from Norfolk, Virginia. The song was originally recorded by Ruby & the Romantics as 'Hey There Lonely Boy' in 1963. Eddie Holman is now an ordained Baptist Minister.

29.   The Love You Save was the 3rd consecutive number one hit for The Jackson 5 in their dynamic debut year. It was obvious that pre-teen Michael Jackson, the group's lead singer was the star. This energetic million seller was a song about a girl who was a little too fast for her age. The songwriting credits were listed as 'The Corporation', although it was written by Freddie Perren, Fonce Mizell, Deke Richards and Berry Gordy Jr, the same as many of their previous chart toppers.

30.   The Rapper by The Jaggerz featured Donnie Iris on lead vocals. He later had a solo hit in 1981 with 'Ah Leah'. The name 'Jaggerz' was inspired by Mick Jagger of the Rolling Stones. 'The Rapper', which peaked at number two on the charts, was their only top 40 hit.

31.   Vehicle by The Ides of March featured the powerful voice of Jim Peterik on lead vocals. The Ides of March formed while in High School in Chicago and were named after a line in Shakespeare's 'Julius Caesar'. Although this was the only hit for the Ides of March, Peterik resurfaced in the 80's as the keyboardist of Survivor, best known for their number one hit 'Eye of the Tiger'.

14

**32.	Spill The Wine** was something completely different for Eric Burdon, the former lead singer of The Animals. This funky, Latin beat hit was the first chart hit for the group War, before they went on to have a successful string of hits on their own. This unusual and unique pop hit also features a woman in the background speaking Spanish to Eric Burdon.

**33.	Candida** by Dawn featured Tony Orlando on lead vocals. When this first 'Dawn' hit was recorded, there was not yet such a group. Therefore, session singers and musicians were featured on a recording of a group that didn't even exist. They included Jay Siegel of the Tokens and Toni Wine, who co-wrote 'Candida'. Hank Medress and The Tokens produced this and other hits by Tony Orlando and Dawn. It wasn't until after this hit, that Tony Orlando met Thelma Hopkins and Joyce Vincent Wilson, who became the backing group 'Dawn'.

**34.	Gypsy Woman** by Brian Hyland was produced by Del Shannon. This remake of the Impressions song from the 60's became Brian Hyland's final top 30 hit.

**35.	In The Summertime** by Mungo Jerry was the only hit in North America for this British Skiffle quartet led by singer/songwriter Ray Dorset.

**36.	Whole Lotta Love** by Led Zeppelin was their first major hit. This progressive recording featured the unique vocals of Robert Plant supported by the guitarist-producer Jimmy Page, bass guitarist John Paul Jones and drummer John Bonham. Some of the lyrics of 'Whole Lotta Love' were borrowed by Robert Plant from the early 60's song 'You Need Love' by Willie Dixon. In 2009, it was named the 3rd greatest Rock song of all time by VH1. The 'B' side of this single was the popular 'Living Loving Maid'.

**37.	Give Me Just A Little More Time** by The Chairman of the Board featured the distinctive lead vocals of 'General' Norman Johnson who fronted the group 'The Showmen' of 'It Will Stand' fame in the early 60's. This was the first and biggest hit for this Detroit Soul group. Although Ron Dunbar is listed as the composer, it was actually written and produced by Holland/Dozier/Holland after leaving Motown while legal proceedings were still in the works.

**38.	Cecilia** by Simon & Garfunkel was their second single release from the album 'Bridge over Troubled Water'. This goodtime, up tempo hit was a rarity for the top pop folk duo of the 60's. There was much tension between the two during the recording of this album and Simon and Garfunkel went their separate ways after the recording was complete.

**39.	Green Eyed Lady** by Sugarloaf was a hit that was certainly ahead of its time with its intricate production and instrumentation. This Denver based rock quartet was fronted by lead singer/ songwriter/keyboardist Jerry Corbetta. The U.S. single of this hit was a little over 3 and a half minutes, while the single released on the Liberty label in Canada of 'Green Eyed Lady' was almost 6 minutes long.

**40.	Fire And Rain** by James Taylor was an autobiographical song about a difficult time in his life when he spent time in a mental institution. This was the first of many major hits for this singer/songwriter from Boston.

41.   **Instant Karma** was John Lennon's first million selling single. Some of the musical guests featured on this recording included George Harrison on guitar, Billy Preston on organ, Klaus Voorman on bass, Andy White on drums and Mal Evans on claps and chimes.

42.   **Love on a Two Way Street** by The Moments was produced and co-written by Sylvia Robinson, who had a million selling solo hit 3 years later with 'Pillow Talk' as simply 'Sylvia'. Although this was the only notable hit by the Moments, they emerged 10 years later as 'Ray, Goodman and Brown' with the Top 10 hit 'Special Lady'.

43.   **Ride Captain Ride** was the only hit for Blues Image, a Florida – based Rock Quintet. They were the House band of 'Thee Image', a South Florida hotspot where 'Cream', 'The Grateful Dead' and 'Blood, Sweat & Tears' once played.

44.   **Get Ready** by Rare Earth was a remake of The Temptations hit from 1966.4 years later, Rare Earth became the first big hit-making act signed by Motown that consisted of only white members. Rare Earth's 1970 version charted even higher than the original version by the Temptations.

45.   **Rainy Night in Georgia** by Brook Benton was written by Tony Joe White, the Louisiana swamp rock singer/songwriter who gave us Polk Salad Annie' in 1969. 'Rainy Night in Georgia' became the final major hit for Brook Benton who achieved many hits during the late 50's and early 60's.

46.   **Signed, Sealed, Delivered, I'm Yours** by Stevie Wonder was popular the year he married singer Syreeta Wright, who also co-write and sang backup on this Motown classic. Their marriage lasted until 1972.This was the first hit single produced by Stevie Wonder and also marked the first time he was nominated for a Grammy Award.

47.   **Hitchin' A Ride** by Britain's Vanity Fare was written by Mitch Murray and Peter Callander, who were also responsible for composing hits which included 'Billy, Don't Be A Hero', 'The Night Chicago Died' and 'The Ballad Of Bonnie and Clyde'. Years after their hit record days, Vanity Fare's guitarist Tony Goulden became mayor of Medway Towns in England, keyboard player Barry Landeman became a school teacher, Tony Jarett, the bass player, became a Carpenter and lead singer Trevor Brice, settled in Denmark, where he continued to perform, write and record.

48.   **Love Grows (Where My Rosemary Goes)** by Edison Lighthouse was the only hit for this British studio group which featured Tony Burrows on lead vocals. He also supplied vocals on the biggest hits by 'The White Plains', 'Brotherhood Of Man', 'The Pipkins' and 'First Class'.

49.   **Don't Cry Daddy** by Elvis Presley was released at the end of 1969, the 6th of 6 top 40 hits during the King's comeback year of 1969. This hit peaked in January of 1970 and was the second Elvis hit written by Mac Davis following the social comment hit 'In the Ghetto'.

50.   **All Right Now** was the only notable hit by the British group known as 'Free', although some of the members resurfaced in the group Bad Company. 'Free' guitarist Paul Kossoff died of drug related problems in 1976. Lead singer Paul Rodgers and drummer Simon Kirke formed Bad Company.

51.   **Ball of Confusion** by The Temptations was a hard hitting social comment hit written and produced by Motown's Norman Whitfield and Barrett Strong. They gave the Temptations a more progressive, psychedelic soul sound which was far removed from the previous mellow, harmonizing Motown sound they were known for during the mid 60's.

52.   **Patches** by Clarence Carter was a top 5 hit in the summer of 1970 for this blind soul singer from Alabama. Clarence Carter did not write the story song 'Patches', but with the opening line, 'I was born and raised down in Alabama', you would think it was. It was originally recorded by the Chairman of the Board as a 'B' side and was co-written by lead singer 'General' Norman Johnson, but it was Clarence Carter who made it a million seller.

53.   **Black Magic Woman** by Santana was a prime cut from their critically acclaimed album, 'Abraxas'. It was Santana's second consecutive top ten hit and like 'Evil Ways', featured group member Gregg Rolie on lead vocals. The song was written by Peter Green and was originally recorded by Fleetwood Mac in 1969 with limited success.

54.   **Turn Back the Hands of Time** was the highest charting pop hit for soul singer Tyrone Davis. This million selling hit also reached number one on the R & B charts. Tyrone Davis died in 2005 at the age of 66 from complications from a stroke he suffered the year before. He was married to his wife Ann for over 40 years.

55.   **Up Around the Bend** by Creedence Clearwater Revival. was an energetic rock song with a prominent guitar intro from John Fogerty, the group's lead singer, guitarist, producer and songwriter. This song and its popular 'B' side, 'Run Through the Jungle' were both included on C.C.R.'s 'Cosmo's Factory' album.

56.   **25 Or 6 To 4** by Chicago featured Peter Cetera on lead vocals. It was Chicago's second hit following 'Make Me Smile', the brass rock group's debut single. This Robert Lamm – penned hit ran 4:50 as an album cut and under 3 minutes on the single.

57.   **Indiana Wants Me** was the first major hit for Toronto singer/songwriter R. Dean Taylor who recorded on the 'Rare Earth' label, a subsidiary of Motown records. R. Dean Taylor previously co-wrote 'Love Child' and "I'm Livin' in Shame" for The Supremes and 'All I Need' for The Temptations.

58.   **No Time** by The Guess Who was composed by lead singer Burton Cummings and Guitarist Randy Bachman. This million seller was popular at the beginning of 1970, just before their biggest hit of all time 'American Woman' was released.

59.   **Ma Belle Amie** was the only hit for Holland's The Tee Set, who were

17

part of the Dutch Mini Music Invasion in 1970, along with The Shocking Blue and The George Baker Selection. All three hits appeared on the 'Colossus' record label in early 1970.

60.   Julie Do Ya Love Me by Bobby Sherman was the final official top ten hit for this popular teen idol. He not only appeared regularly on the covers of teen magazines, and on radio, but starred in the series 'Here Comes the Brides' for two years, until its run ended in April of 1970.

61.   Lay Down (Candles in the Rain) was the first major hit for the singer/ songwriter from Queens, New York known as Melanie. On this top ten hit, Melanie Safka was backed by The Edwin Hawkins Singers, who had a top ten hit of their own in 1969 with 'Oh Happy Day'.

62.   Love Or Let Me Be Lonely by The Friends of Distinction was the 3rd and final hit for this 2 man, 2 woman vocal group from Los Angeles discovered by the great Cleveland Brown's running back Jim Brown.

63.   He Ain't Heavy, He's My Brother by The Hollies featured a then-unknown Elton John on piano. Allan Clarke was featured on lead vocals on this powerful and emotional hit.

64.   Come And Get It by Badfinger was written by Paul McCartney and featured in the film 'The Magic Christian' which starred Ringo Starr and Peter Sellers. This was the first hit for Badfinger after changing their name from The Iveys. Both groups recorded on the Beatles 'Apple' label.

65.   I'll Never Fall In Love Again by Dionne Warwick was yet another top ten hit written by Burt Bacharach and Hal David, the composers of every hit she achieved during the 60's as she entered 1970.

66.   Tighter, Tighter by Alive and Kicking was co-written and produced by Tommy James. This one hit wonder group from New York City also recorded on the Roulette Record Label which produced all of the hits of Tommy James and the Shondells. Originally he was considering having 'Alive and Kicking' record 'Crystal Blue Persuasion', but he liked it so much that he decided to record it himself. He then wrote 'Tighter Tighter' for them.

67.   Snowbird by Anne Murray was the first major hit for the former school teacher from Springhill, Nova Scotia, Canada. 'Snowbird' was written by Gene McLellan, who also wrote 'Put Your Hand in the Hand' for Ocean.

68.   O-O-H Child was the only hit for the Five Stairsteps, a family act from Chicago produced by Curtis Mayfield. The Burke family group consisted of four brothers and one sister. The flip side of this single was a cover of the Beatles 'Dear Prudence' which was a minor hit for this one hit wonder act.

69.   Easy Come, Easy Go by Bobby Sherman was his 3rd consecutive top 10 million seller following 'Little Woman' and 'La La La' (If I Had You) from 1969. Although he was a regular on the 'Shindig' music show in the mid 60's, his teen idol hit recording days arrived later and lasted the two years 1969 to 1971.

70.   Montego Bay was the only hit for Bobby Bloom, who died of an accidental shooting in 1974. Montego Bay, co-written and produced by Jeff Barry, was Bobby Bloom's only hit as a singer, but as a writer, he co-wrote the classic 'Mony Mony' by Tommy James and the Shondells and the Staple Singers' hit 'Heavy Makes You Happy'.

71.   Arizona by Mark Lindsay was the first and biggest solo hit for the lead singer on all the hits of Paul Revere and The Raiders. He also co-wrote and produced their hits from 1968 to 1969.

72.   The Wonder of You by Elvis Presley was recorded 'live' in Las Vegas. This song was originally a hit for Ray Petersen in 1959. The 'B' side of this single was 'Mama Liked the Roses' a well-received heart-warming ballad by the King.

73.   House of the Rising Sun by Frigid Pink was a progressive version of the hit The Animals brought to the top of the charts during the British Music Invasion in 1964. Kelly Green was the lead singer of this 4 man rock band from Detroit.

74.   Without Love (There Is Nothing) by Tom Jones was a remake of an R & B song popular in the late 50's by Clyde McPhatter and in the early 60's for Ray Charles. Tom Jones had a steady string of hits during this time period when he also had his own prime time Variety TV Show.

75.   (I Know) I'm Losing You by Rare Earth was the second consecutive top 10 hit for this Detroit group. It was also the second straight successful remake of a Temptations hit from the late 60's.This one had a psychedelic echo introduction followed by progressive guitars, drums and upfront vocals by drummer/lead singer Pete Rivera.

76.   Does Anybody Really Know What Time It Is by Chicago was their 3rd consecutive top 10 hit in their debut year on the pop charts. This social comment hit was written by Robert Lamm, who also sang lead. It's interesting to note that their first 3 top 10 hits each had different lead singers with Terry Kath on lead on 'Make Me Smile' while Peter Cetera sang lead on '25 Or 6 To 4'.

77.   The Letter by Joe Cocker was his 'live' concert remake of the Box Tops hit which topped the charts in 1967.Keyboardist Leon Russell was one of the featured musicians on this recording. This was actually Joe Cocker's first official top 10 hit in North America, although he had previous success with the Beatles' songs 'With A Little Help From My Friends' and 'She Came In Through The Bathroom Window'.

78.   Domino was Belfast, Ireland-born Van Morrison's first top ten hit since 'Brown Eyed Girl' 3 years earlier in 1967.'Domino' was the opening track of his album 'His band and The Street Choir' and was a perfect example of his 'blue-eyed soul' style.

79.   No Matter What by Badfinger featured one of pop/rock music's most memorable guitar intros. This great production was the first original Badfinger composition, written by Pete Ham, who delivered the lead vocals. This was the 2nd of 4 top 20 hits they recorded on the Beatles' Apple label. Sadly, the 2 main members of the group, Pete Ham and Tom Evans both committed suicide.

80.   **Didn't I (Blow Your Mind)** by The Delfonics was a smooth and mellow soul classic for this Philadelphia R & B vocal group. This hit won the Grammy Award for Best R & B Performance by a Group or Duo. Singer Major Harris joined this group the following year in 1971.

81.   **Make Me Smile** was the first of many hits for Chicago, a brass rock group produced by James William Guercio. 'Make Me Smile' was written by group member James Pankow and was an excerpt from the musical suite "Ballet for a Girl from Buchannon. The lead singer on this hit was Terry Kath, who died in 1978 after accidentally shooting himself in the head. The 'B' side of this single was the popular ballad 'Color My World', which also became the flip side of 'Beginnings' the following year.

82.   **Share The Land** by The Guess Who was their second consecutive social comment hit of 1970, immediately following 'Hand Me Down World'. 'Share The Land' was the Guess Who's 4th consecutive hit of 1970, and their 2nd without Randy Bachman.

83.   **Psychedelic Shack** by The Temptations was yet another successful psychedelic soul hit for the legendary Motown act. This Norman Whitfield/ Barrett Strong production featured the more progressive- sounding Temptations, complete with rock guitars and synthesizer sound effects. The 'B' side of this single was their version of 'That's The Way Love Is' which Marvin Gaye brought into the top 10 in 1969.

84.   **Evil Ways** by Santana was their first notable hit. When you think of the group Santana, you probably think of Carlos Santana, but it was Gregg Rolie who sang lead on 'Evil Ways' and the next two hits which followed, 'Black Magic Woman' and 'Oye Como Va'. Their manager, Bill Graham, who owned The Fillmore where they frequently played, insisted they record 'Evil Ways'.

85.   **Lola** by The Kinks was based on a real life experience by Record Producer Robert Wace who told the story of a 'she' that was a 'he' to Kinks front man and songwriter Ray Davies. Another fascinating fact about this hit was that because the BBC prohibits any sort of advertisements and originally the lyrics mentioned 'Coca Cola', the reference to Coke had to go. Ray Davies, on tour in the U.S., flew all the way back to Britain during a 24 hour break in the tour just to change one word, 'Coca Cola' to 'Cherry Cola'. It was then substituted in the song.

86.   **(If You Let Me Make Love to You Then) Why Can't I Touch You** by Ronnie Dyson was a top 10 hit in the summer of 1970. He played a lead in the Broadway musical 'Hair' and was prominently featured on the Soundtrack. Sadly, Dyson died at the age of 40 of heart failure complicated by chronic lung disease.

87.   **I Just Can't Help Believing** by B.J. Thomas was an easy-going song written by Barry Mann and Cynthia Weil. This was B. J. 's final top 10 hit of the 70's until 5 years later when (Hey Won't You Play) 'Another Somebody Done Somebody Wrong Song' reached number one.

88.   Reflections of My Life was the only North American hit for the Marmalade, even though this Scottish band were hugely successful in Britain. In the mid 60's they were popular in Scotland as the Gaylords. Their biggest hit in Britain was their 1968 version of the Beatles' 'Ob-La-Di-Ob-La-Da'.

89.   Woodstock by Crosby, Stills, Nash and Young was written by Joni Mitchell about the most celebrated outdoor rock concert of all time. Crosby, Stills, Nash along with their new member Neil Young, performed at Woodstock around 3am on what technically was the 4th day of this legendary 3 day festival.

90.   Somebody's Been Sleeping by 100 Proof Aged In Soul was a million seller for this one hit wonder soul group from Detroit. The song was inspired by the fairy tale 'Goldilocks and the Three Bears' and 'Jack and The Beanstalk' with the line 'Fe Fi Fo Fum'.

91.   Gimme Dat Ding by The Pipkins was another one hit wonder British studio group made up of many of the same members of Edison Lighthouse, The White Plains and the Brotherhood of Man. Tony Burrows, who sang lead on the above hits, did the low voice in this wild and wacky novelty hit. 'Gimme Dat Ding' was co-written by Albert Hammond who had a big hit of his own two years later with 'It Never Rains In Southern California'.

92.   Jingle Jangle by The Archie's, (a fictitious group based on the comic book characters for Don Kirshner's Saturday morning cartoon show), was written by Jeff Barry and Andy Kim. Studio singer/songwriter Toni Wine sang the 'Sing me sing me' lines while Ron Dante did the lead vocals in a falsetto voice, which sounded drastically different than his lead on 'Sugar Sugar' their multi-million seller from 1969.

93.   Don't Play That Song by Aretha Franklin was a remake of a hit Ben E. King had in 1962.It's interesting to note that the following year, 1971, Aretha had a top 5 hit with a remake of another Ben E. King classic, 'Spanish Harlem'.

94.   Lay A Little Lovin' on Me was the only hit for Robin McNamera, one of the original cast members of the Rock Musical 'Hair'. The 'Hair' cast members supplied the backing vocals on this happy go lucky hit co-written by Jeff Barry.

95.   It Don't Matter to Me by Bread was their follow up to their first and biggest hit 'Make It with You'. This ballad also featured the mellow side of writer/producer and lead singer, David Gates.

96.   Something's Burning by Kenny Rogers and The First Edition was written by Mac Davis. This song had a brilliant production that kept on building to the chorus. One line in the lyrics which stood out as unique were the words 'I kiss the sleep from your eyes'.

97.   Up The Ladder to the Roof by The Supremes was their first hit without Diana Ross. She left the popular girl group in late 1969 to pursue a solo career. This was the first Supremes hit to feature their new lead vocalist, Jean Terrell upfront. She was backed by Cindy Birdsong and the only original member of the Supremes, Mary Wilson. This was also the first Supremes hit since 1967's 'The Happening' which was listed as simply 'The Supremes' and not 'Diana Ross and the Supremes'.

98. **For The Good Times** by Ray Price was written by Kris Kristofferson. Although Ray Price placed over 80 hits on the Country charts, this was his only major hit on the pop charts during the rock era.

99. **5-10-15-20 (25 – 30 Years of Love)** was the only hit for the soul trio, The Presidents. They recorded on the 'Sussex' label, the same label Bill Withers, Jim Gold and The Gallery and Dennis Coffey had hits with in the early 70's.

100. **My Baby Loves Lovin'** by The White Plains was actually made up of most of the same British studio musicians who were also known as Edison Lighthouse and The Pipkins. Lead singer Tony Burrows was featured on all 3 recordings.

101. **Stoned Love** by The Supremes was the 2nd top 10 hit of 1970 in their first year without Diana Ross. Like their previous hit, 'Up the Ladder to the Roof', Jean Terrell also sang lead on 'Stoned Love', which was originally written and recorded as 'Stone Love', but was mislabeled.

102. **Heaven Help Us All** by Stevie Wonder was an anti-war social comment hit written by Ron Miller, who also composed his hits 'For Once In My Life', 'A Place In The Sun' and 'Yester Me, Yester You, Yesterday'.

103. **It's Only Make Believe** by Glen Campbell was a remake of the 1958 number one hit by Conway Twitty. Glen Campbell had his own weekly hour long music/variety show from 1968 – 1972.

104. **You Don't Have To Say You Love Me** by Elvis Presley was a remake of the hit Dusty Springfield brought into the top 10 in the summer of 1966. The 'B' side of this single was 'Patch It Up' and both were from the soundtrack album 'Elvis-That's The Way It Is'.

105. **Still Water (Love)** by The Four Tops was a progressive soul song co-written by Smokey Robinson and produced by Norman Whitfield. It was taken from their album 'Still Waters Run Deep' which also featured their hit remake of 'It's All in the Game'.

106. **Cry Me a River** by Joe Cocker was recorded 'live' at the Fillmore East earlier that year. Joe Cocker's remake was one of many versions of this song recorded through the years, including the most popular rendition by Julie London back in 1955.

107. **Groovy Situation** was a comeback hit produced, written and recorded by Gene Chandler, the singer best known for his 1962 number one hit 'Duke Of

Earl'. 'Groovy Situation' was the only other million seller for the singer whose real name is Eugene Dixon.

108.   Early in the Morning by Vanity Fare was the first of two popular hits, both from 1970 for this British pop quintet. They took their name from the novel (not the magazine) by William Makepeace Thackeray with the spelling changed from 'Vanity Fair' to 'Vanity Fare'.

109.   Walk a Mile in My Shoes by Joe South was a social comment hit from the singer/songwriter who composed many hits for other music artists. Among his compositions were 'Down In The Boondocks' for Billy Joe Royal, 'Rose Garden' for Lynn Anderson, 'Yo Yo' for The Osmonds and 'Hush' for Deep Purple. In 1969 he won the Grammy Award for Song of the Year for his hit 'Games People Play'.

110.   United We Stand by Brotherhood of Man featured many of the same members as the British studio groups Edison Lighthouse, White Plains and the Pipkins. Tony Burrows was a prominent singer on all of the above. The Brotherhood of Man group that had a hit 6 years later with 'Save Your Kisses for Me' was made up of all new members.

111.   Express Yourself by Charles Wright & The 103rd Street Rhythm Band was the second of two top 20 hits for this R & B group. Charles Wright was born in Clarksdale, Mississippi and his eight-man band was from the Watts section of Los Angeles. Comedian Bill Cosby helped this band get their big break.

112.   See Me, Feel Me by The Who was from the Rock opera 'Tommy' which debuted the previous year with 'Pinball Wizard'. 'See Me, Feel Me' was actually a portion of the song 'We're Not Gonna Take It'. The 'B' side of this single was 'Overture from Tommy' which was a hit single in 1970 by the Philadelphia Studio group 'The Assembled Multitude'.

113.   It's A Shame was the biggest Motown hit for The Spinners before leaving the label for Atlantic Records in 1972. This great upbeat, harmonizing hit was produced and co-written by Stevie Wonder.

114.   For The Love of Him by Bobbi Martin certainly sounds dated in its lyrical content these days and would certainly not be accepted by the women's liberation. This was Bobbi Martin's biggest hit and a number one hit on the Adult Contemporary charts. Sadly, she died of cancer on May 2, 2000 at the age of 56.

115.   The Bells by The Originals was written and produced by Motown label mate Marvin Gaye. The Originals had one other top 20 hit, 'Baby I'm For Real' and it was also a Marvin Gaye creation.

116.   Pay to the Piper by The Chairman of the Board was their 4th of 4 top 40 hits in their debut year, 1970. All of their hits featured the distinctive voice of lead singer 'General' Norman Johnson. Johnson also co-wrote hits for the group 'Honeycone', including their number one million seller 'Want Ads' in 1971.

117.   **Daughter of Darkness** by Tom Jones featured a young Elton John on background vocals. This hit was co-written by Geoff Stephens who was also responsible for 'Winchester Cathedral' by The New Vaudeville Band and 'There's A Kind Of Hush' by Herman's Hermits.

118.   **Call Me** by Aretha Franklin was the first of 4 top 40 hits for lady soul in 1970. This hit was written by Aretha, who also plays piano on this soul song which reached number one on the R & B charts.

119.   **River Deep, Mountain High** by the Supremes & the Four Tops was a great pairing of two of the top current acts at Motown at the time. The original version of this song by Ike and Tina Turner in 1966 was a commercial disappointment and the reason its Producer Phil Spector went into seclusion. The Supremes and Four Tops version peaked at number 14, while the original could only manage to reach number 88.

120.   **A Song of Joy** by Miguel Rios was based on the final movement of famed classical composer Ludwig Von Beethoven's Ninth Symphony. Spanish born Miguel Rios sang while Waldo de Los Rios conducted this standout hit in 1970.

121.   **Superbad Part 1 & 2** by James Brown almost made the top 10 on the pop charts. However, it was a number one hit on the R & B charts in 1970. At around this time period, the Godfather of Soul was releasing approximately half a dozen hit singles every year, many of which were parts one and two for side 'A' and side 'B'.

122.   **The Thrill Is Gone** by B. B. King was the most popular pop hit for the King of the Blues. He and his famous guitar 'Lucille' have been performing for over 50 years. B.B. says the 30 dollar guitar got the name many years ago when a fire broke out in an Arkansas bar. King rushed in to save his guitar because he couldn't afford another. The fire had started over a brawl over a woman named 'Lucille'. B. B. King thought that would be a fine name for his guitar, and it remains today.

123.   **Celebrate** by 3 Dog Night was written by Gary Bonner and Alan Gordon who also created 'Happy Together' and 'She'd Rather Be with Me' for the Turtles. 'Celebrate' was 3 Dog Night's 4th top 20 hit and their first of 4 in 1970.

124.   **Engine Number 9** by Wilson Pickett was written by the legendary Philadelphia team of Gamble and Huff, who wrote and produced well over a hundred big hits from the late 60's on. This song is not to be confused with the Roger Miller hit "Engine Engine Number 9' from 1965.

125.   **Are You Ready** by Pacific Gas & Electric was the only hit for this West Coast blues-rock quintet. They were backed by the powerful gospel soul vocals of the Blackberries. The lead singer of Pacific, Gas and Electric, Charles Allen died in 1990 in Los Angeles at the age of 48.

126.   **I Who Have Nothing** by Tom Jones was originally a hit for Ben E. King in 1963. The soulful sounding Tom Jones made it his 3rd consecutive hit of 1970.

127.	**Ohio** by Crosby, Stills, Nash & Young was Neil Young's song about the Kent State University tragedy where four students were shot and killed by National Guardsmen during an antiwar demonstration in May of 1970.

128.	**Look What They've Done to My Song, Ma** by The New Seekers was written by Melanie. The lead singer of the New Seekers was Eve Graham, whose voice was quite similar to Melanie's on this hit. This was popular just a couple of months after Melanie brought her hit 'Lay Down' (Candles in the Rain) into the top ten.

129.	**Hi De Ho** by Blood, Sweat & Tears was written by Carole King and Gerry Goffin. This prime cut from 'Blood, Sweat and Tears 3' once again featured the powerful and distinctive vocals of David-Clayton Thomas.

130.	**Out in The Country** by 3 Dog Night was an easy going song written by songwriter/actor Paul Williams. The following year 3 Dog Night had a hit with his composition 'An Old Fashioned Love Song'.

131.	**Get Up, I Feel like Being a Sex Machine** by James Brown was another of his hits with 'part 1' listed beside the title. This was the 5th of 6 top 40 hits James Brown charted in 1970 alone.

132.	**Kentucky Rain** by Elvis Presley was co written by a then-unknown Country singer by the name of Eddie Rabbit, who didn't begin his own string of hits until several years later. It's also interesting to note that a then-unknown Ronnie Milsap played piano on this popular recording by Elvis.

133.	**Be My Baby** by Andy Kim was a remake of the Ronettes hit from 1963. The song was co-written by Jeff Barry, who also produced this version. In 1969, Andy Kim had an even bigger hit with his version of another Ronettes hit, 'Baby I Love You'. The 1969 version was also produced by Jeff Barry, who also co-wrote the Archies' hit 'Sugar Sugar' with Andy Kim that year.

134.	**After Midnight** was the first solo hit for legendary guitarist Eric Clapton. Aside from studio musicians, he has been lead guitarist for more popular recording acts than any other commercially successful pop star of our time. He was a member of The Yardbirds, Cream, Blind Faith, Delaney and Bonnie and Friends, Derek and The Dominos and others.

135.	**Little Green Bag** by The George Baker Selection was part of the Mini-Dutch Music Invasion of 1970 which also included the Shocking Blue and The Tee Set. George Baker is actually singer/guitarist/keyboardist Johannes Boewens. George Baker Selection's only other hit in North America was 'Paloma Blanca' in 1976.

136.	**El Condor Pasa** by Simon & Garfunkel featured the music of an 18th century folk melody. Paul Simon wrote the lyrics for this 3rd consecutive hit from their 'Bridge over Troubled Water'. This would be Simon and Garfunkel's final hit together until five years later when they would reunite for 'My Little Town'.

137.	**Walkin' in the Rain** by Jay & The Americans was a great remake of

25

the Ronettes hit from 1964.This was Jay (Black) and The Americans' follow up to their 1969 remake of 'This Magic Moment' which was originally a hit for The Drifters.

138.   Come Saturday Morning by The Sandpipers was a soft pop hit from the movie 'The Sterile Cuckoo' starring Liza Minnelli. The Los Angeles-based trio, The Sandpipers had the biggest hit of their career in 1966 with 'Guantanamera'. They recorded on the A & M record label.

139.   Overture from Tommy was the only hit for The Assembled Multitude, a studio group from Philadelphia. This studio group was arranged and conducted by Tom Sellers, who died at the age of 39 as a result of a fire in his hometown of Wayne, Pennsylvania. The original version of this instrumental by the Who, was the flip side of their single 'See Me, Feel Me' which did not chart as a hit single.

140.   Hand Me Down World was the first hit on the charts for the Guess Who after the departure of Randy Bachman, who was last heard on their biggest hit of all, 'American Woman'. 'Hand Me Down World' was the first hit written by new member guitarist Kurt Winter, who was visionary in this social comment hit about the environment and our need to take better care of our world. Burton Cummings sang lead on this and all of the hits of the Guess Who from 1967 on.

141.   Mississippi Queen by Mountain was a hard rock classic from this New York group led by Leslie West who was the writer, lead singer and guitarist and Felix Pappalardi who produced the band and played bass guitar. Corky Laing supplied the hard hitting drums and the cow bell opening. Sadly, Pappalardi, (who produced the recordings of Cream during the late 60's) was shot and killed by his wife in 1983. He was 44 years old.

142.   Love Land by Charles Wright & The 103rd Street Rhythm Band was one of two top 20 hits they achieved in 1970. Charles Wright was a multi-instrumentalist and leader of this eight man band.

143.   Rubber Duckie by Ernie (Jim Henson) was one of the year's most popular novelty hits. Jim Henson (who died of a sudden virus in 1990) was the creator of the Muppets and the popular 'Sesame Street' kids TV show which made its debut in 1969.Jim Henson was also the voice of many Muppets characters including Ernie and Kermit the frog.

144.   Question by The Moody Blues was a progressive hit from this symphonic rock group from Birmingham, England. Justin Hayward and John Lodge were the nucleus of the Moody Blues during the late 60's, 70's and 80's.

145.   Yellow River was a hit for one hit wonder Christie, a British trio featuring Jeff Christie on lead vocals. This hit, produced by Mike Smith, was originally offered to the Tremeloes' Alan Blakely since Christie member Mike Blakely was his brother. When they stalled on the offer, Jeff Christie decided to record it himself.

146.   Tell It All Brother by Kenny Rogers & the First Edition was a thought-provoking soft pop/country song from the album of the same name. This top 20 hit was their follow up to 'Something's Burning'. Kenny Rogers and most of the First Edition were once members of the New Christy Minstrels.

147.   One Man Band by 3 Dog Night was their 4th of 4 hits in 1970. This harder edged 3 Dog Night song was from their 5th album, 'Naturally' which also produced the hits 'Liar' and their biggest of all, 'Joy to the World'.

148.   Reach out and Touch (Somebody's Hand) by Diana Ross was her first solo hit after leaving the Supremes. This heart warming song was written and produced by Ashford and Simpson, who would also give Diana her follow up and first number one solo hit 'Ain't No Mountain High Enough', a song originally popular in 1967 by Marvin Gaye and Tammi Terrell.

149.   Honey Come Back by Glen Campbell was the fifth and final hit written for him by Jimmy Webb, the composer responsible for 'Galveston', 'Wichita Lineman' and others. Glen Campbell also had a lucrative career as a member of 'The Wrecking Crew', a group of studio musicians who played on hundreds of hits primarily during the 60's by artists such as the Mamas & Papas, Monkees, Byrds, Simon and Garfunkel and the Beach Boys.

150.   Joanne by Michael Nesmith & the First National Band was his first solo hit after leaving the Monkees. This song demonstrated Nesmith's love for country-flavored music and the style he was more comfortable with as a singer/songwriter musician. Michael Nesmith's mother was the inventor of the typewriter correction fluid known as 'liquid paper'. When she died, he inherited millions of dollars. He became one of the forerunners in video production and in 1981 won a Grammy Award for 'Video of the Year' for his hour long 'Elephant Parts' feature.

151.   What Is Truth by Johnny Cash was a social comment hit by the man in black. This self-composed hit was popular during the time his TV show, 'The Johnny Cash Show' aired in prime time from 1969 to 1971.

152.   Gotta Hold On To This Feeling by Jr. Walker & The All Stars featured his great signature 'sax' sound along with flowing back up vocals which complimented Walker's emotional delivery. Jr. Walker was born Autry DeWalt and died in late 1995 at the age of 64.

153.   Long Lonesome Highway by Michael Parks was featured in the TV series 'Then Came Bronson'. The show was inspired by the success of 'Easy Rider' and the NBC series was about a youth, played by Michael Parks and the search for the meaning of life riding the highways on his motorcycle.

154.   He Ain't Heavy, He's My Brother by Neil Diamond was a remake of the Hollies hit less than a year after their version reached the top 10. Diamond's remake was less successful, but still managed to reach the top 20.

155.   Blowing Away by the 5th Dimension was the 4th hit single from the 'Age of Aquarius' album. This was one of 5 hits by the 5th Dimension written by Laura Nyro. The others were 'Stoned Soul Picnic', 'Sweet Blindness', 'Wedding Bell Blues' and 'Save the Country'.

156. **Solitary Man** by Neil Diamond was a re-release of his very first hit from 1966. This was re-issued by his former record label 'Bang' which produced his string of over half a dozen hits from 1966 to 1967. 1970 was the year Neil Diamond had hit singles on both his former label 'Bang' and his current label 'Uni'.

157. **Evil Woman, Don't Play Your Games with Me** by Crow was a high energy brass rock hit from this Minneapolis based band. This was the only top 40 hit for this group which featured the powerful lead vocals of Dave Wagner.

158. **Neanderthal Man** by Hotlegs was a number one hit in Britain by the group that evolved into 10c.c. This was a very abstract song which certainly commanded your attention when it played on the radio.

159. **Oh Me Oh My (I'm A Fool for You Baby)** by Lulu was an emotional ballad from this Scottish songstress. Her real name was Marie McDonald McLaughlin Laurie and is best known for her multi week number one hit 'To Sir with Love' in 1967. Lulu was married to Maurice Gibb of the Bee Gees at the time this song was popular.

160. **Winter World of Love** by Engelbert Humperdinck was the last of his top 40 string of hits from 1967 to 1970. He would have to wait almost seven years before his next and final hit 'After the Lovin' would reach the top 10 in early 1977.

161. **Everybody's Got the Right to Love** by The Supremes was their follow up to 'Up the Ladder to the Roof', their first hit after the departure of Diana Ross. This top 30 hit showcased all 3 Supremes, lead singer Jean Terrell, Mary Wilson and Cindy Birdsong.

162. **You're The One** by Little Sister was a funky hit by one of the family members from Sly & the Family Stone. Sly Stone organized his little sister Vanetta Stewart's soul trio.

163. **God, Love and Rock And Roll** by Teegarden and Van Winkle was their only top 40 hit. This gospel rock song featured David Teegarden on vocals and drums with Skip Knape on vocals and keyboards. Teegarden later appeared as the drummer for Bob Seger's Silver Bullet Band.

164. **Closer to Home** was the first hit for Grand Funk Railroad, a hard rock band from Flint, Michigan. The song is also referred to as 'I'm Your Captain'. Their name was inspired by the Michigan landmark, the Grand Trunk Railroad. The group was produced and managed by Terry Knight (formerly of Terry Knight & The Pack) until 1972. Guitarist/keyboardist Mark Farner and drummer Don Brewer shared lead vocals.

165. **Tennessee Bird Walk** by Jack Blanchard & Misty Morgan was a novelty Country hit which crossed over to the pop charts where it reached the top 30. This country duo were both born in Buffalo, but met in Florida where they became husband and wife.

166. **Baby Take Me in Your Arms** by Jefferson was actually British singer

Geoff Turton. This catchy, happy hit was co-written by Tony Macauley, who was responsible for many of the British hits of that time including 'Build Me Up Buttercup', 'Love Grows, Where My Rosemary Grows', Smile A Little Smile For Me', 'Baby Now That I Found You' and many others.

167. **Westbound # 9** by Flaming Ember was the highest charting hit for this blue-eyed soul group from Detroit. Their first hit was 1969's 'Mind, Body and Soul' with their final top 40 hit arriving in late 1970 with 'I'm Not My Brother's Keeper'. In the U.S. they recorded for Hot Wax Records, the newly-formed label founded by Holland/Dozier/Holland fame, formerly with Motown. In Canada, their hits appeared on the Buddah label.

168. **Up On Cripple Creek** by The Band were Canadian with the exception of Levon Helm, who hailed from Arkansas. The Band was formed in Woodstock, New York and formerly the back up band for Ronnie Hawkins during the 60's. Robbie Robertson was guitarist and songwriter on most of their popular recordings including the 'B' side of this single, 'The Night They Drove Old Dixie Down' which became a top 10 hit for Joan Baez the following year. Drummer Levon Helm was the lead singer on 'Up on Cripple Creek'.

169. **She** by Tommy James & The Shondells was released in late 1969 and peaked on the charts in the top 30 in early 1970. After a successful string of hits in the late 60's, Tommy James would resurface in 1971 as simply 'Tommy James' on 'Draggin' the Line', minus the Shondells.

170. **Deeper And Deeper** by Freda Payne was the follow up to her million selling 'Band of Gold' earlier that year. She was signed to former legendary Motown songwriting team Holland/Dozier/Holland's new label 'Invictus' where she had 3 hit singles. Freda Payne was once married to singer Gregory Abbott.

More Hits of 1970

Long Long Time by Linda Ronstadt was a beautiful and emotional ballad by the former lead singer of the Stone Poneys. This pop country hit was Linda Ronstadt's very first solo hit and her final hit with Capitol Records. She would have to wait 5 more years until her next hit, 'You're No Good', but she would have several throughout the remainder of the 70's.

Never Had a Dream Come True by Stevie Wonder was the first hit of the 70's for this legendary Motown performer. This was a prime cut from Stevie's 'Signed, Sealed, Delivered, I'm Yours' album.

Shilo by Neil Diamond was actually recorded in 1967, but Bert Berns, founder of Bang records did not think that it was compatible with Diamond's current commercial sound. Neil Diamond was so disappointed with Berns decision, that he left the label for 'Uni' records where he would score many major hits. 'Shilo' was a song about an imaginary friend, and eventually became a moderate hit in 1970 when it was released by his former label.

Always Something There to Remind Me by R. B. Greaves was a Burt Bacharach/Hal David composition that was previously recorded by Dionne Warwick, Sandie Shaw and others.

R.B. Greaves, who was the nephew of Sam Cooke, had the biggest hit of his career in late 1969 with 'Take a Letter Maria'.

Viva Tirado – Part One by El Chicano was a popular instrumental from this Mexican-American band formed in Los Angeles.

Cold Turkey by Plastic Ono Band was another John Lennon venture outside of the Beatles while the Fab Four were still together. This song was about John Lennon breaking his brief addiction to heroin. The first public performance of 'Cold Turkey' was recorded on the 'Live Peace in Toronto 1969' album. Eric Clapton was featured on lead guitar.

As The Years Go By by Mashmakhan was the only hit for this Canadian rock quartet from Montreal. Pierre Senecal was Mashmakhan's lead singer and songwriter. Group member Jerry Mercer later joined April Wine.

I've Lost You by Elvis Presley was the 4th of 5 top 40 hits for the King in 1970. 'I've Lost You' was both an emotional and powerful ballad from Elvis which was popular between two 60's remakes, 'The Wonder of You' and 'You Don't Have to Say You Love Me'.

Baby Hold On by The Grassroots barely made the top 40 and was their only charted hit in 1970 after having 5 notable hits in 1969 and 3 in 1971.

Temma Harbour by Mary Hopkin was the 3rd of 3 top 40 hits for this singer from Wales. Paul McCartney produced her first 2 hits 'Those Were the Days' in 1968 and 'Goodbye' in 1969. The warm and tropical feeling 'Temma Harbour' became her final top 40 hit in North America. In 1971 she married producer Tony Visconti and left her music career to start a family.

Come Running by Van Morrison was his first solo hit single since 'Brown Eyed Girl' 3 years earlier in 1967. Surprisingly, this song was his only top 40 hit from his very successful and critically-acclaimed album 'Moondance'. Although the title song was popular, it was never a top 40 hit and it wasn't released as a single until 1977, a full seven years later. 'Crazy Love' and 'Into the Mystic' were two other cuts from the album which received favorable response.

Ain't It Funky Now by James Brown was something different from the Godfather of Soul with great and catchy instrumentation front and centre with his vocals coming in for seconds at a time.

Hey Mister Sun by Bobby Sherman was a moderate hit for the California teen idol whose previous 3 hits each reached the top 10. The teenybopper same-sound formula was wearing thin as this one barely made the top 30.

Sugar Sugar by Wilson Pickett was a remake of the multi-million selling Archies' hit less than a year after they topped the charts with it. Pickett's version of this bubblegum song did not translate well into the soul music genre.

You Need Love like I Do (Don't You) by Gladys Knight & The Pips was a psychedelic soul hit produced by Norman Whitfield who also gave other Motown acts like the Temptations and Edwin Starr a more progressive sound.

Save The Country by the 5th Dimension was another hit written by Laura Nyro, who gave this Los Angeles-based vocal group 5 hit singles.

Silver Bird by Mark Lindsay was the 2nd solo hit of 1970 for the former lead singer on all of the hits of Paul Revere & the Raiders. 'Silver Bird' was used in a popular commercial for an airlines company in the 70's.

It's All in the Game by The Four Tops was a remake of the classic hit originally made popular by Tommy Edwards in 1958. This song was co-written by former U.S. Vice-President Charles Dawes.

Puppet Man by the 5th Dimension was written by Neil Sedaka and Howard Greenfield and was also released as a single by Tom Jones in the early 70's.

Spirit in The Dark by Aretha Franklin was the first of 3 1970 hits from Lady Soul using the Dixie Flyers on backup vocals. This song was written solely by Aretha Franklin.

Can't Stop Loving You by Tom Jones was his 4th hit of 1970. All of his hits from 1965 up to this point in 1970 were produced by Peter Sullivan. Sir Tom Jones was knighted in 2006.

Summertime Blues by The Who was the 3rd hit version of this song in the rock era following Eddie Cochran's original in 1958 and Blue Cheer's hard rock version in 1968. The Who's version was from their 'Live at Leeds' album. John Entwistle is featured doing the deep voice of the boss, the father and the congressman.

That's Where I Went Wrong by The Poppy Family was the follow up to their biggest hit 'Which Way You Going Billy. This Canadian duo consisted of husband and wife Susan and Terry Jacks. When their marriage ended, Susan Jacks moved to Nashville to become a country singer and Terry Jacks (who had the biggest hit of his career in 1974 with 'Seasons In The Sun') settled in British Columbia where he became an environmentalist.

Lucretia Mac Evil by Blood, Sweat & Tears was a high energy brass rock hit delivered with power by lead singer David Clayton-Thomas who also wrote this top 30 hit. This was their 5th hit since their debut year in 1969.

Soolaimon (African Trilogy 2) by Neil Diamond was always a favorite at his 'live' shows, despite the fact that this song barely made the top 30 on the pop charts. Diamond studied African culture and was very interested in its music. This unique recording was arranged by Jazz producer/conductor Marty Paich, father of David Paich of Toto fame.

The Sly, The Slick, The Wicked by Lost Generation was an advice song from this one hit wonder soul group from Chicago. This R & B vocal quartet included brothers Lowrell and Fred Simon.

Fancy by Bobbie Gentry was another story song from the singer/songwriter whose signature hit is 'Ode to Billie Joe' from 1967.This song became a top 10 Country hit for Reba McEntire in 1991.

Wonderful World, Beautiful People by Jimmy Cliff was a feel good song that became one of the first reggae hits to penetrate the pop charts. Jimmy Cliff is legendary in the field of ska and reggae music, and holds the 'Order of Merit', the highest honor that can be granted by the Jamaican government for achievement in the arts and sciences. Jimmy Cliff is also well known for his appearance in the film 'The Harder They Fall'.

Maybe by the Three Degrees was a top 30 hit in the summer of 1970 for this Philadelphia R & B vocal trio. They had to wait 4 more years before they struck gold with both 'When Will I See You Again' and 'TSOP' by MFSB featuring the 3 Degrees.

Our House by Crosby, Stills, Nash & Young was their 4th hit single of the year. Neil Young also had a solo career simultaneously with 1970 hits which included 'Only Love Can Break Your Heart' and 'Cinnamon Girl'. 'Our House' was a warm and relaxing song written by Graham Nash which was one of 3 hits from their album 'DeJa Vu', their first with the addition of Neil Young.

She Came in through the Bathroom Window by Joe Cocker was another Beatles song redone by the wild performer known for his spastic movements onstage. Cocker's first hit single was his version of 'With A Little Help from My Friends' from the Beatles Sgt. Pepper's album. 'She Came in through the Bathroom Window' was a Lennon/ McCartney composition from their 'Abbey Road Album'.

All I Have to Do Is Dream by Glen Campbell & Bobbi Gentry was a remake of the Everly Brothers number one hit from 1958. This was the second hit together for Bobbie and Glen following their 1969 version of another Everly Brothers classic, 'Let It Be Me'.

When Julie Comes Around by The Cuff Links was the follow up to their top ten hit 'Tracy' from 1969. Lead singer Ron Dante, the voice of the Archies, was also all of the voices of the Cuff Links overdubbed to make it sound like an entire group.

Only Love Can Break Your Heart by Neil Young was a popular solo hit while he was an active member with Crosby, Stills and Nash. He was a member of Buffalo Springfield during the late 60's with Stephen Stills who accompanied Neil Young on this solo hit. This single was taken from his 'After the Gold Rush' album which also included the prime cut 'Southern Man', which was never released as a single.

Do It by Neil Diamond was another re-release of earlier material from his 'Bang' record label days, similar to 'Solitary Man' and 'Shilo', which were also revived in 1970. This song was originally featured on his 1966 album 'The Feel of Neil Diamond' and was originally the flip side of 'Solitary Man'.

Cupid by Johnny Nash was a reggae-flavored version of the Sam Cooke classic. This version was originally released as the 'B' side of his 1968 top 5 hit 'Hold Me Tight'.

I Want to Take You Higher by Ike and Tina Turner was a remake of the Sly & the Family Stone original which was also performed at Woodstock in the summer of 1969. Ike and Tina Turner's high energy rendition prominently featured Tina upfront with backing by the Ikettes. This was Ike and Tina Turner's first top 40 hit since 'Poor Fool' eight years earlier.

Do What You Wanna Do by Five Flights Up was the only hit for this 5 man American R & B band.

Jennifer Tompkins by Street People was a song co-written by a then-unknown Rupert Holmes, one of the members of this one hit wonder studio group. The following year he wrote 'Timothy' for the Buoys and at the end of the decade would have a number one solo hit with 'Escape, the Pina Colada Song'.

One Tin Soldier by The Original Caste was written by the popular songwriting team of Dennis Lambert and Brian Potter who also wrote hits for the Four Tops, the Grassroots and Tavares. The Original Caste was a Canadian group which featured Dixie Lee Innes on lead vocals. It was the version of this song by 'Coven' which was featured in the movie 'Billy Jack'.

Airport Love Theme by Vincent Bell featured his 'water sound' guitar which was also featured in Ferrante and Teicher's instrumental 'Midnight Cowboy'. This was the theme from the movie 'Airport' which featured an all star cast including Burt Lancaster, Dean Martin, George Kennedy, Jacqueline Bisset, Jean Seberg and Van Heflin.

I'm Not My Brother's Keeper by Flaming Ember was the 3rd and final hit for this Detroit blue-eyed soul group. Lead singer Jerry Pluck also played drums.

Everything's Tuesday by Chairman of the Board was their 3rd of 4 hits in their debut year of 1970. Once again, the distinctive voice of General Norman Johnson was featured on lead vocals.

Go Back by Crabby Appleton was the only hit for this West Coast rock quintet fronted by singer/songwriter/guitarist Michael Fennelly They got their name from the character of the same name from the Tom Terrific cartoon.

TOP 17 ALBUMS OF 1970

1.	Bridge Over Troubled Water	Simon & Garfunkel
2.	Cosmo's Factory	C. C. R.
3.	Led Zeppelin 2	Led Zeppelin
4.	Abraxas	Santana
5.	Let It Be	Beatles
6.	Woodstock	Soundtrack
7.	Led Zeppelin 3	Led Zeppelin
8.	McCartney	Paul McCartney
9.	Blood, Sweat and Tears 3	Blood, Sweat and Tears
10.	Déjà vu	Crosby, Stills, Nash & Young
11.	Willie and the Poor Boys	C. C. R.
12.	Chicago	Chicago
13.	ABC	Jackson 5
14.	'Live' At Leeds	Who
15.	Third Album	Jackson 5
16.	Band of Gypsies	Jimi Hendrix, Buddy Miles
17.	Chicago 2	Chicago

1.	Hello Darlin'	Conway Twitty
2.	It's Just a Matter of Time	Sonny James
3.	Don't Keep Me Hangin' On	Sonny James
4.	The Fightin' Side of Love	Merle Haggard
5.	My Love	Sonny James
6.	He Loves Me All the Way	Tammy Wynette
7.	Endlessly	Sonny James
8.	A Week in a County Jail	Tom T. Hall
9.	Sunday Morning Comin' Down	Johnny Cash
10.	Tennessee Bird Walk	Jack Blanchard & Misty Morgan
11.	Run Woman Run	Tammy Wynette
12.	Coal Miner's Daughter	Loretta Lynn
13.	Is Anybody Going To San Antone	Charley Pride
14.	There Must Be More To Love	Jerry Lee Lewis
15.	Wonder If I Could Live … Anymore	Charley Pride
16.	All for the Love Of Sunshine	Hank Williams Jr.
17.	I Can't Believe …Stayed Loving Me	Charley Pride

Top 17 R & B/Soul Hits Of 1970

1.	I'll Be There	Jackson 5
2.	The Love You Save	Jackson 5
3.	Signed, Sealed, Delivered…	Stevie Wonder
4.	Thank You	Sly & the Family Stone
5.	Love on a Two Way Street	Moments
6.	I Want You Back	Jackson 5
7.	ABC	Jackson 5
8.	Tears of a Clown	Smokey Robinson & The Miracles
9.	Don't Play That Song	Aretha Franklin
10.	Super Bad Part 1 and 2	James Brown
11.	Turn Back the Hands of Time	Tyrone Davis
12.	Call Me	Aretha Franklin
13.	Ain't No Mountain High Enough	Diana Ross
14.	Rainy Night in Georgia	Brook Benton
15.	Stoned Love	Supremes
16.	War	Edwin Starr
17.	Band of Gold	Freda Payne

1.	Shocking Blue	Venus
2.	Eddie Holman	Hey There Lonely Girl
3.	Ides of March	Vehicle
4.	Mungo Jerry	In The Summertime
5.	Moments	Love on a Two Way Street
6.	Jaggerz	The Rapper
7.	Free	All Right Now
8.	Blues Image	Ride Captain Ride
9.	Edison Lighthouse	Love Grows (Where My Rosemary Goes)
10.	Tee Set	Ma Belle Amie
11.	Alive and Kicking	Tighter, Tighter
12.	Five Stairsteps	O – O –H Child
13.	Bobby Bloom	Montego Bay
14.	Frigid Pink	House of the Rising Sun
15.	Ronnie Dyson	Why Can't I Touch You
16.	100 Proof Aged In Soul	Somebody's Been Sleeping
17.	Pipkins	Gimme Dat Ding

Top 17 Rock/Hard Rock Hits Of 1970

1.	Whole Lotta Love	Led Zeppelin
2.	American Woman	Guess Who
3.	All Right Now	Free
4.	House of the Rising Sun	Frigid Pink
5.	The Letter	Joe Cocker
6.	Mississippi Queen	Mountain
7.	Travelin' Band	C.C.R.
8.	Let's Work Together	Canned Heat
9.	Cry Me a River	Joe Cocker
10.	Summertime Blues	The Who
11.	Evil Woman, Don't Play ... Games	Crow
12.	She Came In Through ...Window	Joe Cocker
13.	Go Back	Crabby Appleton
14.	Monster	Steppenwolf
15.	Paranoid	Black Sabbath
16.	Mongoose	Elephant's Memory
17.	You Make Me Real	Doors

17 Notable 'Lost 45's' of 1970

1.	Neanderthal Man	Hotlegs
2.	Joanne	Michael Nesmith
3.	Love Land	Charles Wright & the 103rd Street R.B.
4.	God, Love and Rock And Roll	Teegarden & Van Winkle
5.	Why Can't I Touch You	Ronnie Dyson
6.	Baby Takes Me in Your Arms	Jefferson
7.	Long Lonesome Highway	Michael Parks
8.	Are You Ready	Pacific Gas & Electric
9.	Wonderful World, Beautiful People	Jimmy Cliff
10.	I'm Not My Brother's Keeper	Flaming Ember
11.	A Little Bit of Soap	Paul Davis
12.	Let's Work Together	Wilbert Harrison
13.	Evil Woman, Don't Play ...Games	Crow
14.	Mississippi	John Phillips
15.	I Want To Take You Higher	Ike & Tina Turner
16.	Jennifer Tompkins	Street People
17.	Everything's Tuesday	Chairman Of the Board

70'S Whatever Became of ...SHAWN AND DAVID CASSIDY

Remember 70's teen idols Shawn and David Cassidy? Shawn Cassidy, who is now over 50, is the eldest son of actress Shirley Jones and the second son of the late actor Jack Cassidy. His older half-brother is David Cassidy. They were both teen idols at separate times during the 70's. Shawn is now married to his third wife, producer Tracy Turner, and they have two sons. Back in the late 70's, while still in high school, he signed with Warner Brothers and had big hits with 'That's Rock and Roll', 'Da Do Ron Ron' and 'Hey Deanie'. At the same time, he starred in The Hardy Boys, which ran for three seasons on NBC. Following his acting career, he moved to creating television shows, including 'American Gothic', 'Roar', 'Cold Case' and fan favorite 'Invasion'. Three time married half brother David Cassidy, who celebrated his 60th birthday in 2010, got his big break when he starred as Keith Partridge in The Partridge Family. He also had many hit singles and albums with and without his TV family. Although approximately $500 million was made from the Partridge Family and David Cassidy merchandising internationally, he was allegedly paid only $15,000. He's been broke on more than one occasion because of bad management. He has written a couple of books about his financial nightmares, along with drug use and wild sex. These days he has many irons in the fire, including David Cassidy Travel. He continues to tour to this day. His official website is www. davidcassidy.com.

70'S Whatever Became of ...JIM STAFFORD

In 1974 Florida –born Jim Stafford had 3 consecutive offbeat hits beginning with the million seller 'Spiders and Snakes', followed by 'My Girl Bill' and 'Wildwood Weed'. This multi-talented singer/songwriter with a great sense of humor was a self-taught musician who played the guitar, fiddle, piano, banjo, organ and harmonica.

The following year, 'The Jim Stafford Show' aired on ABC followed by 'Those Amazing Animals' which he co-hosted with Burgess Meredith and Priscilla Presley.

In the late 70's he was married briefly to Bobbie Gentry, the singer of the number one 1967 hit 'Ode to Billie Joe'

What has Jim Stafford been up to since those days? Well, for the past 20 years or so, he has been the star performer at the Jim Stafford Theatre in Branson, Missouri. He has lots of comedy and music in his show, including a segment where he shines on the classical guitar which gets rave reviews. He's happy on and off stage with his wife and business partner Ann with their 2 children. His official website is www.jimstafford.com

70'S Whatever Became of ...RUPERT HOLMES

Rupert Holmes was born in Cheshire, England on February 24, 1947 and moved to New York at the age of six. He is best known for his number one hit 'Escape', (the Pina Colada Song) which was the final hit of the 70's to top the charts back in December 1979. He followed that with the hits 'Him' and 'Answering Machine'. Back in the early 70's, he wrote the twisted, offbeat hit 'Timothy' by the Buoys, in a song that dealt with cannibilism after 3 guys were trapped in a mine and only 2 were left. After the radio hits, he hit Broadway and the bookshelves where he became an author and playwright. In the 80's, his musical 'Drood', based on an unfinished novel by Charles Dickens, won him a Tony Award for both book and score. He also wrote the Tony Award-nominated 'Best Play 2003' for 'Say Goodnight, Gracie', based on the relationship between George Burns and Gracie Allen. That year,he also published the novel, 'Where The Truth Lies' which became a film starring Kevin Bacon, directed by Atom Egoyan. Rupert Holmes has written several other successful novels and scores for musicals and continues to create more on a regular basis. You can check out his website at www.rupertholmes.com

70'S Whatever Became of ...LINDA RONSTADT

The 70's were the most successful decade for this singer born in Tucson, Arizona on July 15, 1946. She charted a dozen top 40 hit singles during the

70's alone, most of which were remakes, including 'Heatwave', 'You're No Good', 'Blue Bayou', 'When Will I Be Loved' and many others. Linda Ronstadt also had major successes with 70's albums like 'Heart Like A Wheel', 'Prisoner In Disguise', 'Hasten Down The Wind' and 'Simple Dreams', all produced by Peter Asher of Peter and Gordon fame. In the mid 70's, her private life was given major publicity when she began a relationship with then-Governor of California Jerry Brown. In the 80's, she was engaged to Star Wars director George Lucas. On August 3, 2007, Ronstadt headlined the Newport Folk Festival making her debut at this prestigious event, where she incorporated jazz, rock and folk music into her repertoire. On May 9, 2009, Linda Ronstadt received an honorary Doctor of Music degree from Berklee College of Music. Commencement speaker Smokey Robinson addressed more than 850 Berklee graduates and 4000 invited guests. Nowadays Linda Ronstadt lives a quiet life and performs only occasionally.

70'S Whatever Became of ...RANDY NEWMAN

Randy Newman was born in New Orleans on November 28th, 1943 and has been successful as a singer, composer and pianist. His first major success came when he wrote 3 Dog Night's 1970 number one hit 'Mama Told Me (Not to Come)'. In early 1978 he had a major hit of his own with the million selling 'Short People' which some vertically-challenged people took more seriously than he ever intended. His real success came in the 80's when he worked mostly as a film composer, scoring films like 'The Natural', 'Ragtime', 'James and The Giant Peach', 'Seabiscuit' and 'Meet The Parents'. He is most identified with all the Disney movies he scored the music for, including huge successes like 'Monsters Inc', 'Princess and The Frog', 'A Bug's Life' and all of the 'Toy Story' and 'Cars' movies. Randy Newman was inducted into the Songwriters Hall Of Fame in 2002. In 2007, Newman was inducted as a Disney Legend. These days Randy Newman keeps busy writing successful film scores and touring as a solo performer. In 2010 he performed concerts in Norway, Helsinki, Denmark, Germany and played in many other venues around the world. In 2010 he released the album 'Harps and Angels'. More information on this multi-talented performer is available on his official website www.randynewman.com

70'S Whatever Became of ...TERRY JACKS

Terry Jacks gained great fame with the 1974 multi million selling 'Seasons in the Sun', but was previously popular as one half of the Poppy Family prior to that monumental number one hit. Back in the late 60's, this native of Winnipeg, Manitoba, Canada moved to Vancouver, British Columbia where he teamed up with singer Susan Pesklevits whom he married in 1968. Terry wrote and played guitar on most of their hits while Susan sang lead on hits which included 'Which Way You Going Billy', 'That's Where I Went Wrong' 'Good Friends' and 'Where Evil Grows' which featured both on lead vocals. After their hits and their marriage ended, Susan Jacks made Nashville her home and recorded several country songs. In 2010 Susan Jacks underwent a successful kidney transplant, donated by her brother Billy. For more info on Susan Jacks, check out her website at www.susanjacks.com Terry Jacks married Margaret Zittier and gradually withdrew from the music world. In the mid 80's he became involved in the environmental movement and has earned several awards, including one from the United Nations and the Western Canada Wilderness Committee. . He has worked in documentary film and video, producing several shorts on environmental themes. The video production 'The Faceless Ones' earned an Environmental Gold Award from the New York International Film Festival.Terry Jacks has transformed himself into something of a major obstacle for large-scale pulp and logging companies that are suspected of noncompliance with Canadian pollution laws. To that end, he established an organization called Environmental Watch.

70'S Whatever Became of ...RAY STEVENS

Funny man Ray Stevens was born Harold Ray Ragsdale on January 24th, 1939 in Clarkdale, Georgia. During the 60's he had novelty hits with 'Ahab The Arab', 'Harry The Hairy Ape', 'Gitarzan' and 'Along Cames Jones'. During the 70's he had two number one hits, 'Everything Is Beautiful' in 1970, during a time he had his own TV show, and in 1974 he topped the charts with the novelty hit 'The Streak'. After the 70's, his pop music career on the charts was finished, although he had a few country hits. This talented singer/songwriter/ producer continued to perform on stage. In the past few years he has been busy with many projects including a jazzy tribute to the songs of Frank Sinatra in 2008 on an album titled 'Ray Stevens Sings Sinatra...Say What?'. In 2009 he released the CD 'One For The Road' aimed primarily at truckers and that same year he was inducted into the Christian Music Hall Of Fame and appeared in the PBS series 'Legends and Lyrics'. In 2009, Ray Stevens released a holiday collection of serious songs titled 'Ray Stevens Christmas'. In 2010 he did a music video about Sarah Palin called 'Caribou Barbie', followed by his social commentary 'Throw The Bums Out!'. In 2010 he also released a 22-song, 4 music video entitled 'We The People'. Although Ray Stevens is now over 70, he continues to keep busy and continues to keep us laughing. His official website can be found at www.raystevens.com

70'S Whatever Became of ...GILBERT O'SULLIVAN

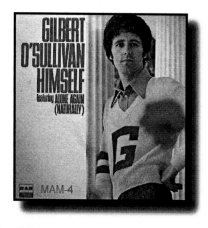

Back in the early 70's, Gilbert O'Sullivan commanded our attention with his unusual look and distinctive voice on hits like 'Alone Again Naturally', 'Clair' and 'Get Down'. This singer/songwriter/pianist born on December 1 1946 in Waterford, Ireland was hot in 1972 and 1973 when he charted 3 million selling singles. Although he continued to release singles and albums, his music could not find the audience it once had. In January of 1980 he married his Norwegian girlfriend Aase and later that year their first of 2 daughters was born. In the early 80's, after living in England for some time, he moved to Ireland because artists are exempt from income tax there. In 1992, he topped the charts in Japan with the new single 'Tomorrow Today' and continued to have success touring there as well. In 2009 ,Gilbert O'Sullivan recorded an album in Nashville and later that year played London's Royal Albert Hall. Even though we don't hear much about Gilbert O'Sullivan anymore here in North America, this singer continues to record and tour . As of 2010, he still bears his trademark big frizzy hair, just like he did in his early 70's heyday. His official website is www.gilbertosullivan. net.

70'S Whatever Became of ...AL GREEN

Soul singer Al Green, who was born Al Greene on April 13th 1946, had one million seller after another in the early 70's beginning with 'Tired Of Being Alone' in 1971, followed by his signature number one hit 'Let's Stay Together' the following year. He had his final million sellling single with 'Sha La La' in 1974, the year his life changed dramatically. That was the year his then-girlfriend, Mary Woodson White, assaulted him before committing suicide at his Memphis home. She doused him with a pan of boiling grits while he was showering, causing 3rd degree burns on his stomach, back and arms. That incident changed his life and he became an ordained pastor of the Full Gospel Tabernacle in 1976. In 1988, he had a top 10 hit with his remake of 'Put A Little Love In Your Heart' with Annie Lennox from the movie 'Scrooged' starring Bill Murray. In 1995 Al Green was inducted into the Rock and Roll Hall of Fame. In 2000, he published the book, 'Take Me To The River', about his life and career. In 2002 he received a Grammy Lifetime Achievement Award and in 2005, Rolling Stone Magazine named him #65 in their list of the '100 Greatest Artists Of All Time'. In 2008 Al Green's album 'Lay It Down' became his most successful album in 35 years. He has sold more than 20 million records and continues to tour and record. His official website is www.algreenmusic.com

70'S Whatever Became of ...THE DEFRANCO FAMILY

The DeFranco Family featured Tony DeFranco, who was only 13 years old when he sang lead on the million selling 'Heartbeat – It's A Lovebeat' back in 1973. They also had hits with 'Abra-Ca-Dabra' and a remake of the Drifters' 'Save The Last Dance For Me'. The 5 members of this teenybopper family act from Port Colborne and Welland, Ontario, Canada moved to California where they struck gold in Los Angeles. In their heyday they appeared on the covers of almost every teen magazine including 'Tiger Beat', one of the most popular of the bunch.They appeared on Dick Clark's American Bandstand nine times along with appearances on The Ed Sullivan Show, Mike Douglas show and many others. Their 2 years of fame ran out and they pursued other interests. In a radio interview I did with Tony and big brother Benny in late 2001, they told me that the sisters were married and stayed at home, Benny had been working for Disney for a couple of decades and Tony DeFranco had a production company, setting up recording sessions. Tony Defranco is currently a very successful Real Estate agent in the Westlake Village in California.The siblings live within an hour drive from each other in California and remain close. Although the DeFranco Family are no longer involved in the music industry, Tony, Benny and Marisa perform on occasion. Their official website is : www.Defranco. com

70'S Whatever Became of ...DEBBY BOONE

When you think of Debby Boone, you most likely think of the 1977 hit 'You Light Up My Life', which spent over two months at the top of the pop charts. It was a huge multi-million seller that won her a Grammy Award the following year in the Best New Artist category. It was also the title song from the movie of the same name which featured actress Didi Conn singing the song, although it was the voice of Kacey Cisyk that you heard singing the tune in the film. Debby Boone was born in Hackensack, New Jersey, the third of four daughters born to singer/actor Pat Boone and Shirley Lee Foley Boone, daughter of country music star Red Foley.'You Light Up My Life' may have been Debby Boone's one and only hit on the pop charts, but she became successful in other areas. In the 80's, her music career first focussed on country music, but later changed to Christian music, where she was much more successful. As well, Debby Boone has appeared in several musical theater productions and has co-authored many children's books with husband, Gabriel Ferrer. In 1981, she wrote her autobiography. 'Debby Boone So Far'. She also spent a year touring the U.S. with the stage adaption of the film 'Seven Brides For Seven Brothers'. Debby Boone continues to record and tour. Her official website is www.debbyboone.net

70'S Whatever Became of ...YVONNE ELLIMAN

Although Yvonne Elliman's career peaked when she had a number one hit with the Saturday Night Fever soundtrack hit 'If I Can't Have You', she previously portrayed Mary Magdalene in the movie, rock opera and album of 'Jesus Christ Superstar'. Her first hit was 'I Don't Know How To Love Him' which was also

49

recorded by Helen Reddy in 1971. Shortly after that, she met and married Bill Oakes, President of RSO Records, the label she recorded her biggest hits on in the late 70's. She also backed labelmate Eric Clapton on his popular album '461 Ocean Boulevard'. Her biggest hits were 'Love Me', 'Hello Stranger' and the Bees Gees' composition 'If I Can't Have You', which their manager Robert Stigwood suggested they give to her to record for the 'Saturday Night Fever' soundtrack'. After the spotlight faded, she remarried and settled for a family life raising her two children and discovering a passion for cooking. Yvonne Elliman now lives where she was born on December 29th, 1951, Honolulu, Hawaii. She performed at a tribute for Sir Tim Rice in 2003 in El Paso, Texas and in 2004 she performed on a PBS special 'Disco Inferno'. In the summer of 2006 she reunited with her former 'Jesus Christ Superstar' performers for Ted Neely's swansong as Jesus at the Ricardo Montalban Theatre. In 2007, an album titled 'Simple Needs' with all songs written by Elliman, was released globally. She continues to perform around the world. For more info, check out her website at www.YvonneElliman.com

70'S Whatever Became of ...ERIC CARMEN

Eric Carmen was successful in the 70's first as the lead singer of the Raspberries and then as a soloist. This classically trained pianist was born in Cleveland, Ohio on August 11th 1949 and found his greatest success in the 70's beginning in 1972 when he sang lead on the high energy hit 'Go All The Way'. After the Raspberries, Eric Carmen launched his solo career with the classical power ballad 'All by Myself' in 1976, followed by 'Never Gonna Fall in Love'. In 1977 when his hit 'She Did It' was in the top 30, his composition 'That's Rock and Roll' reached the top 10 by Shawn Cassidy and later that year another hit he wrote 'Hey Deanie' became a million seller for the teen idol Hardy Boys star. In the early 80's he co-wrote the hit 'Almost Paradise' from the 'Footloose' soundtrack and in the late 80's Eric Carmen came back with the major hit 'Hungry Eyes' from the Dirty Dancing film, followed by 'Make Me Lose Control'. In the year 2000 he resurfaced when he was asked to join Ringo Starr's All Star band, which was a special thrill for him, since seeing the Beatles in his youth, gave him the inspiration to become a rock star. Five years later he reunited with his band the Raspberries to open the new 'House of Blues' in Cleveland, Ohio. Since it sold out in minutes, he decided to add more dates, for a total of ten. These days Eric Carmen works when the mood strikes him. He spends his time supporting his wife and two kids with the royalties from the songs he has written and recorded through the years. His official website is www.ericcarmen.com

70'S Whatever Became of ...JOHNNY RIVERS

The hits of Johnny Rivers started in the 60's with a string of hits which included 'Secret Agent Man', 'Memphis', 'Mountain Of Love' and 'Poor Side Of Town'. He also discovered the 5th Dimension who recorded on his 'Soul City' label and also gave songwriter Jim Webb his first big break writing many of their greatest hits.In the 70's, the singer born John Ramistella on November 7th 1942, continued his hits with 'Rockin' Pneumonia and The Boogie Woogie Flu', 'Help Me Rhonda' (the Beach Boys remake with backup from Brian Wilson) and the million selling 'Swayin' To The Music'(Slow Dancin'). In the 70's he also sang the theme for the late night music show 'The Midnight Special'. Even after the hits stopped, he continued touring. The singer (who was given his show biz name by Mister Rock and Roll Alan Freed) continues touring, doing over 50 shows a year. In early 2000, Johnny Rivers recorded with Eric Clapton, Tom Petty and Paul McCartney on a tribute album dedicated to Buddy Holly's backup band, The Crickets. On June 12, 2009, Johnny Rivers was inducted into the Louisianna Music Hall of Fame. In April of 2010 the 67 year old Rivers performed a benefit concert at his old high school in Baton Rouge, Louisianna where he once saw a young Elvis perform in his very early days. His official website is www.johnnyrivers.com

70'S Whatever Became of...LEO SAYER

The 70's was definitely the decade for British singer/songwriter Leo Sayer whose first hit in the U.K. was the number 2 hit 'The Show Must Go On' in 1973. He co-wrote this hit which he performed in a pierrot style clown outfit with make up. 3 Dog Night had a hit with it the following year when Sayer was back with his first North American hit, 'Long Tall Glasses (I Can Dance)'. The singer born Gerard Hugh Sayer on May 21 1948 had his best year in 1977 when he had 3 top 40 hits, including two number ones, 'You Make Me Feel Like Dancing' and 'When I Need You'. A few years later, Sayer had his last major hit in 1980 with his million selling remake of the Bobby Vee hit 'More Than I Can Say'. That same year he was the voice of Dan The Forest Ranger in 'The Racoons On Ice', the 2nd of 4 specials of the Canadian animated series, 'The Raccoons'. He also sang songs on the soundtrack album 'Lake Freeze' along with Rupert Holmes and Rita Coolidge. Although he had his own British TV Show in 1978 and again in 1983, musically for Leo Sayer, he was inactive on the pop charts. In 2005 he moved to Sydney, Australia where he has remained. His songs have been covered by others including Phil Collins and Meck with his remix of 'Thunder In My Heart' which reached number one in 2006. In 2008 Leo Sayer released a new album in Australia, 'Don't Wait Until Tomorrow', the same year he was featured on 'The Wiggles' DVD 'You Make Me Feel Like Dancing'. 2010 started dramatically for Leo, with him headlining a huge free concert for Australia Day on the water in Sydney's Darling Harbor. His performance was watched by 150,000 people live, and many more on national TV. That same year he traveled to Europe for a series of live shows, re-visiting Britain for an arena tour titled: "Once In a Lifetime", sharing the bill with David Essex, The Osmonds, and The Bay City Rollers. For Leo Sayer, The Show Must Go On! His very creative official website can be found at www. leosayer.com

70'S Whatever Became of ...ALAN O'DAY

Although Alan O'Day may be considered a one hit wonder with his summer 1977 number one hit 'Undercover Angel', that would only be as a singer. As a songwriter, prior to his huge hit, he co-wrote the number one hit 'Angie Baby' for Helen Reddy and the top 5 hit 'Rock and Roll Heaven' for the Righteous Brothers. Alan O'Day was born in Hollywood, California on October 3, 1940, the only child of Earle and Jeannette O'Day, who both worked in journalism. The young O'Day became interested in music at an early age, creating melodies on a xylophone when he was only six years old. By 5th grade he was serenading his classmates with his ukulele and by high school he played in different rock and roll bands. After the 70's, he moved from pop music to television, co-writing over 100 songs for the Saturday morning 'Muppet Babies' series. In the 1990's, he wrote and performed music on the National Geographic series 'Really Wild Animals'. More recently with his pal and children's songwriter Dave Kinnoin, he co-wrote several special songs through an organization called 'Songs of Love'. They would create and produce a song for and about a child with a life-threatening illness. The lyrics are always a positive scenario of their pets, hobbies, parents and friends. O'Day currently lives in Los Angeles, continues to write and perform, and is also a musical and creative consultant. Alan O'Day's official website is at: www.alanoday.com

70'S Whatever Became of ...HELEN REDDY

Helen Reddy was one of the most successful female singers of the 70's, charting 15 top 40 hits including 3 number ones. This Australian singer/songwriter/actress was born on October 25th, 1941 and began her string of 70's-exclusive hits in 1971 with 'I don't know How to Love Him' from 'Jesus Christ Superstar'. In 1972, she co-wrote 'I Am Woman' which became a worldwide feminist anthem and her first North American number one hit. Over the next 5 years, she had more than a dozen notable hits including 'Delta Dawn', 'Leave Me Alone (Ruby Red Dress)', and 'Angie Baby'. When her hits were hot, she was simultaneously acting in movies like 'Airport 1975' and Walt Disney's 'Pete's Dragon'. She was also host and performer between 1973 and 1975 on many episodes of 'The Midnight Special' and hosted her own variety TV program, 'The Helen Reddy Show' in the summer of 1973. Her best-selling memoir 'The Woman I Am' revealed that at the height of her career, her world was shattered by the death of both her parents and, simultaneously the news that she had a rare and incurable disease. In 2002, she retired from performing concerts and recording and now practices as a clinical hypo therapist and motivational speaker. She now resides in Sydney, Australia. Her official website is www.helenreddy.com

♫ This hit became her biggest, reaching number one 5 months after her death.

♫ All 4 Beatles had solo hits in 1971 including Ringo Starr with a song produced and co written by George Harrison.

♫ This number one James Taylor hit was written by his friend Carole King who played piano on this recording.

James Taylor

♫ This story song dealt with cannibalism and was written by a then-unknown Rupert Holmes and recorded by a one hit wonder group.

♫ This pop country singer and actor wrote and played guitar on Elvis Presley's 1968 hit 'Guitar Man' and had the 2 biggest hits of his career in 1971.

♫ This song topped the charts in 1963 and again in 1971 by one of the year's hottest new teen idols.

FIND OUT THAT…AND MUCH MORE INSIDE…1971!

1. Joy to The World by 3 Dog Night was also known to many as 'Jeremiah was a bullfrog'. The biggest hit of 1971 was written by Hoyt Axton 15 years after his mother Mae Axton saw her song 'Heartbreak Hotel' reach number one for Elvis Presley. Hoyt Axton wrote 'Joy to the World' for a children's TV special, but it never went into production, so he offered it to 3 Dog Night. Group member Cory Wells didn't really like it at all, but was convinced by others that it would be a hit. It sold several million copies.

2. Maggie May by Rod Stewart was the first solo hit for the raspy-voiced singer from Britain. The 'B' side of this single 'Reason to Believe', (written by Tim Hardin) was originally the 'A' side. In 1993, Rod Stewart re-released an acoustic version of 'Reason to Believe' and it became a hit again. Both 1971 hits were featured on the number one album 'Every Picture Tells a Story'.

3. It's Too Late by Carole King was the biggest hit from the number one album of the year, 'Tapestry'. Brooklyn, New York born singer/songwriter Carole King had already written dozens of big hits for others by the time this album was released. The 'Tapestry' album was number one for 15 weeks and spent over 300 incredible weeks on the album charts. The 'B' side of the single was 'I Feel the Earth Move', which was also a hit for this talented songstress.

4. How Can You Mend a Broken Heart by the Bee Gees was their first official number one hit in North America, despite the many popular hits they charted during the late 60's. The Bee Gees actually broke up in 1969, almost completely unnoticed, and would have no top 40 hits in 1970. They were back on track and on the charts again in 1971 with 'Lonely Days' and their follow up 'How Can You Mend a Broken Heart' which they originally offered to easy listening singer Andy Williams.

5. Knock Three Times by Tony Orlando and Dawn was the huge follow up to their first hit 'Candida'. 'Knock Three Times' was produced by Dave Appell and Hank Medress of the Tokens and was the first to feature backup singers Telma Hopkins and Joyce Vincent Wilson who became famous as 'Dawn'.

6. Gypsys, Tramps and Thieves by Cher was number one the same year 'The Sonny and Cher Comedy Hour' made its prime time TV debut. This number one solo story song by Cher was produced by Snuff Garrett, who previously gave Bobby Vee and Gary Lewis and the Playboys their biggest hits.

7. Family Affair by Sly and the Family Stone was a prime cut from the album 'There's A Riot Goin' On'. This self-composed number one hit produced by Sly Stone (Sylvester Stewart) was the final hit to reach the top 10 for this popular psychedelic soul group based in San Francisco.

8. You've Got a Friend by James Taylor was written by Carole King and produced by Peter Asher of Peter and Gordon fame. The song was included on Carole King's multi-million selling 'Tapestry' album, but she didn't release it as a single. This number one hit for her musical friend, James Taylor, won 2 major Grammy Awards in 1971, including 'Song of the Year' for Carole King.

9. Uncle Albert/Admiral Halsey by Paul and Linda McCartney was their only hit single from the album 'Ram'. The 'Uncle Albert' in the song was actually inspired by an actual Uncle of Paul's. This number one hit followed 'Another Day', Paul McCartney's first solo hit after the breakup of the Beatles the previous year.

10.   Theme From Shaft by Isaac Hayes won a Best Song Academy Award. Isaac Hayes previously wrote 'Soul Man' and 'Hold On, I'm Comin' with partner Dave Porter for Sam and Dave. In 1971, Isaac Hayes was contacted by MGM executives to discuss a property they had acquired, - the Novel 'Shaft'. Isaac thought he would be considered for the lead role in the movie and agreed to compose the film score. Instead, he received a phone call a few weeks later informing him that Richard Roundtree had been cast as 'Shaft' and production was underway. Isaac may have lost the movie role, but he gained a million selling number one hit.

11.Brown Sugar by The Rolling Stones was popular the year Mick Jagger married Nicaraguan beauty Bianca Perez Mora Macias. 1971 was also the recording debut of Mick Taylor as a member of the Rolling Stones, along with their own record label. This number one hit was taken from the eye- catching 'Sticky Fingers' album with a cover designed by artist Andy Warhol. It featured a real working zipper, on a pair of tight blue jeans many believed belonged to that of Mick Jagger.

12.   Indian Reservation by The Raiders was their only official number one hit. The song's roots go back to 1966 when John D. Loudermilk released his composition of 'Indian Reservation' for RCA Victor. It went nowhere. Don Fardon made the charts in 1968 with the tune listed as 'The Lament of the Cherokee Indian Reservation'. It peaked at number 20. Then, in 1971, The Raiders (formerly Paul Revere and The Raiders) took it all the way to number one.

13.   Me and Bobby McGee by Janis Joplin reached number one 4 months after she died from a drug overdose. This Kris Kristofferson composition became the gem of Janis Joplin's 'Pearl' album.

14.   Brand New Key by Melanie was a multi-week number one hit produced by her husband Peter Schekeryk. This million selling novelty song

58

about a brand new pair of roller skates was apparently written by Melanie Safka in about 15 minutes.

15.   Go Away Little Girl by Donny Osmond was written by Carole King and Gerry Goffin and was previously a number one hit in 1963 by Steve Lawrence. 1971 was a great debut year for both the Osmonds as a group (with Donny on lead vocals) and for Donny as a soloist with each charting 3 notable hits.

16.   Signs by the Five Man Electrical Band featured lead singer, guitarist and songwriter Les Emmerson upfront. 'Signs' was originally released as the 'B' side of 'Hello Melinda Goodbye'.
 At the time of this book publishing, this band from Canada's Capitol city of Ottawa, Ontario continues to perform with most of its original members

17.   Superstar by the Carpenters was a beautiful ballad written by Leon Russell and Bonnie Bramlett of Delaney and Bonnie fame. The song was originally recorded by Delaney and Bonnie in late 1969 as the 'B' side of their single 'Comin' Home' as 'Groupie' (Superstar). The 'B' side of this Carpenters hit was 'Bless the Beasts and Children', the title song of the film directed by Stanley Kramer which starred Billy Mumy.

18.   She's a Lady by Tom Jones was written by Paul Anka. Wales-born Tom Jones began his music career singing in local nightclubs as Tommy Scott. In 1963, he headed his own trio called 'The Senators'. His string of solo hits began in 1965 and 6 years later he had his highest charting North American hit with 'She's A Lady'.

19.   Rose Garden by Lynn Anderson was the number one Country hit of the year. This million selling hit was written by singer/songwriter Joe South. Pete Drake played steel guitar on this mega hit of 1971. The daughter of Country singer Liz Anderson was one of the most popular Country singers of the 70's.

20.   One Bad Apple by the Osmonds was the very first hit for this legendary family act from Utah. Lead singer Donny Osmond was 13 years old when 'One Bad Apple' was shining in the number one position. He also had a successful solo career which began about a month later with the million selling 'Sweet and Innocent'.

21.   Just My Imagination by the Temptations was a return to their ballad sound in the 60's and featured Eddie Kendricks on lead vocals. This Motown hit was number one the year Temptation members Eddie Kendricks and Paul Williams would leave this legendary vocal group. Two years later, Paul Williams committed suicide and Eddie Kendricks died of lung cancer in 1992.

22.   Want Ads by the Honey Cone was a million seller co-written by General Norman Johnson, the lead singer of The Chairman of The Board. The female trio known as 'The Honey Cone' was recruited by the former Motown songwriting team of Holland/Dozier/Holland. Carolyn Willis was a former member of the Girlfriends and Bob. B. Sox and the Blue Jeans, Edna Wright was the sister of Darlene Love and Sheila Clark was a former member of the Ikettes.

23.   What's Going On by Marvin Gaye was the first of 3 consecutive social comment hits from this talented Motown singer/songwriter/producer in 1971. This hit was the title song of the concept album produced solely my Marvin Gaye which ranks as one of the greatest albums of all time. All 3 consecutive hits reached number one on the R & B charts.

24.   Rainy Days and Mondays by the Carpenters was written by Paul Williams and Roger Nichols, who would also give the vocal act from New Haven, Connecticut the hits 'We've Only Just Begun' and 'I Won't Last a Day without You'. All of the hits of the Carpenters featured the beautiful voice of Karen Carpenter on lead vocals.

25.   Put Your Hand in the Hand by Ocean was written by Gene MacLellan, who also composed Anne Murray's claim to fame, 'Snowbird'. This London, Ontario, Canada vocal group featured the lead vocals of Janice Morgan on this million selling hit from early 1971.

26.   Imagine by John Lennon is considered to be his finest solo creation. This thought-provoking ballad was co-produced by Phil Spector and featured John on piano, Klaus Voorman on bass and Andy White on drums.

27.   Never Can Say Goodbye by the Jackson Five was their 6th consecutive top 5 hit. After this hit, they would have to wait 3 years before their next top 5 achievement with 'Dancing Machine', which would reach number 2 in 1974. 'Never Can Say Goodbye' was a more serious song delivered by pre-teen talent Michael Jackson. In 1974, Gloria Gaynor would revive the song disco style and take it to the top 10 again.

28.   Take Me Home Country Roads by John Denver became his first solo hit 2 years after Peter, Paul and Mary had a number one hit with his composition 'Leavin' on a Jet Plane'. This song was written by and featuring Bill Danoff and Taffy Nivert on backing vocals as 'Fat City'. They evolved into the Starland Vocal Band, best known for their 1976 number one hit 'Afternoon Delight'.

29.   Don't Pull Your Love by Hamilton, Joe Frank and Reynolds were formerly known as 'The T-Bones' and had a top 10 instrumental hit in 1966 with the Alka-Seltzer tune 'No Matter What Shape Your Stomach's In'.

30.   Ain't No Sunshine by Bill Withers was produced by Booker T. Jones of Booker T. and The MG's fame. The song came about when Bill Withers originally forgot the lyrics to the song and improvised by adding 'I know, I know, I know'… It sounded so good, that it was left in for the final recording. The words 'I know' can be heard 26 consecutive times on 'Ain't No Sunshine', which featured Steve Stills on lead guitar.

31.   Proud Mary by Ike and Tina Turner was a unique version of the Creedence Clearwater Revival song from 2 years earlier. This was Ike and Tina Turner's biggest hit as a duo. Tina Turner began her very successful solo career in the early 80's. Her rocky marriage lasted until 1976. Ike Turner died in December 2007 at the age of 76.

32.   It Don't Come Easy by Ringo Starr was produced by George Harrison, who also co-wrote and was featured on guitar. This debut top 40 solo hit by Ringo, featured harmony vocals from 'Apple label mates Pete Ham and Tom Evans of Badfinger.

33. **Baby I'm A Want You** by Bread was another million selling ballad by the soft rock group headed by lead singer/songwriter, David Gates. This hit was popular the year Bread man Robb Royer was replaced by Larry Knechtel, one of the top guitar and keyboard session players in the business. Knechtel played the piano on 'Bridge over Troubled Water' by Simon and Garfunkel and bass guitar on the Byrds' 'Mr. Tambourine Man' among hundreds of other recordings during the 60's and 70's.

34. **For All We Know** by The Carpenters was an Academy Award winning Best song from the film 'Lovers and Other Strangers'. This hit was co-written by 2 of the members of the group Bread, James Griffin (Arthur James) and Robb Royer (Robb Wilson).

35. **Treat Her like a Lady** by Cornelius Brothers and Sister Rose was the first of 3 early 70's hits for this family act from Florida. Their next and final 2 hits would arrive in 1972 with 'Too Late to Turn Back Now' and 'Don't Ever Be Lonely'.

36. **The Night They Drove Old Dixie Down** by Joan Baez was written by J. Robbie Robertson of the Band, and originally featured on the 'B' side of their hit 'Up on Cripple Creek' from 1970.

37. **Lonely Days** by the Bee Gees was their return to the top 10 where they last appeared in early 1969 with 'I Started a Joke'. 'Lonely Days' was a more progressive song by the brothers Gibb with innovative changes, production and effects. After their next hit, 'How Can You Mend a Broken Heart', they would not return to the top again until 4 years later when 'Jive Talkin'' would kick off their disco music career.

38. **Yo Yo** by The Osmonds was another million seller featuring Donny Osmond on lead vocals. This song was written by Joe South and originally recorded by Billy Joe Royal in 1966, the year after 'Down In The Boondocks', also written by South.

39. **Spanish Harlem** by Aretha Franklin was a remake of Ben E. King's hit from 10 years earlier. Dr. John played keyboards on this hit which was Aretha's 3rd of 4 in 1971.

40. **Mr. Big Stuff** by Jean Knight was the only hit for this R & B singer from New Orleans, although she continued to tour successfully afterwards.

41. **Smiling Faces Sometimes** by the Undisputed Truth was the only hit for this Motown Act assembled by Norman Whitfield, producer and co-writer of many of the psychedelic late 60's hits of the Temptations. The Temps originally recorded the social comment song 'Smiling Faces Sometimes' as an album cut, but Whitfield suggested his new act record it as a single where it succeeded into the top 5 on the pop charts.

42.   Draggin' The Line by Tommy James was his first hit without The Shondells. 'Draggin' the Line' was originally released as the 'B' side of 'Church Street Soul Revival'. Tommy James co-wrote, produced and arranged his final top 10 hit 'Draggin' the Line' with Bob King.

43.   Stay Awhile by The Bells was a million selling hit for this Canadian quintet which featured Jacki Ralph and Cliff Edwards on lead vocals. Frank Mills, the 'Music Box Dancer' man was once a member of this vocal group.

44.   Groove Me by King Floyd was the only hit for this soul singer from New Orleans. He was a postal worker up until 'Groove Me' became a million seller and number one hit on the R & B charts. King Floyd died in 2006 at the age of 61 from complications from a stroke and diabetes.

45.   An Old Fashioned Love Song by 3 Dog Night was a mellow, easy listening song written by Paul Williams, who also composed their hit 'Out in the Country' from 1970. 'An Old Fashioned Love Song' was the first of 3 hit singles from their 7th album 'Harmony', with others being 'Never Been To Spain' and 'The Family Of Man', both from 1972.

46.   Got to Be There by Michael Jackson was his very first solo hit. He continued to have the best of both worlds with a career on his own as well as lead singer of the multi-talented family act, The Jackson Five. This was the title song of his debut solo album of the same name which was released a couple of months later in January of 1972.

47.   Another Day by Paul McCartney was his first solo hit after the breakup of the Beatles. This self-produced top 10 hit was backed with 'Oh Woman Oh Why' on the single.

48.   Do You Know What I Mean by Lee Michaels was the only hit for this singer from Los Angeles. His use of the Hammond organ caught the ears of many on this hit, but his follow up remake of Marvin Gaye's 'Can I Get A Witness' failed to impress the record buyers.

49.   If You Could Read My Mind by Gordon Lightfoot was this Canadian singer/songwriter's breakthrough hit outside of his own country, although he had many hits there during the 60's. The song has been recorded by more than a hundred music artists through the years. During the 60's, Gordon Lightfoot wrote 'Early Morning Rain' and 'For Lovin' Me' for Peter, Paul and Mary.

50.   I Am...I Said by Neil Diamond was one of his most personal and emotional songs. He sang about his frustrations being torn between his birthplace in New York and his home in L.A. This single from his 'Stones' album resulted in Neil Diamond's first Grammy Award nomination in the Best Pop Performance, Male category.

51.   I Hear You Knocking by Dave Edmunds was a remake of a song popular by both Smiley Lewis and Fats Domino in the mid- 50's. This Welsh-born singer was previously the master guitarist with the group 'Love Sculpture'. He later formed the group 'Rockpile'. During the 80's he produced the hits of the 'Stray Cats' and the hit 'On the Wings of a Nightingale' by the Everly

Brothers, written by Paul McCartney.

52.   **Amos Moses** by Jerry Reed was one of 2 top 10 hits he achieved in 1971.Atlanta born Jerry Hubbard, better known as Jerry Reed wrote and played guitar on 2 Elvis Hits in the late 60's, 'U.S. Male' and 'Guitar Man'. Jerry Reed was also an actor who starred in the movie 'Smokey and the Bandit' and Adam Sandler's 'Waterboy' as the mean-spirited coach.

53.   **Mama's Pearl** by The Jackson Five was the 5th of 6 consecutive top 5 hits for this Motown family act. This bubblegum/pop/soul hit was the first for 1971 and once again featured Michael Jackson front and centre on lead vocals.

54.   **Have You Seen Her** by the Chi-Lites was a major hit for this Chicago-based vocal group which featured Eugene Record on lead vocals. This number one hit on the R & B charts was written by Eugene Record and his partner Barbara Acklin, who had a big hit of her own in 1968 with 'Love Makes a Woman'. Barbara Acklin died of pneumonia in 1998 at the age of 54.

55.   **If** by Bread was one of the most beautiful love songs of the 70's and another extraordinary song from the soft rock group fronted by singer/ songwriter David Gates.

56.   **Mercy Mercy Me** by Marvin Gaye was the 2nd of 3 powerful social comment hits from the critically-acclaimed album 'What's Going On'. In 'Mercy Mercy Me (The Ecology)', Marvin expressed his environmental concerns in this hit which reached top 5 on the pop charts and number one on the R & B charts. Marvin recruited some musicians outside of Motown to obtain the unique sound created for this song and entire album.

57.   **I've Found Someone of My Own** by Free Movement was an assemblage of members from various mostly-gospel groups united as one. Unfortunately the group was short-lived and the first hit for this Los Angeles based vocal group, was also their last.

58.   **Me and You and a Dog Named Boo** by Lobo was the first of a few hits for the pop singer from Tallahassee, Florida whose real name was Kent Lavoie. Many believed Lobo was a group, when in fact, it was a solo singer who played guitar, sang and wrote his own songs which later included 'I'd Love You to Want Me' and 'Don't Expect Me to Be Your Friend'.

59.   **Sweet City Woman** by The Stampeders was a top 10 hit for this Canadian trio from Calgary, Alberta. This hook-laden hit featured the song's composer, Rich Dodson on lead vocals and banjo. In Canada, this multi-week number one hit won the Juno Award (Canadian equivalent of the Grammy Award) for Single of the Year.

60.   **Doesn't Somebody Want to Be Wanted** by the Partridge Family was their follow up to their first and biggest hit 'I Think I Love You' from 1970. This million seller also prominently featured teen idol David Cassidy on lead vocals.

61.   **Sweet and Innocent** by Donny Osmond was his very first solo hit.

The squeaky voiced Donny, the seventh son of George and Olive Osmond was only 13 when this hit was in the top 10.

62. **Beginnings** by Chicago was written by band member Robert Lamm, who also sang lead on this upbeat hit. The 'B' side was 'Color My World', which was originally the flip side of their first hit 'Make Me Smile' in 1970.

63. **Your Song** by Elton John was the breakthrough hit for this future superstar. This timeless song was originally released as the 'B' side to 'Take Me to Your Pilot', but radio disc jockeys preferred 'Your Song' as the hit. It was taken from Elton John's self-titled second album.

64. **Have You Ever Seen the Rain** by C.C.R. was backed with '**Hey Tonight**', a rockin' good upbeat hit which prominently featured the voice and guitar of John Fogerty. There was much speculation about what 'Have You Ever Seen the Rain' was about, but according to what John Fogerty has said in interviews, it was about the rising tension within C.C.R. and the departure of his brother Tom from the group.

65. **Scorpio** by Dennis Coffey was a top 10 instrumental hit by one of Detroit's top session guitarists. Dennis Coffey introduced the 'wah wah' guitar sound to Motown producer Norman Whitfield and can be heard prominently on The Temptations 'Cloud Nine', as well as The Isley Brothers 'It's Your Thing' and Freda Payne's 'Band Of Gold'.

66. **Stoney End** by Barbara Streisand was written by Laura Nyro and was a much hipper sound for the singer who hadn't had a top 10 hit since 1964's 'People'. Laura Nyro previously wrote many hits for the 5th Dimension as well as 'And When I Die' for Blood, Sweat and Tears and 'Eli's Coming' for 3 Dog Night. 'Stoney End' was produced by Richard Perry.

67. **Help Me Make It through the Night** by Sammi Smith was a million seller and number one Country hit for the singer who made Nashville her home. The biggest hit of her career was 1 of 3 major hits Kris Kristofferson wrote for others popular in 1971. The other 2 were 'Me and Bobby McGee' for Janis Joplin and 'For the Good Times' for Ray Price. Sammi Smith, who dropped out of school at 11 and was married at 15, died at the age of 61 in February of 2005.

68. **Bridge over Troubled Water** by Aretha Franklin was a gospel inspired cover version of the Simon and Garfunkel hit from 1970. Lady Soul's version was top 10 on the pop charts and number one on the R & B charts. Aretha Franklin's version won a Grammy Award Best Female R & B Vocal performance.

69. **Sweet Mary** by Wadsworth Mansion was the only hit from this group from Providence, Rhode Island which featured Steve Jablecki on lead vocals. His brother Mike was also part of this four man band.

70. **Sweet Hitch Hiker** by C.C.R. was their final hit to reach the top 10. In 1971, John Fogerty's brother Tom departed from the group due to creative differences. The 'B' side of 'Sweet Hitch Hiker was 'Door To Door' which was written by bass player Stu Cook, who also composed it. It was the first C.C.R.

recording which didn't headline the talents of John Fogerty and the decline of group began, resulting in disbanding the following year.

71.   Peace Train by Cat Stevens was his 3rd consecutive hit of 1971 and his first to reach the top 10 in the United States. Cat Stevens had several hits prior to the 70's in Britain and Canada on the 'Deram' record label. His hits of the 70's were all recorded on 'A & M". 'Peace Train' was 1 of 3 hit singles from his best selling album 'Teaser and The Firecat'.

72.   I Just Want to Celebrate by Rare Earth was the 3rd top 10 hit by this Detroit rock group which recorded on the Motown subsidiary label which bares their name. Of their 3 top 10 hits, this was the only one which was not a remake of a 60's hit by the Temptations. 'I Just Want To Celebrate' was a feel good party song delivered with the powerful vocals of drummer Pete Rivera.

73.   Mr. Bojangles by The Nitty Gritty Dirt Band was written by and originally recorded by Jerry Jeff Walker in 1968. The song was inspired by Bill 'Bojangles' Robinson, an American tap dancer and actor who was popular in the early 1900's. He died in 1949 at the age of 71.

74.   If You Really Love Me by Stevie Wonder was a top 10 hit he co-wrote with his wife Syreeta Wright, whom he was married to from 1970 to 1972. This hit was from the album 'Where I'm Coming From'; his 13th studio album and his first which he had complete artistic freedom. He produced the entire album, and with Syreeta, wrote all of the songs.

75.   Desiderata by Les Crane was a spoken word hit with lyrics that were originally from a piece of prose, written in 1906 by Max Ehrmann. Les Crane hosted the TV talk Show 'ABC's Nightlife' in the 60's and was once married to Tina Louise of 'Gilligan's Island' fame.

76.   Rock Steady was written and performed by Aretha Franklin and was a danceable, upbeat hit by one of the most awarded singers of our time. Aretha Franklin, who is often referred to as 'Lady Soul' and 'The Queen of Soul' has been awarded numerous Grammy Awards, including 'The Living Legend' and 'Lifetime Achievement Awards'. In 1987, she became the first female artist to be entered into the Rock and Roll Hall of Fame. In 2009, Aretha Franklin was the only featured singer at the Presidential Inauguration ceremony for Barack Obama.

77.   Chick a Boom (Don't Ya Just Love It) by Daddy Dewdrop was a novelty hit from this one hit wonder singer from Cleveland, Ohio whose real name is Richard Monda.

78.   Sooner or Later by The Grassroots was their final official top 10 hit. It was the 2nd of 3 1971 hits, their final year in the top 20. All of their hits were produced by Steve Barri, who with P.F. Sloan wrote hits which included 'Eve of Destruction' for Barry McGuire, 'Secret Agent Man' for Johnny Rivers and 'You Baby' for the Turtles.

79.   Tired of Being Alone by Al Green was the first of a string of hits for this Soul and Gospel singer/songwriter born in Arkansas who later became an ordained Pastor, but never gave up performing.

80. **Whatcha See Is Whatcha Get** by The Dramatics featured all of the members of this Detroit soul group sharing lead vocals, although Ron Banks was their lead singer. This message song was also a popular catch phrase delivered by Flip Wilson's character 'Geraldine' on the Flip Wilson show.

81. **Riders on the Storm** by the Doors was cruisin' up the charts at the time their legendary lead singer Jim Morrison died on July 3rd, 1971 at the age of 27. He was found dead in an apartment bathtub in Paris, France under mysterious circumstances.

82. **When You're Hot, You're Hot** by Jerry Reed was the 2nd hot pop hit of 1971 for this singer/songwriter/guitarist /actor from Atlanta, Georgia. He died in September of 2008 at the age of 71.

83. **What Is Life** by George Harrison was the second single from his triple album 'All Things Must Pass' which produced his biggest hit, 'My Sweet Lord'. Harrison's friend Eric Clapton was a featured guitarist on this Top 10 hit.

84. **If I Were Your Woman** by Gladys Knight and the Pips was a top 10 pop hit and a number one hit on the R & B charts for Motown's most popular male/female group. The song was written by Gloria Jones and Pam Sawyer in 30 minutes one afternoon after a barbecue lunch as they were discussing how women, when they fall in love, can't hold back. This legendary R & B family act from Atlanta, Georgia headed by Gladys Knight, delivered it with emotion and it became a classic.

85. **One Toke over the Line** by Brewer and Shipley was the only notable hit from this pop folk duo who recorded on the Kama Sutra label, best known as the home of all the Lovin' Spoonful hits of the 60's. Mike Brewer and Tom Shipley's song was about a 'toke' from marijuana cigarette or pipe, but they use it as a metaphor for excess, and that too much of anything is not good for you. Apparently Jerry Garcia of Grateful Dead was a session musician on this song, playing the steel guitar.

86. **Wild World** by Cat Stevens was his very first hit in the United States and one of the prime cuts from his critically-acclaimed album 'Tea for the Tillerman'. All of Cat Stevens' most successful albums were produced by Paul Samwell-Smith, former bass and keyboard player for the Yardbirds.

87. **Love the One You're With** by Steve Stills was his first solo hit while actively a member of C, S, N, & Y. David Crosby, Graham Nash, Rita Coolidge and John Sebastian supplied backup vocals on this catchy upbeat hit.

88. **Hey Girl** by Donny Osmond was a remake of the 1963 Freddie Scott hit written by Carole King and Gerry Goffin. This 3rd top 10 solo hit for Donny in 1971, was backed with 'I Knew You When' which was originally a hit for Billy Joe Royal in 1965.

89. **It's Impossible** by Perry Como was one of the surprise hits of 1971. Who would have thought that one of the most popular singers of the 40's and 50's would have a top 10 hit for the first time in over 12 years? 'It's Impossible' was originally a Spanish song from 1968 which was translated into English and presented to the legendary easy listening singer and TV Show host, Perry Como.

90. **She's Not Just another Woman** by 8th Day was a million seller for this 5 man, 3 woman Detroit group of session musicians assembled by producers Holland/Dozier/Holland. The HDH team was formerly the top composers for Motown and launched two record labels of their own 'Hot Wax' and 'Invictus'. Besides the studio group '8th Day', the Chairman of The Board and Freda Payne had all their hits on this label.

91. **Love Her Madly** by The Doors was popular 3 months prior to the death of their dynamic lead singer, Jim Morrison. Guitarist Robby Krieger wrote this hit from their 6th and last studio album 'L.A. Woman'.

92. **That's The Way I've Always Heard It Should Be** by Carly Simon was the first hit from this singer/songwriter from New York City. Thanks to this song, she also won the 'Best New Artist' Grammy Award. Her father, Richard L. Simon is the co-founder of Simon and Schuster publishing.

93. **Watching Scotty Grow** by Bobby Goldsboro was written by Mac 'Scott' Davis about his own son Scotty. After writing hits for Elvis Presley, Kenny Rogers, Bobby Goldsboro and others, Mac Davis began his own hit recording career in 1972 with 'Baby Don't Get Hooked on Me'.

94. **I'll Meet You Halfway** by The Partridge Family was their 3rd consecutive hit to reach the top 10. David Cassidy was the featured lead singer on all of their hits which were produced and mostly co-written by Wes Farrell, who also created the TV show theme, 'Come On, Get Happy'.

95. **Inner City Blues (Make Me Wanna Holler)** by Marvin Gaye was the 3rd of 3 hits from his concept album 'What's Going On'. 'Inner City Blues', which featured Marvin on piano, was about the ghettos of inner city America. Like his previous 2 single releases from this album, this single also reached number one on the R & B chart.

96. **Respect Yourself** by the Staple Singers was a great message song from the Family soul group from Mississippi. This song was co- written by Luther Ingram, who would have his own major hit the following year with '(If Loving You Is Wrong) I Don't Want to Be Right'.

97. **Cherish** by David Cassidy was a remake of the number one hit by the Association from 1966. This was teen idol and Partridge Family star David Cassidy's first and only top 10 solo hit. David was the son of actor Jack Cassidy, stepson of Shirley Jones and half-brother of Shaun Cassidy.

98. **What the World Needs Now/Abraham, Martin and John** by Tom Clay was an attention-grabbing medley of 2 songs interspersed with narration and actual news clips of the tragedies involving Martin Luther King Jr., as well as John and Bobby Kennedy. This top 10 Motown hit ran over 6 minutes, but received lots of radio station airplay due to huge requests and sales. Tom Clay was a Radio announcer in Los Angeles and the singing vocal backup was supplied by the Blackberries.

99. **Temptation Eyes** by the Grassroots was their 1st of 3 1971 hits after achieving 8 top 40 hits during the late 60's.Most of their hits, including this one , were produced by Steve Barri with horns arranged by Jimmie Haskell.

100. **All I Ever Need Is You** by Sonny and Cher was their first top 10 hit together since 'The Beat Goes On' in 1967. This hit was in the top 10 the year their own TV variety series made its debut. 'All I Ever Need is You' was originally offered to Kenny Rogers, but although he turned it down, he eventually recorded it as a duo with Dottie West 8 years later. The song was written by Jimmy Holiday and Eddie Reeves and produced by Snuff Garrett.

101. **Liar** by 3 Dog Night was the follow up single to their mega hit 'Joy to the World' and was featured on their album 'Naturally'. The more progressive 3 Dog Night 'Liar', was written by Russ Ballard of Argent fame and featured Danny Hutton on lead vocals.

102. **(Where Do I Begin) Love Story** by Andy Williams was the vocal version of the theme from the tear-jerking movie which starred Ryan O'Neal and Ali McGraw. Andy Williams was one of the most consistent easy listening singers of the 50's and 60's and 'Love Story' was his first official top 10 hit since 1963, and his final to achieve that status.

103. **Stick Up** by The Honey Cone was originally the title of their first and biggest hit 'Want Ads'. Although 'Stick Up' didn't quite make the top 10, it became a number one hit on the R & B charts.

104. **Power to the People** by John Lennon and The Plastic Ono Band was co-produced by Phil Spector. Backup vocals were provided by 45 singers including Rosetta Hightower, the former lead singer of the early 60's group The Orlons.

105. **Won't Get Fooled Again** by the Who was one of their most powerful and lasting hits. This song, which featured guitar power chords, organ and synthesizer, was written by Pete Townsend with lead vocals delivered by Roger Daltry. This was featured as the final track on their 'Who's Next' album.

106. **I Don't Know How to Love Him** by Helen Reddy was from the rock opera 'Jesus Christ Superstar' written by Andrew Lloyd Webber and Tim Rice. This was the first of several 70's hits for Australian singer Helen Reddy, which included 3 official number ones, 'I Am Woman', 'Delta Dawn' and 'Angie Baby'.

107. **Everybody's Everything** by Santana was their 4th consecutive top 20 hit and the first to feature guest musicians, 'The Tower of Power' horn section. The title of this high energy hit is not mentioned anywhere in the song. A then-teenaged new member Neal Schon played guitar on this hit, but left 2 years later to form the group Journey. He also recruited Santana member Greg Rolie to join this new band.

108. **Never Ending Song of Love** by Delaney and Bonnie and Friends was the highest charted hit for this husband and wife team which included friends which included at various times, Eric Clapton, Leon Russell, Rita Coolidge and Duane Allman among others.

109.   Never My Love by the 5th Dimension was a remake of the 1967 hit by The Association. Marilyn McCoo was prominently featured on this loving ballad written by Don and Dick Addrisi who would surface in 1972 with 'We've Got to Get It on Again' as The Addrisi Brothers.

110.   Immigrant Song by Led Zeppelin was the follow up to their classic 'Whole Lotta Love'. This British heavy metal group wrote 'Immigrant Song' during their tour of Iceland, Bath and Germany in 1970. The 'B' side of this single 'Hey Hey What Can I Do' was not available on any Led Zeppelin album until it was released in 1990 as a boxed set.

111.   Oye Como Va by Santana was their 3rd consecutive hit to feature keyboardist Greg Rolie on lead vocals. This hit was featured on their signature album 'Abraxas'.

112.   Eigtheen by Alice Cooper was the breakthrough hit for this shock rocker from Detroit whose real name is Vincent Furnier. He got his stage name from a 16th century witch. Bob Ezrin, the Canadian producer of this and many other Alice Cooper recordings, also produced hits for Kiss and Pink Floyd.

113.   Bring the Boys Home by Freda Payne was a protest song during the war in Vietnam to stop the war and send the boys home. This was Freda Payne's second gold record and was popular the summer after 'Band of Gold'.

114.   Superstar by Murray Head and the Trinidad Singers, was originally released as a single in 1969, but didn't become a hit until 1971. This Andrew Lloyd Webber/Tim Rice composition was the title song from the popular 'Jesus Christ Superstar' rock opera. It's interesting to note that there were 3 hits in 1971 with the title 'Superstar', each a different song. Besides this one, there was also 'Superstar' by the Carpenters as well as one from the Temptations.

115.   Timothy by the Buoys was written by a then-unknown Rupert Holmes, best known for his number one 1979 hit 'Escape' (The Pina Colada Song). The Buoys were a one hit wonder group from Wilkes-Barre, Pennsylvania and the song was about cannibalism.

116.   I Woke up in Love This Morning by the Partridge Family was another popular 1971 hit from the TV family act. The show was created by Canadian Bernard Slade who was also responsible for 'The Flying Nun' and 'Bridget Loves Bernie'.

117.   Trapped by This Thing Called Love by Denise LaSalle was a number one hit on the R & B charts and top 20 on the pop charts. She was a soul singer/songwriter from Mississippi who scored the biggest hit of her career with this song.

118.   Here Comes That Rainy Day Feeling Again by the Fortunes was another great harmonizing hit from the British group that had a hit in 1965 with 'You've Got Your Troubles', also written by Roger Cook and Roger Greenaway. The Fortunes also sang the popular late 60's Coca Cola jingle 'It's The Real Thing'. Sadly, lead singer Rod Allen died of cancer in January of 2008 at the age of 63.

119. **One Monkey Don't Stop No Show** by The Honey Cone was the 3rd consecutive hit for this trio in their debut chart year. This hit was a Latin-influenced dance favorite at the nightclubs in late '71 and early '72.

120. **Don't Knock My Love** by Wilson Pickett was a number one hit on the R & B charts and his final top 20 hit on the pop charts. Wilson Pickett co-wrote this funky soul hit which featured the Memphis horns, background vocals and the distinctive guitar of Dennis Coffey, who scored a top 10 hit of his own in 1971 with 'Scorpio'.

121. **So Far Away** by Carole King was another prime cut from her monumental 'Tapestry' album. This song featured her friend James Taylor on acoustic guitar in the same year he would have a number one hit with her composition 'You've Got a Friend'. The 'B' side of this single was the popular 'Smackwater Jack'.

122. **We Can Work It Out** by Stevie Wonder was his soul remake of the Beatles classic from early 1966 featured on his album 'Signed, Sealed, Delivered, I'm Yours'.

123. **Easy Loving** by Freddie Hart was a multi-week number one hit on the Country charts and top 20 on the pop charts. This song was so popular in the Country Music format that it won the Country Music Association's Song of the Year two years in a row, in 1971 and 1972.

124. **Theme from Love Story** by Henry Mancini was one of 2 popular instrumental versions from the film which made popular the line 'Love means never having to say you're sorry'. Although Henry Mancini is best known for all the films he scored the music for, it was Francis Lai who composed this instrumental.

125. **Amazing Grace** by Judy Collins was recorded at St. Paul's Chapel at Columbia University. The words for 'Amazing Grace' were written in 1779 by Reverend John Newton with the music being composed in 1884.

126. **Born to Wander** by Rare Earth was one of their hits produced by Tom Baird, who also wrote this follow up to their single '(I Know) I'm Losing You'.

127. **Stones** by Neil Diamond was the title song from his album which also featured his top 10 hit 'I Am...I Said'. Aside from his self-composed songs on this album, he recorded compositions by Joni Mitchell, Randy Newman, Leonard Cohen and Roger Miller.

128. **Double Lovin'** by The Osmonds was the 2nd of 3 1971 hits by this popular family act which centered on a young Donny Osmond.

129. **Funky Nassau** by The Beginning of the End could also describe their career, because this was their first and last hit. This happy-go-lucky funky hit by this group from the Bahamas graced the dance floors and radio airwaves during the spring and summer of 1971.

130. **Where Did Our Love** Go by Donnie Elbert was a remake of the first

Supremes hit to reach number one. This New Orleans born singer and multi-instrumentalist would also revive the Four Tops 'I Can't Help Myself' and bring it into the top 30 in 1972.

131. Two Divided by Love by the Grassroots was their final top 20 hit. This goodtime brassy pop rock band was fronted by lead singer Rob Grill. All of their major hits were recorded on the Dunhill label in the U.S.

132. Thin Line between Love and Hate by The Persuaders was a million seller and number one R & B hit for this one hit wonder soul group from New York City. The lead singer was Douglas 'Smokey' Scott.

133. No Love At All by B.J. Thomas was a social comment hit about people, breakups and relationships. After many personal ups and downs, B. J. Thomas became a born again Christian in the late 70's and also became a Gospel music singer.

134. Hot Pants part 1 by James Brown was a dance hit about the hottest fashion on women in 1971. It was also the year James Brown left 'King' Records, the independent label that put over 60 of his singles on the charts. 'Hot Pants' was James Brown's last recording for 'King' and the 2nd release on his newly established label 'People', before he switched to Polydor records.

135. Remember Me by Diana Ross was her follow up to 'Ain't No Mountain High Enough' which became her first number one solo hit. This was also written by Ashford and Simpson, who supplied background vocals.

136. Here Comes the Sun by Ritchie Havens was a remake of a Beatles song written by George Harrison. Ritchie Havens was best known for opening 'Woodstock' 2 years earlier with his distinctive voice and performance playing an acoustic guitar.

137. Nathan Jones by the Supremes was another hit for the popular Motown girl group after the departure of Diana Ross. This hit was produced by Frank Wilson and featured all 3 Supremes, Jean Terrell, Mary Wilson and Cindy Birdsong singing in unison, and was also unusual with the 'phasing' effect used on this Motown hit.

138. A Natural Man by Lou Rawls was a social comment hit from the man with the golden voice. 1971 was the year he left Capitol records and then signed with 'MGM', which gave him his first and final hit until he had the biggest hit of his career with Columbia records in 1976 with 'You'll Never Find Another Love Like Mine'. Lou Rawls died of cancer in early 2006 at the age of 72.

139. Rings by Cymarron was a soft rock hit from this one hit wonder group from Memphis produced by Chips Moman who helped make hits for B.J.Thomas, Willie Nelson, Waylon Jennings and Tammy Wynette. 'Rings' was a catchy play on words which became a minor hit for Lobo in 1974.

140. Cried like a Baby by Bobby Sherman was his follow up to 'Julie Do Ya Love Me' and his final hit to reach the top 20. 1971 was the year teen idol

Bobby Sherman made an appearance on the Partridge Family Show with the other top teen idol of the day, David Cassidy. The ratings were so good, Bobby Sherman was given his own show on ABC, 'Getting Together'.

141. **Don't Let the Green Grass Fool You** by Wilson Pickett was an advice song from the R & B singer who had many personal problems later in life with arrests involving guns, assault and drunk driving charges. He died in early 2006 at the age of 64, but left behind some great soul classics.

142. **Raindance** by The Guess Who was a social comment hit popular in the same year they had hits with 'Albert Flasher' and 'Sour Suite', all featuring Burton Cummings on lead vocals.

143. **Woodstock** by Matthews Southern Comfort was popular 2 years after the event and 1 year after Crosby, Stills, Nash and Young had a hit with this song. This version of the Joni Mitchell composition was a much mellower and slower paced rendition of the song. Mathews Southern Comfort lead singer Ian Matthews had a solo hit in 1978 with 'Shake It'.

144. **Chirpy Chirpy Cheep Cheep** by Mac and Katie Kissoon was the only hit for this brother and sister duo that was originally from Port-Of-Spain, but moved to England in the late 50's. The version of this song by 'Middle of the Road' reached number one in Britain, but this was the most popular version in North America.

145. **We Gotta Get You a Woman** by Runt was actually Todd Rundgren. Todd, who formerly headed the band 'Nazz,' was a multi-instrumentalist who was also a master at producing and writing.

146. **Toast and Marmalade for Tea** by Tin Tin was produced by Maurice Gibb of the Bee Gees. This Australian trio had a very unusual and distinctive sound on what would be their only hit.

147. **I Don't Want to Do Wrong** by Gladys Knight and the Pips was their follow up to 'If I Were Your Woman'. The group got their name 'Pips' from their Manager Cousin James 'Pips' Woods.

148. **I Don't Blame You At All** by Smokey Robinson and The Miracles was their final hit before their lead singer/songwriter/producer left the group for a solo career.

149. **Theme from the Summer of '42** by Peter Nero was the title tune from the movie starring Jennifer O'Neill. Peter Nero was a Brooklyn-born Pop/Jazz// classical pianist who has released almost 70 albums through the years.

150. **Love the One You're With** by The Isley Brothers was a hit just 6 months after the original by Steve Stills was enjoying chart success. The Isleys' brought their special soul treatment of the song into the top 20 again.

151. **Superstar (Remember How You Got Where You Are)** by the Temptations was the 3rd hit in 1971 with the 'Superstar' title, but each was a completely different song. This song was apparently an attack on the 2 former

Temptations members David Ruffin and Eddie Kendricks.

152. **Love Lines, Angles and Rhymes** by the 5th Dimension was another ballad which featured Marilyn McCoo on lead vocals. This was the title song from their 6th album and was the only top 20 hit featured on it.

153. **Only You Know and I Know** by Delaney & Bonnie and Friends was their final top 20 hit. This song was originally recorded by Dave Mason in 1970. Delaney and Bonnie's musical roots go back to the 60's when Delaney Bramlett was a member of the TV house band the 'Shindogs' on the 'Shindig' music TV show while Bonnie performed as a teenager as a member of Ike and Tina Turner's revue. Delaney and Bonnie dissolved their marriage and group in 1972.

154. **Double Barrel** by Dave and Ansil Collins was the only hit for this Jamaican duo known for this catchy reggae-flavored hit with a great echo effect and the 'I Am the Magnificent, W. 0. 0. 0.'

155. **You're All I Need to Get By** from Aretha Franklin was a remake of the Motown song made famous by Marvin Gaye and Tammi Terrell in 1968.

156. **High Time We Went** by Joe Cocker was a rockin' hit from the wild singer from Sheffield, England. This was his first original hit, and one he co-wrote with Chris Stainton. The 'B' side of this single, 'Black Eyed Blues' also received some attention.

157. **Get It On** by Chase was a great horn-filled super fast hit from this one hit wonder Jazz-Rock Band. Trumpeter Bill Chase, who was formerly with Woody Herman and Stan Kenton, was killed in a plane crash in the summer of 1974.

158. **Right On the Tip of My Tongue** by Brenda and the Tabulations was a hit in the spring of 1971 for this Philadelphia R & B vocal group.

159. **The Wedding Song (There is Love)** by Paul Stookey of Peter, Paul and Mary fame, became a popular ballad played at wedding receptions everywhere.

160. **Blue Money** by Van Morrison was his 2nd hit from the album 'His Band and the Street Choir', while its 'B' side 'Sweet Thing' was from Van's album 'Astral Weeks'.

161. **I Love You for All Seasons** by Fuzz was the only hit for this female trio from Washington. The 'B' side of the single was an instrumental version of the song.

162. **Free** by Chicago was the first of 3 hits from 1971 by this Jazz-Brass Rock band from the city that bears their name. This hit was from 'Chicago 3' and was written by Robert Lamm.

163. **I Really Don't Want to Know** by Elvis Presley was originally a hit in 1954 for Les Paul and Mary Ford and again in 1960 for Tommy Edwards.

164.   Maybe Tomorrow by The Jackson Five was their first hit that failed to reach the top 5 after half a dozen consecutive big hit singles. This was the title song of the album which also included their hit 'Never Can Say Goodbye'.

165.   Make It Funky by James Brown was his first hit on his new label 'Polydor' and this Godfather of Soul offering with a party groove, reached number one on the R & B charts. James Brown produced and co-wrote 'Make It Funky'.

166.   The Story in Your Eyes by The Moody Blues was their only charted hit in 1971.This fast-paced hit featured lead singer/songwriter/guitarist Justin Hayward and prominently highlighted the melotron played by Mike Pinder. This single was from their album 'Every Good Boy Deserves Favour'.

167.   Never Can Say Goodbye by Isaac Hayes was his version of a song the Jackson Five had great success with. The biggest hit of his career would follow a few months later with 'Theme from Shaft'.

168.   One Fine Morning by Lighthouse was the biggest hit in the U.S. for this Canadian brass rock band from Toronto. Bob McBride was the lead singer on this powerful song written by drummer and co-founder Skip Prokop.

169.   Birds of a Feather by The Raiders, written by Joe South, was the final top 30 hit for this pop/rock band from Portland, Oregon. This was the follow up to their biggest hit of all, 'Indian Reservation' from earlier in 1971.

170.   Bangla Desh by George Harrison was co-produced by Phil Spector and featured his Beatle buddy Ringo Starr on drums. George Harrison organized the Bangladesh benefit concerts at Madison Square Garden in 1971.

More hits from 1971

(I Know) I'm Losing You by Rod Stewart with Faces was a remake of the Rare Earth hit from 1970, which was a remake of the Temptations hit from 1966.

Absolutely Right by the Five Man Electrical Band was the high energy follow up to 'Signs' from earlier in 1971. Lead singer/songwriter Les Emmerson fronted this and other hits they charted during the 70's.

Moon Shadow by Cat Stevens was his 2nd of 3 hits in 1971 and was taken from his album 'Teaser and The Firecat', which was also a successful children's book he wrote and illustrated. 'Moon Shadow' was another of Cat Stevens' philosophical songs and one he noted as his personal favorites. Cat Stevens was born Steven Georgiou in London, England and since his conversion to the Muslim religion in the late 70's, is known as 'Yusef Islam'.

Albert Flasher by the Guess Who was a rockin' good hit which featured Burton Cummings on lead vocals and piano. Canada's most successful Rock band continued their winning ways from the late 60's into the early 70's with one hit right after another.

Heavy Makes You Happy (Sha-na-boom-boom) by The Staple Singers was co-written by Bobby Bloom of 'Montego Bay' fame. This was the first of a string of hits for this family gospel soul group from Mississippi.

Cool Aid by Paul Humphrey and the Cool Aid Chemists was a moderately successful instrumental hit for this one hit wonder music act.

Games by Redeye was the only hit for this rock quartet led by Dave Hodgkins and Douglas 'Red' Mark. On this hit, they had a great harmonizing sound similar to Crosby, Stills, Nash and Young.

Wild Night by Van Morrison was a very upbeat song from this Northern Irish singer/songwriter. This hit from the 'Tupelo Honey' album was produced by Van Morrison and Ted Templeman, producer of the Doobie Brothers and Van Halen. This was remade and popularized again in 1994 by John Mellencamp.

If Not for You by Olivia-Newton John, written by Bob Dylan, was the very first hit for this pop singer from Australia. Her next hit would not arrive until 2 and half years later with 'Let Me Be There', and that was followed by a long string of hits and an acting career.

Questions 67 and 68 by Chicago was originally released as a single in 1969 with very little success. It was re-released as a single in the fall of 1971 backed with a great version of 'I'm A Man' which was originally a hit in 1967 for the Spencer Davis Group.

Saturday Morning Confusion by Bobby Russell was a fun social comment hit from a talent known primarily as a songwriter. As a composer, he wrote 'Honey' for Bobby Goldsboro, 'Little Green Apples' for O.C.Smith, 'The Joker Went Wild' for Brian Hyland and 'The Night The Lights Went Out In Georgia' for his former wife, Vicki Lawrence. Bobby Russell died in 1992 at the age of 52.

Stagger Lee by Tommy Roe, produced by Steve Barri, was the final top 40 hit from this Atlanta, Georgia born singer who had a string of hits in the 60's which included 'Sheila', 'Sweet Pea' and 'Dizzy'. This was the 3rd time out for the song 'Stagger Lee' which was a hit in the 50's by Lloyd Price and a hit in the 60's for Wilson Pickett.

Chicago by Graham Nash was the first solo hit from the member of Crosby, Stills, Nash and Young. This social comment hit was about Black Panther leader Bobby Seale and the Chicago Seven who were on trial for conspiracy to riot at the 1968 Democratic convention.

I Ain't Got Time Anymore by the Glass Bottle was the only top 40 hit for this American group fronted by Gary Criss. This hit was co-produced by novelty artist Dickie Goodman.

1900 Yesterday by Liz Damon's Orient Express was the only hit for this 3 woman, 6 man group from Hawaii. They recorded this dreamy, easy listening hit on the White Whale record label where the Turtles placed their hits of the 60's.

Burning Bridges by the Mike Curb Congregation was from the movie 'Kelly's Heroes', which starred Clint Eastwood and many other notable actors. Mike Curb was the President of MGM records at the time this hit was released and a few years later he started up his own record label, 'Curb Records'. He was also a politician and was elected Lieutenant Governor of California in 1978. 'Burning Bridges' was composed by Lalo Schifrin, the creator of the 'Mission: Impossible' theme.

(Do The) Push and Pull by Rufus Thomas was a number one hit on the R & B charts and was a favorite at the dance clubs. He was previously known for his top 10 1963 hit 'Walking the Dog'. The father of singer Carla Thomas was 84 when he died in December of 2001.

(For God's Sake) Give More Power To The People by the Chi-Lites was a protest song from this R & B group primarily known for their 2 big hits that followed, 'Have You Seen Her' and 'Oh Girl'.

Wild Horses by The Rolling Stones was their follow up to 'Brown Sugar', also from the 'Sticky Fingers' album. The song was originally recorded over a 3 day time period at Muscle Shoals Sound Studio in Alabama in December of 1969, but legal problems with their former label prevented the Stones from releasing it then.

One Tin Soldier (Legend of Billy Jack) by Coven was the version featured in the movie 'Billy Jack' starring Tom Laughlin. The version by Canadian group 'Original Caste' was popular over a year before the 'Coven' version.

The Drum by Bobby Sherman was the final top 30 hit for this teen idol singer and TV star. This hit was co-written by Alan O'Day who not only wrote hits for others, but had a number one hit of his own with 'Undercover Angel' in 1977.

Puppet Man by Tom Jones was a hit for the 5th Dimension the year before, in 1970. Neil Sedaka co-wrote this moderately successful hit.

I Play and Sing by Tony Orlando and Dawn was a very similar-sounding hit as their previous 'Candida' and 'Knock 3 Times' and had very limited success.

Theme from Love Story by Francis Lai was the original version of the instrumental featured in the film which starred Ryan O'Neal and Ali McGraw.

Lucky Man by Emerson, Lake and Palmer was a progressive hit from this British classical-oriented rock trio. Keith Emerson came from the group 'Nice', Greg Lake came from 'King Crimson' and Carl Palmer came from 'Atomic Rooster and 'The Crazy World of Arthur Brown'.

It's A Cryin' Shame by Gayle McCormick was the only solo hit from the singer who fronted 'Smith' on their powerful 1969 remake of 'Baby Its You', which was produced by Del Shannon.

Resurrection Shuffle by Ashton, Gardner and Dyke was a much bigger hit in England for this British trio than it was in North America. Unfortunately, this was the only hit for the trio that gave us this great hit from '71.

Where Evil Grows by the Poppy Family, featured Terry Jacks on lead vocals, accompanied by his wife Susan. The original 'A' side, 'I Was Wondering' became the 'B' side of this single.

Love Means (You Never Have to Say you're Sorry) by Sounds of Sunshine was inspired by the catchphrase from the movie 'Love Story'. This one hit wonder group, which sounded very much like the Lettermen on this recording, were actually 3 brothers, Walt, Warner and George Wilder from Los Angeles.

Mighty Clouds of Joy by B.J. Thomas was the first of his gospel-influenced recordings, which he would explore more during the late 70's.

I'd Love to Change the World by Ten Years After was the only top 40 hit for this British rock quartet which featured Alvin Lee on lead vocals. Their breakthrough North American performance was at Woodstock in the summer of '69 when they performed 'I'm Going Home'.

Loving Her Was Easier by Kris Kristofferson was the first solo pop for this singer/songwriter from the year 3 of his compositions did well for Janis Joplin, Ray Price and Sammi Smith. He was married to Rita Coolidge from 1973 to 1980 and he starred in several movies including 'A Star Is Born' with Barbara Streisand.

I Don't Know How To Love Him by Yvonne Elliman was the original version of the song from 'Jesus Christ Superstar' in which she played the part of Mary Magdalene. Helen Reddy also had a hit with this song in 1971.

Let Your Love Go by Bread was their venture into an upbeat rock style, which failed to catch on with the radio listeners and record buyers who preferred their familiar soft pop ballads.

You've Got a Friend by Roberta Flack and Donny Hathaway was the first charted single for both singers, but failed to do well since it was directly competing at the same time with the James Taylor version of this Carole King composition which went to number one.

Soul Power part 1 by James Brown was the 2nd of 9 singles released by James Brown in 1971 and his 19th hit since 1965 which had a 'Part 1' listed beside its title.

Precious, Precious by Jackie Moore was a million seller for this female soul singer from Jacksonville, Florida, despite only reaching number 30 on the pop charts.

Long Ago and Far Away by James Taylor was the follow up to the biggest hit of his career, 'You've Got a Friend'. This song featured Carole King on piano and Joni Mitchell on backing vocals.

Somebody's Watching You by Little Sister was written and produced by big brother, Sly (Sylvester Stewart) Stone. This was Little Sister's 2nd hit, following 'You're The One' in 1970.

Summer Sand by Dawn was a feel good summer beach tune delivered by Tony Orlando and his backup vocalists.

D.O.A. by Bloodrock was the only hit for this rock group from Fort Worth, Texas headed by lead singer Jim Rutledge. This was quite a morbid song when it was released in early 1971.

Battle Hymn of Lt. Calley by C.Company featuring Terry Nelson was a controversial hit which offered a heroic description of Lt. William Calley, who was sentenced and convicted to life in prison for murdering Vietnamese civilians in the My Lai. It was a spoken word recording with vocals by Terry Nelson to the tune of 'Battle Hymn of The Republic'.

Just Seven Numbers (Can Straighten out My Life) by The Four Tops barely made the top 40, although it was another great hit which featured the distinctive voice of lead singer Levi Stubbs. Levi died in October of 2008 at the age of 72, after battling cancer for several years.

Marianne by Stephen Stills was his 2nd and final solo hit, although it featured great guitar accompaniment by the legendary Eric Clapton and Nils Lofgren.

So Long Marianne by Brian Hyland was written by Leonard Cohen and became the final hit for the singer from Queens, New York, whose first hit 'Itsy Bitsy Teenie Weenie Yellow Polka Dot Bikini' became his biggest hit at the age of 16.

Silver Moon by Michael Nesmith was his follow up to his first solo hit 'Joanne'. This hit was featured on his RCA album 'Loose Salute'. The piano on this song was played by Glen Hardin, who wrote 3 hits for Gary Lewis and the Playboys including 'Count Me In'. He played with Elvis during the 70's and arranged some of his hits including 'The Wonder of You'.

Do Me Right by Detroit Emeralds was an almost hypnotic soul hit from this band originally from Little Rock, Arkansas. They were known as 'The Emeralds' until they moved to Detroit.

Rainy Jane by Davy Jones was co-written by Neil Sedaka. This was the former Monkees most successful solo hit.

I Hear Those Church Bells Ringing by Dusk was the opposite of Dawn and was created by the same producers, Hank Medress and Dave Appell. The lead singer was Peggy Santiglia, who was lead singer of the Angels of 'My Boyfriend's Back' fame in the 60's. 'Dusk' also had a minor hit with the similar sounding 'Angel Baby' (not the same as Rosie & The Originals song) in 1971.

Do I Love You by Paul Anka was his first hit of the 70's. This love ballad was very popular in Canada.

Mammy Blue by the Pop Tops was a very unique sounding song by this vocal/instrumental group which formed in Madrid, Spain in 1967 with lead vocals by Phil Trim who was from the West Indies. This group was also known as 'Los Pop Tops'.

Whole Lotta Love by C.C.S. was an instrumental remake of the classic Led Zeppelin song. The British jazz/rock band led by Alexis Korner, C.C.S., was short for 'Collective Consciousness Society'. They were produced by Mickie Most.

Chairman of the Board by The Chairman of The Board was a salute to them, but just missed the top 40.

I'm Comin' Home by Tommy James was his final hit of the 70's. This hit was produced by Jimmy 'Wiz' Wisner and featured backing vocals by the Stephentown Singers.

Top 17 Albums of 1971

1.	Tapestry	Carole King
2.	Pearl	Janis Joplin
3.	All Things Must Pass	George Harrison
4.	Sticky Fingers	Rolling Stones
5.	Every Picture Tells a Story	Rod Stewart
6.	Santana	Santana
7.	Jesus Christ Superstar	Various Artists
8.	4 Way Street	Crosby, Stills, Nash & Young
9.	Imagine	John Lennon
10.	Shaft	Isaac Hayes
11.	Chicago 3	Chicago
12.	Love Story	Soundtrack
13.	Up To Date	Partridge Family
14.	Ram	Paul and Linda McCartney
15.	Every Good Boy Deserves…	Moody Blues
16.	Santana 3	Santana
17.	There's A Riot Goin' On	Sly & the Family Stone

Top 17 Country Hits of 1971

1.	Rose Garden	Lynn Anderson
2.	Kiss an Angel Good Morning	Charley Pride
3.	When you're Hot, You're Hot	Jerry Reed
4.	Empty Arms	Sonny James
5.	I'm Just Me	Charley Pride
6.	Easy Loving	Freddie Hart
7.	Help Me Make It thru ...Night	Sammi Smith
8.	I'd Rather Love You	Charley Pride
9.	I Won't Mention It Again	Ray Price
10.	How Can I Unlove You	Lynn Anderson
11.	The Year That Clayton D...Died	Tom T. Hall
12.	After The Fire Is Gone	Conway Twitty & Loretta Lynn
13.	You're My Man	Lynn Anderson
14.	Good Lovin' (Makes It Right)	Tammy Wynette
15.	Daddy Frank (Guitar Man)	Merle Haggard
16.	Flesh and Blood	Johnny Cash
17.	Lead Me On	Conway Twitty & Loretta Lynn

Top 17 One Hit Wonders of 1971

1.	Jean Knight	Mr. Big Stuff
2.	Undisputed Truth	Smiling Faces Sometimes
3.	Free Movement	I've Found Someone of My Own
4.	King Floyd	Groove Me
5.	Lee Michaels	Do You Know What I Mean
6.	Wadsworth Mansion	Sweet Mary
7.	Daddy Dewdrop	Chick A Boom
8.	Les Crane	Desiderata
9.	Brewer and Shipley	One Toke over the Line
10.	Buoys	Timothy
11.	The 8th Day	She's Not Just Another Woman
12.	Beginning Of the End	Funky Nassau
13.	Cymarron	Rings
14.	Mac and Katie Kissoon	Chirpy Chirpy Cheep Cheep
15.	Tin Tin	Toast and Marmalade for Tea
16.	Dave and Ansil Collins	Double Barrel
17.	Chase	Get It On

Top 17 R & B/Soul Hits of 1971

1.	What's Going On	Marvin Gaye
2.	Family Affair	Sly & the Family Stone
3.	Mr. Big Stuff	Jean Knight
4.	Groove Me	King Floyd
5.	Just My Imagination	Temptations
6.	Want Ads	Honey Cone
7.	Spanish Harlem	Aretha Franklin
8.	Never Can Say Goodbye	Jackson Five
9.	Mercy Mercy Me	Marvin Gaye
10.	Bridge Over Troubled Water	Aretha Franklin
11.	Stick Up	Honey Cone
12.	Have You Seen Her	Chi-Lites
13.	Make It Funky	James Brown
14.	(Do The) Push and Pull	Rufus Thomas
15.	Inner City Blues	Marvin Gaye
16.	Jody's Got Your Girl and Gone	Johnny Taylor
17.	If I Were Your Woman	Gladys Knight & the Pips

Top 17 Rock/Hard Rock Hits of 1971

1.	Brown Sugar	Rolling Stones
2.	Immigrant Song	Led Zeppelin
3.	Won't Get Fooled Again	Who
4.	Eighteen	Alice Cooper
5.	Power to the People	John Lennon/Plastic Ono Band
6.	I Just Want To Celebrate	Rare Earth
7.	High Time We Went	Joe Cocker
8.	Sweet Hitch Hiker	C.C.R.
9.	Love Her Madly	Doors
10.	The Story in Your Eyes	Moody Blues
11.	D. O. A.	Bloodrock
12.	I'd Love to Change the World	Ten Years After
13.	Do You Know What I Mean	Lee Michaels
14.	Hey Tonight	C.C.R.
15.	I'm A Man	Chicago
16.	Wild Horses	Rolling Stones
17.	Behind Blue Eyes	Who

17 Notable Lost 45's of 1971

1.	Chirpy Chirpy Cheep Cheep	Mac and Katie Kisoon
2.	Get It On	Chase
3.	Marianne	Steve Stills
4.	Toast and Marmalade for Tea	Tin Tin
5.	Timothy	Buoys
6.	Sweet Mary	Wadsworth Mansion
7.	Double Barrel	Dave and Ansil Collins
8.	Burning Bridges	Mike Curb Congregation
9.	Rings	Cymarron
10.	Funky Nassau	Beginning Of the End
11.	Pushbike Song	Mixtures
12.	Saturday Morning Confusion	Bobby Russell
13.	I Hear Those Church Bells …	Dusk
14.	Games	Redeye
15.	Just Seven Numbers	Four Tops
16.	1900 Yesterday	Liz Damon's Orient Express
17.	Resurrection Shuffle	Ashton, Gardner & Dyke

1.	You Light Up My Life	Debby Boone	1977
2.	Joy to the World	3 Dog Night	1971
3.	Bridge Over Troubled Water	Simon and Garfunkel	1970
4.	My Sharona	Knack	1979
5.	The First Time Ever I Saw Your Face	Roberta Flack	1972
6.	American Pie	Don McLean	1972
7.	Le Freak	Chic	1978
8.	Tie A Yellow Ribbon …Old Oak Tree	Tony Orlando and Dawn	1973
9.	The Way We Were	Barbara Streisand	1974
10.	I'll Be There	Jackson Five	1970
11.	Love Will Keep Us Together	Captain and Tennille	1975
12.	Killing Me Softly With His Song	Roberta Flack	1973
13.	Bad Girls	Donna Summer	1979
14.	It's Too Late	Carole King	1971
15.	Kiss You All Over	Exile	1978
16.	Raindrops Keep Fallin' On My Head	B.J. Thomas	1970
17.	Best Of My Love	Emotions	1977
18.	(They Long To Be) Close To You	Carpenters	1970
19.	Disco Lady	Johnny Taylor	1976
20.	Reunited	Peaches and Herb	1979
21.	I Can See Clearly Now	Johnny Nash	1972
22.	I Will Survive	Gloria Gaynor	1979
23.	Afternoon Delight	Starland Vocal Band	1976
24.	Without You	Nilsson	1972
25.	Love Theme from 'A Star Is Born'	Barbara Streisand	1977
26.	I Think I Love You	Partridge Family	1970
27.	Bad Blood	Neil Sedaka	1975
28.	Hot Stuff	Donna Summer	1979
29.	Lean On Me	Bill Withers	1972
30.	Kiss And Say Goodbye	Manhattens	1976
31.	Boogie Oogie Oogie	A Taste Of Honey	1978
32.	Ain't No Mountain High Enough	Diana Ross	1970

33.	Rhinestone Cowboy	Glen Campbell	1975
34.	December 1963 (Oh What A Night)	Four Seasons	1976
35.	Knock Three Times	Tony Orlando and Dawn	1971
36.	You're So Vain	Carly Simon	1973
37.	Play That Funky Music	Wild Cherry	1976
38.	Escape (The Pina Colada Song)	Rupert Holmes	1979
39.	Sir Duke	Stevie Wonder	1977
40.	Bad Bad Leroy Brown	Jim Croce	1973
41.	War	Edwin Starr	1970
42.	I Want You Back	Jackson Five	1970
43.	The Streak	Ray Stevens	1974
44.	Billy Don't Be A Hero	Bo Donaldson & the Heywoods	1974
45.	Babe	Styx	1979
46.	Gypsies, Tramps and Thieves	Cher	1971
47.	The Candy Man	Sammy Davis Junior	1972
48.	50 Ways to Leave Your Lover	Paul Simon	1976
49.	The Tears of A Clown	Smokey Robinson & Miracles	1970
50.	Kung Fu Fighting	Carl Douglas	1974
51.	Cracklin' Rosie	Neil Diamond	1970
52.	Fly Robin Fly	Silver Convention	1975
53.	If You Leave Me Now	Chicago	1976
54.	Me and Mrs. Jones	Billy Paul	1972
55.	The Nights the Lights ...in Georgia	Vicki Lawrence	1973
56.	MacArthur Park	Donna Summer	1978
57.	Thank You	Sly and the Family Stone	1970
58.	Will It Go Round in Circles	Billy Preston	1973
59.	T.S.O.P.	M.F.S.B. with the 3 Degrees	1974
60.	Laughter In The Rain	Neil Sedaka	1975
61.	Everything Is Beautiful	Ray Stevens	1970
62.	Midnight Train To Georgia	Gladys Knight and the Pips	1973
63.	Family Affair	Sly and the Family Stone	1971
64.	The Locomotion	Grand Funk	1974
65.	Star Wars Theme/Cantina Band	Meco	1977
66.	You've Got A Friend	James Taylor	1971
67.	Theme from Shaft	Isaac Hayes	1971
68.	Baby Come Back	Player	1978
69.	I Can Help	Billy Swan	1974
70.	Brand New Key	Melanie	1971
71.	Torn Between Two Lovers	Mary MacGregor	1977
72.	Make It with You	Bread	1970
73.	Indian Reservation	Raiders	1971
74.	Me and Bobby McGee	Janis Joplin	1971
75.	5th of Beethoven	Walter Murphy	1976
76.	Grease	Frankie Valli	1978
77.	3 Times A Lady	Commodores	1978
78.	Baby Don't Get Hooked On Me	Mac Davis	1972
79.	Cats in the Cradle	Harry Chapin	1974
80.	A Horse with No Name	America	1972

81. You Don't Bring Me Flowers	Barbara Streisand & N.Diamond	1978
82. Rock Your Baby	George McCrae	1974
83. Too Much, Too Little, Too Late	Johnny Mathis & Den.Williams	1978
84. ABC	Jackson Five	1970
85. My Ding A Ling	Chuck Berry	1972
86. Rise	Herb Alpert	1979
87. He Don't Love You (Like I Do)	Tony Orlando and Dawn	1975
88. Want Ads	Honeycone	1971
89. Brandy (You're A Fine Girl)	Looking Glass	1972
90. No More Tears (Enough Is Enough)	Barbara Streisand & D.Summer	1979
91. Rich Girl	Hall and Oates	1977
92. Let's Stay Together	Al Green	1972
93. Brother Louie	Stories	1973
94. Love's Theme	Love Unlimited Orchestra	1974
95. Superstar	Carpenters	1971
96. Disco Duck	Rick Dees & His Cast of Idiots	1976
97. Ring My Bell	Anita Ward	1979
98. Rose Garden	Lynn Anderson	1971
99. My Eyes Adored You	Frankie Valli	1975
100. The Joker	Steve Miller Band	1974
101. Rock the Boat	Hues Corporation	1974
102. Love Hangover	Diana Ross	1976
103. What A Fool Believes	Doobie Brothers	1979
104. One Bad Apple	Osmonds	1971
105. Best Of My Love	Eagles	1975
106. I Write the Songs	Barry Manilow	1976
107. Just My Imagination	Temptations	1971
108. The Most Beautiful Girl	Charlie Rich	1973
109. Hotel California	Eagles	1977
110. Papa Was A Rolling Stone	Temptations	1972
111. That's The Way I Like It	K.C. & the Sunshine Band	1975
112. Car Wash	Rose Royce	1977
113. Black and White	3 Dog Night	1972
114. Go Away Little Girl	Donny Osmond	1971
115. Thank God I'm A Country Boy	John Denver	1975
116. You Don't Have To Be A Star	Marilyn McCoo & Billy Davis Jr.	1977
117. Oh Girl	Chi-Lites	1972

♫ This novelty hit was the legendary Chuck Berry's only number one hit.

♫ George Harrison produced and played slide guitar on this top 10 hit for Badfinger

♫ Michael Jackson's first number one solo hit was from a movie about a rat.

♫ Johann Sebastian Bach inspired this top 10 instrumental hit from 1972.

♫ This hit by the Moody Blues did not become a hit until 5 years after it was recorded.

♫ A toy piano was used on this hit by this popular duo.

FIND OUT THAT...AND MUCH MORE INSIDE 1972!

1.   **Alone Again (Naturally)** by Gilbert O'Sullivan was the debut North American hit for this singer/songwriter from Ireland. His real name is Raymond O'Sullivan, but it was changed as a play on words to 'Gilbert and Sullivan', the famous composers from the Victorian era. Although this multi-week number one hit was written by Gilbert O'Sullivan, none of the situations in the song ever happened to him. He didn't cry when his father died, and his mother was very much alive.

2.   **The First Time Ever I Saw Your Face** by Roberta Flack got its break when it was featured in the movie 'Play Misty for Me' starring Clint Eastwood. The song sat idle until Clint Eastwood wanted it to underscore a romantic scene with Donna Mills in his new thriller. Once he got permission to use it in the film, fans rushed from the movie theatres to the record stores. Atlantic records rushed it out and it was soon on the radio climbing the charts to number one where it remained for 6 weeks.

3.   **American Pie** by Don McLean was an epic song with references to Buddy Holly and the day the music died. Don McLean described the song as 'a perfect metaphor for the music of the 60's and for my own youth'. This 8 and a half minute masterpiece was divided into parts 1 and 2 for side 'A' and side 'B' on the United Artists single.

4.   **I Can See Clearly Now** by Johnny Nash was one of the first mass appeal pop reggae hits of the era selling millions of copies and topping the charts for a full month in the Fall of 1972. Johnny Nash went to Jamaica and recorded this song with Bob Marley's backing band, the Wailers. Jimmy Cliff revived the song and made it a big hit all over again in 1993.

5.   **Without You** by Nilsson was written by Pete Ham and Tom Evans of Badfinger, who originally recorded this song on one of their albums. Nilsson discovered the song while drinking at a friend's house listening to songs to include on his next album. After one too many drinks, the next day he couldn't remember who did it, and thought it was John Lennon or The Beatles. His friend identified that it belonged to Badfinger, and Nilsson recorded it with

great success. Gary Wright, then a member of the group Spooky Tooth played the piano on the opening of this hit.

6.   **Lean on Me** by Bill Withers was the biggest hit from his 2nd album, 'Still Bill'. Bill Withers installed toilets in Boeing 747's before hitting it big, but wrote this song while still working at that job and got the inspiration to write the song by his co-workers willingness to help each other. In 2007, 'Lean on Me' was inducted into the Grammy Hall Of Fame.

7.   **The Candy Man** by Sammy Davis Jr. was co- written by actor/singer Anthony Newley. The song was featured in the film 'Willie Wonka and The Chocolate Factory' starring Gene Wilder. Producer Mike Curb was the one who suggested Sammy Davis Jr. record the main song. The result was a million seller and multi-week number one hit.

8.   **Me and Mrs. Jones** by Billy Paul was a soulful ballad story song about an extramarital affair. This million selling hit was produced and written by the popular Philadelphia soul team of Gamble and Huff, who gave the O'Jays and Harold Melvin and The Blue Notes their biggest hits. Billy Paul was born Paul Williams, but that would have been confusing, since there were already 2 other popular singers by that name, one of the Temptations with the other being the white singer/actor/pianist/composer.

9.   **Baby Don't Get Hooked on Me** by Mac Davis was written the night before he recorded it and it became the biggest hit for the singer who was only known to most as a songwriter. Under the name Scott Davis, Mac previously wrote hits which included 'In the Ghetto' and 'Don't Cry Daddy' for Elvis Presley and 'Something's Burning' for Kenny Rogers. In the 70's, Mac Davis also hosted his own TV Variety Show and became active as an actor.

10.   **A Horse With No Name** by America was written by Dewey Bunnell, who sang lead vocals on their debut hit, which topped the charts replacing Neil Young's 'Heart Of Gold'. Coincidentally, many believed it was the voice of Neil Young on the radio when they first heard this new recording. It's interesting to note that all of 'America's hit albums began with the letter 'H', except for their debut album, simply titled 'America'. The group won the 1972 Best New Artist Grammy Award.

11.   **My Ding a Ling** by Chuck Berry was surprisingly this legendary Rock and Roll pioneer's only number one hit! This rude novelty hit which Chuck Berry previously recorded as 'My Tambourine' was performed years before by Dave Bartholomew as 'Little Girl Sing Ding a Ling'. The song was changed and recorded live by Chuck Berry at the 1972 Lanchester Arts Festival in England. The 'B' side of the single was a 'live' version of 'Reelin' and Rockin'.

12.   **Brandy (You're A Fine Girl)** by the Looking Glass was written by the group's lead singer, Elliot Lurie. Most of the group met while students at Rutgers University in New Jersey. CBS Records President Clive Davis saw them perform at a showcase and signed them to his Epic record label. This number one hit was unlike the music the Looking Glass performed at bars, which was usually hard rock. They had one other hit, 'Jimmy Loves Mary-Anne' and that was the last appearance on the pop charts for this 70's group,

although Elliot Lurie became a Music Supervisor on many movies including 'Spanglish', 'Something's Gotta Give' and dozens of others.

13. Heart of Gold by Neil Young was recorded in Nashville and featured backing vocals by James Taylor and Linda Ronstadt. This number one hit was from his 4th album 'Harvest' and most of it was recorded while he was in a brace because of a problem with a weak side with his muscles, which kept him in and out of hospitals during this time period. This was the Toronto-born singer/guitarist/songwriter's biggest solo hit of his career.

14. Let's Stay Together by Al Green became his signature hit and a multi-million seller in early 1972. Al Green was originally a Gospel singer until his Memphis soul career took off like wildfire. He had 4 major hits in 1972 alone.

15. I Am Woman by Helen Reddy was the anthem song for the Women's Liberation Movement in 1972 and was featured in the film 'Stand Up and Be Counted'. Helen Reddy wrote the lyrics to this hit which not only went to number one, but put her hit career into high gear. She would have 2 more number one hits before the end of 1974.

16. Papa Was a Rollin' Stone by the Temptations featured group member Dennis Edwards on lead vocals. At first he was hesitant about singing the song because he got upset the first time he saw the lyrics, 'It was the 3rd of September, that day I'll always remember, 'cause that was the day my daddy died'. His father had passed away on the 3rd of September and he found the words upsetting. The song reached number one in December of 1972.

17. Black and White by 3 Dog Night was written back in 1955 by Earl Robinson and David Arkin, the late father of actor Alan Arkin. The song was written in response to the 1954 ruling the United States Supreme Court handed down in its landmark decision banning segregation in public schools. 3 Dog Night carried the song to number one almost 20 years later.

18. Oh Girl by Chi-Lites was referred by some as 'western soul' because of the use of the harmonica in this number one hit. Group leader Eugene Record wrote, produced and sang lead on this timeless love song.

19. Ben by Michael Jackson was the title song from the movie of the same name about an ailing youngster who befriends the leader of a pack of rats. The lyrics to 'Ben' were written by Don Black who previously co-wrote both 'To Sir with Love' for Lulu and 'Born Free' for Roger Williams. The later was from a movie about a lion. It was Don Black who suggested Michael Jackson record the song, which he agreed to do immediately after hearing it. Soon after, it became his first official solo number one hit.

20. I'll Take You There by the Staple Singers was a number one hit for this gospel family soul group from Mississippi. Roebuck 'Pop' Staples was the leader of this family act consisting of his daughters Cleo, Yvonne and Mavis on lead vocals. Their hits were recorded at the famous Muscle Shoals Studios in Memphis for the Stax record label. Pops died just short of his 86th birthday in December of 2000.

21.   **Song Sung Blue** by Neil Diamond was the 2nd of 3 official number one hits in the 70's for the superstar singer/songwriter from Brooklyn, New York. 'Song Sung Blue' was nominated for both Grammy Award Song and Record of the year, but lost on both to 'The First Time Ever I Saw Your Face' by Roberta Flack.

22.   **Long Cool Woman (In a Black Dress)** by The Hollies was inspired by C.C.R in the writing and production of this hit. Lead singer Allan Clarke recruited British composers Roger Cook and Roger Greenaway to breathe some life back into the group. With Allan Clarke, the song was written around the piano in less than 2 hours after a liquid lunch and recorded with a rocked up echo effect and a strong C.C.R influence.

23.   **Burning Love** by Elvis Presley was the final official top 10 hit for the King of Rock and Roll. This hit peaked at number 2, perhaps because Michael Jackson, the future son-in-law he never knew, was holding on to the top spot with 'Ben'.

24.   **Nights in White Satin** by the Moody Blues was originally released in 1968 from their 'Days of Future Passed' album, but didn't become a hit until 4 years later in 1972. Group member Justin Hayward wrote this song when he was a teenager after a friend gave him a gift of satin bed sheets. The London Festival Orchestra is featured on this recording, along with band member Mike Pinder's mellotron.

25.   **Clair** by Gilbert O'Sullivan was the follow up to his first and biggest hit 'Alone Again Naturally'. This million seller was written by Gilbert O'Sullivan and Gordon Mills, his Producer and Manager. Mills also did the same for Tom Jones and Engelbert Humperdinck. The 'real' Clair was in fact the daughter of Gordon Mills and it is her that you hear giggling at the end of this hit.

26.   **I Gotcha** by Joe Tex was the biggest hit for this Texas-born soul singer who had major hits in the 60's with 'Hold What You've Got' and 'Skinny Legs and All'. 'I Gotcha' was an accidental hit. First, it was intended for the 'Groove Me' singer King Floyd, and then when Tex recorded it, it was placed as the 'B' side of 'A Mother's Prayer'. Radio DJ's started playing 'I Gotcha' instead and it became a multi-million selling number 2 hit on the pop charts and number one on the R & B charts.

27.   **Too Late to Turn Back Now** by Cornelius Bros and Sister Rose was a family act from Florida, and this was their follow up to their other million seller, 'Treat Her Like A Lady'. Both hits were 'advice' songs written by Eddie Cornelius, who later became a born-again Christian and an ordained pastor.

28.   **Outa Space** by Billy Preston was the first major hit for the keyboardist/vocalist once described as 'the 5th Beatle'. This energetic instrumental was a million seller for this talented music artist born in Houston, Texas who got his start as a regular on TV's 'Shindig' show back in the 60's. Sadly, he died of kidney failure at age 59 in June of 2006.

29.   **I'd Love You to Want Me** by Lobo was the biggest hit for this Florida – born singer /songwriter/guitarist whose real name was Kent Lavoie. This hit,

which stalled at number 2, didn't reach the top spot on the charts because 'I Can See Clearly Now' by Johnny Nash occupied the number one position for a full month in the fall of 1972.

30.   **Use Me** by Bill Withers was the 3rd and final solo hit for this singer/ songwriter/guitarist born in Slab Fork, West Virginia. The following year, Bill Withers married actress Denise Nicholas, but they divorced in 1974. Due to a legal dispute with his record label, 'Sussex', he was unable to record thereafter as a solo performer.

31.   **Rockin' Robin** by Michael Jackson was a remake of the Bobby Day hit from 1958. This was Michael Jackson's 2nd solo hit following 'Got to Be There'. Later in 1972, Michael Jackson had his first number one solo hit with 'Ben', from the movie of the same name.

32.   **Precious and Few** by Climax was the only hit for this Los Angeles-based band, however the lead singer, Sonny Geraci was the front man for The Outsiders in the 60's. He was the voice you heard singing lead on their 1966 top 10 hit 'Time Won't Let Me'.

33.   **I'll Be Around** by the Spinners was their first hit on their new label, 'Atlantic' after leaving Motown. This Detroit R & B vocal group had 3 consecutive million sellers beginning with this one produced and co-written by Thom Bell, who also gave the Delfonics and Stylistics some of their biggest hits.

34.   **Everybody Plays the Fool** by the Main Ingredient featured group member Cuba Gooding Senior, the father of the future actor who was only 4 years old when this hit was in the top 5. The Main Ingredient was a 3 man R & B vocal group that formed in Harlem, New York and recorded on the RCA record label.

35.   **The Lion Sleeps Tonight** by Robert John was not only a top 10 remake of the Tokens 1961 number one hit, but some of the members of the original group sang backup on this updated version which was also produced by the Tokens. The remake was almost identical to the original from 11 years prior.

36.   **If You Don't Know Me by Now** by Harold Melvin and the Bluenotes featured Teddy Pendergrass on lead vocals. This was a million seller for this popular Philadelphia soul group led by Harold Melvin, who got top billing, despite the fact that it was the voice of Teddy Pendergrass featured as their lead singer. After a successful solo career, Teddy Pendergrass was left paralyzed and confined to a wheelchair after a car accident in 1982. Harold Melvin, in 1997, died at the age of 57 after suffering a stroke the year before.

37.   **Saturday in the Park** by Chicago was written by group member Robert Lamm, who also played piano and sang lead on this song inspired by the sights and sounds he experienced a couple of years earlier while visiting New York City around the 4th of July. This was the biggest hit from their album 'Chicago 5'.

38.   **(If Loving You Is Wrong) I Don't Want to Be Right** by Luther Ingram

was a number one hit on the R & B charts for a full month in the summer of 1972. This song about an extramarital affair was a hit the same year as Billy Paul's 'Me and Mrs. Jones', another multi-million selling infidelity song. Luther Ingram passed away at age 69 in 2007, as a result of heart failure.

39. **Betcha by Golly Wow** by the Stylistics was the 2nd consecutive 1972 top 10 hit for this Philadelphia soul group, which featured Russell Thompkins Jr. on lead vocals. Like their previous hit, 'You Are Everything', this song was also written by Thom Bell and Linda Creed. Sadly, Linda Creed died of breast cancer at age 36, in 1986, just weeks before her song 'The Greatest Love of All' by Whitney Houston reached number one.

40. **Puppy Love** by Donny Osmond was the first of 3 consecutive solo hits for this young teen idol. 'Puppy Love' was a remake of the Paul Anka hit from 1960. Donny Osmond was crowned winner of the popular 'Dancing with The Stars' competition on the top rated TV show on November 24, 2009.

41. **Backstabbers** by the O'Jays was another soul hit that was part of the Philadelphia sound produced and written by the team of Gamble and Huff. The trio of singers featured Eddie Levert, whose son Gerald had a successful solo career until his death at age 40 in 2006. The O'Jays were inducted into the Rock and Roll Hall Of Fame in 2005.

42. **I'm Still in Love with You** by Al Green was his 3rd of 4 major hits in 1972 which all followed the same rhythm and tempo. Willie Mitchell produced his hits as well as co-wrote them with Al Green along with Al Jackson in many cases.

43. **Nice to Be with You** by Jim Gold and The Gallery was a million seller for this pop group from Detroit. He was discovered by 'Sussex' label mate Dennis Coffey, the session guitarist on many hits of the day and maker of his own instrumental hit 'Scorpio'.

44. **Sunshine** by Jonathan Edwards was the only major hit for this Minnesota born singer/ songwriter. He moved to Nova Scotia in Canada in the 70's, but moved back to the United States later in the decade where he continued to perform and act. In 2008 he scored the music and appeared as Reverend Purly in the movie 'Golden Boys' which starred David Carradine, Bruce Dern and Mariel Hemingway.

45. **Day After Day** by Badfinger was produced by George Harrison, who is also featured on guitar. This Badfinger hit, which featured Pete Ham on lead vocals, was the highest charting of the 4 hits they achieved during the early 70's.

46. **Daddy Don't You Walk So Fast** by Wayne Newton was the biggest chart hit of all for one of the most popular Las Vegas performers of all time. This emotional, yet sappy hit was written by British songwriters Peter Callander and Geoff Stephens. Composers Stephens was also the voice and writer of 'Winchester Cathedral' by The New Vaudeville Band.

47. **Down By the Lazy River** by the Osmonds was a high energy hit for the family act from Utah. This was their final million seller as a group and the first hit which didn't feature Donny on lead vocals.

48. **It Never Rains In Southern California** by Albert Hammond was a million selling top 5 hit for this British singer/songwriter. Hammond is also known as the co-writer of the hits 'When I Need You' by Leo Sayer, 'The Air That I Breathe' by the Hollies and 'Gimme Dat Ding' by the Pipkins, among other notable songs.

49. **Freddie's Dead** by Curtis Mayfield was the first top 10 solo hit for the former voice of the Impressions. This million seller was the 1st of 2 in 1972 from the film 'Superfly'. Curtis Mayfield died in December of 1999 at age 57 after a decade of ill-health which began when he was struck and paralyzed from the neck down when stage lighting equipment at an outdoor concert fell on him at Wingate Field in Flatbush, Brooklyn, New York.

50. **Sylvia's Mother** by Dr Hook and the Traveling Medicine Show was written by cartoonist, author and songwriter Shel Silverstein, who also composed their hit 'The Cover of the Rolling Stone'. He also wrote the offbeat hits 'A Boy Named Sue' for Johnny Cash and 'The Unicorn' for The Irish Rovers'.

51. **You Oughta Be with Me** by Al Green was the 4th of 4 major 1972 hits for the Memphis soul singer who later became a Pastor at the Full Tabernacle Church in Memphis. The Reverend Al Green co-wrote all of his hits during this time period.

52. **Mother and Child Reunion** by Paul Simon was the first solo hit for this very successful singer/songwriter of 'Simon and Garfunkel' fame. Paul Simon came up with the idea for the song title after seeing a chicken and egg dish called 'Mother and Child Reunion' while eating at a Chinese Food Restaurant in Chinatown in New York City.

53. **Go All The Way** by the Raspberries featured Eric Carmen on lead vocals. This Jimmy Ienner produced hit was the biggest of their hits before Eric Carmen launched a successful solo hit with 'All By Myself', 'Hungry Eyes', 'Make Me Lose Control' and others. 'Go All The Way', with its sexually explicit lyrics, great guitar hooks and harmony, reached the top 5 and sold over a million copies for this group from Ohio.

54. **Funny Face** by Donna Fargo was the biggest of her hits on both the Country and Pop charts. Her first hit; 'The Happiest Girl in the Whole U.S.A.' was also a major hit and million seller. Up until 1972, Donna Fargo, whose real name is Yvonne Vaughn, worked as a high school teacher. In 1979, she was diagnosed with multiple sclerosis, but continued to be active as a recording artist and author.

55. **Look What You've Done for Me** by Al Green was another copy of his familiar string of soul ballads in 1972. This was the second of 4 hits that year to the singer now known as the Reverend Al Green.

56. **Where Is the Love** by Roberta Flack and Donny Hathaway was a Grammy Award Winning Best Pop Vocal Performance by a Duo or Group hit.

It was from the year Roberta Flack made her debut with 'The First Time Ever I Saw Your Face'. Multi-Instrumentalist Donny Hathaway was a schoolmate of Roberta Flack and they recorded one more major hit together in 1978 with 'The Closer I Get to You'. Sadly, Donny Hathaway committed suicide in 1979 by jumping from the 15th floor of New York's City's Essex hotel.

57.   Garden Party by Rick Nelson was inspired by his Madison Square Garden concert where fans gave him a negative response because he was performing his newer Country Pop songs, and not the 50's and 60's hits he was best known for. The line 'you can't please everyone, so you've got to please yourself', summed up his thoughts in this million seller. The former teen idol and TV star died in a plane crash on New Year's Eve in 1985.

58.   Hold Your Head Up by Argent, a British rock quartet formed by Rod Argent, the former keyboardist for the Zombies and composer of their hits 'She's Not There' and 'Tell Her No'. Argent guitarist Russ Ballard later went on the write hits for Kiss, America, 3 Dog Night and others. 'Hold Your Head Up' was Argent's only top 40 hit.

59.   Daydreaming by Aretha Franklin reached the top 10 on the Pop charts and number one on the R & B charts in 1972. This hit from her album 'Young, Gifted and Black' featured Donny Hathaway on electric piano in the same year he shared a top 10 duet with Roberta Flack on 'Where Is the Love'.

60.   Everything I Own by Bread was another great soft pop hit by the group led by Oklahoma born singer/songwriter David Gates. Many thought that this song was about a woman with lyrics about giving up everything he owned to have 'you' back again. However, the 'you' David Gates was referring to was his late father.

61.   Rockin' Pneumonia and the Boogie Woogie Flu by Johnny Rivers returned this New York City born singer/songwriter to the top 10 for the first time since 1967. This remake was originally a minor hit for Huey 'Piano' Smith and the Clowns back in 1957. This was Johnny Rivers' only top 10 hit on the 'United Artists' record label.

62.   Clean up Woman by Betty Wright was a million seller for this soul singer from Miami, Florida. The guitar riff of this hit has been sampled on many hits through the years.

63.   Summer Breeze by Seals and Crofts was the first major hit for this pop duo from Texas. Jim Seals (brother of 'England' Dan Seals) and Dash Crofts had a string of hits during the 70's which included 'Diamond Girl' and 'Get Closer'. One of the distinctive instruments used in 'Summer Breeze' is a child's toy piano, played by session musician Larry Knechtel. The song was remixed in 2004 and received airplay on many Adult Contemporary radio stations across North America all over again.

64.   Never Been to Spain by 3 Dog Night was their 2nd major hit written by Hoyt Axton, following 'Joy to the World'. This hit was from their 'Harmony' album and was one of over 20 top 40 hits they achieved during the late 60's and early 70's.

65.   **Troglodyte** by the Jimmy Castor Bunch was a million selling novelty hit in the spring of 1972. This New York City born R & B singer/saxophonist/composer/arranger previously had a solo hit in 1966 with 'Hey Leroy, Your Mama's Calling You'. The follow up to 'Troglodyte (Caveman) was the similar sounding 'Bertha Butt Boogie', inspired by a character introduced in the aforementioned million seller.

66.   **School's Out** by Alice Cooper is a hit the singer describes as a joyful song about the happy time when kids are out on summer vacation for over 2 months of fun. It was the title track of Alice Cooper's 5th album and featured the childhood rhyme 'No more pencils, no more books, no more teacher's dirty looks' accompanied by children singing along.

67.   **I'd Like to Teach the World to Sing** by the New Seekers was adapted from a popular Coca Cola jingle. This top 10 million seller was written by Roger Cook, Roger Greenaway, Bill Backer and Billy Davis. British songwriters Cook and Greenaway are also known for writing 'You've Got Your Troubles' for the Fortunes, 'Green Grass' for Gary Lewis and the Playboys, 'My Baby Loves Lovin' for the White Plains and several other hits of that era.

68.   **Morning Has Broken** by Cat Stevens was his highest charting hit in the United States. The piano arrangement on this hit was performed by Rick Wakeman of 'Yes' fame. The song itself dates back to 1931 as a Christian hymn known as 'Bunessan' arranged by the composer Martin Shaw.

69.   **Joy** by Apollo 100 was an adaptation of Bach's 'Jesus, Joy of Man's Desiring'. This one hit wonder British studio band featured keyboardist Tom Parker.

70.   **Rocket Man** by Elton John was the first of 2 consecutive top 10 singles from the album 'Honky Chateau' with 'Honky Cat' being the second. 'Rocket Man', written by Elton John and Bernie Taupin, was loosely based on Ray Bradbury's book 'The Illustrated Man' and inspired by David Bowie's hit 'Space Oddity' which was also produced by Gus Dudgeon.

71.   **The Way of Love** by Cher was a remake of a minor hit from 1965 by British singer Kathy Kirby and was originally a song written in French. Cher's version was produced by Snuff Garrett and popular during the time the weekly 'Sonny and Cher Show' was in prime time.

72.   **In The Rain** by The Dramatics was number one on the R & B charts for a month back in the spring of 1972 and top 5 on the pop charts, scoring higher than their previous hit 'Whatcha See Is Whatcha Get'. Ron Banks was the lead singer of this early 70's soul group from Detroit.

73.   **Rock and Roll Part 2** by Gary Glitter was a favorite at sporting events and was known as 'the hey song'. This rockin' hit with an energetic beat was the only notable hit in North America for this British Glam rock singer who was born Paul Gadd. In 1999, Gary Glitter was sentenced to four months imprisonment when he was listed as a sex offender in the UK following conviction of downloading thousands of items of child pornography. Many radio stations have avoided playing this hit since Glitter's conviction.

74.   Goodbye to Love by The Carpenters was inspired by an old movie. One night Richard Carpenter happened to catch the 1935 movie 'Mississippi' with W.C. Fields, Bing Crosby and Joan Bennett. Throughout the movie, Bing Crosby referred to a tune he's supposedly written called 'Goodbye to Love'. He never actually sang it though, he just talked about it. Richard Carpenter decided that he would write the song and his sister Karen would sing it. It became a big hit in the summer of '72.

75.   How Do You Do by Mouth and MacNeal was the only hit for this Dutch duo. Their names were Willem Duyn and Maggie MacNeal. In 1974, they parted ways. Willem 'Mouth' Duyn died of a heart attack in 2004 at the age of 67.

76.   Tumbling Dice by the Rolling Stones was a song about gambling and love written by Mick Jagger and Keith Richards from their double album, 'Exile on Main Street'. Both Charlie Watts and producer Jimmy Miller played drums simultaneously on this recording and Mick Taylor, the group's lead guitarist, filled in on bass for Bill Wyman, who was absent on the session recording this song.

77.   Last Night I Didn't Get to Sleep by the 5th Dimension prominently featured Marilyn McCoo on lead vocals on this ballad written by British songwriter Tony MacAuley. He previously co-wrote many hits including 'Build Me Up Buttercup', 'Love Grows (Where My Rosemary Grows)' and 'Baby, Now That I've Found You' to name just a few.

78.   You Don't Mess around with Jim by Jim Croce was the very first hit for this Louisiana born singer/songwriter/guitarist. This was one of Croce's self-penned story songs produced by Terry Cashman and Tommy West, who also provide backing vocals. They were previously known as the songwriters of Spanky and Our Gang's top 10 hit 'Sunday Will Never Be the Same', and as members of the one hit wonder act 'The Buchanan Brothers, known for the hit 'Medicine Man'.

79.   Ventura Highway by America was the 3rd consecutive hit for this soft rock trio in their debut year on the charts. Group member Dewey Bunnell, who wrote the song, sang lead on this hit with backing vocals and guitars by Dan Peek and Gerry Beckley. Janet Jackson later sampled this song in her hit single 'Someone to Call My Lover'.

80.   Doctor My Eyes by Jackson Browne was the first hit for this singer/ songwriter/guitarist/pianist born in Heidelberg, Germany. He co-wrote the Eagles' debut hit 'Take It Easy', which was popular a few months after 'Doctor My Eyes' reached the top 10. Both artists recorded on the 'Asylum' record label.

81.   Honky Cat by Elton John was the 2nd hit single from the 'Honky Chateau' album, which also produced 'Rocket Man'. 'Honky Cat' is dominated by Elton John's piano and an extensive horn section, with no guitars featured on this summer of 1972 hit. The album 'Honky Chateau' is a reference to where the album was recorded 30 miles outside of Paris

82. **Jungle Fever** by Chakachas was a one hit wonder act which consisted of Latin soul studio musicians from Belgian. This sexy disco hit featured the suggestive voice of Kari Kenton, who also played the maracas. This hit was later prominently featured in the movie 'Boogie Nights' starring Mark Wahlberg and Wililam H. Macy.

83. **Popcorn** by Hot Butter was a top 10 novelty instrumental which featured a moog synthesizer played by Stan Free. This one hit wonder was number one in both Australia and Switzerland for an incredible 10 weeks! The 'B' side of 'Popcorn' was appropriately titled 'At the Movies'.

84. **You Are Everything** by The Stylistics was the first of a string of silky smooth ballads by this Philadelphia soul group which featured the voice of Russell Thompkins Jr. Their hits were produced by Thom Bell, who previously gave another Philadelphia group, The Delfonics, their biggest hits.

85. **Layla** by Derek and the Dominos was originally released as a single in early 1971 with little success. Both Eric Clapton and Duane Allman are featured on guitars with Jim Gordon playing the memorable piano part of the song. 'Layla' was the nickname of Patti Boyd, whom Eric Clapton later married after she divorced George Harrison. Sadly Duane Allman was killed in a motorcycle accident on October 29th 1971 at age 24, almost a year *before* 'Layla' became a top 10 hit in the summer of 1972.

86. **Hot Rod Lincoln** by Commander Cody & His Lost Planet Airman was a remake of a song that was a hit for both Johnny Bond and Charlie Ryan. Commander Cody was actually George Frayne who formed the group while attending the University of Michigan. He moved to San Francisco and had his one and only hit with this fast-paced cruisin' hit.

87. **Coconut** by Nilsson was an unusual song from the Brooklyn-born singer/composer. Harry Nilsson has many musical accomplishments to his credit. He wrote 3 Dog Night's first notable hit 'One', he performed the theme for the TV series 'The Courtship of Eddie's Father' and had his first major hit with 'Everybody's Talkin' from the movie 'Midnight Cowboy'. Nilsson died at the age of 52 of heart failure in January of 1994.

88. **Superfly** by Curtis Mayfield was his 2nd consecutive million seller from the film of the same name. The former lead singer/songwriter of The Impressions was inducted into the Rock and Roll Hall Of Fame in March of 1999, 9 months before he died at the age of 57.

89. **Witchy Woman** by The Eagles was their top 10 follow up to their debut hit 'Take It Easy'. Don Henley sang lead on this hit which he co-wrote with group member Bernie Leadon, who left the band in 1975 and was replaced by Joe Walsh.

90. **I'm Stone in Love with You** by The Stylistics was their 3rd top 10 hit of 1972. Thom Bell and Linda Creed wrote this silky smooth ballad delivered in fine style by Russell Thompkins Jr. This song was about giving everything up for love. All of their hits were recorded on the 'Avco' record label.

91. **Goodtime Charlie's got the Blues** by Danny O'Keefe was the only hit for this folk/pop singer/songwriter from Spokane, Washington. Danny O'Keefe also plays guitar and harmonica on this top 10 hit which was later recorded by Elvis Presley.

92. **A Cowboy's Work Is Never Done** by Sonny and Cher was on the charts simultaneously with Cher's solo hit 'The Way of Love'. 'Cowboy', written by Sonny Bono and produced by Snuff Garrett, was Sonny and Cher's final top 10 hit together. As 'Sonny and Cher' they sold 80 million records together.

93. **Back Off Boogaloo** by Ringo Starr was produced by George Harrison, who also played guitar on this hit. Ringo solely wrote this song, but not only got by with a little help from his friend George, but Gary Wright played keyboards, Klaus Voorman played bass and 3 female singers, including Madeline Bell, sang backup.

94. **Bang a Gong (Get It On)** by T. Rex was the biggest North American hit for this British group led by singer/songwriter Marc Bolan. The 2 main members of the Turtles, Mark Volman and Howard Kaylan sang backing vocals on this hit which reached number one in Britain titled as 'Get It On'. It was re-titled in North America to avoid any confusion with the song by 'Chase' of the same title. Marc Bolan was killed in a car accident September 16th 1977 at the age of 30.

95. **I Need You** by America was the 2nd of 3 consecutive hits for this successful 70's trio. Gerry Beckley played keyboards and sang lead vocals with Dewey Bunnell and Dan Peek on backing vocals and guitars.

96. **Take It Easy** by The Eagles was the first hit for this very successful Los Angeles-based Rock Country band. Glenn Frey was the featured lead singer on this goodtime hit co-written by Jackson Browne, who had his first hit that same year with 'Doctor My Eyes'.

97. **Sweet Seasons** by Carole King was a top 10 hit from her 'Music' album, which was the follow up to the iconic 'Tapestry' album. 'Sweet Seasons' was co-written by Carole, who is featured on piano with backing by musicians who include James Taylor on guitar and backing vocals. The album was produced by Lou Adler.

98. **The Guitar Man** by Bread featured group member and top session player Larry Knechtel on the prominently featured guitar on this hit. The following year, in 1973, Bread called it quits. They reunited for an album in late 1976 which produced their final hit 'Lost without Your Love'.

99. **Listen to the Music** by The Doobie Brothers was their very first hit. It was produced by Ted Templeman, (the lead singer of Harper's Bizarre in the 60's) who decided to use the two multi-track machine effect, and use of the very effective 'phasing' sound. The first notable hit to use it was Miss Toni Fisher's 1959 top ten hit 'The Big Hurt'.

100. **The Happiest Girl in the Whole U.S.A.** by Donna Fargo was the first of 2 major back-to-back hits from this Country singer from North Carolina. This song written by Donna Fargo was the point of view of a newlywed singing it to her new husband. It became her signature hit.

101. **If I Could Reach You** by the 5th Dimension was the final top 10 hit for this Los Angeles based vocal group consisting of 2 girls and 3 guys. Group members Marilyn McCoo (featured as lead singer on this ballad) and Billy Davis Junior celebrated their 40th wedding anniversary together in 2009. The 5th Dimension were inducted into the Vocal Group Hall Of Fame in 2002.

102. **Convention '72** by The Delegates was a novelty hit in the same style as Dickie Goodman's humorous narrative with excerpts from current hits. This one hit wonder act featured Bob DeCarlo who was the Morning Man on a radio station in Tampa, Florida. 3 years later, Dickie Goodman revisited the concept on his big hit 'Mr. Jaws'.

103. **Keeper of the Castle** by The Four Tops was the first of 3 consecutive hits for the former Motown group on their new label, Dunhill records. This was the title song of their album which also included their next big hit 'Ain't No Woman like the One I've Got'.

104. **Drowning in the Sea of Love** by Joe Simon was a million seller for this Louisiana born R & B artist who began singing in his father's Baptist church. This hit was from the talented team of Gamble and Huff.

105. **Amazing Grace** by the Royal Scots Dragoon Guards was the first major hit to feature bagpipes as its predominant instrument. The tune originated in 1779 and became a million seller in 1972 by the military band of Scotland's armored regiment, led by bagpipe soloist Major Tony Crease. In this surprise instrumental hit, there were 20 pipes piping and 10 drums drumming.

106. **Play Me** by Neil Diamond was his follow up to the number one 'Song Sung Blue'. Both hits and the next single release 'Walk on Water' were from his album 'Moods'. These would be his final releases on the 'Uni' label, before switching to Columbia, where he would also have great success.

107. **Sugar Daddy** by the Jackson 5 was another sweet bubblegum hit from the family act from Gary, Indiana. Lead vocals on this hit were shared by Michael, Jermaine and Tito Jackson. This single was from their Greatest Hits album and was top 10 at the beginning of 1972.

108. **Tightrope** by Leon Russell was the first notable hit as an artist for this keyboardist/composer/arranger from Oklahoma who played on hundreds of recordings by other music artists. He was a regular session player on Phil Spector's 'Wall of Sound' hits, as well as keyboardist/arranger on many of the hits of Gary Lewis and the Playboys and Brian Hyland.

109. **Beautiful Sunday** by Daniel Boone was the only hit for this British singer whose real name was Peter Lee Stirling. In Britain, his version of 'Daddy Don't You Walk So Fast' was released as a single. In North America, it was a top 5 hit for Wayne Newton in 1972.

110. **Roundabout** by Yes was the breakthrough hit for this progressive 70's British group which featured Rick Wakeman on keyboards and Jon Anderson on lead vocals. This song was co-written by guitarist Steve Howe and was edited for single release from its origin 8 minutes plus. This was from the 'Fragile' album, the first to feature new member Rick Wakeman.

111.   **Motorcycle Mama** by Sailcat was an easy-going hit for this duo from Alabama consisting of Court Pickett and John Wyker. This one hit wonder act recorded on the Elektra record label.

112.   **Vincent** by Don McLean was about artist Vincent Van Gogh and 'Starry Night' was one of his most famous paintings. The line 'you suffered for your sanity' referred to Van Gogh's schizophrenic disorder which he suffered from. 'Vincent' was Don McLean's follow up to his legendary 'American Pie' from earlier in 1972.

113.   **It's Going to Take Some Time** by The Carpenters was written by Carole King and Toni Stern. Carole King included this song on her album 'Music' which contained her hit single 'Sweet Seasons'.

114.   **Anticipation** by Carly Simon was her follow up to her first hit 'That's The Way I've Always Heard It Should Be and the title song from her album released in late 1971.The album was produced by Paul Samwell- Smith, who produced all of Cat Stevens albums during that time period. 'Anticipation' was used in a popular commercial for Heinz Ketchup in the 70's.

115.   **Something's Wrong with Me** by Austin Roberts was co-written by Bobby Hart of Boyce and Hart fame, best known for writing many of the Monkees' biggest hits. Austin Roberts had the biggest hit of his career with the story song 'Rocky' in the summer of 1975, but was also known for writing country hits for others and collaborating on the music for the cartoons 'Scooby Doo' and 'Josie and The Pussycats' in the 70's.

116.   **Walkin' in the Rain (With the One I Love)** by Love Unlimited was a California female soul trio managed, produced and written by Barry White. Barry's voice is the one you hear on the telephone part way through this million seller from the spring of 1972. Barry White's career as the leader of the Love Unlimited Orchestra and the singer of his solo hits began the following year.

117.   **You Wear It Well** by Rod Stewart was a song he co-wrote and featured on his 'Never a Dull Moment' album. He was still a member of the Faces when he recorded this solo hit which reached number one in Britain and top 20 in North America. His follow up single from the same album was his version of the Jimi Hendrix song 'Angel'.

118.   **Little Bitty Pretty One** by the Jackson Five was a remake of the 1957 hit by Thurston Harris. This Jackson 5 hit just missed the top 10. This was the 9th hit single by the Jackson 5, and the first that was a remake. It's interesting to note that the other popular teen idol act, the Osmonds would have hits with many remakes in the early 70's, particularly Donny, as a soloist.

119.   **Power of Love** by Joe Simon was a number one hit on the R & B charts and his 2nd million seller of 1972 written by Gamble and Huff. Joe Simon also had a hand in writing this hit which was to be his final million seller.

120.   **Black Dog** by Led Zeppelin was produced by guitarist Jimmy Page, who co-wrote this fan favorite with bass player John Paul Jones and lead singer Robert Plant. This was the lead off single from 'Led Zeppelin 1V', one of

the best selling rock albums of all time. The title doesn't actually appear on the album which shows a picture of an old man slumped down with a cane with a pile of sticks on his back.

121.   Don't Say You Don't Remember by Beverly Bremers, was an emotional ballad for this singer from Chicago. Although this was her only top 20 hit, she acted in Broadway shows, and later voiced and appeared in commercials and taught others how to sing.

122.   Rock and Roll Lullaby by B.J. Thomas was written by the popular songwriting team of Barry Mann and Cynthia Weil. This well-produced ballad featured the twangy guitar of Duane Eddy with backup vocals by David Somerville of the Diamonds and Darlene Love with the Blossoms. Although some believed it was the Beach Boys who did the background singing, it was session singers, although Brian Wilson was approached.

123.   The Family of Man by 3 Dog Night was the 2nd of 3 notable hits they achieved in 1972 alone. All 3 singers took turns singing lead on this hit which was one of 3 singles from their 'Harmony 'album. This was 1 of 3 hit singles for 3 Dog Night co-written by Paul Williams with the other 2 being 'Out in the Country' and 'An Old Fashioned Love Song'.

124.   Day By Day by Godspell was the most popular song from this successful Broadway musical. Original cast member Robin Lamont is featured on lead vocals on this inspirational hit.

125.   Too Young by Donny Osmond was another remake of a 50's hit for the lead singer of the Osmonds. This was originally a number one hit for Nat 'King' Cole back in 1951.This was Donny's follow up to another oldie, 'Puppy Love', originally by Paul Anka in 1960.

126.   Baby Blue by Badfinger was the 4th and final top 40 hit for this British rock quartet. This hit was produced by Todd Rundgren, and written by Pete Ham (who also sang lead on this hit) about a former girlfriend. Like the other hits by Badfinger, this was also recorded on the Beatles' Apple label.

127.   Why/Lonely Boy by Donny Osmond was a double-sided hit single of remakes by one of the top teen idols of the early 70's, along with Bobby Sherman and David Cassidy. It's interesting that both of the songs on this single were originally popular by teen idols from the previous era. The song 'Why' was a number one hit for Frankie Avalon in 1959, the same year the original 'Lonely Boy' was number one for Paul Anka.

128.   I Saw the Light by Todd Rundgren was the first notable solo hit for this multi-instrumentalist singer/songwriter/producer from Pennsylvania. This hit was from his double album 'Something/Anything' in which he played all the instruments and sang all the vocals. This was Todd Rundgren's best selling album and it also contained his biggest hit 'Hello It's Me'.

129.   I'd Like to Teach the World to Sing by The Hillside Singers was the original version of the song taken from the TV Coca Cola commercial which the New Seekers turned into a million selling hit. This version was produced and arranged by Al Ham and the one hit wonder Hillside Singers included his daughter Lori and wife Mary Mayo.

130.   Diary by Bread was the 4th single from their 'Baby I'm A Want You' album. 'Diary' was a song about a boy who is love with a girl, finds and reads her diary, only to discover that she is in love with someone else. Like all other hits by Bread, this was written by lead singer David Gates.

131.   Slippin' Into Darkness by War was the first of a half a dozen notable hits for this California band that fused funk, latin, rock, reggae, jazz and soul into this multi-ethnic group. They started out as Eric Burdon and War, backing the former lead singer of the Animals on the summer of 1970 hit 'Spill the Wine'. They sold several million records during the 70's.

132.   Conquistador by Procol Harum was recorded 'live' with the Edmonton Symphony Orchestra in Canada. This British group which featured the distinctive voice of Gary Brooker on lead vocals was best known for their 1967 classic, 'A Whiter Shade of Pale'.

133.   Sweet Surrender by Bread was the only song lead singer/songwriter wrote for the group while on the road. Later in the decade David Gates would have a solo hit with 'Goodbye Girl', the title song of the Neil Simon film which starred Richard Dreyfuss and Marsha Mason.

134.   Speak to the Sky by Rick Springfield was the very first North American hit for this singer/actor/songwriter from Australia. His next hit didn't arrive until almost 10 years later when 'Jessie's Girl' topped the charts in 1981, when he also starred in the TV soap 'General Hospital' as Dr. Noah Drake.

135.   Hold Her Tight by The Osmonds was the 2nd of 3 top 20 hits for this family act in 1972. This hit was more of a rock style than their previous hit singles and all the Osmond brothers sang together and played their instruments, including Donny on keyboards.

136.   Run to Me by The Bee Gees was a top 20 hit for the Gibb brothers in the summer of 1972. This Bee Gees hit from the album 'To Whom It May Concern' featured Barry Gibb on lead vocals. After this hit, they were in a slump until they resurfaced with a new sound, new label (RSO) and a number one hit with 'Jive Talkin' in 1975.

137.   Walk on Water by Neil Diamond was the 3rd single release from his 'Moods' album. 'Walk on Water', was his last single release on the 'Uni' record label, and one of his most creative recordings up to that period in his career. Before becoming a successful singer/songwriter, Neil Diamond received a scholarship in fencing. He continued his swordsmanship skills and used fencing exercises while warming up before concerts.

138.   Floy Joy by the Supremes was the final top 20 hit for the legendary Motown group once fronted by Diana Ross. Mary Wilson and Jean Terrell share lead vocals on this hit with backup from Cindy Birdsong. This was the title track of the album which was produced by the miracle man Smokey Robinson, who was also Vice-President of Motown Records at that time.

139.   My World by The Bee Gees featured Robin Gibb on lead vocals and was not available on any of their albums until they released 'The Best of the Bee Gees Volume 2 in 1973. This top 20 hit was released while they were still in the process of recording their album 'To Whom the Bell Tolls' which included their next single, 'Run To Me'.

140.   Thunder and Lightning by Chi Coltrane was the only hit for this dynamic voiced pianist/singer from Racine, Wisconsin. It is unfortunate that lightning did not strike twice for this singer who began her music career early with classical piano studies at the age of 7. She sang in her church choir, and at the age of 12 gave her first public keyboard performance.

141.   Sitting by Cat Stevens was the only single from his very successful album 'Catch Bull at Four'. This album, like his previous best sellers, was produced by Paul Samwell-Smith, formerly of the Yardbirds. After this, Cat Stevens produced or co-produced all of his own recordings.

142.   Operator (That's Not the Way It Feels) by Jim Croce was the follow up to his first hit 'You Don't Mess around with Jim'. This was one of his wife Ingrid's favorite songs by her late husband. His guitarist and backup singer, Maury Muehleisen, was also killed in the plane crash that took Croce's life on September 20th 1973.

143.   Stay with Me by Faces featured Rod Stewart on lead vocals while he was enjoying a successful solo career simultaneously. The Faces were formerly the 'Small Faces' and included Ronnie Lane, Ronnie Wood, Ian McLagan and Kenney Jones. Ron Wood later joined the Rolling Stones and Kenney Jones joined the Who after the death of Keith Moon.

144.   The City of New Orleans by Arlo Guthrie was the biggest hit for the son of legendary folk singer Woody Guthrie. Arlo Guthrie performed at Woodstock 3 years earlier, the same year he starred in the film 'Alice's Restaurant'. This song was written by folk singer Steve Goodman while on the train of the same name.

145.   Crazy Horses by The Osmonds was a totally out of character hit for the group formerly known for its sweet bubblegum sound with Donny taking centre stage. This heavy rock style hit was apparently a protest song about air pollution. It was written by Alan, Merrill and Wayne Osmond, who are all featured front and centre on this very different hit for the Osmonds.

146.   Looking through the Windows by The Jackson Five was their 3rd of 4 top 20 singles in 1972 and was taken from their 5th studio album of the same name. This song was the beginning of a more mature sounding Michael Jackson as his voice was changing and the material was less of a bubblegum sound now.

147.   Get on the Good Foot by James Brown was number one on the R & B charts for a full month and one of his biggest selling singles of all time. This funky dance hit was the 5th of 7 charted hits for the Godfather of soul.

148.   I Wanna Be Where You Are by Michael Jackson was the 3rd of 3 hit singles from his debut solo album 'Got to Be There' which went on the sell close to a million copies worldwide. The album also included covers of Bill Withers 'Ain't No Sunshine', Carole King's 'You've Got a Friend' and the Supremes' 'Love Is Here and Now You're Gone. 'I Wanna Be Where You Are' was his first solo hit which fail to reach the top 10.

149.   Sealed with a Kiss by Bobby Vinton was a remake of the Brian Hyland hit from 1962. This summer of 1972 hit was from Bobby Vinton's 23rd and final studio album with Epic records. Two years later he resurfaced on ABC records and had his first top 10 hit in 6 years with 'My Melody of Love'.

150.   Suavacito by Malo was the only hit for this group formed by Jorge Santana, the brother of legendary guitarist Carlos Santana. 'Suavacito' is Spanish for Bad, but is also Mayan for Good.

151.   Starting All over Again by Mel and Tim was the 2nd hit for the cousins from Mississippi whose full names were Mel Hardin and Tim McPherson. This song later became a hit for Hall and Oates. Mel and Tim's previous hit was 1969's 'Backfield in Motion', produced by Gene Chandler, who discovered this R & B duo.

152.   Join Together by The Who was a top 20 single that was not included on an album until it was released on a compilation several years later. The Who were inducted into the Rock and Roll Hall Of Fame in 1990, their first year of eligibility.

153.   It's One of Those Nights by the Partridge Family was the 5th and final top 20 hit for this prime time family act which featured teen idol David Cassidy on lead vocals. This hit was written by Tony Romeo, who also composed their biggest hit 'I Think I Love You'. He also wrote 'I'm Gonna Make You Mine' by Lou Christie and 'Indian Lake' for the Cowsills, the real life family act from Rhode Island which inspired the creation of the TV family act, the Partridge Family.

154.   Hey Big Brother by Rare Earth was the final hit for this Detroit Rock group whose biggest hits were the remakes of the Temptations hits 'Get Ready' and '(I Know) I'm Losing You' in 1970. Pete Rivera, whose real name is Pete Hoorelbeke, was the lead singer and drummer for this high energy rock band.

155.   Kiss an Angel Good Morning by Charley Pride was the biggest hit of this legendary country singer's career. This million seller was number one on the country charts for 5 weeks and was his only top 40 hit on the pop charts. In total, Charley Pride achieved 29 number one country hits. He was discovered by Red Sovine in 1963

156.   Taxi by Harry Chapin was the hit that launched the career of this folk rock storyteller from New York City. He studied film and actually worked as a taxi driver for a few months, trying to make ends meet and also hoping the experience would be good for his writing career, hearing the stories from his passengers. Harry Chapin died in an accident with a truck while driving his Volkswagen on the Long Island Expressway on his way to a charity concert on July 16, 1981. This talented and generous entertainer was 38 when he died.

157. **Corner of the Sky** by The Jackson Five was a song from the Broadway musical 'Pippin' starring Ben Vereen. This hit was from their 6th studio album 'Skywriter', which demonstrated a more mature sound as they were departing from the bubblegum sound and image. This was their 3rd consecutive hit which failed to reach the top 10. They would get out of their slump in 1974 when 'Dancing Machine' would become a million selling major hit.

158. **Taurus** by Dennis Coffey was his follow up to his top 10 instrumental 'Scorpio'. Although 'Taurus' was not nearly as successful, Coffey was a major player as a session player on numerous Motown and other hits.

159. **The Witch Queen of New Orleans** by Redbone was the first top 30 hit for this American Indian 'swamp rock' group which was headed by the Vegas brothers, Lolly and Pat. Prior to this hit, they were session musicians and wrote the hit 'Niki Hoeky in 1966 for P.J. Proby. Redbone was inducted into the Native American Music Association Hall Of Fame in 2008.

160. **Me and Julio down by the Schoolyard** by Paul Simon was his follow up to his first solo hit 'Mother and Child Reunion' from the self-titled album. There have been many debates over what this song is really about from an anti-war protest to something sexual. Paul Simon has never really confirmed it either way.

161. **Ain't Understanding Mellow** by Jerry Butler and Brenda Le Eager was a million seller, despite the fact that this hit did not reach the top 20 on the pop charts. This was Jerry Butler's final notable hit and the 1st of 2 he would release as singles with soul singer Brenda Lee Eager, with a remake of the Carpenters' hit 'Close To You' being the other.

162. **I Believe in Music** by The Gallery was written by Mac Davis and was the follow up to their million seller 'Nice To Be With You' from earlier in 1972. Although he was also lead singer on this hit, Jim Gold was dropped from the name of the group on this top 30 hit.

163. **Give Ireland Back to the Irish** by Paul McCartney and Wings was completely banned in Britain from airplay on the BBC. This controversial social comment song was written by Paul and Linda McCartney in response to Bloody Sunday in Northern Ireland on January 30, 1972. The 'B' side was the instrumental version of the tune.

164. **I Can't Help Myself** by Donnie Elbert was the 2nd of 2 Motown remakes in the early 70's. Before this Four Tops recycled hit, he scored with his reworking of the Supremes song 'Where Did Our Love Go' in 1971.He later became an A & R Director for Polygram records in Canada in the 80's, but he died of a massive stroke in 1989 at the age of 52.

165. **Crazy Mama** by J.J. Cale was the only top 40 hit for this Oklahoma City born singer/songwriter/guitarist who wrote 'After Midnight' and 'Cocaine' for Eric Clapton. He did session work with Bob Seger, Neil Young, Art Garfunkel and Phil Spector among others.

166. **Don't Ever Be Lonely (A Poor little Fool like Me)** by Cornelius

Brothers and Sister Rose was their follow up to the similar sounding 'Too Late to Turn Back Now'. The hits of this family act from Dania, Florida were recorded on the United Artists record label.

167. **Happy** by the Rolling Stones was unusual in the fact that Keith Richards is the lead singer on this single. This was their follow up to 'Tumbling Dice' and was also featured on the 'Exile on Main Street' album. Keith Richards wrote this song in France and since 1972 will often sing it in concert, giving Mick Jagger a chance to rest his vocal chords, while at the same time giving Keith the spotlight. On this recording, their producer Jimmy Miller played drums, Bobby Keyes plays saxophone and maracas and Nicky Hopkins played the electric piano.

168. **The Day I Found Myself** by Honey Cone was the final hit from this soul trio of singers who started their 4 hit run with 'Want Ads', followed by 'Stick Up' and 'One Monkey Don't Stop No Show'. All 3 singers, Carolyn Willis, Edna Wright and Shellie Clark had previous careers in the 60's as members of other girl groups.

169. **Once You Understand** by Think was a thought-provoking hit which featured dialogue between a teenager and his parents. This one hit wonder studio group was assembled by producers Lou Stallman and Bobby Susser. The voice of the father, was Lou Stallman who co-wrote 'Round and Round' for Perry Como, 'Yogi' for The Ivy Three and 'It's Gonna Take a Miracle' by Deniece Williams.

170. **Runnin' Away** by Sly and the Family Stone featured piano player Rose Stone on lead vocals on this follow up to their number one hit 'Family Affair'. Both hits were featured on the album 'There's a Riot Goin' On', and all songs were written, produced and arranged by Sylvester Stewart, better known as Sly Stone.

More hits of 1972

We've Got to Get It on Again by the Addrisi Brothers was a top 30 hit for the brothers from Massachusetts who wrote the million seller 'Never My Love' for the Association in 1967.'We've Got to Get It on Again' was a great underrated song from Don and Dick Addrisi whose parents were part of the Flying Addrisi Acrobatic act. Don Addrisi died of cancer in 1984 at the age of 45.

Living in a House Divided by Cher was the first single from her album 'Foxey Lady' produced by Snuff Garrett. This follow up to her top 10 1972 hit 'The Way of Love' just missed the top 20.

Pieces of April by 3 Dog Night featured Chuck Negron front and centre on this follow up to their number one hit 'Black and White'. 'Pieces of April' from the album 'Seven Separate Fools' was written by Dave Loggins of 'Please Come to Boston' fame.

Someday Never Comes by C.C.R. was the final hit single from this legendary California band led by John Fogerty. This mediocre hit was from their swan song album 'Mardi Gras' was certainly not up to par compared with the previous releases by Creedence Clearwater Revival. Front man John Fogerty contributed only 3 songs to this album with Stu Cook and Doug Clifford contributing writing, performing and producing duties. John's brother Tom had just quit the band. He died in 1990 of respiratory failure at the age of 48. Creedence Clearwater Revival was inducted into the Rock and Roll Hall of Fame in 1993.

How Can I Be Sure by David Cassidy was a remake of the Young Rascals hit from 1967. He was also having hits with the Partridge Family simultaneously. In 1971 he scored his first top 10 solo hit with a remake of the Association's 1966 hit 'Cherish'. After 1972, David Cassidy did not have a hit again until 1990 with the song 'Lyin' To Myself'. His half-brother Shaun began a string of 3 consecutive million sellers in 1977 beginning with 'Da Do Ron Ron', another 60's remake.

Isn't Life Strange by the Moody Blues was a philosophical song written by bassist John Lodge from their album 'Seventh Sojourn'. The production, orchestra and vocals were all superb on this Moody Blues single which was one of their longer hit singles, running over 6 minutes.

Softly Whispering I Love You by English Congregation was the only hit for this British ensemble which featured the powerful and distinctive vocals of Brian Keith. This song was written by Roger Cook and Roger Greenaway, who also recorded under 'David and Jonathan' during the 60's. As songwriters they wrote numerous hits including 'My Baby Loves Lovin', 'Green Grass', 'Long Cool Woman , 'You've Got Your Troubles' and many others.

Old Man by Neil Young was the follow up to 'Heart of Gold' which was the first single from his most successful album 'Harvest'. James Taylor and Linda Ronstadt sang backup on this song inspired by the caretaker of the ranch Neil Young purchased in Northern California in 1970.

You Could Have Been a Lady by April Wine was the first hit in the United States for this Canadian rock group headed by Myles Goodwyn. This song was written by Erroll Brown and Tony Wilson of the British group Hot Chocolate and was one of the few non-original hits for this popular band during the 70's and 80's.

Superwoman (Where Were You When I Needed You) by Stevie Wonder was inspired by Syreeta Wright, the former Motown secretary whom he was married to from 1970 to 1972. This was the only top 40 hit from his album 'Music of the Mind', the first which showcased Stevie Wonder's experimentation with the synthesizer.

Spaceman by Nilsson featured Peter Frampton on guitar and was featured on the album 'Son of Schmilsson', the follow up to the very successful 'Nilsson Schmilsson'. 'Spaceman' was written by Nilsson and produced by Richard Perry.

Gone by Joey Heatherton was a remake of the Ferlin Husky Country hit from the 50's. She was a popular movie and TV actress during the 60's and appeared nude in Playboy in April of 1997 at the age of 52.

George Jackson by Bob Dylan was a song about the black militant shot to death in a prison riot. Three years later, Bob Dylan would have another hit based on a controversial person, boxer Rubin 'Hurricane' Carter, who was convicted of murder.

All the Young Dudes by Mott the Hoople was the best known hit from this British glitter-rock band led by vocalist Ian Hunter. They took their name from the Willard Manus novel. David Bowie not only wrote and produced this song, but was also featured on rhythm guitar and backing vocals.

Sunny Days by Lighthouse was written by drummer and lead singer Skip Prokop while relaxing in a child's pool stoned one summer afternoon. This was a major hit in Canada for this brass rock band from Toronto. One of the original members of this group was Howard Shore, who went on to score the music for over 40 films including 'Lords of the Rings' and 'The Aviator'.

Long Haired Lover from Liverpool by Little Jimmy Osmond was popular when the youngest member of the Osmond family was only 8 years old. The Mike Curb Congregation accompanied him on this hit produced by Mike Curb and Perry Botkin Jr. This hit was number one in Britain for over a month in late 1972.

Daisy Mae by Hamilton, Joe Frank and Reynolds was a lesser known hit for the group that scored big in the summer of 1971 with 'Don't Pull Your Love'. Although Tommy Reynolds left the group in 1972, and was replaced by Alan Dennison, the group still recorded under its original name. Sadly, Dan Hamilton, who sang lead on 'Don't Pull Your Love' died in 1994 at the age of 48.

Son of My Father by Giorgio was actually Giorgio Moroder an Oscar and Grammy award winning Italian composer/conductor/producer who later scored music for many films, including 'Midnight Express', 'Scarface', 'Flashdance' and produced for many artists including Donna Summer. This song prominently features a very distinctive synthesizer and was also a hit around the same time by 'Chicory' or 'Chicory Tip'.

Iron Man by Black Sabbath was an early hit for this heavy metal group which formed in Birmingham, England back in the late 60's, featuring lead singer Ozzy Osbourne. Although this hit failed to reach the top 40 on the pop charts, it became a heavy metal classic and in 2006 was awarded the number 1 spot on VH1's Greatest Metal Songs of All Time. 30 years after it was originally recorded, it won a Grammy Award for Best Metal Performance.

Beautiful by Gordon Lightfoot was a moderate hit from his 8th studio album 'Don Quixote'. This Canadian singer songwriter's songs have been recorded by Elvis Presley, Peter, Paul and Mary, Johnny Cash, Marty Robbins, Judy Collins, Barbra Streisand and many others.

Pop That Thang by the Isley Brothers featured Ronald on lead vocals on this soul/funk hit from their album 'Brother, Brother, Brother'. It was a top 5 hit on the R & B charts and top 30 on the pop charts in the summer of 1972.

Levon by Elton John was the first of 5 hits that appeared on the pop charts in 1972 for this superstar singer/songwriter/pianist and also the first hit from his album 'Madman across the Water'. 'Levon' was inspired by Levon Helm of the Band, one of Elton John and Bernie Taupin's favorite groups back then.

You're Still a Young Man by Tower Of Power was the first charted hit for this interracial Oakland - based soul/funk group known for its great horn section. The founder of the group, Emilio Castillo co-wrote this song based on a true story of a then-girlfriend who was 6 years older than him.

Until it's Time for You to Go by Elvis Presley was co-written by Canadian Buffy Sainte-Marie and was featured on the album 'Elvis Now'. She later co-wrote the Academy Award winning song 'Up Where We Belong' which was made popular by Joe Cocker and Jennifer Warnes from the movie 'An Officer and A Gentlemen'.

Tiny Dancer by Elton John has become a classic, despite the fact that it just missed making the top 40 on the pop charts. Lyricist Bernie Taupin was inspired to write this song for his then- girlfriend and later wife Maxine Feibelman (whom he married in 1971 and later divorced in 1976) who was a dancer and seamstress for the band who also accompanied them on their first tour of North America. At the time this book was published, Bernie Taupin is married to his 4th wife, Heather Kidd with 2 daughters.

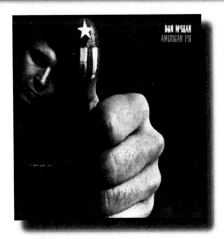

1.	American Pie	Don McLean
2.	Chicago 5	Chicago
3.	Honky Chateau	Elton John
4.	First Time	Roberta Flack
5.	Seventh Sojourn	Moody Blues
6.	Exile on Main Street	Rolling Stones
7.	Superfly	Curtis Mayfield
8.	America	America
9.	Music	Carole King
10.	Harvest	Neil Young
11.	Catch Bull at Four	Cat Stevens
12.	Thick as a Brick	Jethro Tull
13.	Concert for Bangla Desh	George Harrison and Friends
14.	Fragile	Yes
15.	Carney	Leon Russell
16.	Days of Future Passed	Moody Blues
17.	All Directions	Temptations

Top 17 Country Hits of 1972

1.	My Hang Up Is You	Freddie Hart
2.	Funny Face	Donna Fargo
3.	She's Too Good to Be True	Charley Pride
4.	One's On the Way	Loretta Lynn
5.	The Happiest Girl in The Whole U.S.A.	Donna Fargo
6.	Chantilly Lace	Jerry Lee Lewis
7.	He's Gonna Take A Little Bit Longer	Charley Pride
8.	Carolyn	Merle Haggard
9.	If You Leave Me Tonight I'll Cry	Jerry Wallace
10.	Bless Your Heart	Freddie Hart & the Heartbeats
11.	I Ain't Never	Mel Tillis
12.	Eleven Roses	Hank Williams Jr.
13.	Grandma Harp	Merle Haggard
14.	It's Four in the Morning	Faron Young
15.	My Man	Tammy Wynette
16.	That's Why I Love You like I Do	Sonny James
17.	(Lost Her Love) On Our Last Date	Conway Twitty

Top 17 Soul/R & B Hits of 1972

1. Let's Stay Together — Al Green
2. I'll Be Around — Spinners
3. I'll Take You There — Staple Singers
4. (If Loving You Is Wrong) I Don't…Right — Luther Ingram
5. Get On the Good Foot — James Brown
6. In The Rain — Dramatics
7. Me and Mrs. Jones — Billy Paul
8. If You Don't Know Me by Now — Harold Melvin & the Bluenotes
9. Oh Girl — Chi-Lites
10. Daydreaming — Aretha Franklin
11. Power of Love — Joe Simon
12. I'm Still in Love with You — Al Green
13. Lean On Me — Bill Withers
14. Outa Space — Billy Preston
15. Where Is the Love — Roberta Flack & Donny Hathaway
16. I Gotcha — Joe Tex
17. Backstabbers — O'Jays

Top 17 One Hit Wonders of 1972

360 Degrees Of Billy Paul

1.	Billy Paul	Me and Mrs. Jones
2.	Luther Ingram	(If Loving You Is Wrong) I Don't... ...Right
3.	Betty Wright	Clean Up Woman
4.	Climax	Precious and Few
5.	Apollo 100	Joy
6.	Mouth and MacNeal	How Do You Do
7.	Argent	Hold Your Head Up
8.	Chacachas	Jungle Fever
9.	Hot Butter	Popcorn
10.	Commander Cody	Hot Rod Lincoln
11.	Danny O'Keefe	Good Time Charlie's Got The Blues
12.	Sailcat	Motorcycle Mama
13.	Daniel Boone	Beautiful Sunday
14.	Chi Coltrane	Thunder and Lightning
15.	Royal Scots Dragoon Guard	Amazing Grace
16.	Malo	Suavacito
17.	Think	Once You Understand

Top 17 Rock/Hard Rock Hits of 1972

1.	School's Out	Alice Cooper
2.	Layla	Derek and the Dominos
3.	Tumbling Dice	Rolling Stones
4.	Bang A Gong (Get It On)	T. Rex
5.	Listen To the Music	Doobie Brothers
6.	Roundabout	Yes
7.	Black Dog	Led Zeppelin
8.	Stay With Me	Faces
9.	Elected	Alice Cooper
10.	Happy	Rolling Stones.
11.	You Could Have Been A Lady	April Wine
12.	Footstompin' Music	Grand Funk
13.	All the Young Dudes	Mott the Hoople
14.	Easy Livin'	Uriah Heep
15.	Lookin' For a Love	J. Geils Band
16.	Rock and Roll	Led Zeppelin
17.	Iron Man	Black Sabbath

1. Thunder and Lightning — Chi Coltrane
2. Don't Say You Don't Remember — Beverly Bremers
3. The Witch Queen of New Orleans — Redbone
4. We've Got to Get It on Again — Addrisi Brothers
5. Isn't Life Strange — Moody Blues
6. Something's Wrong with Me — Austin Roberts
7. Softly Whispering I Love You — English Congregation
8. Suavacito — Malo
9. You're Still A Young Man — Tower Of Power
10. Goodtime Charlie's Got The Blues — Danny O'Keefe
11. Tightrope — Leon Russell
12. Motorcycle Mama — Sailcat
13. Baby Blue — Badfinger
14. One Monkey Don't Stop No Show — Honey Cone
15. I Need You — America
16. Diary — Bread
17. Superwoman — Stevie Wonder

(* indicates number one only in Britain)

1.	Bohemian Rhapsody	Queen	1976
2.	Mull of Kintyre/Girl's School*	Wings	1977
3.	My Sweet Lord	George Harrison	1971
4.	Maggie May	Rod Stewart	1971
5.	Amazing Grace	Royal Scots Dragoon	1972
6.	Don't Go Breaking My Heart	Elton John and Kiki Dee	1976
7.	In The Summertime*	Mungo Jerry	1970
8.	I Hear You Knocking*	Dave Edmunds	1970
9.	Bye Bye Baby*	Bay City Rollers	1975
10.	Hot Love*	T.Rex	1971
11.	Save Your Kisses for Me*	Brotherhood of Man	1976
12.	Love Grows	Edison Lighthouse	1970
13.	Blockbuster*	Sweet	1973
14.	He Ain't Heavy, He's My Brother	Hollies	1970
15.	Sailing*	Rod Stewart	1975
16.	Imagine	John Lennon	1971
17.	Chirpy Chirpy Cheep Cheep*	Middle of the Road	1971
18.	All Right Now*	Free	1970
19.	Let It Be	Beatles	1970
20.	Alone Again (Naturally)	Gilbert O'Sullivan	1972
21.	My Love	Paul McCartney	1973
22.	Do Ya Think I'm Sexy	Rod Stewart	1979
23.	Night Fever	Bee Gees	1978
24.	Tonight's The Night	Rod Stewart	1976
25.	How Deep Is Your Love	Bee Gees	1977
26.	Philadelphia Freedom	Elton John	1975
27.	Cum On Feel the Noise*	Slade	1973
28.	I'd Like to Teach the World to Sing*	New Seekers (British/Australian)	1971

29. Billy Don't Be A Hero*	Paperlace	1974
30. I Don't Want To Talk About It	Rod Stewart	1977
31. Stayin' Alive	Bee Gees	1978
32. Get It On (Bang A Gong)*	T. Rex	1971
33. I Don't Like Mondays*	Boomtown Rats	1979
34. Cuz I Love You*	Slade	1971
35. I'm The Leader of the Gang (I Am)*	Gary Glitter	1973
36. Jive Talkin'	Bee Gees	1975
37. Silly Love Songs	Paul McCartney and Wings	1976
38. The Long and Winding Road	Beatles	1970
39. Metal Guru*	T. Rex	1972
40. Eye Level*	Simon Park Orchestra	1973
41. Tiger Feet*	Mud	1974
42. Wuthering Heights*	Kate Bush	1978
43. Woodstock*	Matthew's Southern Comfort	1971
44. I Love You Love Me Love*	Gary Glitter	1973
45. Crocodile Rock	Elton John	1973
46. The Air That I Breathe	Hollies	1974
47. Mississippi*	Pussycat	1976
48. Are 'Friends' Electric	Tubeway Army	1979
49. Whole Lotta Love	Led Zeppelin	1970
50. Ernie (The Fastest Milkman in the…)*	Benny Hill	1971
51. Mouldy Old Dough*	Lieutenant Pigeon	1972
52. Angie	Rolling Stones	1973
53. Give A Little Love*	Bay City Rollers	1975
54. Hold Me Close*	David Essex	1975
55. I Love To Love*	Tina Charles	1976
56. So You Win Again*	Hot Chocolate	1977
57. Escape (The Pina Colada Song)	Rupert Holmes	1979
58. Message in a Bottle	Police	1979
59. Instant Karma	John Lennon/Plastic Ono Band	1970
60. Back Home*	England World Cup Squad	1970
61. Photograph	Ringo Starr	1973
62. Band on the Run	Paul McCartney and Wings	1974
63. January*	Pilot	1975
64. We Don't Talk Anymore	Cliff Richard	1979
65. Matchstick Men and Matchstalk Cats…*	Brian and Michael	1978
66. Grandad*	Clive Dunn	1971
67. Long Cool Woman (In A Black Dress)	Hollies	1972
68. Ballroom Blitz	Sweet	1975
69. Give Me Love (Give Me Peace…)	George Harrison	1973
70. When I Need You	Leo Sayer	1977
71. All Kinds of Everything*	Dana	1970
72. How Can You Mend A Broken Heart	Bee Gees	1971
73. Mama Weer All Crazee Now*	Slade	1972
74. I'm Not In Love	10 C.C.	1975
75. Whispering Grass*	Windsor Davies and Don Estelle	1975
76. I Just Want To Be Your Everything	Andy Gibb	1977

77. Tragedy	Bee Gees	1979
78. Uncle Albert/Admiral Halsey	Paul and Linda McCartney	1971
79. Brown Sugar	Rolling Stones	1971
80. Gonna Make You A Star*	David Essex	1974
81. Shadow Dancing	Andy Gibb	1978
82. Dreams	Fleetwood Mac	1977
83. Telegram Sam*	T. Rex	1972
84. It Never Rains In Southern California	Albert Hammond	1972
85. Hey Rock and Roll*	Showaddywaddy	1974
86. Oh Boy*	Mud	1975
87. You Should Be Dancing	Bee Gees	1976
88. You to Me Are Everything*	Real Thing	1976
89. Combine Harvester*	Wurzels	1976
90. Sultans of Swing	Dire Straits	1979
91. Neanderthal Man	Hotlegs	1970
92. It Don't Come Easy	Ringo Starr	1971
93. Never Ending Song of Love	New Seekers (British/Aust.)	1971
94. Angel Fingers*	Wizzard	1973
95. Sad Sweet Dreamer*	Sweet Sensation	1974
96. Devil Woman	Cliff Richard	1976
97. Baker Street	Gerry Rafferty	1978
98. Hitchin' a Ride	Vanity Fare	1970
99. Your Song	Elton John	1971
100. Space Oddity	David Bowie	73/75
101. Nights in White Satin	Moody Blues	1972
102. Baby Jump*	Mungo Jerry	1971
103. Get Down*	Gilbert O'Sullivan	1973
104. Welcome Home*	Peters and Lee	1973
105. Fame	David Bowie	1975
106. Blinded by the Light	Manfred Mann's Earth Band	1977
107. Rat Trap*	Boomtown Rats	1978
108. Another Day	Paul McCartney	1971
109. Day after Day	Badfinger	1972
110. Bennie and the Jets	Elton John	1974
111. Streets of London*	Ralph McTell	1975
112. Forever and Ever*	Silk	1976
113. Lucy in the Sky with Diamonds	Elton John	1974
114. Miss You	Rolling Stones	1978
115. Pop Muzik	M	1979
116. Too Much Heaven	Bee Gees	1979
117. Come and Get It	Badfinger	1970

♫ This Paul McCartney hit was the theme for the first James Bond film starring Roger Moore as agent 007.

♫ A then-unknown David Foster was the keyboardist for this one hit wonder Canadian group.

♫ This million selling story song was originally offered to Cher, but Sonny turned it down.

♫ This number one hit from a disaster film won the Academy Award for Best Song.

♫ Bette Midler's first major hit was a remake of a song the Andrew Sisters made popular in 1941.

♫ This re released novelty hit sold a million copies in 1973 exactly as it did 11 years earlier when it topped the charts.

FIND OUT THAT…AND MUCH MORE INSIDE…1973!

1.   **Tie a Yellow Ribbon Round the Old Oak Tree** by Tony Orlando and Dawn was based on a true story about a man who had served 3 years in prison and was returning home on a bus. He had written a letter to his wife that if she still loved him that she could let him know by tying a yellow ribbon around the old oak tree in the city square of their hometown. The question was answered in this song which became the biggest hit of the year.

2.   **Killing Me Softly with His Song** by Roberta Flack was inspired by another singer, Lori Lieberman after hearing Don McLean's 'American Pie'. This song was written by Norman Gimbel and Charles Fox who won major Grammy Awards for Record and Song of the Year, as well as the Grammy for Best Pop Female for Roberta Flack

3.   **You're So Vain** by Carly Simon featured Mick Jagger on backing vocals, so that pretty much eliminates him as the one this song is about. Speculation on who the song was about ran from Warren Beatty to Kris Kristofferson and even Carly Simon's husband James Taylor. She married Taylor and she said that it is definitely not about him.

4.   **My Love** by Paul McCartney and Wings was written for his wife Linda, the one true love of his life. They were married in 1969, the same year John Lennon wed Yoko Ono. 'My Love' was the only hit single released from the 'Red Rose Speedway' album.

5.   **Crocodile Rock** by Elton John was a very nostalgic song which was inspired by many hits of the 50's and 60's including the very obvious 'Speedy Gonzales' recorded by Pat Boone in 1962. This number one hit was the first single released from his forthcoming album 'Don't Shoot Me, I'm Only the Piano Player' which also included the follow up hit 'Daniel'.

6.   **Bad Bad Leroy Brown** by Jim Croce was inspired by someone he met in his short time in the army and the line 'meaner than a junkyard dog' came from his experience when he used to frequent junkyards in search of old car parts. This became Jim Croce's signature hit and one that was still on the

charts at the time of his death from a plane crash on September 20th that year. He was 30 years old when he died.

7.   **The Night the Lights Went out in Georgia** by Vicki Lawrence was written by her husband Bobby Russell who previously wrote 'Honey' for Bobby Goldsboro and 'Little Green Apples' for O. C. Smith. The song was originally turned down by Cher, but Vicki liked the song and told her husband that it was a hit, despite the fact that he didn't think much of it. It became a number one million seller for the singer who is best known as the actress who played Carol Burnett's sister on TV.

8.   **Will It Go Round in Circles** by Billy Preston was a number one million seller for the singer/songwriter/keyboardist known as 'the 5th Beatle' before his solo career. His musical relationship with the Beatles began shortly after George Harrison discovered him in 1967 while Preston accompanied Ray Charles on tour. 'Will It Go Round in Circles' was produced and co-written by Billy Preston with Bruce Fisher.

9.   **Midnight Train to Georgia** by Gladys Knight and The Pips was originally titled 'Midnight Plane to Houston' as a country song. This number one hit was written by Jim Weatherly, who also wrote 'Neither One Of Us', a number 2 hit earlier in 1973.'Midnight Train to Georgia' won the 1974 Grammy Award for Best R & B Group or Duo. This was the first major hit by Gladys Knight and The Pips on the Buddah label, after leaving Motown records.

10.   **Brother Louie** by The Stories was a song about an interracial relationship between a black girl, her white boyfriend and his racist parents. The song was written by Errol Brown and Tony Wilson of Hot Chocolate who originally recorded it, but without much success. They would score later in the 70's with 'Emma' and 'You Sexy Thing'. Although this was the only hit for the Stories, (featuring the distinctive voice of Ian Lloyd) group co-founder Michael Brown was a founding member of the Left Banke during the 60's, best known for their hit 'Walk Away Renee'.

11.   **The Most Beautiful Girl** by Charlie Rich was number one on both the pop charts and the country charts for the singer known as 'The Silver Fox'. This pianist/singer was born in Colt, Arkansas and had hits in 1960 with the Elvis influenced 'Lonely Weekends' and the upbeat piano-driven 'Mohair Sam' in 1965.He would have to wait 8 years before his next pop hit would arrive with 'Behind Closed Doors' which opened up the door to great success in the next couple of years.

12.   **Top Of The World** by The Carpenters became the 2nd official number one hit for the popular brother and sister soft rock duo, although they had 5 hits that stalled at number 2 between 'Close To You' and this one. 'Top of the World' was written by Richard Carpenter and their musical friend John Bettis, who also co-wrote 'Goodbye to Love' and 'Yesterday Once More'. 'Top of the World' which was also a major Country hit in 1973 for Lynn Anderson, was originally intended to be only an album cut.

13.   **Half-breed** by Cher was about the tale of the daughter of a Cherokee

mother and white father written specially for her by songwriter Mary Dean. By 1973, Cher had fully established herself as a solo act, and in 1974 both her marriage to Sonny Bono and their weekly Comedy Variety TV Show ended.

14.   **Time in a Bottle** by Jim Croce became a hit single after his death along with 'I Got a Name', 'I'll Have to Say I Love You in a Song' and 'Workin' at the Car Wash Blues'. 'Time in a Bottle' was featured in a made-for-TV movie starring Desi Arnaz Jr. and Season Hubley and was telecast September 12, 1973, the night Jim Croce had just completed his 3rd album. Viewer response to the song was so great, it was released as a single, but that didn't happen until after Croce lost his life in a plane crash on September 20th 1973.

15.   **The Morning After** by Maureen McGovern was an Academy Award winning song from the all-star disaster film 'The Poseidon Adventure'. Maureen McGovern was a secretary who worked as a folksinger part time when she was asked to sing the song that would put her into the limelight.

16.   **Delta Dawn** by Helen Reddy was previously recorded by Tanya Tucker, Bette Midler and a few other music artists, but was only a major hit by the singer from Australia who first hit number one in 1972 with 'I Am Woman'.

17.   **We're An American Band** by Grand Funk was the first of two number one hits produced by Todd Rundgren for this rock band from Flint, Michigan. Although guitarist Mark Farner sang lead on many of their hits, it was drummer Don Brewer who wrote and sang lead on this title track from their 7th studio album.

18.   **Angie** by the Rolling Stones from their 'Goat's Head Soup' album was primarily written by Keith Richards. The song title was inspired by his daughter 'Angela', not about Mick Jagger's relationship with David Bowie's wife 'Angela', which was the rumor at the time.

19.   **Frankenstein** by the Edgar Winter Group was a high energy instrumental produced by Rick Derringer who was the lead singer of the McCoys during the 60's. Edgar Winter, the long haired albino brother of older brother Johnny, was a multi-talented instrumentalist who played saxophone, keyboards and drums on this self-composed number one hit.

20.   **Photograph** by Ringo Starr was co-written with George Harrison, who played a 12-string guitar and sang harmony vocals on this number one hit. Ringo followed this hit with another hit that topped the charts, 'You're Sixteen'. A 3rd top 10 hit, 'Oh My My' from his self-titled album 'Ringo' would be released the following year in early 1974.

21.   **Love Train** by the O'Jays was the biggest hit from this soul group from Ohio which at various stages was a duo, a quintet, a quartet and a trio when they recorded this number one million seller. This goodtime song about love and togetherness was their 3rd single from the 'Backstabbers' album and was both written and produced by Kenny Gamble and Leon Huff.

22.   **You Are the Sunshine of My Life** by Stevie Wonder became one of his most popular love songs and it was covered by dozens of music artists

including Frank Sinatra, Ella Fitzgerald, Mel Torme, Tom Jones and many others. This hit was number one the year after his marriage to Syreeta Wright ended, although they occasionally continued their professional relationship. 'You Are the Sunshine of My life' won a 1974 Grammy Award for Best Male Pop Vocal Performance.

23. **Touch Me in the Morning** by Diana Ross was the 2nd official number one hit for the former super Supreme. This song was written by Ron Miller and newcomer Michael Masser, who would later write some of Whitney Houston's biggest hits. Diana Ross was juggling her acting career as her role as Billie Holiday in 'Lady Sings The Blues' was getting rave reviews when this hit was recorded.

24. **Give Me Love, Give Me Peace on Earth** by George Harrison was the only single released from his album 'Living in the Material World'. George Harrison once described this song as 'a prayer and personal statement between me, the Lord and whoever likes it'. This song replaced another former Beatle, Paul McCartney's 'My Love' and George was replaced at number one with 'Will It Go Round in Circles' by Billy Preston, who played with the Beatles.

25. **Goodbye Yellow Brick Road** by Elton John was the title track of this best selling double album which also included the hit singles 'Saturday Night's Alright For Fighting', and 'Bennie and The Jets'. The album also included the popular cuts 'Funeral for a Friend' and his tribute to Marilyn Monroe, 'Candle in the Wind'.

26. **Playground in My Mind** by Clint Holmes was the only hit for this British born singer who moved to Buffalo, New York as a child. This million seller was written by Paul Vance and Lee Pockriss who previously wrote 'Itsy Bitsy Teenie Weenie Yellow Polka Dot Bikini' for Brian Hyland, 'Catch a Falling Star' for Perry Como and 'Tracy' for the Cuff Links. It is Paul Vance's son Philip who is the child heard singing on this popular hit,

27. **Let's Get It On** by Marvin Gaye was one of 34 chart singles as a soloist and 15 more in duets during his Motown years. 'Let's Get It On' was a sexy number one hit which Marvin Gaye co-wrote and co-produced with Ed Townsend who was best known for his classic 1958 hit 'For Your Love'.

28. **Superstition** by Stevie Wonder was the first of 2 number one hits from his 'Talking Book' album with 'You Are the Sunshine of My Life' following in the footsteps climbing to the top spot. Both songs won Grammy Awards with 'Superstition' winning both 'Best R & B Vocal Performance and Best R & B Song.' This hit was written, produced and arranged by Stevie Wonder, who also played many of the instruments on this multi-layered masterpiece.

29. **Dueling Banjos** by Eric Weissburg and Steve Mandell was from the movie 'Deliverance' starring Burt Reynolds and Jon Voight. This instrumental was written in 1955 as 'Feuding Banjos' by Arthur 'guitar boogie' Smith.

30. **Live And Let Die** by Paul McCartney and Wings was the title song of the 1973 James Bond film and reunited the former Beatle with producer George Martin, who also arranged the orchestral break. 'Live and Let Die' was the first James Bond film to star Roger Moore as agent 007.

31. **Kodachrome** by Paul Simon was a goodtime summer 1973 hit named after the Kodak 35mm film. It was a million seller in North America, but was not played on radio in Britain because the BBC banned the song due to the trademarked name. In 2009, Paul Simon reunited with his former partner Art Garfunkel for a tour and a concert at Madison Square Gardens in celebration of the Rock and Rock Hall of Fame's 25th Anniversary.

32. **Cisco Kid** by War was their highest charting of their 8 top 20 hits during the 70's. The song was inspired by the popular TV series from the 50's which starred Duncan Renaldo as the Cisco Kid. There was also 'Cisco Kid' movies and comic books.

33. **Neither One Of Us (Wants To Be The First)** by Gladys Knight and the Pips was number one for a full month on the R & B charts and it almost made the top spot on the pop charts in early 1973.This hit was their final major hit for Motown before switching to the Buddah label. This Grammy Award Winning Best Pop Vocal Duo or Group Song was written by Jim Weatherly, who would also write the biggest hit of their career, 'Midnight Train to Georgia'.

34. **Daniel** by Elton John was written and recorded on the same day, with Bernie Taupin writing the lyrics and Elton composing the music. This was the follow up to 'Crocodile Rock', also from the album 'Don't Shoot Me, I'm Only The Piano Player'. Elton John has sold more than 200 million records since 'Your Song' was released in early 1971.

35. **Loves Me like a Rock** by Paul Simon featured vocal accompaniment by the Gospel singing group the Dixie Hummingbirds. This follow up to 'Kodachrome' was also featured on his album 'There Goes Rhymin' Simon' which was recorded at Muscle Shoals Studios in Alabama.

36. **Keep On Truckin'** by Eddie Kendricks was the biggest solo hit by this former member and lead singer of the Temptations. He was the lead voice you heard on The Temptations hits 'Get Ready', 'The Way You Do the Things You Do' and 'Just My Imagination'. Eddie Kendricks left the Temptations in 1971 because he was not allowed to have a solo career while being a member of this legendary Motown group. Sadly, Eddie Kendricks died of lung cancer in 1992 at age 52.

37. **Yesterday Once More** by The Carpenters was a song about listening to music on the radio in the carefree days of the 50's and 60's. This was from their 'Now and Then' album which featured a medley of oldies on the 'then' side which included 'Deadman's Curve', 'Fun Fun Fun', 'One Fine Day' and others. Karen Carpenter's smooth vocals brought warmth to 'Yesterday Once More', co-written by brother Richard, who's 1973 Red Ferrari, is prominently pictured on the album cover.

38. **Last Song** by Edward Bear was a Canadian group based in Toronto headed by lead singer/songwriter Larry Evoy. This trio got their name from the A. A. Milne's Winnie the Pooh, whose proper name is 'Edward Bear'. They also had hits with 'You, Me and Mexico', 'Close Your Eyes' and 'Masquerade' among others.

39.   Shambala by 3 Dog Night was a million seller from their 10th studio album 'Cyan'. Singer B.W. Stevenson debuted on the charts with his version a week before 3 Dog Night brought their more popular version to the top 5. B.W. Stevenson would have his one and only hit later in the year with 'My Maria'. 'Shambala' is a song about the mythical kingdom where life is filled with joy, kindness and good fortune.

40.   Little Willy by The Sweet was a bubblegum hit by the British group later known for their glam-rock hits 'Ballroom Blitz' and 'Fox on the Run'. Nicky Chinn and Mike Chapman not only wrote most of the Sweet's biggest hits, but also composed 'Kiss You All Over' for Exile', 'Mickey' for Toni Basil, 'Stumblin' In for Suzi Quatro and Chris Norman among other hits during the 70's and 80's.

41.   Ramblin' Man by the Allman Brothers was the biggest hit for this group that formed in Macon, Georgia back in '69. The Allman brothers, Greg and Duane, were the nucleus of this southern rock group, along with guitarist Dickey Betts, who sang lead on their signature hit. Sadly, Duane Allman was killed in a motorcycle accident on September 29th, 1971 at the age of 24, and group member Berry Oakley also died in a motorcycle accident a little over a year later in the same area at the same age.

42.   Also Sprach Zarathustra (2001) by Deodato was a piece of classical music composed by Richard Strauss in 1896 which later became the theme for the movie '2001: A Space Odyssey'. 'Deodato' was Eumir De Almeida Deodato, a keyboardist/composer/producer/arranger from Rio de Janeiro, Brazil. This Grammy Award Winning producer/arranger produced many of the hits for Kool and The Gang.

43.   Pillow Talk by Sylvia was a sultry, sexy and smooth soul hit by the lady who 2 decades earlier was half of the duo 'Mickey and Sylvia' She was born Sylvia Vanderpool and in 1964 married Joe Robinson. As Sylvia Robinson, she co- wrote the 1970 hit 'Love On A Two Way Street' for the Moments and was the driving force behind one of rap music's first major hits 'Rapper's Delight' by The Sugarhill Gang.

44.   Heartbeat, It's a Lovebeat by the Defranco Family were a Canadian act which featured 13 year old lead singer Tony DeFranco on this 1973 million seller bubblegum hit. The group moved to California, where they all still live, and at last report lead singer Tony DeFranco is a successful real estate agent in Westlake Village, California.

45.   Say, Has Anybody Seen My Sweet Gypsy Rose by Tony Orlando and Dawn was a million selling follow up to their biggest hit of all, 'Tie a Yellow Ribbon Round the Old Oak Tree,' written and produced by the same group of musicians. This hit was delivered in a style from the 'Al Jolson' era and was featured on their latest album 'Dawn's Ragtime Follies'. The follow up single was the similar-sounding 'Who's In the Strawberry Patch with Sally'.

46.   I'm Gonna Love You Just A Little Bit More Baby by Barry White was the first of many solo million sellers for one of the smoothest and deepest voices in music. Barry White was a soul singer/songwriter/producer/arranger/

128

keyboardist and leader of his own 40-piece Love Unlimited Orchestra. He recorded all of his solo hits on the 20th Century record label.

47. **Leave Me Alone (Ruby Red Dress)** by Helen Reddy was the follow up million seller to the number one hit 'Delta Dawn'. 'Leave Me Alone' was written by Linda Laurie, the former novelty artist of the 1959 hit 'Ambrose (part 5)', recorded when she was a teenager. Linda Laurie passed away in November of 2009.

48. **Your Mama Don't Dance** by Loggins and Messina was the first and biggest hit of their career together as a duo. Kenny Loggins played in a few bands before meeting up with former Poco and Buffalo Springfield member 'Jim Messina. In 1973 they charted 3 top 20 hits and failed to reach the top 40 again, although Kenny Loggins had a very successful solo career which included over a dozen notable hits. Loggins and Messina reunited for a tour in 2009.

49. **Drift Away** by Dobie Gray was the biggest hit for this Texas born singer/songwriter/actor who had to wait 8 years between this hit and his prior top 20 hit 'The 'In' Crowd' in 1965.Dobie Gray, had a hit again with 'Drift Away' when Uncle Kracker included him in a duet of the song in 2003.

50. **Smoke on the Water** by Deep Purple was about the burning of the Montreux Casino in December of 1971 during a Frank Zappa concert which they opened. This hit from their 'Machine Head' album which was released in early 1972 wasn't released as a single until over a year later, in the spring of 1973. This classic rock hit featured the lead vocals of Ian Gillan, the guitar of Richie Blackmore, the organ of Jon Lord, the bass of Roger Glover and the drums of Ian Paice.

51. **Could It Be I'm Falling In Love** by the Spinners was the 2nd of 3 consecutive million selling singles in a row for this Detroit R & B group discovered by Harvey Fuqua, former lead singer of the Moonglows, back in 1961.Bobby Smith and Phillip Wynne shared lead vocals on this love song which also featured 3 female singers on background vocals. This number hit on the R & B charts was produced by Thom Bell and written by twin brothers Mervin and Melvin Steals.

52. **Ain't No Woman (Like the One I Got)** by The Four Tops was the biggest of the 3 hits they had on the Dunhill record label after leaving Motown after a decade of hits. This love song was written by Dennis Lambert and Brian Potter, who previously wrote successful hits like 'Don't Pull Your Love', 'One Tin Soldier', 'It Only Takes a Minute' and 'Two Divided By Love'.

53. **Why Can't We Live Together** by Timmy Thomas was the only major hit for this soul singer/songwriter/keyboardist from Evansville, Indiana. Timmy Thomas, a minister's son, wrote this song out of frustration of the problems that were going on in the world. His soulful voice, a Lowery organ and a rhythm machine took this hit to the top of the R & B charts and near the top of the pop charts in early 1973.

54. **Sing** by The Carpenters was actually a song created for the popular 'Sesame Street' children's TV show and performed in English, Spanish and sign language. Richard Carpenter produced and played keyboards, while Karen played drums and sang lead, backed by the Jimmy Joyce Children's Choir. This was the first of 2 major hits from their 'Then and Now' album with 'Yesterday Once More' being the other.

55.   Just You 'N Me by Chicago featured Peter Cetera on lead vocals and was written by James Pankow, trombonist, songwriter and one of the founding members of this popular 70's brass rock band. This hit was taken from the album 'Chicago 6' which also included 'Feelin' Stronger Everyday'.

56.   Oh Babe, What Would You Say by Hurricane Smith was his only hit as a singer. However, Norman 'Hurricane' Smith was the sound engineer of many of the recordings by the Beatles and producer of several of the early albums by Pink Floyd. He hit on the 'Hurricane' idea as a result of seeing the 1952 Yvonne De Carlo film 'Hurricane' Smith. Norman 'Hurricane' Smith died at the age of 85 in early March of 2008.

57.   Stuck in the Middle with You by Stealer's Wheel featured a then-unknown Gerry Rafferty on lead vocals. The song was later known for being featured in a violent scene in the film 'Reservoir Dogs'. The Scottish group Stealer's Wheel broke up in 1975 and Gerry Rafferty had a string of solo hits beginning with 'Baker Street' in 1978.

58.   Do It Again by Steely Dan was the debut hit from this Los Angeles based pop/jazz group featuring Donald Fagen and Walter Becker. This was the first of 2 consecutive hits from the album 'Can't Buy a Thrill' which featured a cover showing a line of prostitutes standing in a red light area waiting for clients.

59.   That Lady by The Isley Brothers was their first top 10 hit since 'It's Your Thing' in 1969 and became a top 10 million seller in the summer of 1973. This song, inspired by The Impressions, was actually one they performed a decade earlier as 'Who's That Lady', but decided to rearrange it with a Latin rock feel, which was popular for Santana at the time.

60.   The Cover Of The Rolling Stone by Dr. Hook and The Medicine Show was written by writer/cartoonist Shel Silverstein, who also composed their debut hit 'Sylvia's Mother' in 1972.The group got their name from the eye patch worn by Ray Sawyer who was featured on lead vocals on this top 10 hit. They got their wish to appear on the cover of Rolling Stone magazine in late March of 1973, while this hit was on the pop charts.

61.   Space Race by Billy Preston was an instrumental and the top 10 follow up to his number one hit 'Will It Go Round in Circles'. Aside from Tony Sheridan, he was the only artist to receive billing alongside the Beatles on their records. The Beatles 1969 hit 'Get Back' is credited as 'The Beatles with Billy Preston.'

62.   Paper Roses by Marie Osmond was a remake of a song Anita Bryant took to the top 5 hit in 1960. Marie Osmond was only 13 years old when she had a hit with 'Paper Roses', which reached number one on the Country charts and top 5 on the pop charts. Three years later, she and her brother Donny began hosting their own TV Variety Show.

63.   **Hello Its Me** by Todd Rundgren was a song he released originally with his group 'Nazz' in 1969.This was the biggest charted hit for the singer/songwriter/producer/musician and was from his biggest selling album 'Something/Anything' which also included 'I Saw The Light'. In the 70's Todd Rundgren also produced hits for other artists including Badfinger, Grand Funk and Meatloaf's most successful album, 'Bat Out Of Hell'.

64.   **Higher Ground** by Stevie Wonder was a social comment song and the first of 3 hits from his critically acclaimed 'Innervisions' album. Background singers on this song included Minnie Ripperton, Deniece Williams and Syreeta Wright, his wife from 1970 to 1972.At the time this song was on the charts, Stevie Wonder was in a serious car accident that left him in a coma for 4 days. He fully recovered with the exception of the partial loss of his sense of smell.

65.   **Danny's Song** by Anne Murray was written by Kenny Loggins, who also wrote 'Love Song' which was also released as a hit single for Canada's sweetheart in 1973.

66.   **Diamond Girl** by Seals and Crofts were once members of the 50's group 'The Champs', best known for their hit 'Tequila'. The jazzy, pop folk 'Diamond Girl' was the title song from their 5th album, which also produced the hit single 'We May Never Pass This Way Again'.

67.   **The Twelfth of Never** by Donny Osmond was a remake of a Johnny Mathis hit from the 50's. The title comes from the popular expression of a date in the future that will never come. 'The Twelfth of Never' was co-written by Jerry Livingston who composed many tunes through the years including the theme for 'Casper the Friendly Ghost' with Mack David.

68.   **Monster Mash** by Bobby 'Boris' Pickett was the surprise hit of 1973, because it was totally unchanged from the hit that topped the charts and sold millions back in 1962. The inspiration of the song started when Bobby 'Boris' Pickett would perform a clubs at night and would do his impression of Boris Karloff as if he was doing the song 'Little Darlin'. Fellow band member Leonard Capizzi encouraged Bobby to do more with it and record producer Gary Paxton made it happen. This hit was a million seller in 1962 and again in 1973.

69.   **Get Down** by Gilbert O'Sullivan was the 3rd and final million selling top 10 hit in North America for this singer/songwriter from Waterford, Ireland. This hit reached number one in Britain for the singer who continued to perform decades after the hits, and in late 2009 performed at London's Royal Albert Hall.

70.   **Wildflower** by Skylark was a one hit wonder Canadian group which featured a then-unknown future super producer David Foster on keyboards. The soulful voice of Donny Gerrard was the lead singer for this Vancouver, British Columbia vocal group.

71.   **My Maria** by B.W. Stevenson which featured the guitar of Larry Carlton, was the only notable hit for this singer/songwriter from Dallas, Texas. This song later became a number one hit on the Country charts for Brooks and Dunn. Sadly, B.W. Stevenson died at the age of 38 in 1988 after heart surgery.

72.   Long Train Runnin' by The Doobie Brothers was their first official top 10 hit after their debut hit 'Listen to the Music', which also featured Tom Johnston on lead vocals. He also wrote most of their early hits including 'China Grove', the follow up to 'Long Train Runnin', both were featured on the album 'The Captain and Me'.

73.   I Got a Name by Jim Croce was released as a single just days after he died in a plane crash. The album 'I Got a Name' was completed just 8 days before his death and also included his future hits 'I'll Have To Say I Love You In A Song' and 'Workin' At The Car Wash Blues'. 'I Got a Name' was from the movie 'Last American Hero' starring Jeff Bridges and was one of the few songs not written by Jim Croce. This song was composed by Norman Gimbel and Charles Fox, who also wrote the 70's hits 'Killing Me Softly with His Song' and the themes for both 'Happy Days' and 'Laverne and Shirley.'

74.   Reeling in the Years by Steely Dan was the second single release from their debut album 'Can't Buy a Thrill'. This hit featured Donald Fagen on lead vocals and Elliot Randall on the memorable guitar solo. The name 'Steely Dan' came from the steam-powered dildo in William Burrough's novel 'The Naked Lunch'.

75.   Feelin' Stronger Everyday by Chicago was written by group members James Pankow and the lead singer on this hit, Peter Cetera. This hit was one of two hits from the 'Chicago 6' album, and both were written or co-written by James Pankow.

76.   One of a Kind (Love Affair) by The Spinners was the 3rd of 3 consecutive million sellers. Bobby Smith and Philip Wynne share lead vocals on their 70's hits, although it was Wynne who sang lead on this soul classic. Sadly, Wynne died of a heart attack while performing at a nightclub in 1984. He was 43 years old.

77.   Break up To Make Up by The Stylistics was their follow up to the top 10 hit 'I'm Stone in Love with You'. Most of their hits, which were produced by Thom Bell, were ballads featuring the silky smooth voice of Russell Thompkins Jr, known for his high pitch tenor and falsetto voice.

78.   China Grove by the Doobie Brothers had a very distinctive guitar riff that has been used in many TV shows and movies through the years. Lead singer and guitarist Tom Johnston wrote this follow up single to 'Long Train Runnin' and both were from the album 'The Captain and Me'.

79.   Dancing in the Moonlight by King Harvest was the only hit for this 6 man band from Olcott, New York. This one hit wonder was written in 1968 by Sherman Kelly, the brother of King Harvest's former drummer Wells Kelly. This is one group that does not sound at all like what you would imagine. The album cover photo of this group would not be out of place to be perceived as a heavy metal group or 6 guys that would like comfortable as bikers.

80.   Boogie Woogie Bugle Boy by Bette Midler was the claim to fame hit for the Divine Miss M. 'Boogie Woogie Bugle Boy' was a remake of a World War 2 song popularized by the Andrew Sisters. Bette Midler's 'Divine Miss

M' album was co-produced by her musical friend Barry Manilow, who would accompany her on piano before they became major stars.

81.   The Love I Lost by Harold Melvin and The Blue Notes was their 2nd and only other top 10 million seller following their 1972 hit 'If You Don't Know Me By Now'. Both songs featured Teddy Pendergrass on lead vocals. 'The Love I Lost', written and produced by Gamble and Huff, was originally intended to be a ballad, but was transformed into a disco song.

82.   Hi Hi Hi by Paul McCartney and Wings was banned on many radio stations because of its sexual and drug references which include 'getting high', 'gonna do it to ya', 'sweet banana' and 'get you ready for my polygun.' This high energy rocker was produced by Paul and co-written with his wife Linda.

83.   Daddy's Home by Jermaine Jackson was a remake of the Shep and The Limelites top 5 hit from 1961. In 1973, Jermaine Jackson, married Hazel Joy Gordy, daughter of Motown President Berry Gordy Jr. They separated a few years later. Jermaine Jackson was the family spokesperson for much of the public interviews regarding the death of his brother Michael, June 25th 2009.

84.   Don't Expect Me to Be Your Friend by Lobo was the 3rd of 3 top 10 hits for this pop singer/songwriter/guitarist whose full name was Roland Kent Lavoie. Lobo's hits were produced by Phil Gernhard, who also produced (and co-wrote) 'Snoopy Vs. The Red Baron' for the Royal Guardsmen, 'Abraham, Martin and John' for Dion, Let Your Love Flow' by the Bellamy Brothers and 'Spiders and Snakes' for Jim Stafford.

85.   Right Place, Wrong Time by Dr. John was the biggest pop hit for the New Orleans 'swamp rock' pioneer whose real name is Malcolm 'Mac' Rebennack. This top 10 hit was produced by Allen Toussaint, also from New Orleans, who also played various instruments and supplied background vocals on this song from one of rock music's most unusual voices.

86.   Hocus Pocus by Focus was a totally offbeat, abstract hit by this one hit wonder progressive rock Dutch group. This mostly-instrumental hit featured an amazing performance by Thijs van Leer yodeling, playing keyboards, flute and whistling.

87.   Rocky Mountain High by John Denver was inspired by his move to Aspen, Colorado and his love of the area. This song is one of 2 official state songs for Colorado and a 'Rocky Mountain High' ski run at the Snowmass Ski Resort near Aspen has been named in John Denver's honor.

88.   Behind Closed Doors by Charlie Rich was the first of 2 major 1973 hits for the singer known as 'The Silver Fox'. This song was written by Kenny O'Dell, who had a hit of his own in 1967 with 'Beautiful People'. Both 'Behind Closed Doors' and 'The Most Beautiful Girl' topped the Country charts for Charlie Rich in 1973. This Grammy and Country Music award winner died in his sleep at the age of 62 in 1995.

89.   Free Ride by Edgar Winter Group was written by Dan Hartman and produced by Rick Derringer. This high energy hit has been used in numerous films as well as video games. 1973 was a banner year for the Edgar Winter group with 'Free Ride' hot on the heels of their number one monster instrumental hit 'Frankenstein'.

90.   **All I Know** by Art Garfunkel, written by Jim Webb, was the first and biggest solo hit for the former half of Simon and Garfunkel. This song was popular after he appeared in the movies 'Catch 22' and 'Carnal Knowledge' with Jack Nicholson. In 2009, he re-united once again for a tour with his former music partner Paul Simon.

91.   **Never, Never Gonna Give You Up** by Barry White was the 2nd top 10 million seller in his debut year as a solo soul music artist. Most of his big hits in the 70's had the same sexy sound that his female fans adored. He would have 4 more major hits in the 70's, including the 1974 number one hit 'Can't Get Enough of Your Love, Babe'.

92.   **Natural High** by Bloodstone was the only hit for this soul group from Kansas City, Missouri. Bloodstone's soul ballad was similar to the style of other smooth R & B vocal groups of the time like the Stylistics, the Moments and the Chi-Lites.

93.   **Knockin' on Heaven's Door** by Bob Dylan was featured in the Sam Peckinpah movie 'Pat Garrett and Billy the Kid' which also starred this iconic singer/songwriter, along with Kris Kristofferson and James Coburn. This song has been recorded by various music artists through the years, including Guns 'N Roses.

94.   **Stir It Up** by Johnny Nash was written by Bob Marley and recorded in Jamaica with the Wailers. This became Bob Marley's first composition to become popular outside of Jamaica. The following year, Eric Clapton had a number one hit with Marley's 'I Shot the Sheriff'. 'Stir It Up' was Johnny Nash's follow up to his multi million seller 'I Can See Clearly Now'.

95.   **Money** by Pink Floyd was the first major hit in North America for this legendary British band. This was Pink Floyd's only hit from their classic album 'Dark Side of the Moon' which charted for an incredible 741 weeks on the album chart. In December of 2009 it actually re-entered that same chart.

96.   **Saturday Night's Alright for Fighting** by Elton John was the first of 3 hit singles from his 'Goodbye Yellow Brick Road' album, and one of his few hits to miss the mark of the top 10 during this era. This hit was a departure from his previous hits with a style much harder and heavier, which would explain why the Who covered it in 1991.

97.   **Space Oddity** by David Bowie was originally released in 1969, without success, to coincide with man's first walk on the moon. However, it was re-released in 1973 and it became his first North American top 40 hit. This hit was produced by Gus Dudgeon, who also produced over a dozen albums for Elton John.

98.   **Why Me** by Kris Kristofferson was a number one country hit for this singer/songwriter/actor and his first hit to reach top 20 on the pop charts. This song was popular the year he married Rita Coolidge, who he later divorced in 1980.

99.   Dead Skunk by Loudon Wainwright 3rd was a fun novelty song from this satirical folk singer/songwriter from North Carolina who scored with only one hit. He was married briefly to Kate McGarrigle and has appeared in many movies through the years including 'The 40 Year Old Virgin', 'The Aviator' and 'The Slugger's Wife'.

100.   Walk on the Wild Side by Lou Reed was co-produced by David Bowie and was the biggest 70's solo hit for this former member of The Velvet Underground. This hit from his 'Transformer' album, was about New York City transvestites and prostitutes. The saxophone solo was played by Ronnie Ross, who taught David Bowie how to play the instrument when he was just a kid.

101.   Living in the Past by Jethro Tull prominently featured leader Ian Anderson on lead vocals and flute. This progressive British rock group took their name from an 18th century agriculturist. This hit was originally recorded in 1969, but didn't become a hit until early 1973 when it was featured in the album 'Living in the Past'.

102.   Masterpiece by the Temptations was actually their final hit to reach the top 10. This was another progressive Motown hit written and produced by Norman Whitfield for this legendary group previously known for their tight harmonies and choreographed dance moves on stage.

103.   Uneasy Rider by Charlie Daniels was the first pop hit for this guitar and fiddling singer based in Nashville. 'Uneasy Rider' was a narrative story hit about an encounter at a bar in the Southern States with a culture different than the traveling visitor.

104.   The World Is a Ghetto by War was the first of 3 top 10 1973 hits for this funk/latin/rock band from Long Beach, California. The title track was over 10 minutes in length on the album.

105.   Trouble Man by Marvin Gaye featured the multi-talented Motown artist on drums, piano and all the vocals on this song, which he also wrote and produced. The song was used in the crime/drama film starring Robert Hooks as 'Mr. T', not to be confused with the character who surfaced years later.

106.   Yes We Can Can by the Pointer Sisters was the first chart success from this soul act from Oakland. Allen Toussaint wrote this funk/soul debut hit which featured Anita Pointer on lead vocals backed by sisters, Bonnie, Ruth and June. The song was originally recorded by Lee Dorsey, in 1970 as 'Yes We Can'. Lee Dorsey's biggest hit 'Working in a Coal Mine' was also written by Allen Toussaint.

107.   Peaceful by Helen Reddy was written and originally recorded by Kenny Rankin and was a song about escaping to a tranquil, more relaxing place. This hit single was the one that followed 'I Am Woman' and the one just before 'Delta Dawn', both of which reached number one.

108.   Here I Am (Come and Take Me) by Al Green was his 7th million selling single between late 1971 and this hit in the summer of '73. Al Green's 70's hits were produced and co-written by Willie Mitchell who helped nurture this talented singer/songwriter, who was the 6th of 10 children born to Robert and Cora Green.

109.   **D'yer Maker** by Led Zeppelin was a reggae-influenced song which all 4 band members were credited for writing. The title 'D'yer Maker' is probably the most mispronounced song title in pop music history. It is actually a play on words of 'Jamaica' or 'did you make her', based on the old joke. The song title was most often pronounced as 'dire maker'.

110.   **I Believe in You** by Johnny Taylor was number one on the R & B charts and was a Sam Cooke-inspired hit written and produced by Don Davis. Johnny Taylor replaced Sam Cooke when he left the Soul Stirrers in 1957. Johnny Taylor died of a heart attack in 2000 at the age of 63.

111.   **Peaceful Easy Feeling** by the Eagles became a popular song, despite the fact that it did not achieve great success on the pop charts. This Eagles hit, which featured Glenn Frey on lead vocals, was written by Jack Tempchin was also co-wrote other Eagles and Glenn Frey solo hits including 'You Belong to the City'. 'Peaceful Easy Feeling' was the 3rd single, following 'Take It Easy' and 'Witchy Woman' from their self-titled 'Eagles' debut album.

112.   **Gypsy Man** by War followed their biggest chart success 'Cisco Kid'. 'Gypsy Man' was from their album 'Deliver the Word' which sold over a million copies.

113.   **You're A Special Part of Me** by Diana Ross and Marvin Gaye was the first of 3 singles from their duet album 'Diana and Marvin' which was produced by Motown boss Berry Gordy.

114.   **Jambalaya** by The Blue Ridge Rangers was actually John Fogerty playing all instruments and vocals on this remake of a Hank Williams song from the 50's.In 2009, the former C.C.R. front man released a sequel album 'The Blue Ridge Rangers Rides Again'.

115.   **If You're Ready (Come Go with Me)** by the Staple Singers was produced by Al Bell, the president of Stax records. The songwriters got the inspiration of the title of this song when they were getting ready to go for lunch when Raymond Jackson called out 'If You're Ready', Come Go With Me.' The other two writers thought it would be a nice title. It became another million selling hit for the family act from Mississippi.

116.   **I'm Just a Singer (In A Rock and Roll Band)** by The Moody Blues was the final top 30 hit of the 70's before members of this progressive, symphonic band went their separate ways. This hit written by John Lodge, was the 2nd hit from the 'Seventh Sojourn' album, and was in response to the many fans that were looking at the group as spiritual leaders.

117.   **Rockin' Roll Baby** by the Stylistics was the only up tempo hit for the smooth, soul group known for their ballads. The Stylistics was created by remaining members of two defunct Philadelphia soul groups, The Monarchs and the Percussions and was united as one.

118.   Don't Let Me Be Lonely Tonight by James Taylor featured Michael Brecker on tenor saxophone. This ballad was the only hit from his 'One Man Dog' concept album which was primarily recorded at his home studio. Guests featured on the album include Carole King, Linda Ronstadt, Dash Crofts and his wife Carly Simon.

119.   Funky Worm by the Ohio Players was the first top 40 hit on the pop charts for the R & B group that would score million sellers with 'Fire', 'Skin Tight' and 'Love Rollercoaster'. 'Funky Worm' was a novelty hit which featured keyboardist Walter 'Junie' Morrison doing the voice of a granny singing about a worm. It reached number one on the R & B charts.

120.   Call Me (Come Back Home) by Al Green was another million selling Memphis soul single by the man inducted into the Rock and Roll Hall Of Fame in 1995.

121.   My Music by Loggins and Messina was the 3rd and final hit for this pop/rock duo in the first and final year in the top 40 on the charts. This song was from their third album 'Full Sail' which also included 'Love Song', which Anne Murray made popular.

122.   Love Jones by the Brighter Side of Darkness was a million seller for this one hit wonder R & B/soul group from Chicago which featured 12 year old lead singer Daryl Lamont. Cheech and Chong did a parody of this song later in 1973 as 'Basketball Jones'.

123.   Aubrey by Bread was the last charted hit by this soft rock group in the year they disbanded. They briefly reunited and had one more hit in the 70's with 'Lost Without Your Love' in 1977.

124.   Are You Man Enough by The Four Tops was from the movie 'Shaft in Africa' starring Richard Roundtree. This was their 3rd and final 1973 hit from their short-lived years on the 'ABC Dunhill' record label after leaving Motown. This would also be their final top 40 hit of the 70's.

125.   I Wanna Be with You by the Raspberries was the follow up to their powerhouse hit 'Go All The Way'. This similar style high energy rocker was also co - written by lead singer Eric Carmen. 'I Wanna Be With You' was featured on their album 'Fresh Raspberries', their follow up to 'Raspberries', both released in 1972 and produced by Jimmy Ienner.

126.   Out of the Question by Gilbert O'Sullivan was a moderate hit for the Irish born singer/songwriter who had a unique style which was demonstrated in his previous hits 'Alone Again Naturally' and 'Clair'. His hits were produced by Gordon Mills, the man who managed both Tom Jones and Engelbert Humperdinck.

127.   I'm Doing Fine Now by New York City was the only top 40 hit for this R & B quartet based in the Big Apple. Tim McQueen was the lead singer of this hit co-written and produced by Thom Bell who was known for his work with the Delfonics, The Spinners and the Stylistics.

128.   The Right Thing to Do by Carly Simon was her follow up to her signature hit 'You're So Vain'.' The Right Thing To Do' was the opening track from her number one album 'No Secrets' which included guest musicians Klauss Voormann, Nicky Hopkins, Paul and Linda McCartney, Bonnie Bramlett and her husband James Taylor.

129.   Mind Games by John Lennon was the title track from his 4th post-Beatles album release which he produced entirely on his own. John Lennon also designed the cover of 'Mind Games'. This album was recorded during his 18 month separation from Yoko at a time that May Pang was his companion and lover.

130.   Basketball Jones by Cheech and Chong was a parody of the 1973 million seller 'Love Jones' by the Brighter Side of Darkness. This song by the popular comedians featured an all star cast of performers including George Harrison, Billy Preston, Carole King, Michelle Phillips and others.

131.   Daisy a Day by Jud Strunk was a sentimental pop/country song about a relationship between a boy and girl who grow up and grow old together. Jud Strunk died in a plane crash as a result of a heart attack while piloting his single engine plane in 1981 at the age of 45. He was a regular on 'Laugh In' and made several appearances on Johnny Carson's 'Tonight Show'.

132.   Cheaper to Keep Her by Johnny Taylor was his follow up to his million selling 'I Believe in You'. 'Cheaper To Keep Her' was written by Mack Rice, who is best known for composing the soul classic 'Mustang Sally', one of Wilson Pickett's best known hits and for co-writing 'Respect Yourself' for the Staple Singers.

133.   Steamroller Blues by Elvis Presley was written by James Taylor. This hit was featured in the TV special and album 'Aloha from Hawaii via Satellite'. The song 'Fool' was the 'B' side.

134.   Summer (The First Time) by Bobby Goldsboro was the final top 40 hit for this singer/songwriter known for a string of hits during the 60's. This song was about losing one's virginity to an older woman and was popular the year his syndicated TV variety show made its debut.

135.   Let Me Serenade You by 3 Dog Night was a moderate hit from their album 'Cyan' which also included the million selling 'Shambala'. 'Let Me Serenade You' was written by Canadian John Finley, who was previously a member and writer for the group Rhinoceros, known for the instrumental hit 'Apricot Brandy'.

136.   Thinking of You by Loggins and Messina was their 2nd hit following 'Your Mama Don't Dance', also from their self titled album. Musical guests on the album included Steve Stills and Rusty Young.

137.   Do You Wanna Dance by Bette Midler was a slowed-down version of the hit originally popular by Bobby Freeman in 1958 and Del Shannon and The Beach Boys in the 60's. This was Bette Midler's first charted hit from her debut album 'The Divine Miss M'.

138.   So Very Hard to Do by The Tower of Power was their most successful single and the first of 3 from their self-titled album. This soul/funk band was famous for its very impressive horn section.

139.   Rocky Mountain Way by Joe Walsh was the first solo hit for the former James Gang member who joined the Eagles 2 years later. This classic rock hit was taken from his album 'The Smoker You Drink, The Player You Get'.

140.   If You Want Me to Stay by Sly and The Family Stone was the final million seller for this psychedelic soul group that had a respectable string of hits from 1968 to 1973.Sly (Sylvester Stewart) Stone wrote and produced all of their hits. In 1974, Sly married actress/model Kathy Silva on stage at Madison Square Gardens in one of the most talked about weddings of the 70's.

141.   You'll Never Get to Heaven by The Stylistics was a remake of the Burt Bacharach/Hal David composition made popular in the 60's by Dionne Warwick.

142.   A Million to One by Donny Osmond was a remake of the 1960 hit by Jimmy Charles. Most of Donny's early 70's hits were recycled hits from the 50's and 60's.The 'B' side of this double-sided hit single was 'Young Love' , which was a million seller for both Sonny James and Tab Hunter in the late 50's.

143.   Hummingbird by Seals and Crofts was sandwiched between their top 10 hits 'Summer Breeze' and 'Diamond Girl'. 'Hummingbird' was the opening track from the 'Summer Breeze' album which featured guest musicians Larry Knechtel, John Hartford, Marty Paich, Jim Gordon and John Ford Coley.

144.   Separate Ways by Elvis Presley was the King of Rock and Roll's follow up single to 'Burning Love', his final official top 10 hit. 'Separate Ways', which was the title song from his latest album, was featured in the movie 'Elvis on Tour'. The 'B' side of this single was 'Always on My Mind' which later became a huge hit for Willie Nelson.

145.   Angel by Aretha Franklin was a soul ballad co-written by Lady Soul's sister Carolyn and co-produced by Quincy Jones. This song was from the album 'Hey Now Hey', the first by Aretha Franklin which was not produced by Jerry Wexler and his associates.

146.   Leaving Me by the Independants was a million seller co-written and co-produced by Chuck Jackson, the brother of civil rights leader Jesse Jackson. This Chuck Jackson is not to be confused with the solo singer from the 60's.The other writer and producer of this song was group member Marvin Yancy, who later co-wrote Natalie Cole's first hit 'This Will Be'. They were married in 1976, but divorced in 1980.

147.   We May Never Pass This Way Again by Seals and Crofts was the second hit single from the 'Diamond Girl' album and their 3rd hit of 1973.Both members of this pop/folk duo were members of the Baha'i faith, emphasizing the spiritual unity of all humankind.

148. **Driedel** by Don McLean was a moderate hit from his album simply titled 'Don Mclean', which was the follow up to the legendary 'American Pie' album. 'Driedel' is a 4 sided spinning top played with during the Jewish holiday of Hanukkah.

149. **You Turn Me On, I'm A Radio** by Joni Mitchell featured Graham Nash on harmonica. Canadian Joni Mitchell is a singer/songwriter and painter who found fame in 1970 with her hit 'Big Yellow Taxi' and for the hit 'Woodstock' which became a major hit for Crosby, Stills, Nash and Young. The biggest album of her career, 'Court and Spark' would arrive the year after this hit was popular.

150. **Nutbush City Limits** by Ike and Tina Turner was the final top 40 hit for this soul duo whose troubled marriage finally ended in 1976. They were inducted into the Rock and Roll Hall of Fame in 1991. Tina became a superstar solo performer beginning with a string of hits in 1984.

151. **Come Get to This** by Marvin Gaye was from his album 'Let's Get It On' and was produced and written by this Motown legend. This was the 4th of 4 hit singles for Marvin Gaye in 1973, including his duet with Diana Ross, 'You're A Special Part of Me'.

152. **Daddy Could Swear, I Declare** by Gladys Knight and the Pips was the follow up single to 'Neither One Of Us' and 1 of 6 singles they charted in 1973, a banner year for this family group from Atlanta, Georgia.

153. **Theme from Cleopatra Jones** by Joe Simon was the title song from the movie which starred Tamara Dobson as the Special Agent assigned to crack down on drug trafficking in the United States.

154. **You've Never Been This Way Before** by Conway Twitty reached number one on the country charts and top 30 on the pop charts. Some radio stations refused to play the song because of its suggestive lyrics. He died in 1993 at the age of 59 from abdominal aortic aneurysm.

155. **How Can I Tell Her** by Lobo was one of 3 moderately successful singles from his album 'Calumet'. Roland Kent Lavoie took the stage name 'Lobo' which is Spanish for wolf.

156. **Hurts So Good** by Millie Jackson was another hit from the film 'Cleopatra Jones'. This was the most popular hit for the soul singer from Thompson, Georgia.

157. **Doing It to Death** by Fred Wesley and the JB's was written, produced and arranged by the Godfather of soul, James Brown. This hit reached number one the R & B charts for the James Brown's back up band.

158. **Misdemeanor** by Foster Sylvers of the family act best known 2 years later for 'Boogie Fever' was only 11 years old when he had a hit with this song. He was the youngest member of the group which numbered 9 when they signed with Capitol records a couple of years later. This song was written by Foster's big brother Leon Sylvers.

159. **Big City Miss Ruth** by The Gallery was the final charted hit for the short-lived group whose biggest hit was 'Nice to Be with You' the year before.

160. **No More Mr. Nice Guy** by Alice Cooper was the 3rd of 4 singles from his album 'Billion Dollar Babies'. This song was later covered by Megadeth and featured in the movie 'Shocker'. Pat Boone recorded his own version on the 1997 album 'In a Metal Mood: No More Mr. Nice Guy'.

161. **Reelin' and Rockin'** by Chuck Berry was the follow up to his biggest hit of all 'My Ding a Ding'. Both songs were recorded 'live' in Manchester, England. 'Reelin' and Rockin' was originally popular in 1958 as the 'B' side of 'Sweet Little Sixteen'.

162. **Ooh Baby** by Gilbert O'Sullivan was the final top 30 hit in North America for Gilbert O'Sullivan, although he continued to have a music career in Britain.

163. **Who's In the Strawberry Patch with Sally** by Tony Orlando and Dawn was the follow up to the similar sounding "Say, Has Anybody Seen My Sweet Gypsy Rose' also from the album 'New Ragtime Follies'. The following year, Tony Orlando and Dawn began the first of 3 years with their own prime time TV weekly variety show.

164. **I Got Ants in My Pants** by James Brown was his only hit to reach the top 30 of the 6 hit singles he charted in 1973, although his backing group, The J.B's led by Fred Wesley had a number one R & B hit.

165. **Smoke Gets in Your Eyes** by Blue Haze was a disco style version of a song originally popular in 1934 by Paul Whiteman and again in 1959 by the Platters. This was the only hit for this British group which recorded on the A & M record label.

166. **It Sure Took a Long Long Time** by Lobo was the 2nd of 5 singles charted in 1973, although only 'Don't Expect Me to Be Your Friend' reached the top 10. All of Lobo's hits were on the Big Tree label, but after the heyday, Lobo recorded on 'Curb', 'MCA' and finally his own label, 'Lobo' records.

167. **Satin Sheets** by Jeanne Pruett was a number one hit on the country charts and the biggest hit of all for this singer born in Alabama who moved to Nashville in the late 50's. She joined the Grand Ole Opry in the same year that 'Satin Sheets' caressed the top spot.

168. **Believe in Humanity** by Carole King was from her album 'Fantasy' the first which contained songs she wrote alone. This album produced by Lou Adler, contained 2 singles, but no major hits.

169. **And I Love You So** by Perry Como was written by the American Pie guy Don McLean. This was the final top 40 hit for the singer and TV personality who was popular during the 40's and 50's.

170. **The Hurt** by Cat Stevens was the only single from his first self-produced album, 'Foreigner', which was recorded in Jamaica. Some of the contributing singers and musicians on this album included Patti Austin, Phillip Upchurch, Herbie Flowers and the Tower Of Power horns.

More Hits of 1973

Jimmy Loves Mary-Anne by The Looking Glass was the only other hit for the group that gave us the great number one hit 'Brandy (You're A Fine Girl) in the summer of '72.This bubblegum song was along the same pattern, but not as strong. Lead singer Elliot Lurie later became a music supervisor for movies.

Soul Makossa by Manu Dibango was an unusual and unique hit which blended disco, funk, jazz and Cameroonian music. He was born in Douala, Cameroon to a father who was a civil servant and a mother who was a fashion designer.

I'm A Stranger Here by the 5 Man Electrical Band was an extraterrestrial song from the Canadian group that scored a million seller in 1971 with 'Signs'. This band was known in the 60's as The Staccatos and was best known for their 1967 hit 'Half Past Midnight'.

Tequila Sunrise by the Eagles was an easy going feel good song from their album 'Desperado' written by Glenn Frey and Don Henley. Although this song didn't make it into the top 40, it became a classic for this Los Angeles based Rock Country group.

Been to Canaan by Carole King was the only single released from her album 'Rhymes and Reasons'. The legendary singer/songwriter from Brooklyn, New York was also featured on this album playing piano, clavinet, Fender Rhodes and Wurlitzer.

What About Me by Anne Murray was written by Scott McKenzie, the singer who gave us the anthem song of the summer of love, 'San Francisco' (Be Sure to Wear Flowers in Your Hair'). This 'live' concert recording was her follow up to her top 10 hit 'Danny's Song' written by Kenny Loggins.

Give It to Me by The J. Geils Band featured Peter 'Wolf' Blankfield on lead vocals. This moderately successful single came from their 'Bloodshot' album. Their biggest hit arrived in 1980 with the multi-week number one hit and million seller 'Centerfold'.

Harry Hippie by Bobby Womack and his backing group 'Peace' was written by Jim Ford for Bobby's brother Harry. Tragically, the following year, in 1974, Harry Womack was killed by his girlfriend during a fight.

Let's Pretend by the Raspberries was a mellower sound than their previous 2 energetic rockers, 'Go All The Way' and 'I Wanna Be with You'. This hit which featured lead singer and songwriter Eric Carmen also had great lyrics, melody and harmony.

Pretty Lady by Lighthouse featured drummer and songwriter Skip Prokop on lead vocals. This Toronto based band had over half a dozen notable hits in Canada including 'One Fine Morning' and 'Sunny Days'.

142

Give Your Baby a Standing Ovation by The Dells was a much bigger hit on the R & B charts than it was on the pop charts for this legendary vocal group which formed back in 1952. Although they had bigger charting hits with 'Stay in My Corner' and 'Oh What a Night', this hit sold a million copies, which the others did not.

Could You Ever Love Me Again by Gary and Dave was a big hit in Canada for the singer/songwriters who were both pilots before their music careers took flight. This Canadian duo had a string of hits with this one being their most successful.

One Less Set of Footsteps by Jim Croce was a mid chart success between his singles 'Operator' and 'Bad Bad Leroy Brown'. Croce's guitarist sidekick on stage was Maury Muehleisen was also killed in the plane crash later that year on September 20th 1973.

The First Cut Is the Deepest by Keith Hampshire was written by Cat Stevens in 1967. Rod Stewart also had a hit with this song. Canadian Keith Hampshire was a former radio D.J. and TV personality who had 3 notable hits during the early 70's.

Country Sunshine by Dottie West featured Elvis Presley's backup singers, the Jordinaires. She wrote this song specifically for a Coca Cola commercial and released it as single. 'Country Sunshine' became her signature hit. She died in 1991 at the age of 58 as a result of injuries suffered in a car accident.

Close Your Eyes by Edward Bear was the follow up to their biggest hit 'Last Song', a million seller from earlier in 1973. Larry Evoy was the lead singer of this Toronto- based Canadian group.

Control of Me by Les Emmerson was a ballad from the lead singer and songwriter of the 5 Man Electrical Band, best known for their hits 'Signs' and 'Absolutely Right'.

Twistin' the Night Away by Rod Stewart was a remake of the Sam Cooke song originally popular in 1962. This hit was from Rod Stewart's album 'Never a Dull Moment' which also included 'You Wear It Well'.

Blue Collar by Bachman-Turner Overdrive was the first notable hit single for this hard rocking Canadian group led by former Guess Who member guitarist/ songwriter Randy Bachman. This song was a jazzy, easy listening hit, unlike the next 3 hits that followed, 'Let It Ride', 'Takin' Care Of Business' and 'You Ain't Seen Nothin' Yet'.

Top 17 Albums of 1973

1.	Goodbye Yellow Brick Road	Elton John
2.	Living In a Material World	George Harrison
3.	Brothers and Sisters	Allman Brothers
4.	No Secrets	Carly Simon
5.	Chicago 6	Chicago
6.	Goat's Head Soup	Rolling Stones
7.	Red Rose Speedway	Paul McCartney
8.	Houses of the Holy	Led Zeppelin
9.	Dark Side of the Moon	Pink Floyd
10.	Billion Dollar Babies	Alice Cooper
11.	Don't Shoot Me; I'm Only the Piano Player	Elton John
12.	The World Is a Ghetto	War
13.	Dueling Banjos from Deliverance Sdtk	Eric Weissberg and Steve Mandell
14.	Lady Sings the Blues	Diana Ross
15.	The Beatles 1967 – 1970	Beatles
16.	Aloha From Hawaii Via Satellite	Elvis Presley
17.	A Passion Play	Jethro Tull

Top 17 Country Hits of 1973

1.	The Most Beautiful Girl	Charlie Rich
2.	Satin Sheets	Jeanne Pruett
3.	She's Got to Be a Saint	Ray Price
4.	You've Never Been This Far Before	Conway Twitty
5.	Behind Closed Doors	Charlie Rich
6.	Paper Roses	Marie Osmond
7.	Teddy Bear Song	Barbara Fairchild
8.	She Needs Someone to Hold Her	Conway Twitty
9.	We're Gonna Hold On	George Jones and Tammy Wynette
10.	Love Is the Foundation	Loretta Lynn
11.	Everybody's had the Blues	Merle Haggard
12.	A Shoulder to Cry On	Charley Pride
13.	Come Live With Me	Roy Clark
14.	Kids Say the Darndest Things	Tammy Wynette
15.	Amazing Love	Charley Pride
16.	Super Kind of Woman	Freddie Hart and the Heartbeats
17.	Blood Red and Goin' Down	Tanya Tucker

Top 17 R & B/Soul hits of 1973

1. Let's Get It On   Marvin Gaye
2. Love Train   O'Jays
3. Midnight Train to Georgia   Gladys Knight and the Pips
4. Could It Be I'm Falling in Love   Spinners
5. Neither One of Us (Wants to Be the First...) Gladys Knight and the Pips
6. One of Kind (Love Affair)   Spinners
7. Superstition   Stevie Wonder
8. If You're Ready (Come Go With Me)   Staple Singers
9. Why Can't We Live Together   Timmy Thomas
10. Pillow Talk   Sylvia
11. I'm Gonna Love You Just A Little Bit More Barry White
12. Keep On Truckin'   Eddie Kendricks
13. The Love I Lost (Part 1)   Harold Melvin and the Bluenotes
14. Masterpiece   The Temptations
15. I Believe In You (You Believe In Me)   Johnny Taylor
16. Angel   Aretha Franklin
17. Doing It To Death   Fred Wesley and The J.B.'s

Top 17 One Hit Wonders of 1973

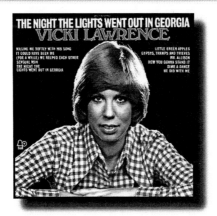

1. Vicki Lawrence — The Night The Lights Went Out In Georgia
2. Stories — Brother Louie
3. Clint Holmes — Playground in My Mind
4. Deodato — Also Sprach Zarathustra (2001)
5. Timmy Thomas — Why Can't We Live Together
6. Hurricane Smith — Oh Babe What Would You Say
7. Skylark — Wildflower
8. B.W. Stevenson — My Maria
9. Focus — Hocus Pocus
10. King Harvest — Dancing In The Moonlight
11. Brighter Side of Darkness — Love Jones
12. Bloodstone — Natural High
13. Jud Strunk — Daisy A Day
14. Blue Haze — Smoke Gets In Your Eyes
15. New York City — I'm Doin' Fine Now
16. Manu Dibango — Soul Makossa
17. Foster Sylvers — Misdemeanor

Top 17 Rock/Hard Rock Hits of 1973

1.	We're An American Band	Grand Funk
2.	Frankenstein	Edgar Winter Group
3.	Smoke on the Water	Deep Purple
4.	Reeling In the Years	Steely Dan
5.	China Grove	Doobie Brothers
6.	Money	Pink Floyd
7.	Hocus Pocus	Focus
8.	Long Train Runnin'	Doobie Brothers
9.	Hi Hi Hi	Paul McCartney and Wings
10.	Saturday Night's Alright for Fighting	Elton John
11.	Space Oddity	David Bowie
12.	Free Ride	Edgar Winter Group
13.	D'yer Maker	Led Zeppelin
14.	Rocky Mountain Way	Joe Walsh
15.	Right Place, Wrong Time	Dr. John
16.	Walk On the Wild Side	Lou Reed
17.	Over The Hills and Far Away	Led Zeppelin

1.	I Wanna Be With You	Raspberries
2.	My Music	Loggins and Messina
3.	Don't Expect Me to Be Your Friend	Lobo
4.	Keeper of the Castle	Four Tops
5.	Get Down	Gilbert O'Sullivan
6.	Dead Skunk	Loudon Wainwright the 3rd
7.	Hocus Pocus	Focus
8.	Yes We Can Can	Pointer Sisters
9.	Blockbuster	Sweet
10.	Sitting	Cat Stevens
11.	Jambalaya	Blue Ridge Rangers
12.	Thinking Of You	Loggins and Messina
13.	Living In the Past	Jethro Tull
14.	Out of the Question	Gilbert O'Sullivan
15.	Jimmy Loves Mary-Anne	Looking Glass
16.	Summer (The First Time)	Bobby Goldsboro
17.	Who's In The Strawberry Patch With Sally	Tony Orlando and Dawn

(* Indicates American Band with Canadian lead singer)

1.	American Woman	Guess Who	1970
2.	Seasons in the Sun	Terry Jacks	1974
3.	Heart of Gold	Neil Young	1972
4.	Sundown	Gordon Lightfoot	1974
5.	Rock Me Gently	Andy Kim	1974
6.	Signs	5 Man Electrical Band	1971
7.	You Ain't Seen Nothin' Yet	Bachman-Turner Overdrive	1974
8.	Sweet City Woman	Stampeders	1971
9.	Snowbird	Anne Murray	1970
10.	No Time	Guess Who	1970
11.	Takin' Care of Business	Bachman-Turner Overdrive	1974
12.	Last Song	Edward Bear	1973
13.	One Fine Morning	Lighthouse	1971
14.	Hot Child in the City	Nick Gilder	1978
15.	If You Could Read My Mind	Gordon Lightfoot	1971
16.	I Just Wanna Stop	Gino Vannelli	1979
17.	Sunny Days	Lighthouse	1972
18.	Big Yellow Taxi	Joni Mitchell	1970
19.	Put Your Hand In The Hand	Ocean	1971
20.	You're Having My Baby	Paul Anka	1974
21.	As The Years Go By	Mashmakkan	1970
22.	Stay Awhile	Bells	1971
23.	Oh What a Feeling	Crowbar	1971
24.	Painted Ladies	Ian Thomas	1973
25.	Up On Cripple Creek	Band	1970
26.	You, Me and Mexico	Edward Bear	1970
27.	Raise A Little Hell	Trooper	1978
28.	Albert Flasher	Guess Who	1971
29.	Indiana Wants Me	R. Dean Taylor	1970
30.	Stand Tall	Burton Cummings	1976
31.	Carry Me	Stampeders	1971

32.	Sometimes When We Touch	Dan Hill	1977
33.	You Could Have Been A Lady	April Wine	1972
34.	Be My Baby	Andy Kim	1970
35.	You Needed Me	Anne Murray	1978
36.	Wildflower	Skylark	1973
37.	Roxy Roller	Sweeney Todd	1976
38.	Wreck of The Edmund Fitzgerald	Gordon Lightfoot	1976
39.	We're Here for a Good Time	Trooper	1979
40.	Pretty Lady	Lighthouse	1973
41.	Carefree Highway	Gordon Lightfoot	1974
42.	People Gotta Move	Gino Vannelli	1974
43.	Only Love Can Break Your Heart	Neil Young	1970
44.	Daytime Nighttime	Keith Hampshire	1972
45.	Break It to Them Gently	Burton Cummings	1978
46.	Music Box Dancer	Frank Mills	1979
47.	Share the Land	Guess Who	1970
48.	Absolutely Right	5 Man Electrical Band	1971
49.	Could You Ever Love Me Again	Gary and Dave	1973
50.	Two for the Show	Trooper	1976
51.	Beautiful	Gordon Lightfoot	1972
52.	Danny's Song	Anne Murray	1973
53.	Gotta See Jane	R. Dean Taylor	1971
54.	Hand Me Down World	Guess Who	1970
55.	That's Where I Went Wrong	Poppy Family	1970
56.	Lovin' You Ain't Easy	Pagliaro	1971
57.	Old Man	Neil Young	1972
58.	Let It Ride	Bachman-Turner Overdrive	1974
59.	Virginia (Touch Me Like You Do)	Bill Amesbury	1974
60.	You Won't Dance With Me	April Wine	1977
61.	Oh Pretty Lady	Trooper	1978
62.	Where Evil Grows	Poppy Family	1971
63.	I'm Scared	Burton Cummings	1976
64.	First Cut Is the Deepest	Keith Hampshire	1973
65.	Runnin' Back To Saskatoon	Guess Who	1972
66.	Every Bit of Love	Ken Tobias	1975
67.	Flip, Flop and Fly	Downchild Blues Band	1974
68.	Close Your Eyes	Edward Bear	1973
69.	Devil You	Stampeders	1971
70.	Right Before Your Eyes	Ian Thomas	1977
71.	Help Me	Joni Mitchell	1974
72.	I'm On Fire for You Baby	April Wine	1974
73.	No Sugar Tonight	Guess Who	1970
74.	Coming Home	Ian Thomas	1978
75.	Cinnamon Girl	Neil Young	1970
76.	Wheels of Life	Gino Vannelli	1979
77.	Oh My Lady	Stampeders	1973
78.	Do I Love You	Paul Anka	1971
79.	From New York To L.A.	Patsy Gallant	1976

80.	Hi De Ho	Blood, Sweat and Tears *	1970
81.	I Will Still Love You	Stonebolt	1978
82.	Freedom for the Stallion	Edward Bear	1974
83.	I'm A Stranger Here	5 Man Electrical Band	1973
84.	Cousin Mary	Fludd	1973
85.	Raindance	Guess Who	1971
86.	Last Kiss	Wednesday	1973
87.	You're Still the One	Copperpenny	1973
88.	Lucretia Mac Evil	Blood, Sweat and Tears *	1970
89.	Just As Bad As You	Shawne Jackson	1974
90.	It Wouldn't Have Made Any Difference	Tom Middleton	1973
91.	Rock And Roll Song	Valdy	1972
92.	Dancing On A Saturday Night	Bond	1975
93.	Clap For the Wolfman	Guess Who	1974
94.	One Night Lovers	Tom Middleton	1976
95.	Mr. Monday	Original Caste	1970
96.	I Just Want To Make Music	Ken Tobias	1973
97.	(Make Me Do) Anything You Want	A Foot in Coldwater	1972
98.	Blue Collar	Bachman-Turner Overdrive	1973
99.	Wondering Where the Lions Are	Bruce Cockburn	1979
100.	The Homecoming	Hagoode Hardy	1975
101.	Fly Little White Dove Fly	Bells	1970
102.	The Farmer's Song	Murray McLauchlan	1973
103.	Take Me in Your Arms	Charity Brown	1975
104.	My Own Way To Rock	Burton Cummings	1977
105.	Werewolf	5 Man Electrical Band	1973
106.	Jodie	Joey Gregorash	1971
107.	Raised On Robbery	Joni Mitchell	1974
108.	Love Song	Anne Murray	1974
109.	Can You Give It All To Me	Myles and Lenny	1974
110.	Take It Slow (Out In The Country)	Lighthouse	1971
111.	Theme From S.W.A.T.	T.H.P. Orchestra	1976
112.	Calling Occupants	Klaatu	1977
113.	Jimmy Mack	Charity Brown	1974
114.	Turned 21	Fludd	1971
115.	Some Sing Some Dance	Pagliaro	1972
116.	Ain't It A Sad Thing	R. Dean Taylor	1971
117.	I Wouldn't Want To Lose Your Love	April Wine	1975

♪ This number one remake by Ringo Starr featured Paul McCartney playing the kazoo.

♪ This 1974 number one rock hit originally topped the charts 12 years earlier by Carole King's former baby sitter.

♪ Bob Marley wrote this hit which became Eric Clapton's first number one single.

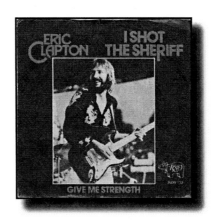

♪ K.C. & the Sunshine band wrote and backed this singer on his number one hit a year before they had their first hit.

♪ The wildest and craziest new fad of the year was the inspiration for this number one novelty hit.

153

FIND OUT THAT…AND MUCH MORE INSIDE…1974!

1. The Way We Were by Barbra Streisand was the title song of the movie in which she starred with Robert Redford. The song, written by Marvin Hamlisch with Alan and Marilyn Bergman, won both Best Song in both the Grammy and Academy Awards.

2. Seasons in the Sun by Terry Jacks was a Rod McKuen/Jacques Brel composition which was turned down by the Beach Boys. Terry Jacks, who was previously known as half of the Poppy Family with wife Susan, decided to record it solo and it not only went to number one, but sold over 5 million copies worldwide.

3. The Streak by Ray Stevens was written and recorded quickly to take advantage of the latest big fad which really got a lot of attention. That year, on the Academy Awards, millions of viewers watched when a naked man streaked past host David Niven on live television. Like his other hits which included 'Gitarzan', 'Ahab the Arab' and 'Harry the Hairy Ape', Ray Stevens performed the voices of all the characters on this number one hit.

4. Billy Don't Be a Hero by Bo Donaldson & the Heywoods was a civil war story song written by British songwriters Mitch Murray and Peter Callander. The original version was recorded by Paper lace and topped the pop charts in Britain. Just before that version was to be released in North America, Cincinnati's Bo Donaldson & the Heywoods' producer Steve Barri had it rush released, beating the version by Paper lace in North America.

5. You're Having My Baby by Paul Anka was a duet with Odia Coates whom he had just recently met. He wrote the song for his wife and their 4 daughters while he was performing in Lake Tahoe, California. This multi-week number one hit was met with controversy because of the title and line 'You're Having *My* Baby', which Anka later changed to 'You're Having *Our* Baby' when performing it in concert.

6. Kung Fu Fighting by Carl Douglas was apparently recorded in 10 minutes and was originally intended to be the 'B' side of his single produced by Biddu.

Jamaican-born and California-raised Carl Douglas wrote this song which was released when kung fu movies were at their peak in popularity. The timing was right for this novelty disco hit which sold millions and spent multiple weeks at number one.

7. T.S.O.P. by M.F.S.B. and the Three Degrees was an assemblage of almost 40 session musicians who played on many of the Philadelphia soul hits by the O'Jays, Harold Melvin and The Bluenotes, The Delfonics and others during the early 70's. This number one million seller was written and produced by the team of Gamble and Huff and featured the vocal trio 'The Three Degrees on this mostly instrumental masterpiece. T.S.O.P. was short for 'The Sound of Philadelphia' and MFSB was 'mothers, fathers, sisters, brothers.'

8. The Locomotion by Grand Funk was a rock remake of the number one hit by Little Eva from 1962 written by Carole King and Gerry Goffin. Todd Rundgren produced this number one hit from the 'Shinin' On' album.

9. Band on the Run by Paul McCartney & Wings was recorded in Lagos, Nigeria and did not include 2 of the Wing men, Henry McCullough and Denny Seiwell who failed to show up at the airport before departure time. The title song of the album featured a star-studded cover which included actors James Coburn and Christopher Lee dressed as convicts caught in the spotlight of a prison searchlight.

10.   I Can Help by Billy Swan was written quickly and naturally after he received a little RMI organ for a wedding present from Kris Kristofferson and Rita Coolidge. The organ he received was prominently featured on this number one hit in late 1974. When Billy Swan was a teenager he wrote the top 10 hit 'Lover Please' for Clyde McPhatter and in 1969 produced 'Polk Salad Annie' for Tony Joe White.

11.Cats in the Cradle by Harry Chapin was a story suggested by his wife Sandy, who co-wrote this strong message song which was delivered to number one on the pop charts. The song is about a father and son who can't schedule time to be with each other, at any time during their lives.

12.   Rock Your Baby by George McCrae was written by Harry Casey (K.C.) and Richard Finch, the nucleus of K.C. & the Sunshine band, who did the backing instrumentation on this number one hit. This may be the most inexpensive made million seller ever recorded because this track took less than an hour to complete at an estimated cost of $15. This was the only major hit for Florida-born George McCrae who was once married to Gwen McCrae, who had a top 10 hit with 'Rockin' Chair' in 1975.

13.   I Honestly Love You by Olivia Newton- John was written by Jeff Barry and Peter Allen and became the first of 5 official number one hits for this talented entertainer. The song was originally going to be recorded by co-writer Peter Allen, but Olivia heard it on a demo, loved it and wanted to record it. It became her 3rd million selling single of 1974, her first major year on the pop charts.

14.   Bennie & Jets by Elton John was the 3rd hit single from the 'Goodbye

Yellow Brick Road' album, and the only one to top the charts. In Britain, Elton's tribute to Marilyn Monroe, 'Candle in the Wind' was originally the 'A' side, but the response to 'Bennie' was so great that it was flipped. The 'live' sounds from previous concerts, including whistles, were added after the recording by producer Gus Dudgeon.

15.   Sundown by Gordon Lightfoot was the title track of his 10th studio album which also topped the charts in the spring of 1974.He wrote this song while he was living on a farm north of Toronto. There have been many interpretations and theories about what and whom this song is about. One of them is that it is about his former girlfriend Cathy Smith, who was later sentenced for delivering a lethal dose of heroin to comedian John Belushi.

16.   Love's Theme by Love Unlimited Orchestra was a million selling number one instrumental hit for the 40 piece act created by Barry White. He was the writer/producer/conductor for the Love Unlimited Orchestra and also had a very successful solo career simultaneously.

17.   The Joker by Steve Miller was also written and produced by the Milwaukee, Wisconsin-born, Dallas, Texas-raised rock guitarist. The song is sometimes confused with 'space cowboy', the title of a song he recorded on an earlier album. In this number one hit, during the song, Steve Miller makes references to the lines from the 1954 Clovers song "Lovey Dovey" when he sings "You're the cutest thing that I ever did see/ Really love your peaches, wanna shake your tree / Lovey dovey, lovey dovey all the time.'

18.   Rock The Boat by Hues Corporation was one of 3 number one hit 3 word titles from 1974 which began with the word 'Rock', along with George McCrae's 'Rock Your Baby' and 'Andy Kim's 'Rock Me Gently.' The name of this Los Angeles-based soul trio, Hues Corporation, was inspired by Howard Hughes, but they decided to keep the name spelling different to prevent any legal problems.

19.   Rock Me Gently by Andy Kim was totally financed and recorded on his own 'Ice' record label, which Capitol records picked up and released in the United States. 'Rock Me Gently' became Andy Kim's biggest hit and his first major chart success since 1970's 'Be My Baby'. His late 60's hits were in collaboration with writer/producer Jeff Barry, whom he co-wrote the multi-million selling Archies' hit 'Sugar, Sugar'.

20.   You Ain't Seen Nothin' Yet by Bachman Turner Overdrive was an accidental hit for this powerhouse Canadian rock group. Randy Bachman never wanted the public to hear the song he wrote for his stuttering brother Gary, but when Charlie Fach of Mercury Records was looking for a hit he didn't hear in the other songs they recorded, Randy Bachman pulled out this one and Fach loved it. This became B. T. O.'s biggest hit.

21.   Annie's Song by John Denver was written in about 10 minutes on a ski lift for his wife Annie Martell. They were college sweethearts who married in 1967. Unfortunately their marriage ended in divorce in 1983.This hit , which does not mention the title anywhere in the song, was his 2nd consecutive number one hit in 1974 following 'Sunshine On My Shoulders'.

22. Nothing from Nothing by Billy Preston was written one night after a Rolling Stones tour when he was in his dressing room while playing in a night club in Atlanta, Georgia. The room had a piano and he started playing around with a saying he heard, 'nothing from nothing' and gave it a sing a long feeling and a saloon piano to add character. He brought it to his co-writer Bruce Fisher who wrote the 2nd verse, and the song went to number one in the fall of 1974.

23. Then Came You by Dionne Warwick & the Spinners came about when producer Thom Bell suggested both acts record this song together after their double bill summer tour. The Spinners were having one hit after another at that time and Dionne Warwick had not had a top 10 hit since 1970. 'Then Came You' featured Dionne with Spinners' lead singer Phillip Wynne on this smooth soul classic number one hit.

24. Show and Tell by Al Wilson reached number one in early 1974 for the soul singer previously known for his 1968 tale 'The Snake'. This hit was produced and written by Jerry Fuller, who previously wrote over 20 songs for Rick Nelson including 'Travelin' Man' and most of Gary Puckett's biggest hits including 'Young Girl' and 'Lady Willpower' which he also produced. Al Wilson died on April 21 2008 at the age of 68, just hours before another singer from Meridian, Mississippi, Paul Davis died at age 60.

25. The Night Chicago Died by Paper lace was the follow up to 'Billy, Don't Be a Hero' which they originally charted and took to number one in Britain. Songwriters/producers Mitch Murray and Peter Callandar weren't about to have another number one hit taken from them. They rushed it out before anyone could record a cover of the song and it shot to number one. This was a story song about a fictional account of a shootout between Al Capone and the police. This was not the first such gangster story song written by the songwriting duo that also composed the 1968 hit 'The Ballad of Bonnie and Clyde' for Georgie Fame.

26. Sunshine on My Shoulders by John Denver was originally the 'B' side of a single he released the previous year, but in 1974 it became his first official number one hit. The singer/songwriter born Henry John Deutschendorf, Jr., was now enjoying a steady stream of hit songs written from his personal experiences. A television series using 'Sunshine On My Shoulders' as a theme song was telecast on NBC during the 1974-75 season starring Cliff DeYoung, who had a hit with the John Denver song 'My Sweet Lady'.

27. You're Sixteen by Ringo Starr featured Paul McCartney playing kazoo and Harry Nilsson on backing vocals on this remake of Johnny Burnette's hit from 1960. Ringo Starr's version, produced by Richard Perry, was his 2nd consecutive number one hit following 'Photograph' from his self-titled album 'Ringo'.

28. Hooked on a Feeling by Blue Suede was a very offbeat remake of the B.J. Thomas hit from 1969. This version Swedish pop group Blue Swede, featuring lead singer Bjorn Skifs began with a wild a capela 'Ooga-Chaga Ooga- Ooga Chaga. The song was written by Mark James, who also wrote Elvis Presley's final number one hit 'Suspicious Minds.'

158

29.   Dark Lady by Cher was a story song written by John Durrill, the keyboard player for the popular 60's instrumental group, 'The Ventures'. Producer Snuff Garrett had Durrill rewrite the ending of the song so that the woman who caught her boyfriend with her fortune teller would shoot them both dead.

30.   You Make Me Feel Brand New by The Stylistics was the most successful of their string of silky smooth soul songs which graced the airwaves of pop radio everywhere during the 70's.This million seller which featured lead singer Russell Thompkins Jr., was written by Thom Bell and Linda Creed. The group Simply Red recycled it and made it a hit again in 2003.

31.   I Shot the Sheriff by Eric Clapton was written and originally recorded by Bob Marley. Clapton had just returned to recording after a 2 year battle with heroin when he recorded the album '461 Ocean Boulevard'. It included his number one treatment of 'I Shot the Sheriff' which became his highest charting solo hit. Singer Yvonne Elliman supplied backing vocals.

32.   Angie Baby by Helen Reddy was a story song written by Alan O'Day, who also co-wrote the Righteous Brothers 1974 hit 'Rock And Roll Heaven'. Three years later, he had a number one hit with 'Undercover Angel'. 'Angie Baby' was the 3rd and final official number one hit for Helen Reddy and the first hit taken from her album 'Free and Easy'.

33.   Feel Like Makin' Love by Roberta Flack was written by Eugene McDaniels, who was best known in the early 60's as Gene McDaniels who had major hits with 'A Hundred Pounds Of Clay' and 'Tower Of Strength'. This was Roberta Flack's 3rd official number one hit and by accident was her first as a producer. Her producer Joel Dorn left the sessions, so she hastily took over and produced the session under the name Rubina Flack.

34.   Can't Get Enough of Your Love by Barry White was a very special love song because it was the only one he wrote for his wife. It was the first official number one hit (and 3rd million seller) for the singer who grew up in a high crime area in Los Angeles. As a teenager, he was once put in jail for stealing several thousands of dollars of Cadillac tires.

35.   Whatever Gets You through the Night by John Lennon features Elton John on piano, organ and backing vocals. It's hard to imagine that this was John Lennon's first official number one solo hit in the United States. Elton John bet John Lennon at the recording session that it would top the charts, and if it did, Lennon would make an appearance at one of Elton's concerts. Lennon honored the lost bet and the winning song by performing with Elton John at his Madison Square Gardens concert Thanksgiving weekend later that same year.

36.   Do It (Till You're Satisfied) by B.T. Express was the first and biggest hit for this Brooklyn, New York R & B/disco band formerly known as Brooklyn Trucking Express before their name was shortened. Billy Nichols claims he wrote this million selling number one hit R & B hit because it motivated him. He was not a member of the group, but a saxophonist/guitarist who traveled with Marvin Gaye and the Spinners.

37. **Don't Let the Sun Go down on Me** by Elton John featured Beach Boys' Carl Wilson and Bruce Johnston on backing vocals, along with Toni Tennille. This was the first hit from the 'Caribou' album, which was written over a 10 day period in January of 1974.In 1991 it became a hit again when Elton John re recorded it as a duet with George Michael.

38. **When Will I See You Again** by the Three Degrees was the biggest hit for this Philadelphia female soul trio which accompanied MFSB on the number one million seller TSOP from earlier in 1974.The Three Degrees recorded since the mid 60's and had a top 30 hit in the summer of 1970 with 'Maybe' on the Roulette record label.

39. **Spiders and Snakes** by Jim Stafford was co-written by David Bellamy of the Bellamy Brothers and was the 1st of 3 consecutive 1974 hits for this singer/songwriter and multi-instrumentalist from Florida. He was later married briefly to Bobbie Gentry of 'Ode to Billie Joe' fame.

40. **My Melody of Love** by Bobby Vinton was a major comeback and a million selling hit for the singer known as 'the Polish Prince'. This adaptation of a German song by Henry Mayer gave Bobby Vinton his biggest hit since 'Mr. Lonely' 10 years earlier.

41. **You're the First, the Last, My Everything** by Barry White was a song he completely re-wrote which a friend, Sterling Radcliffe had composed as a country and western song 21 years earlier called 'You're The First, The Last, In Between'. After Barry White reworked and released the song, it became another million seller for the multi-talented soul singer from Texas.

42. **You Haven't Done Nothin'** by Stevie Wonder featured the Jackson Five on backing vocals. This social comment hit was aimed at U.S. President Richard Nixon and was the first of 2 major hits from the album 'Fulfillingness First Finale'.

43. **Dancing Machine** by The Jackson Five was their first top 10 hit in 3 years. The song was produced and co-written by Hal Davis who was inspired to create the song after a girl who liked him would dance to anything at anytime. She was a dancing machine. This was the only major hit from the Jackson Five's album 'Get It Together'.

44. **Best Thing That Ever Happened to Me** by Gladys Knight & The Pips was another of their major hits written by Jim Weatherly, who also composed 'Midnight Train to Georgia' and 'Neither One of Us'. This song was a number one hit on the country charts for Ray Price in 1973 and a number one hit on the R & B charts for Gladys Knight & The Pips in 1974.

45. **Smokin' in the Boys Room** by Brownsville Station was the only notable hit for this rock trio from Ann Arbor, Michigan. This teen rebellion hit was written by group members Michael 'Cub' Koda and Michael Lutz and was later featured in the 1979 movie 'Rock and Roll High School.' In 1985 Motley Crue launched their career with this song.

46. **The Show Must Go On** by 3 Dog Night, co-written by Leo Sayer, was the final top 10 hit for this pop rock trio from Los Angeles. Chuck Negron sang lead on this prime cut from their album 'Hard Labor', the first 3 Dog Night recording produced by Jimmy Ienner.

47. **Boogie Down** by Eddie Kendricks was the follow up to the former lead singer of the Temptations biggest solo hit 'Keep on Truckin'. 'Boogie Down' reached number one on the R & B charts and was very popular at the clubs. Along with his former Temptations' members, he was inducted into the Rock and Roll Hall of Fame in 1989. Sadly, he died of lung cancer in 1992 at the age of 52.

48. **Tell Me Something Good** by Rufus, written by Stevie Wonder, was the hit that launched the career of this soulful group led by Chaka Khan. Two of the members of Rufus came from the group American Breed, best known for their 1968 hit 'Bend Me, Shape Me.'

49. **I'm Leaving It up To You** by Donny & Marie Osmond was a remake of the number one hit from 1963 by Dale and Grace. Together, Donny and Marie hosted their own weekly musical/variety show from 1976 to 1978.

50. **Rock On** by David Essex was a tribute to the early days of rock and roll and most notably iconic teen rebel James Dean. This was the only hit in North America for David Essex, although he had many in his native Britain. David Essex starred with Ringo Starr in the film 'That'll Be the Day' which featured hits from the early to mid-60's. David Essex also starred in the sequel 'Stardust' which co-starred Adam Faith, Larry Hagman, Keith Moon, and Edd Byrnes.

51. **Come and Get Your Love** by Redbone was a million seller for this American/Indian swamp rock group headed by brothers Lolly and Pat (Vasquez) Vegas. The brothers were session musicians and also worked on the 'Shindig' music TV show in the mid-60's before launching their own group in 1969.

52. **Rock And Roll Heaven** by the Righteous Brothers was a comeback hit for this blue-eyed soul duo who had not achieved a top 10 hit since '(You're My) Soul And Inspiration' 8 years earlier in 1966. This hit was co-written by Alan O'Day, who had a number one hit later in the decade with 'Undercover Angel'. Bobby Hatfield of the Righteous Brothers joined rock and roll heaven in 2003 at the age of 63 from a heart attack as a result of an apparent cocaine overdose.

53. **Jazz man** by Carole King featured the saxophone of Tom Scott on this major hit for this singer/songwriter extraordinaire. This was the biggest hit from her 'Wrap around Joy' album which she wrote with former Steely Dan member Dave Palmer. This Lou Adler-produced album also featured the hit 'Nightingale'.

54. **Until You Come Back To Me (That's What I'm Gonna Do)** by Aretha Franklin was co-written by Stevie Wonder and became her final top 10 hit until 11 years later when 'Freeway Of Love' sped up to the top 5 on the pop charts. This hit reached number one on the R & B charts.

55.   The Entertainer by Marvin Hamlisch was written in 1902 by Scott Joplin and became the theme of the film 'The Sting' starring Paul Newman and Robert Redford. Pianist/composer Marvin Hamlisch also won the Grammy Award for Best Song for 'The Way We Were' which topped the charts for Barbra Streisand in 1974. Back in the 60's Marvin Hamlisch co-wrote Lesley Gore's top 10 hit 'Sunshine, Lollipops and Rainbows. Marvin Hamlisch won the Best New Artist Grammy in 1974.

56.   Rikki Don't Lose That Number by Steely Dan was a prime cut from their 'Pretzel Logic' album. This hit featured Donald Fagen on lead vocals and Walter Becker on guitar and vocals and also featured guest drummer Jim Gordon with backing vocals by Timothy B. Scmidt of Poco and Eagles fame. Steely Dan quit touring the following year to concentrate on writing and studio recordings.

57.   Junior's Farm by Paul McCartney & Wings was actually recorded in Nashville, Tennessee while they were staying at the farm of Curly Putman Junior, whose claim to fame was writing the song 'Green Green Grass of Home'. The 'B' side was the country-inspired 'Sally G'. Both songs were written and produced by Paul McCartney.

58.   If You Love Me (Let Me Know) by Olivia Newton-John was the follow up to 'Let Me Be There'. Both songs were written by John Rostill, produced by John Farrar and both were top 10 on both the pop and country charts. This was the 2nd of 3 major hits for Olivia Newton-John in 1974.

59. Mockingbird by James Taylor and Carly Simon was a remake of the top 10 hit from 1963 by Inez and Charlie Foxx. Taylor and Simon were happily married to one another when this million seller was in the top 10 on the pop charts.

60.   Jungle Boogie by Kool & the Gang was the first major hit for this R & B group from Jersey City, New Jersey. This hit was used in Quentin Tarantino's 1994 film Pulp Fiction on the car radio while John Travolta and Samuel L. Jackson were driving around in the early part of the movie. Kool and The Gang's next major hit didn't arrive until 1979 when they added lead singer "J.T." Taylor to the lineup beginning with 'Ladies Night'.

61.   Tin Man by America was inspired by the character in the 1939 classic film 'The Wizard of Oz'. This hit was produced by Sir George Martin and written by guitarist/singer Dewey Bunnell, who also composed their hits 'A Horse with No Name' and 'Ventura Highway'. After 3 major hits in their debut year of 1972, and no notables hits in 1973, 'Tin Man' got them back on track again as it began a string of 4 top 20 hits for this soft rock 70's trio.

62.   Be Thankful for What You Got by William De Vaughn was a one hit wonder singer/songwriter guitarist from Washington, D.C. He was a drafting technician for the Government when he paid around a $1,000. to record a song he wrote. After its million selling success, he lost interest in the music business and his newfound career died as quickly as it arrived.

63.   The Bitch Is Back by Elton John was the 3rd of 4 major hit singles he released in 1974. This rock hit by Elton was from the album 'Caribou', named

162

by Caribou Ranch Recording studio where it was recorded. Elton John would say the word 'Bitch' again in the number one hit the following year, 'Bad Blood' backing Neil Sedaka.

64.   Please Come Home to Boston by Dave Loggins was the only major hit for the cousin of singer/songwriter Kenny Loggins. As a songwriter, Dave Loggins also wrote 'Pieces of April' for 3 Dog Night and 'Morning Desire' for Kenny Rogers. He also shared a 1984 duet hit with Anne Murray with 'Nobody Loves Me like You Do', which won a CMA Award.

65.   Back Home Again by John Denver was his 3rd consecutive million selling hit of 1974 following back-to-back number one hits with 'Sunshine On My Shoulders' and 'Annie's Song'. 'Back Home Again' was the title song from the multi-platinum album which contained 4 hit singles. This song won the CMA award for Song of the Year in 1975 at which time John Denver also won the 'Entertainer of the Year' award.

66.   Beach Baby by First Class was a one hit wonder British studio band which featured Tony Burrows, who was previously the lead singer on 'Love Grows (Where My Rosemary Goes)" by Edison Lighthouse. This goodtime nostalgic hit was recorded on Jonathan King's 'UK Records' record label.

67.   I've Got to Use My Imagination by Gladys Knight & The Pips was co-written by Carole King's former husband and songwriting partner Gerry Goffin. This million seller had a very different sound than their other big hits at the time, probably because it was the first one produced by Kenny Kerner and Richie Wise, who produced the number one hit 'Brother Louie' for the Stories.

68.   The Air That I Breathe by The Hollies was co-written by Albert Hammond and became the final major hit from this popular British group from Manchester, England. This hit, engineered by Alan Parsons, was originally recorded by the Everly Brothers with little success the year before. The Hollies were inducted into the Rock and Roll Hall of Fame in 2010.

69.   Let Me Be There by Olivia Newton –John was the first of 5 consecutive million sellers for the British-born, Australian-raised singer/actress. Although her first hit was 'If Not for You', (written by Bob Dylan) from 1971, 'Let Me Be There' was her first official top 10 hit. The bass singer on this hit was Mike Sammes of the Mike Sammes Singers, who sang backing vocals of Tom Jones' hit 'Green Green Grass of Home' and 'Delilah', among other British hits.

70.   On and On by Gladys Knight & The Pips was like a description of their red hot career at this time…the hits just kept on coming on and on with one right after the other. This was their 4th consecutive million seller in less than 9 months. This song was written and produced by Curtis Mayfield and was from the album and movie 'Claudine' starring Diahann Carroll and James Earl Jones.

71.   The Lord's Prayer by Sister Janet Mead was the only hit for this singer who became a member of the Sisters of Mercy Convent when she was 17 years old. This Australia born music lover had a unit she called her Rock Band and provided music for a weekly rock mass at the Adelaide Cathedral.

Her music began attracting attention and she was asked to make some recordings. Her recording of 'The Lord's Prayer' sold over a million copies and she donated all her royalties to charity.

72.   Midnight at the Oasis by Maria Muldaur was a sensuous spring 1974 hit for this New York City born singer who was part of the 60's Greenwich Village folk/jazz music scene. This Italian singer's real name is Maria D'Amato.

73.   Waterloo by Abba was the first of many hits for this iconic quartet from Sweden. 'ABBA' is an acronym formed from the first letters of each group member's first name: Agnetha, Björn, Benny and Anni-Frid.'Waterloo' won Abba the Eurovision Song Contest in 1974.

74.   Everlasting Love by Carl Carlton was a remake of the 1967 hit originally popular by Robert Knight. Detroit born Carl Carlton had his first hit at the age of 16 as 'Little Carl Carlton' with 'Competition Ain't Nothin' in 1968.

75.   Clap for the Wolfman by The Guess Who was a tribute to one of the most popular and original sounding radio personalities of the 50's, 60's and 70's. Wolfman Jack, whose real name was Bob Smith, was prominently featured on this top 10 hit from the summer of 1974. Wolfman Jack died suddenly as a result of a heart attack at the age of 57 on July 1st 1995.

76.   Can't Get Enough by Bad Company was the first and biggest hit for this British rock group which featured lead vocalist Paul Rodgers and drummer Simon Kirke from the group Free, as well as Mick Ralphs from Mott The Hoople and Boz Burrell from King Crimson.

77.   Americans by Byron MacGregor was a million selling spoken word hit delivered by the News Director at CKLW-Detroit (in Windsor, Ontario, Canada) backed by an instrumental version of 'America The Beautiful'. The narration was originally written and delivered as an editorial by Gordon Sinclair on CFRB Radio station in Toronto, Ontario. He pointed out that when many countries faced economic crises or natural disasters, Americans were among the most generous people in the world at offering assistance, but when America faced a crisis, it often faced that crisis alone.

78.   Longfellow Serenade by Neil Diamond was a reference to the 19th century poet Henry Wadsworth Longfellow and is the story of a man who woos his girl with poetry. This was the biggest hit single from his 'Serenade' album, produced by Tom Catalano.

79.   Another Saturday Night by Cat Stevens was a remake of the Sam Cooke classic hit from 1963. This was Cat Stevens' final top 10 hit. Later in the decade he converted to the Muslim religion and took the name Yusef Islam.

80.   Jet by Paul McCartney & Wings was the 2nd of 3 major hits from the 'Band on the Run' album. This high energy hit was written by Paul and Linda McCartney and mostly recorded at EMI's studios in Lagos, Nigeria. This hit was originally written about Paul and Linda's little black puppy named 'Jet'.

81.   For the Love of Money by The O'Jays has a distinctive echo and 'swishing' bass guitar sound which Gamble and Huff produced in this million selling hit. The title was inspired by a well known Bible verse in 1 Timothy which begins with 'For the Love of Money, the root of all evil...'This hit was later used as the theme for the reality show 'The Apprentice with Donald Trump.'

82.   **Call on Me** by Chicago featured Peter Cetera on lead vocals and was the 2nd of 3 notable hits from the album 'Chicago 7'. This was the only hit by Chicago written by trumpeter Lee Loughnane, one of the founding members of this legendary brass rock band.

83.   **Oh My My** by Ringo Starr was the former Beatles' 3rd consecutive hit from his 3rd solo album 'Ringo' which included his consecutive number one hits 'Photograph' and 'You're Sixteen'. Ringo got by with a little help from his friends Billy Preston, Martha Reeves and Merry Clayton on this hit which he co-wrote with Vini Poncia, who also supplied backup vocals.

84.   **Help Me** by Joni Mitchell was the biggest hit from her most successful album, 'Court and Spark', which produced 3 hit singles. This hit was written and produced by Joni Mitchell and features the backing group Tom Scott's L.A. Express. The other notable hits from this album were 'Raised on Robbery' and 'Free Man in Paris'.

85.   **Sideshow** by Blue Magic was the only hit for this soul group from Philadelphia. Songwriters Vinnie Barrett and Bobby Eli were inspired to write this song after a visit to an antique museum that had all kinds of circus toys. This million selling love ballad was followed by the similarly themed '3 Ring Circus', which failed to reach the top 30.

86.   **Tubular Bells** by Mike Oldfield was a haunting instrumental theme from the shocking movie 'The Exorcist' starring Linda Blair. The album version from this British multi-instrumentalist/composer was almost 50 minutes in length.

87.   **Sweet Home Alabama** by Lynyrd Skynyrd was the highest charting hit for this Southern rock group headed by lead singer Ronnie Van Zant. They took the group name from their gym teacher Leonard Skinner. It's interesting to note that there is also a character in the 1963 top 10 hit 'Hello Muddah, Hello Faddah' by Allan Sherman named Leonard Skinner. A plane crash on October 20th 1977 killed Ronnie Van Zant and members Steve Gaines and his sister Cassie Gaines.

88.   **Life Is A Rock (But The Radio Rolled Me)** by Reunion featured Joey Levine, the lead singer of 'Yummy Yummy Yummy' and 'Chewy Chewy' by The Ohio Express on lead vocals. This one hit wonder studio group rattled off over a hundred music artists' names, dances, song titles or record labels in this very unique and fun hit from the fall of 1974.

89.   **Wildwood Weed** by Jim Stafford was the 3rd of 3 consecutive twisted comedic hits for this singer/ songwriter in 1974, his only year in the top 20 on the pop charts. The following year he had his own prime time summer variety TV show and in the early 80's he was the co-host of 'Those Amazing Animals'.

90.   **Erus Tu** by Mocedades was the only hit for this group from Spain which featured the Amezaga sisters, Amya and Izaskum on vocals. It was released as a single after it was used as Spain's entry in the Eurovision Song Contest, where it placed second. The 'B' side of the single featured English lyrics.

91.   **I'll Have to Say I Love You in a Song** by Jim Croce was one of the posthumous hits for this popular singer/songwriter who lost his life in a single engine plane crash on September 20, 1973.This song was written by Jim for his wife Ingrid one night after a confrontation with her about their finances and problems making ends meet. This hit was featured on the album 'I Got a Name' which also included his next and final hit single 'Workin' at the Car Wash Blues'.

92.   **Hollywood Swinging** by Kool & the Gang was a number one hit on the R & B charts taken from their album 'Wild and Peaceful' and was inspired by the unusual song 'Soul Makossa' by Manu Dibango. This was the 2nd major hit for Kool and the Gang, following 'Jungle Fever' which also sold a million copies.

93.   **Just Don't Want to Be Lonely** by The Main Ingredient was the 2nd million seller for this New York City soul trio which included Cuba Gooding Sr. as a member. Their first and only other top 10 hit was 'Everybody Plays the Fool' from 1972.

94.   **You Won't See Me** by Anne Murray was her remake of a Beatles song which they never released as a single. This hit by Anne was one of 3 from her 8th studio album, 'Love Song'.

95.   **Stop and Smell the Roses** by Mac Davis was co-written with Tonight Show Bandleader and Trumpeter Doc Severinsen. The song offers advice to take time out of your busy schedule to stop and smell the roses along the way. Doc and Mac became acquainted after Davis made frequent appearances on Johnny Carson's 'Tonight Show' and suggested writing a song with a phrase he recently heard a physician use.

96.   **Only You (And You Alone)** by Ringo Starr was a remake of the Platters hit from 1955. John Lennon, who played acoustic guitar on this hit, was the one who suggested that Ringo record this classic. This hit from Ringo's 'Goodnight Vienna' album also featured musical guests Billy Preston and Harry Nilsson.

97.   **Carefree Highway** by Gordon Lightfoot was the follow up to his biggest hit 'Sundown' which reached number one in the spring of 1974.Gordon Lightfoot was born in Orillia, Ontario, North of Toronto.

98.   **Helen Wheels** by Paul McCartney & Wings was inspired by Paul and Linda's Land Rover which they called 'Hell on Wheels'. This single was released prior to the release of their 'Band on the Run' album and was included on the North American release, but not the initial British release of the monumental LP.

99.   Never My Love by Blue Suede was their follow up to their number one abstract remake of 'Hooked on a Feeling' from earlier this year. 'Never My Love' was an upbeat version of the Association hit from 1967 written by the Addrisi Brothers, Don and Dick.

100.   Sha La La (Make Me Happy) by Al Green was his final top 10 hit of the 70's after achieving 7 previous million selling singles. Al Green's producer and co-writer, Willie Mitchell died on January 5, 2010 of cardiac arrest at the age of 81.

101.   Never, Never Gonna Give Ya Up by Barry White was the 2nd of 6 million sellers for the singer/songwriter/producer with the deep sexy voice that women found irresistible. Barry White started his career in music at a very young age and at 11 years old played the piano on Jesse Belvin's hit 'Goodnight My Love'.

102.   Steppin' Out (Gonna Boogie Tonight) by Tony Orlando & Dawn was one of 3 hit singles from the album 'New Ragtime Follies'. This top 10 hit was popular the year their weekly TV music/variety show made its debut.

103.   You and Me against the World by Helen Reddy was co-written by singer/composer/actor/pianist Paul Williams and was the 2nd hit from the album 'A Song for Jeffrey'. Helen Reddy interpreted the song from the standpoint of a mother singing to her daughter.

104.   Living for the City by Stevie Wonder was a very strong social commentary song from his critically-acclaimed 'Innervisions' album, which also included the hits 'Higher Ground' and 'Don't You Worry 'Bout a Thing'. Minnie Ripperton, Deniece Williams and his former wife Syreeta Wright sang background vocals on this hit which was over 7 minutes in length on the album and 3:41 on the single.

105.   Hang on in There Baby by Johnny Bristol was his only major hit as a singer, although he co-produced and co-wrote many Motown hits through the years. Among the hits he co-wrote was Diana Ross and The Supremes' final number one hit 'Someday We'll Be Together', in which he supplied the male voice singing alongside Diana. Johnny Bristol died on March 21, 2004.

106.   Radar Love by Golden Earring was the only North American 70's hit for this Dutch rock group, although they had many that charted in their homeland. This great 'driving' hit makes reference to 'Brenda Lee is coming on strong', the top 10 hit from 1966.In late 1982, Golden Earring returned to the pop charts in North America with their top 10 entry, 'Twilight Zone'.

107.   (I've Been) Searchin' for So Long by Chicago was the 1st of 3 hit singles from their double album 'Chicago 7'. This hit, written by James Pankow, begins as a ballad and builds as it progresses. Pankow also wrote Chicago's hits 'Make Me Smile', 'Colour My World', and 'Old Days' among others.

108.   Earache My Eye by Cheech & Chong was a top 10 novelty hit which featured Cheech Marin's character 'Alice Bowie'. This comedy routine/song first appeared on 'Cheech and Chong's Wedding Album'. The famed international percussionist Airto Moreira plays drums on this hit.

109.   Keep on Smiling by Wet Willie was the first and biggest hit by this Southern rock band from Mobile, Alabama led by Brothers Jack and lead singer Jimmy Hall.

110.   Oh Very Young by Cat Stevens was the first of 2 top 10 hits in 1974 for the singer born Steven Georgiou. This philosophical song was taken from his album 'Buddha and The Chocolate Box' and was his final top 10 original hit. His follow up single was his 1974 remake of the Sam Cooke classic, 'Another Saturday Night'.

111.   Lookin' for a Love by Bobby Womack was a minor hit originally when he was lead singer of a group called the Valentinos recorded on Sam Cooke's SAR record label back in 1962. The J. Geils Band had a hit with it in 1971 and 2 years later Bobby Womack decided to use the song as a warm up while recording new material, not planning on releasing it commercially. After he listened to it again, it was decided that it deserved another chance. It then sold a million copies and reached number one on the R & B charts. Bobby Womack was inducted into the Rock and Roll Hall of Fame in 2009.

112.   Takin' Care of Business by Bachman Turner Overdrive featured former Guess Who member Randy Bachman on lead vocals. The song was originally going to be called 'White Collar Worker', but Randy Bachman changed it after he heard a Vancouver radio DJ say the catch phrase 'we're takin' care of business'.

113.   Love Me for a Reason by The Osmonds was the final top 10 hit for the group as a family. This love ballad was produced by Mike Curb and co-written by Johnny Bristol, who scored his biggest hit in 1974 with the R & B hit 'Hang on in There Baby'. 'Love Me for a Reason' by The Osmonds featured Merrill Osmond on lead vocals.

114.   Put Your Hands Together by the O'Jays was the first of 2 top 10 hits from their album 'Ship Ahoy'. Like most of their hits, this was also written and produced by Kenny Gamble and Leon Huff. The O'Jays were inducted into the Vocal Group Hall of Fame in 2004 and The Rock and Roll Hall of Fame in 2005.

115.   Wishin' You Were Here by Chicago featured backing vocals by The Beach Boys. This ballad was written by Peter Cetera, who was featured on lead vocals alongside Terry Kath on this hit from 'Chicago 7'.

116.   A Very Special Love Song by Charlie Rich was a multi-week number one hit on the country charts and the Grammy Award winning Country Song of the Year of 1974. The song was co-written by his producer Billy Sherrill. Although 1973 was the most successful year on the pop charts for Charlie Rich, 1974 was his biggest year on the country charts when he had 5 hits reach number one.

117.   One Hell of a Woman by Mac Davis was one of 2 notable hit this singer/songwriter/actor from Lubbock, Texas achieved in 1974.It was also the year he began hosting his own variety TV Show which ran until 1976. He also later appeared in several movies.

168

118.   I've Got the Music in Me by Kiki Dee was the most successful solo hit for this singer from Yorkshire, England whose real name is Pauline Matthews. Her best known hit is the one she shared with Elton John in 1976, 'Don't Go Breaking My Heart'. Both hits were recorded on Elton John's own record label, 'Rocket'Records.

119.   My Girl Bill by Jim Stafford was the 2nd of 3 notable hits in 1974, his exclusive year in the top 20 on the pop charts. This was an offbeat play-on-words song and like his other hits, was produced by Phil Gernhard and Kent Lavoie, who was also the singer known as Lobo.

120.   I Love by Tom T. Hall was the biggest hit as a pop singer for this Country artist best known for giving Jeannie C. Riley her number one 1968 hit 'Harper Valley P.T.A.' On February 12, 2008, Tom T. Hall was inducted into the Country Music Hall Of Fame.

121.   Wild Thing by Fancy was a remake of the number one hit by The Troggs from 1966.This British one hit wonder group featured Helen Court on lead vocals. The song was written by Chip Taylor, the brother of actor Jon Voight.

122.   Bungle in the Jungle by Jethro Tull was written and produced by lead singer Ian Anderson and taken from their 7th studio album 'War Child'. This progressive rock group was named after the 18th century agriculturalist Jethro Tull.

123.   The Need to Be by Jim Weatherly was the only notable hit as a singer for this former All-American quarterback, who chose songwriting as a career over pro football. As a songwriter, he wrote many hits for several music artists including 'Midnight Train to Georgia' and 'The Best Thing That Ever Happened to Me' for Gladys Knight and The Pips among others.

124.   You Got the Love by Rufus was the follow up to their first and biggest hit 'Tell Me Something Good' and the first to be billed as 'Rufus featuring Chaka Khan'. This song was co-written by Ray Parker Jr. who began his string of hits in the late 70's with the group Raydio before going solo and having a number one hit with 'Ghostbusters'.

125.   I Won't Last a Day without You by The Carpenters was written by Paul Williams and Roger Nichols who also wrote their hits 'We've Only Just Begun' and 'Rainy Days and Mondays'. The Carpenters did not release a new album in 1974, instead releasing their first Greatest Hits 1969 – 1973 collection, partly because they were too busy on their first world tour. 'I Won't Last a Day without You' was taken from their 1972 album 'A' Song for You'

126.   Who Do You Think You Are by Bo Donaldson & the Heywoods was the only other hit for this Cincinnati-based group known for their million seller, 'Billy Don't Be A Hero'. The group was discovered while touring with the Osmonds in the early 70's, eventually signing with 'ABC Records', where Steve Barri produced their hits.

127.   Love Song by Anne Murray won a Grammy Award for Best Female Country Performance for this singer from Springhill, Nova Scotia, Canada.

This song was co-written by Kenny Loggins and originally recorded by Loggins and Messina, although it never became a hit for them.

128.   You Little Trustmaker by The Tymes was the first major hit in over 10 years for this Philadelphia soul group who first hit the top of the pop charts with 'So Much in Love' in 1963. In 2005 The Tymes were inducted into the Vocal Group Hall Of Fame.

129.   Shinin' On by Grand Funk was the title song from the album produced by Todd Rundgren which included their rockin' version of 'The Locomotion'. This hit was written by the nucleus of the group, guitarist Mark Farner and drummer Don Brewer.

130.   Skin Tight by Ohio Players was the title cut from the 7th studio album and their first for Mercury records. This group originated in 1959 as an instrumental group called the 'Ohio Untouchables'. They resurfaced in the early 70's with a soul funk sound and had major hits with 'Fire' and 'Love Rollercoaster', as well as this hit recorded in Chicago which ran almost 8 minutes on the album.

131.   Doo Doo Doo Doo Heartbreaker by The Rolling Stones was the follow up to their number one hit 'Angie' from 'Goats Head Soup', the final album produced by Jimmy Miller. Billy Preston played keyboards on this social comment hit popular in early 1974.

132.   Don't You Worry 'Bout a Thing by Stevie Wonder was the 3rd hit single from his 'Innervisions' album written and produced by the Motown genius. This song was more positive than the other hits from this intricate album with flawless production and heavy use of the synthesizer performed by Wonder.

133.   Do It Baby by The Miracles was their first top 30 hit since the departure of Smokey Robinson in 1972. Billy Griffin replaced Smokey as the lead singer of this legendary Motown group. Griffin along with the other members of The Miracles, received a Star on the Hollywood Walk of Fame in March of 2009.

134.   Last Time I Saw Him by Diana Ross was a moderate hit for the singer who fronted the most successful girl group of all time. This song was co-written by Michael Masser who also co-wrote the number one hits 'Touch Me in the Morning' from 1973 and 'Theme from Mahogany' (Do You Know Where You're Going To' in 1976.

135.   Fairytale by The Pointer Sisters was written by Anita and Bonnie and was a prime cut from their album 'That's A Plenty'. This hit not only reached top 20 on the pop charts, but also reached top 40 on the country charts helping the Pointer Sisters become the first black American group to perform on the Grand Ole Opry.

136.   Promised Land by Elvis Presley was written by Chuck Berry who recorded it in 1964. The King of Rock and Roll's remake of this song was recorded at Stax studios in Memphis. This was the title song of the album which he recorded in the city where his recording career began.

137.   Are You Lonesome Tonight by Donny Osmond was a remake of a song recorded originally in 1927 by Vaughn Deleath, but made most popular by Elvis Presley in 1960.

138.   Haven't Got Time for the Pain by Carly Simon featured her husband James Taylor on acoustic guitar on this prime cut from her 'Hotcakes' album. This song demonstrated her upbeat mood while pregnant with her first child. This album also included the hit duet 'Mockingbird' with hubby James Taylor.

139.   Must of Got Lost by J. Geils Band was the first top 20 hit for this Boston rock group which featured Peter 'Wolf' Blankfield on lead vocals. This was their final top 40 hit on the Atlantic label before switching to EMI America where they had 2 consecutive million sellers in the early 80's with 'Centrefold' and 'Freeze-Frame'.

140.   Keep on Singing by Helen Reddy was co-written by Bobby Hart of Tommy Boyce and Bobby Hart fame and was originally recorded by Austin Roberts. This was the first of 3 notable 1974 hits for Helen Reddy.

141.   It's Only Rock And Roll (But I Like It) by The Rolling Stones was the title song of the first single from what was Mick Taylor's last appearance as a group member. Although not credited, future Stones member Ronnie Wood collaborated with Jagger and Richards on this song. It was originally recorded at his home studio with David Bowie featured backing Mick Jagger's vocals and Kenney Jones on drums.

142.   Tryin' to Hold On To My Woman by Lamont Dozier was a moderate hit for this songwriter best known in the team of Holland/Dozier/Holland, who created dozens of major Motown hits for the Supremes, The Four Tops and Martha and The Vandellas among others. In the 80's he wrote the number one hit 'Two Hearts' with Phil Collins for the movie 'Buster'.

143.   Rub It In by Billy 'Crash' Craddock was the biggest country and pop hit for the singer once referred to as 'Mr. Country Rock'. This song was written and originally recorded by singer/songwriter Layng Martine Jr., who had a minor hit with it in 1971.

144.   Dark Horse by George Harrison was a dark song from the 'quiet' Beatle inspired by his failing marriage to Patti Boyd who left him for their mutual friend Eric Clapton. Billy Preston was featured on the electric piano on this hit from the album of the same name.

145.   Me and Baby Brother by War was their follow up to 'Gypsy Man' and was also included on their album 'Deliver the Word'. Their music has been described as California 'funk vibe' and certainly delivers a feel good, cruisin' sound with an infectious beat and rhythm.

146.   Love Don't Love Nobody by The Spinners was the 4th hit single for this Detroit R & B vocal group in 1974.In Britain they were known as the Detroit Spinners to avoid confusion with the British group known as The Spinners.

147.   Ain't Too Proud to Beg by The Rolling Stones was a remake of the

1966 hit by the Temptations. This hit was the follow up the album's title song 'It's Only Rock and Roll', which was the last for Stones member Mick Taylor. Ronnie Wood would eventually replace Mick Taylor 2 years later in 1976.

148.   People Gotta Move by Gino Vannelli was the first of a string of hits for this Montreal born singer songwriter. His biggest hit 'I Just Wanna Stop' in 1978 makes reference to 'those nights in Montreal'.

149.   Sure as I'm Sittin' Here by 3 Dog Night was the final top 30 hit of their 5 year span of continuous success on the pop charts. This was their 2nd hit from their album 'Hard Labor' and was written by John Hiatt, who later wrote the hit 'Angel Eyes' for the Jeff Healey Band.

150.   Free Man in Paris by Joni Mitchell was the 3rd single release from her 'Court and Spark' album and featured backing vocals by David Crosby and Graham Nash and guitars by Jose Feliciano and Larry Carlton. Neil Diamond covered this song in 1977 on his album 'I'm Glad You're Here With Me Tonight'.

151.   Finally Got Myself Together by The Impressions was a number one hit on the R & B charts, despite the fact that their former lead singer, songwriter and producer Curtis Mayfield left the act in 1970. This hit was written and produced by Ed Townsend who previously co-wrote and co-produced Marvin Gaye's number one hit 'Let's Get It On'. In 1958 Ed Townsend had a hit with the ballad 'For Your Love'.

152.   Overnight Sensation by The Raspberries was the final hit single for this energetic pop/rock group from Ohio fronted by singer/songwriter Eric Carmen. 'Overnight Sensation (Hit record) was an ambitious production by Jimmy Ienner from 'Starting Over', their 4th and final album. The following year Eric Carmen launched a successful solo career beginning with the hit 'All By Myself'.

153.   My Sweet Lady by Cliff De Young was from the made- for -TV movie 'Sunshine' which was about a young mother dying of cancer and featured songs by John Denver. Cliff DeYoung appeared in several movies and TV shows through the years, including a short-lived TV series based on the film 'Sunshine'.

154.   After the Gold Rush by Prelude was an a cappella version of the Neil Young song by this one hit wonder act from Britain. Two of the members of this trio consisted of Brian and Irene Hume, a husband and wife who later became a successful country music act in Britain.

155.   If You Talk in Your Sleep by Elvis Presley was recorded at Stax studios with Wayne Jackson and the Memphis horns. This hit was co-written by Red West, who was Presley's bodyguard and friend since high school days.

156.   So You Are a Star by The Hudson Brothers was popular the year they hosted their own TV variety show which ran in the summer of 1974. Bill, Brett and Mark Hudson also hosted the children's TV show 'The Hudson Brothers Razzle Dazzle Comedy Show.' Bill Hudson was married to actress Goldie Hawn from 1976 to 1980 and is the father of Kate Hudson.

157. **Sexy Mama** by The Moments was their 2nd biggest hit next to their million seller 'Love On A Two Way Street' in 1970. Due to contractual problems, they changed their name to 'Ray, Goodman and Brown'. The biggest hit under their new name arrived in 1979 with 'Special Lady'.

158. **There Won't Be Anymore** by Charlie Rich was the first of 6 consecutive 1974 hits on the country charts, 5 of which reached number one for 'the Silver Fox'. Billy Sherrill, one of country music's most talented and respected producers gave Charlie Rich most of his hits, as well as other country stars including Tammy Wynette, with whom he co-wrote her most famous song, 'Stand by Your Man'.

159. **Save the Last Dance for Me** by The DeFranco Family was a remake of the number one hit by the Drifters from 1960. This was the 3rd and final top 40 hit for the family act which featured a young Tony DeFranco on lead vocals.

160. **Machine Gun** by The Commodores was an instrumental and the first chart entry for this Motown act which made Lionel Richie a superstar. Keyboardist Milan Williams wrote this funk instrumental which featured Richie on saxophone.

161. **I'm Coming Home** by The Spinners was the follow up to the title song from the album 'Mighty Love' which also included this top 20 hit.

162. **Rockin' Soul** by Hues Corporation was the follow up to their mega hit 'Rock the Boat' which topped the charts in the summer of 1974. They could not repeat the success of their only major hit, although 'Rockin' Soul' just made the top 20. This California trio broke up in 1978.

163. **Midnight Rider** by Gregg Allman was the first solo hit single for the popular member of the Allman Brothers band. The following year he married Cher, but that union lasted for only 2 years. Gregg Allman was inducted with the band into the Rock and Roll Hall of Fame in 1995.

164. **Let's Put It All Together** by The Stylistics was their final top 40 hit and was the follow up to their biggest hit 'You Make Me Feel Brand New'. Their producer Thom Bell stopped working with the Stylistics in 1974 and Hugo and Luigi, known for producing hits in the 50's and early 60's took over with limited success.

165. **Tell Me a Lie** by Sami Jo was the only notable hit for this country pop singer from Batesville, Arkansas. The song became more popular when Janie Fricke brought it to the top of the Country charts 9 years later in 1983.

166. **My Mistake (Was to Love You)** by Diana Ross & Marvin Gaye was the second single from their Duets album, with 'You're A Special Part of Me' being the first. Their next single release from the album, a cover of Wilson Pickett's 'Don't Knock My Love' failed to reach the top 40.

167. **Piano Man** by Billy Joel was inspired by his pre-fame days playing the piano bars and watching the characters that frequented the nightspot. Although this was Billy Joel's first hit, and is considered to be a signature recording, it failed to reach the top 20 on the pop charts. It did however, become a timeless classic.

168.   I'm in Love by Aretha Franklin was a Bobby Womack composition which Wilson Pickett charted in 1967 as the 'B' side to his hit 'Stag-O-Lee'. Both versions were recorded at the same Memphis studio. Lady's soul version featured backup singers Cissy Houston and Judy Clay, as well as bass guitarist Stanley Clarke and keyboardist Bob James.

169.   If You Wanna Get to Heaven by The Ozark Mountain Daredevils was a mixture of country, bluegrass, rock and pop in this upbeat hit from group from Springfield, Missouri. Their only other top 40 hit was the very different 'Jackie Blue' which reached the top 5 in 1975.

170.   **Livin' For You** by Al Green was written with Willie Mitchell in about an hour just before their Thanksgiving dinner back in 1973. This hit reached number one on the R & B chart and was more of a gospel- sounding hit at a time when religion began occupying a greater place in Al Green's life.

More Hits of 1974

Mighty Love – Part 1 by The Spinners was a mighty big number one hit on the R & B charts, even though it barely made the top 20 on the pop charts. Although the Spinners had several big hits in the 70's, the only one to reach number one on the pop charts was the one they shared with Dionne Warwick, 'Then Came You', from 1974.

Touch Me by Fancy was the only other hit single for this British group best known for their 1974 remake of the Troggs' 'Wild Thing'.

I Feel a Song (In My Heart) by Gladys Knight & The Pips didn't quite reach the top 20 on the pop charts, but reached number one on the R & B charts. This hit was produced and co-written by Tony Camillo, who would resurface on his own in 1975 with the top 10 hit 'Dynomite', inspired by the phrase used by J. J. Walker in the TV series 'Good Times'.

Woman to Woman by Shirley Brown was the swan song on the legendary Stax record label out of Memphis. This number one R & B hit was co-produced by the legendary Al Jackson, who also played drums.

Jim Dandy by Black Oak Arkansas was a Southern Rock group named after their hometown. This remake of Lavern Baker's 1957 hit featured group member Jim 'Dandy' Mangrum and the raspy voice of Ruby Starr on vocals.

Honey Honey by Abba was the 2nd charted North American hit for the Swedish pop quartet, following their claim to fame, 'Waterloo', earlier in 1974.

Touch a Hand, Make a Friend by The Staple Singers was the follow up to their top 10 hit 'If You're Ready (Come Go with Me) from late 1973. This family soul group were inducted into the Rock and Roll Hall of Fame in 1999, the year before their mentor 'Pops' Staples died a week before his 85th birthday.

Rock and Roll Hoochie Koo by Rick Derringer was the most successful solo hit for the singer who fronted the popular 60's group 'The McCoys' when he was a teenager as Rick Zehringer. This singer/guitarist also performed and produced hits for the Edgar Winter Group and Weird 'Al' Yankovic. Rick Derringer became a member of Ringo Starr's All-Starr band in 2010.

Let It Ride by Bachman Turner Overdrive was the first rock hit single by the group fronted by former Guess Who member Randy Bachman, along with Fred Turner who sang lead on this top 30 hit. In 1974, Bachman Turner Overdrive won the Most Promising New Group Juno Award, Canada's equivalent to the Grammys.

Walk like a Man by Grand Funk was a moderate hit sandwiched between their 2 number one hits 'We're An American Band' and 'The Locomotion'. 'Walk like a Man' was a Mark Farner and Don Brewer composition, not to be confused with the Four Seasons hit which bears the same title.

This Heart by Gene Redding is a one hit wonder singer from Anderson, Indiana who was discovered at a USO Club in Anchorage, Alaska by singer Etta James.

Come Monday by Jimmy Buffet was the first hit from this singer/songwriter from Mobile, Alabama who has a devoted base of fans known as 'parrot heads'. He wrote 'Come Monday' for his wife while he was on tour, and has been performing it on tour ever since.

Workin' at the Car Wash Blues by Jim Croce was the final charted top 40 hit popular after his death in September of 1973.

I Love My Friend by Charlie Rich was a number one hit on the country charts from the year he won the 1974 CMA Entertainer of the Year award. He first played jazz and blues, then rockabilly and finally in the 70's became best known as a country singer.

I'm a Train by Albert Hammond was the only other top 40 hit by this singer/ songwriter known primarily for his hit 'It Never Rains in Southern California'. As a songwriter he co-wrote many successful songs including 'Little Arrows', 'The Air That I Breathe', 'Gimme Dat Ding' and 'When I Need You' among others.

Sister Mary Elephant (Shudd-Up) by Cheech & Chong was a comedic hit featuring a prissy, substitute nun teaching in a school of noisy teenage boys until she yells 'Shudd-up' to get their attention. This follow up to 'Basketball Jones' was featured on their 2nd album 'Big Bambu'.

Already Gone by The Eagles was only a moderate hit for the group that was about to hit superstardom. This hit was the first single to feature new member Don Felder while founding member Glenn Frey provided lead vocals.

Train of Thought by Cher was written by Alan O'Day of 'Undercover Angel' fame who also wrote 'Angie Baby' for Helen Reddy and 'Rock and Roll Heaven' for the Righteous Brothers. 'Train of Thought' was the moderately successful follow up to her number one hit 'Dark Lady'

The Americans (A Canadian's Opinion) by Gordon Sinclair was the original from the broadcast as an editorial in 1973 on CFRB radio in Toronto. News Director Byron Macgregor from CKLW-Windsor/Detroit had a million seller with it in 1974, the same year Sinclair's version hit the charts.

Willie and the Hand Jive by Eric Clapton was a remake of the Johnny Otis Show top 10 hit from 1958. The hand jive was a popular 50's dance which involved complicated hand moves and claps involved around various parts around the body. This was Eric Clapton's follow up to the number one hit 'I Shot The Sheriff', also from the album '461 Ocean Boulevard'.

Fire, Baby I'm on Fire by Andy Kim was the follow up to his number one hit 'Rock Me Gently'. In the mid 80's he changed his stage name to Baron Longfellow, but returned to his original stage name the following decade.

Sugar Baby Love by The Rubettes was a huge number one hit in the U.K. for this British pop bubblegum group which featured the distinctive falsetto of lead singer Paul DaVinci. This goodtime hit was written by Wayne Bickerton and Tony Waddington who also wrote the 1969 hit 'Nothing but Heartache' for the Flirtations.

Last Kiss by Wednesday was a remake of the 1964 J. Frank Wilson hit by this Canadian group. Their next single was a remake of Mark Dinning's 'Teen Angel', another teen tragedy song of the era.

WOLD by Harry Chapin was a story song inspired by a morning radio DJ Jim Connors, who was one of the first to play Harry's records on radio. Harry got the idea for the song after overhearing a phone conversation with Jim and the discussion the two of them would have later about 'life as a jock' and the effects it would have on his everyday life. Like Harry Chapin, Jim Connors would also die as a result of a fatal car accident. For Harry Chapin it happened in 1981 and for Jim Connors life would end in 1987.

Painted Ladies by Ian Thomas was the first solo for this Canadian singer/ songwriter/author/actor who is the brother of Dave Thomas of SCTV and the Mackenzie Brothers fame with Rick Moranis.

Virginia (Touch Me Like You Do) by Bill Amesbury was a goodtime, upbeat hit with a party atmosphere by this singer/songwriter from Toronto who has since had a sex change and is now known as 'Barbara' Amesbury.

It Doesn't Have to Be That Way by Jim Croce was released after his death and was a minor hit from his 'Life and Times' album. Jim Croce's widow, Ingrid operates 'Croce's Restaurant and Jazz Bar in San Diego, California.

Raised on Robbery by Joni Mitchell was one of 3 hit singles from her 'Court and Spark' album which Rolling Stone Magazine listed in 2003 at #111 on the 500 Greatest Albums of all time. Robbie Robertson of the Band played guitar on this fast paced Joni Mitchell hit.

Werewolf by The 5 Man Electrical Band was a story song from the group from Ottawa, Ontario, Canada that scored their biggest hit with 'Signs' in 1971. Prior to that, they were known as The Staccatos.

176

Top 17 Albums of 1974

1.	Greatest Hits	Elton John
2.	The Sting	Soundtrack
3.	Band on the Run	Paul McCartney & Wings
4.	Caribou	Elton John
5.	You Don't Mess Around With Jim	Jim Croce
6.	John Denver's Greatest Hits	John Denver
7.	Planet Waves	Bob Dylan
8.	461 Ocean Boulevard	Eric Clapton
9.	Sundown	Gordon Lightfoot
10.	Fullingness' First Finale	Stevie Wonder
11.	The Way We Were	Barbra Streisand
12.	Not Fragile	Bachman Turner Overdrive
13.	So Far	Crosby, Stills, Nash & Young
14.	Walls and Bridges	John Lennon
15.	It's Only Rock And Roll	Rolling Stones
16.	Endless Summer	Beach Boys
17.	Back Home Again	John Denver

Top 17 Country Hits of 1974

1. A Very Special Love Song — Charlie Rich
2. I Love — Tom T. Hall
3. I Can Help — Billy Swan
4. Rub It In — Billy 'Crash' Craddock
5. Another Lonely Song — Tammy Wynette
6. There Won't Be Anymore — Charlie Rich
7. He Still Thinks I Care — Anne Murray
8. Please Tell Her How the Story Ends — Ronnie Milsap
9. I See the Want in Your Eyes — Conway Twitty
10. Jolene — Dolly Parton
11. The Grand Tour — George Jones
12. I Will Always Love You — Dolly Parton
13. Back Home Again — John Denver
14. Please Don't Stop Loving Me — Porter Wagoner & Dolly Parton
15. I Love My Friend — Charlie Rich
16. Room Full of Roses — Mickey Gilley
17. Pure Love — Ronnie Milsap

Top 17 Disco Hits Of 1974

1.	T. S. O. P.	M. F. S. B.
2.	Rock Your Baby	George McCrae
3.	Rock the Boat	Hues Corporation
4.	Can't Get Enough of Your Love Babe	Barry White
5.	Do It (Till You're Satisfied)	B. T. Express
6.	You're The First, The Last, My Everything	Barry White
7.	Dancing Queen	Abba
8.	Boogie Down	Eddie Kendricks
9.	Jungle Boogie	Kool & the Gang
10.	Kung Fu Fighting	Carl Douglas
11.	For The Love of Money	O'Jays
12.	Hollywood Swinging	Kool & the Gang
13.	Dancing Machine	Jackson Five
14.	Never, Never Gonna Give Ya Up	Barry White
15.	Hang On In There Baby	Johnny Bristol
16.	You Got the Love	Rufus
17.	Skin Tight	Ohio Players

Top 17 One Hit Wonders of 1974

1. Carl Douglas   Kung Fu Fighting
2. George McCrae   Rock Your Baby
3. Billy Swan   I Can Help
4. Hues Corporation   Rock the Boat
5. M. F. S. B.   T.S.O.P.
6. Brownsville Station   Smokin' In the Boys Room
7. Dave Loggins   Please Come To Boston
8. First Class   Beach Baby
9. Reunion   Life Is a Rock (But the Radio Rolled Me)
10. Mocedades   Erus Tu (Touch the Wind)
11. Fancy   Wild Thing
12. Johnny Bristol   Hang On In There Baby
13. Sister Janet Mead   The Lord's Prayer
14. William De Vaughn   Be Thankful For What You Got
15. Jim Weatherly   The Need To Be
16. Prelude   After The Gold Rush
17. Rubettes   Sugar Baby Love

Top 17 Rock/Hard Rock Hits of 1974

1.	Radar Love	Golden Earring
2.	Can't Get Enough	Bad Company
3.	Smokin' In the Boys Room	Brownsville Station
4.	Yoy Ain't Seen Nothin' Yet	B. T. O.
5.	The Locomotion	Grand Funk
6.	Jet	Paul McCartney & Wings
7.	The Bitch Is Back	Elton John
8.	Takin' Care of Business	B. T. O.
9.	It's Only Rock and Roll (But I like It)	Rolling Stones
10.	Helen Wheels	Paul McCartney & Wings
11.	The Joker	Steve Miller Band
12.	Rock and Roll Hootchie Koo	Rick Derringer
13.	Midnight Rider	Greg Allman
14.	Walk like A Man	Grand Funk
15.	Rock on	David Essex
16.	Sweet Home Alabama	Lynyrd Skynyrd
17.	Shinin' On	Grand Funk

17 Notable 'Lost 45'S' from 1974

1. Life Is A Rock (But the Radio Rolled Me)   Reunion
2. If You Wanna Get To Heaven   Ozark Mountain Daredevils
3. Jim Dandy   Black Oak Arkansas
4. Keep On Smiling   Wet Willie
5. WOLD   Harry Chapin
6. Sugar Baby Love   Rubettes
7. Overnight Sensation   Raspberries
8. Thanks for Saving My Love   Billy Paul
9. You Little Trustmaker   Tymes
10. Wishin' You Were Here   Chicago
11. I've got the Music in Me   Kiki Dee
12. So You Are A Star   Hudson Brothers
13. Who Do You Think You Are   Bo Donaldson & the Heywoods
14. I'm A Train   Albert Hammond
15. I Shall Sing   Art Garfunkel
16. Rings   Lobo
17. Train of Thought   Cher

TOP 17 HITS OF THE 70's

1.	You Light Up My Life	Debby Boone	1977
2.	Night Fever	Bee Gees	1978
3.	Joy to the World	3 Dog Night	1971
4.	Bridge Over Troubled Water	Simon & Garfunkel	1970
5.	Tonight's The Night	Rod Stewart	1976
6.	My Sharona	The Knack	1979
7.	Alone Again Naturally	Gilbert O'Sullivan	1972
8.	Love Will Keep Us Together	Captain & Tennille	1975
9.	Tie A Yellow Ribbon 'Round the Old Oak Tree	Tony Orlando & Dawn	1973
10.	The Way We Were	Barbra Streisand	1974
11.	Shadow Dancing	Andy Gibb	1978
12.	The First Time Ever I Saw Your Face	Roberta Flack	1972
13.	I'll Be There	Jackson 5	1970
14.	My Sweet Lord	George Harrison	1970
15.	It's Too Late	Carole King	1971
16.	American Pie	Don McLean	1972
17.	Maggie May	Rod Stewart	1971

TOP 17 ARTISTS OF THE 70's

1.   Elton John
2.   Paul McCartney
3.   Bee Gees
4.   Jackson 5
5.   Carpenters
6.   Stevie Wonder
7.   Chicago
8.   3 Dog Night
9.   Barry Manilow
10. Olivia Newton-John
11. The Eagles
12. Neil Diamond
13. John Denver
14. Diana Ross
15. Rod Stewart
16. Donna Summer
17. Marvin Gaye

TOP 17 ALBUMS OF THE 70's

1.	Rumours	Fleetwood Mac	1977
2.	Saturday Night Fever	Soundtrack	1978
3.	Tapestry	Carole King	1971

4.	Frampton Comes Alive	Peter Frampton	1976
5.	Captain Fantastic & the Brown Dirt Cowboy	Elton John	1975
6.	American Pie	Don McLean	1972
7.	Bridge Over Troubled Water	Simon & Garfunkel	1970
8.	Goodbye Yellow Brick Road	Elton John	1973
9.	Hotel California	The Eagles	1977
10.	Led Zeppelin 2	Led Zeppelin	1970
11.	Band On The Run	Paul McCartney & Wings	1974
12.	Pearl	Janis Joplin	1971
13.	The Long Run	The Eagles	1979
14.	Songs in the Key Of Life	Stevie Wonder	1976
15.	Physical Graffiti	Led Zeppelin	1975
16.	All Things Must Pass	George Harrison	1971
17.	Cosmo's Factory	C. C. R.	1970

TOP 17 COUNTRY HITS OF THE 70's

1.	Luckenbach, Texas	Waylon Jennings	1977
2.	Rose Garden	Lynn Anderson	1971
3.	My Hang Up Is You	Freddie Hart	1972
4.	Hello Darlin'	Conway Twitty	1970
5.	Kiss an Angel Good Morning	Charley Pride	1971
6.	The Most Beautiful Girl	Charlie Rich	1973
7.	Rhinestone Cowboy	Glen Campbell	1975
8.	Convoy	C.W. McCall	1976
9.	Mammas Don't Let Your Babies …Cowboys	Waylon & Willie	1978
10.	A Very Special Love Song	Charlie Rich	1974
11.	Amanda	Waylon Jennings	1979
12.	It's Just a Matter of Time	Sonny James	1970
13.	Funny Face	Donna Fargo	1972
14.	Easy Loving	Freddie Hart	1971
15.	Here You Come Again	Dolly Parton	1977
16.	Good Hearted Woman	Waylon & Willie	1976
17.	Before The Next Teardrop Falls	Freddie Fender	1975

TOP 17 R & B/SOUL HITS OF THE EARLY 70's
(Excluding Motown)

1.	Let's Stay Together	Al Green	1972
2.	Midnight Train To Georgia	Gladys Knight & Pips	1973
3.	Family Affair	Sly & the Family Stone	1971
4.	I'll Take You There	Staple Singers	1972
5.	Mr. Big Stuff	Jean Knight	1971
6.	I'll Be Around	The Spinners	1972
7.	Thank You (Falettinme Be Mice Elf Agin)	Sly & the Family Stone	1970
8.	Band of Gold	Freda Payne	1970
9.	Love on A Two Way Street	The Moments	1970
10.	Groove Me	King Floyd	1971
11.	Don't Play That Song	Aretha Franklin	1970
12.	Could It Be I'm Falling In Love	The Spinners	1973
13.	Best Thing That Ever Happened To Me	Gladys Knight & Pips	1974
14.	Turn Back the Hands of Time	Tyrone Davis	1970
15.	Love Train	O'Jays	1973
16.	Want Ads	Honeycone	1971
17.	Spanish Harlem	Aretha Franklin	1971

TOP 17 DISCO HITS 1974 – 1979

1.	Night Fever	Bee Gees	1978
2.	Stayin' Alive	Bee Gees	1978
3.	Bad Girls	Donna Summer	1979

4.	Disco Lady	Johnnie Taylor	1976
5.	Le Freak	Chic	1978
6.	I Will Survive	Gloria Gaynor	1979
7.	TSOP	MFSB	1974
8.	Jive Talkin'	Bee Gees	1975
9.	How Deep Is Your Love	Bee Gees	1977
10.	Best Of My Love	The Emotions	1977
11.	Hot Stuff	Donna Summer	1979
12.	5th Of Beethoven	Walter Murphy	1976
13.	Rock Your Baby	George McCrae	1974
14.	Fly Robin Fly	Silver Convention	1975
15.	That's The Way I like It	K.C. & Sunshine Band	1975
16.	You Should Be Dancing	Bee Gees	1976
17.	The Hustle	Van McCoy	1975

TOP 17 MOTOWN HITS OF THE 70's

1.	I'll Be There	Jackson 5	1970
2.	What's Going On	Marvin Gaye	1971
3.	Superstition	Stevie Wonder	1973
4.	Let's Get It On	Marvin Gaye	1973
5.	Love Hangover	Diana Ross	1976
6.	Sir Duke	Stevie Wonder	1977
7.	The Love You Save	Jackson 5	1970
8.	Dancing Machine	Jackson 5	1974
9.	I Wish	Stevie Wonder	1977
10.	Got To Give It Up	Marvin Gaye	1977
11.	I Want You Back	Jackson 5	1970
12.	Signed, Sealed, Delivered, I'm Yours	Stevie Wonder	1970
13.	Keep On Truckin'	Eddie Kendricks	1973
14.	The Tears of A Clown	S. Robinson & Miracles	1970
15.	3 Times A Lady	Commodores	1978
16.	Just My Imagination	Temptations	1971
17.	Don't Leave Me This Way	Thelma Houston	1977

TOP 17 NOVELTY HITS OF THE 70's

1.	The Streak	Ray Stevens	1974
2.	Disco Duck	Rick Dees	1976
3.	Kung Fu Fighting	Carl Douglas	1974
4.	The Candy Man	Sammy Davis Jr.	1972
5.	Convoy	C.W. McCall	1976
6.	My Ding A Ling	Chuck Berry	1972
7.	Troglodyte (Caveman)	Jimmy Castor Bunch	1972
8.	Monster Mash	Bobby 'Boris' Pickett	62/73
9.	Popcorn	Hot Butter	1972
10.	Spiders & Snakes	Jim Stafford	1974
11.	Chick A Boom	Daddy Dewdrop	1971
12.	Short People	Randy Newman	1978
13.	Cover Of the Rolling Stone	Dr. Hook	1973
14.	Gimme Dat Ding	Pipkins	1970
15.	Mr. Jaws	Dickie Goodman	1975
16.	Dead Skunk	Loudon Wainwright 3rd	1973
17.	Run Joey Run	David Geddes	1975

TOP 17 ONE HIT WONDERS OF THE 70's

1.	Debby Boone	You Light Up My Life	1977
2.	Starland Vocal Band	Afternoon Delight	1976
3.	Shocking Blue	Venus	1970
4.	Vicki Lawrence	Night the Lights...Geor.	1973

5.	Carl Douglas	Kung Fu Fighting	1974
6.	Billy Paul	Me and Mrs. Jones	1972
7.	M	Pop Muzik	1979
8.	Stories	Brother Louie	1973
9.	Wild Cherry	Play That Funky Music	1976
10.	Jean Knight	Mr. Big Stuff	1971
11.	Minnie Ripperton	Lovin' You	1975
12.	George McCrae	Rock Your Baby	1974
13.	Meco	Star Wars	1977
14.	Anita Ward	Ring My Bell	1979
15.	Undisputed Truth	Smiling Faces Sometimes	1971
16.	Eddie Holman	Hey There Lonely Girl	1970
17.	Billy Swan	I Can Help	1974

TOP 17 ROCK/HARD ROCK HITS OF THE 70's

1.	Whole Lotta Love	Led Zeppelin	1970
2.	Brown Sugar	Rolling Stones	1971
3.	Bohemian Rhapsody	Queen	1976
4.	School's Out	Alice Cooper	1972
5.	We're An American Band	Grand Funk	1973
6.	Radar Love	Golden Earring	1974
7.	Fame	David Bowie	1975
8.	Frankenstein	Edgar Winter Group	1973
9.	My Sharona	The Knack	1979
10.	Immigrant Song	Led Zeppelin	1971
11.	Layla	Derek & the Dominos	1972
12.	American Woman	Guess Who	1970
13.	Won't Get Fooled Again	Who	1971
14.	All Right Now	Free	1970
15.	Smoke on the Water	Deep Purple	1973
16.	Blinded by the Light	Manfred Mann's E.B.	1977
17.	Miss You	Rolling Stones	1978

TOP 17 FEMALE ARTISTS OF THE 70's

1.	Olivia Newton-John
2.	Diana Ross
3.	Donna Summer
4.	Barbra Streisand
5.	Linda Ronstadt
6.	Aretha Franklin
7.	Cher
8.	Roberta Flack
9.	Helen Reddy
10.	Anne Murray
11.	Carly Simon
12.	Gladys Knight
13.	Carole King
14.	Dionne Warwick
15.	Natalie Cole
16.	Marie Osmond
17.	Rita Collidge

TOP 17 MALE ARTISTS OF THE 70's

1.	Elton John
2.	Paul McCartney
3.	Stevie Wonder

4.	Barry Manilow
5.	Neil Diamond
6.	John Denver
7.	Rod Stewart
8.	Marvin Gaye
9.	Ringo Starr
10.	James Taylor
11.	Barry White
12.	Jim Croce
13.	Donny Osmond
14.	Kenny Rogers
15.	Paul Simon
16.	Al Green
17.	Cat Stevens

TOP 17 DUOS OF THE 70's

1.	The Carpenters
2.	The Captain and Tennille
3.	Hall and Oates
4.	Simon and Garfunkel
5.	Seals and Crofts
6.	Loggins and Messina
7.	England Dan and John Ford Coley
8.	Sonny and Cher
9.	Ike and Tina Turner
10.	Donny and Marie Osmond
11.	The Poppy Family
12.	Waylon and Willie
13.	Peaches and Herb
14.	John Travolta and Olivia Newton-John
15.	Marilyn McCoo and Billy Davis Jr.
16.	Roberta Flack and Donny Hathaway
17.	James Taylor and Carly Simon

TOP 17 MOVIE HITS OF THE 70's

1.	The Way We Were	Barbra Streisand	1974
2.	Raindrops Keep Fallin' On My Head	B. J. Thomas	1970
3.	Theme from Shaft	Isaac Hayes	1971
4.	Grease	Frankie Valli	1978
5.	Stayin' Alive	Bee Gees	1978
6.	A Star Is Born (Evergreen)	Barbra Streisand	s1977
7.	The Candy Man	Sammy Davis Jr.	1972
8.	The Morning After	Maureen McGovern	1973
9.	Car Wash	Rose Royce	1977
10.	Nobody Does It Better	Carly Simon	1977
11.	The Entertainer	Marvin Hamlisch	1974
12.	Do You Know Where You're Going (Mahogany)	Diana Ross	1976
13.	Ben	Michael Jackson	1972
14.	Gonna Fly Now (Theme from Rocky)	Bill Conti	1977
15.	Dueling Banjos	Eric Weissberg/S.Mand.	1973
16.	Theme from Love Story	Henry Mancini	1971
17.	Come and Get It	Badfinger	1970

TOP 17 INSTRUMENTAL HITS OF THE 70'S

1.	Star Wars	Meco	1977
2.	5th of Beethoven	Walter Murphy	1976
3.	Rise	Herb Alpert	1979
4.	Love's Theme	Love Unlimited Orch.	1974
5.	Frankenstein	Edgar Winter Group	1973

6.	Pick Up the Pieces	Average White Band	1975
7.	Feels So Good	Chuck Mangione	1978
8.	Outa Space	Billy Preston	1972
9.	Theme from S.W.A.T.	Rhythm Heritage	1976
10.	Also Sprach Zarathustra (2001)	Deodato	1973
11.	Dueling Banjos	Eric Weissberg & S.Ma.	1973
12.	The Entertainer	Marvin Hamlisch	1974
13.	Music Box Dancer	Frank Mills	1979
14.	Joy	Apollo 100	1972
15.	Popcorn	Hot Butter	1972
16.	Scorpio	Dennis Coffey	1971
17.	Amazing Grace	Royal Scots Dragoon	1972

TOP 17 BUBBLEGUM HITS OF THE 70's

1.	I Think I Love You	Partridge Family	1970
2.	Billy, Don't Be A Hero	Bo Donaldson & Heyw.	1974
3.	Saturday Night	Bay City Rollers	1975
4.	ABC	Jackson 5	1970
5.	Brand New Key	Melanie	1972
6.	One Bad Apple	Osmonds	1971
7.	Puppy Love	Donny Osmond	1972
8.	The Love You Save	Jackson 5	1970
9.	Da Do Ron Ron	Shawn Cassidy	1977
10.	Yo Yo	Osmonds	1971
11.	Heartbeat it's A Love beat	Defranco Family	1973
12.	Easy Come Easy Go	Bobby Sherman	1970
13.	That's Rock and Roll	Shawn Cassidy	1977
14.	Hot Line	Sylvers	1977
15.	Hey Deanie	Shawn Cassidy	1978
16.	Jingle Jangle	Archies	1970
17.	My Baby Loves Lovin'	White Plains	1970

♪ In his comeback year, Neil Sedaka had 3 number one hits, including one he co wrote which launched the career of the Captain and Tennille.

♪ This number one American hit was produced by George Martin, the genius who gave the Beatles their sound.

♪ This number one David Bowie hit was co written by John Lennon, who also sang on this recording.

♪ The Bee Gees were inspired to write this number one hit by the sound their car tires made driving over the bridge on the way to their recording studio everyday.

♪ The title of this girl's name song was changed to avoid confusion with another song with the same title.

♪ This offbeat Ringo Starr hit was written by the same guy who gave 3 Dog Night their biggest hit 4 years earlier.

FIND OUT THAT...AND MUCH MORE INSIDE...1975!

1. Love Will Keep Us Together by the Captain and Tennille was the first and biggest hit for this husband and wife musical couple. The Captain was keyboardist Daryl Dragon and his wife Toni Tennille was the voice of the group on all of their hits. This multi week number one hit was written by Neil Sedaka and Howard Greenfield and was featured on the 'Sedaka's Back's album. Toni Tennille can be heard singing 'Sedaka is Back' as the song is fading at the end.

2. Jive Talkin' by the Bee Gees was a comeback hit for the brothers Gibb and their first of many disco-flavored hits. This prime cut from their 'Main Course' album was recorded at Criteria studios in Miami. The song 'Jive Talkin'' was inspired by their nightly drive over the Sunny Isles Bridge as the tires of their car made a 'chunka chunka' sound crossing some railroad tracks. One night Barry Gibbs' wife Linda, turned to her husband and said 'Hey listen to that sound, it's our drive talking.' Barry looked at her and started singing what evolved into their next number one hit.

3. Philadelphia Freedom by Elton John was written for Billie Jean King, who was the player/coach of the World Team Tennis League in Philadelphia known as the Freedoms. Elton John was one of her biggest fans. The 'B' side of this single was a 'live' duet with John Lennon of the Beatles song 'I Saw Her Standing There'.

4. Island Girl by Elton John was his 4th major hit single of 1975, and the biggest hit from his 2nd major album of the year. This number one hit replaced 'Bad Blood' at the top spot by Neil Sedaka, which of course featured Elton on accompanying vocals. 'Island Girl' from the album 'Rock of the Westies' was a song about a prostitute and a man who wants to take her back to Jamaica. This album also featured Elton John's new back up band which replaced Nigel Olsson on drums and Dee Murray on bass guitar.

5. Bad Blood by Neil Sedaka featured backing vocals by Elton John. He brought Sedaka back and signed him to his own 'Rocket Records' label in 1974. It's interesting to note that this song was knocked out of the number one spot on the charts by Elton John's own 'Island Girl.'

6. Fame by David Bowie was co-written by John Lennon, who could be heard singing near the end of this number one hit. David Bowie was born David Robert Jones on Elvis Presley's 12th birthday on January 8th 1947 in the Brixton section of London, England. Fame came his way in the early 70's and after this disco tinged song became a hit, he was invited to sing the song on the 'Soul Train' television show.

7. Rhinestone Cowboy by Glen Campbell was the first official number one hit for the pop country singer who was previously known as one of the members of 'the Wrecking Crew', the top session musicians during the 60's and early 70's who played on hundreds of hits. 'Rhinestone Cowboy' was produced by the popular team Lambert and Potter and written by the relatively unknown Larry Weiss.

8. Fly Robin Fly by the Silver Convention was the first and biggest hit for this German studio disco act which became a real group of singers after this multi million seller. This song was originally to be called 'Run Rabbit Run', but was changed at the last minute to 'Fly Robin Fly' when co writer Silvester Levay heard a song called 'Run Rabbit' on Armed Forces radio just before the song was to be recorded.

9. Lucy in the Sky with Diamonds by Elton John featured background vocals and guitar by John Lennon under the name of 'Dr. Winston's O'Boogie'. This song was originally recorded by the Beatles on their 1967 masterpiece 'Sgt. Pepper's Lonely Hearts Club Band' album. It's interesting to note that in 1975, Elton John played a 2-day spectacular concert at Dodger Stadium in Los Angeles, the first time that venue had allowed concerts since outlawing rock shows after the Beatles played there in 1966.

10.   Laughter in the Rain by Neil Sedaka became his first number one hit since 'Breaking up Is Hard to Do' 13 years earlier in 1962 and his first top 40 hit in a dozen years. This was the first single from his great comeback album 'Sedaka's Back' which included backing vocals by all 4 members of the group 10 C.C.

11.He Don't Love You (Like I Love You) by Tony Orlando and Dawn was a remake of the Jerry Butler 1960 hit 'He Will Only Break Your Heart' written by Butler, Clarence Carter and Curtis Mayfield. They changed the title of the song, and in the spring of 1975, it became Tony Orlando and Dawn's 3rd and final number one hit. This hit was popular when their TV music/variety show was in the middle of its 3 year run in prime time.

12.   My Eyes Adored You by Frankie Valli was the first major solo hit for the lead singer of the Four Seasons since 1967's 'Can't Take My Eyes off You'. Producer Bob Crewe and co writer Kenny Nolan originally titled this song 'Blue Eyes in Georgia', but changed it for Frankie Valli to 'My Eyes Adored You'. Kenny Nolan co wrote 2 other major hits in 1975, 'Lady Marmalade' and 'Get Dancin'. He also had hits of his own in the late 70's with 'I Like Dreaming' and 'Love's Grown Deep'.

13.   Saturday Night by The Bay City Rollers was the breakthrough hit in North America for the Scottish group that caused hysteria and excitement

196

in the United Kingdom not seen since the Beatles arrived on the scene over a dozen years earlier. This tartan-clad teenybopper group had already had major success in Britain before 'Saturday Night' arrived. They got their name from sticking a pin in a map. It landed on Bay City, Michigan, and they decided that the Bay City Rollers sounded like a good name for the group.

14.   **Best of My Love** by the Eagles was the first of 2 official number one hits for this Los Angeles based rock country group in 1975. This hit from the 'On the Border' album was written by Glenn Frey, J.D. Souther and Don Henley who provided lead vocals on this love ballad.

15.   **That's the Way I like It** by K. C. & the Sunshine Band was the 2nd number one hit for this Florida-based pop/disco band in their debut year. Lead singer and co writer K.C. originally used moaning and groaning where the 'ah-ha ah-has' were, but he thought it would be a little too risqué for the public.

16.   **Thank God I'm a Country Boy** by John Denver was originally a studio recording from the 1974 'Back Home Again' album. However, when he performed it in concert, the response was so great, he decided to re-release it as a 'live' recording from a concert at the Universal City Amphitheatre in California. It became his 3rd of 4 number one hits

17.**One of These Nights** by the Eagles was a more aggressive sounding rock song than their previous number one hit 'Best of My Love'. The title track of their album 'One Of These Nights' was written by Glenn Frey and Don Henley, with Henley and Randy Meisner sharing lead vocals. 1975 was the year guitarist Bernie Leadon left the group and Don Felder and Joe Walsh joined.

18.   **The Hustle** by Van McCoy was written before he even saw the dance at a disco. It became a number one, multi million seller and Grammy Award winning 'Best Pop Instrumental' of 1975. Van McCoy previously wrote 'Baby I'm Yours', which was a substantial hit for Barbara Lewis in 1965. Sadly, Van McCoy died in 1979 of a heart attack at the young age of 39.

19.   **Before the Next Teardrop Falls** by Freddy Fender was the claim to fame for this unique-voiced Texas singer. The song was written in the 60's, but revived when producer Huey P. Meaux had Tex-Mex singer Freddy Fender record the song in half English and half Spanish with his fluttering tenor voice. The song topped both the pop and country charts and was named the Single of the Year by the Country Music Association for 1975.

20.   **Lady Marmalade** by Labelle was produced by the legendary Allen Toussaint and written by Bob Crewe and Kenny Nolan. When Patti Labelle first heard the lyrics 'Voulez-vous couches avec mo ice soir' she had no idea what it meant. She didn't realize at first that it was a song about a hooker and the line meant 'will you sleep with me tonight?' She did know that it sounded like a hit, and she was right when it went all the way to number one.

21.   **Listen to What the Man Said** by Wings was written and produced by Paul McCartney and released 2 weeks before the album 'Venus and Mars' hit the store shelves. This happy go lucky hit recorded in New Orleans featured guest musicians Tom Scott on saxophone and Dave Mason on guitar.

22. **Lovin' You** by Minnie Ripperton was produced by her friend Stevie Wonder, whom she toured with and backed, in his group Wonderlove. The lady with the voice of an angel died of cancer in 1979. She was just 31 years old.

23. **Mandy** by Barry Manilow was a remake of the song 'Brandy' which Scott English had a moderate hit with in 1972. This became Barry Manilow's very first hit, thanks to Clive Davis who suggested he record it and release it as a single. Most of Manilow's hits were produced by Ron Dante who was the voice of the Archies on the multi million seller 'Sugar Sugar' in 1969.

24. **Shining Star** by Earth, Wind & Fire was a million selling funk/R & B single produced and co written by group leader and founder Maurice White. This hit from their album 'That's The Way of the World' won Earth, Wind and Fire a Grammy Award for Best R & B Performance by a Duo or Group.

25. **(Hey Won't You Play) Another Somebody Done Somebody Wrong Song** by B. J. Thomas is one of the longest titles for a song that reached number one. In his autobiography, B. J. admits to barely remembering recording this hit because he was spending upwards of $3,000. a day to feed a drug habit. After hitting rock bottom, he turned his life around in 1976 and began a drug-free life. His gospel music career began in 1977.

26. **Black Water** by The Doobie Brothers featured a great a cappella section where producer Ted Templeman pulled the music track out. He got the idea when he was the lead singer of Harper's Bizarre back in the late 60's when it was used in the hit '59th Street Bridge Song (Feelin' Groovy).Originally this song was on the 'B' side of the single 'Another Park, another Sunday' but was flipped over when it started getting airplay on radio stations in the South. The song became the Doobie Brothers first official number one hit.

27. **Fallin' in Love** by Hamilton, Joe Frank & Reynolds was the biggest hit from the group known for their million seller 'Don't Pull Your Love' in 1971. They were previously known as the T-Bones on the top 10 1966 instrumental 'No Matter What Shape Your Stomach's in' which was a commercial for Alka Seltzer. Even though (Tommy) Reynolds left the group in 1972, the group decided to keep the name the same for this ballad written by Dan Hamilton and his then-wife Ann.

28. **Please Mr. Postman** by the Carpenters was a remake of the Marvelettes' number one hit from 1961.The inspiration to redo an oldie came after critics heard the oldies but goodies featured in a medley on their 'Now and Then' album and suggested Karen's voice was so well-suited to the pop songs that she should consider doing it more often. The advice was taken and the result was their 3rd number one hit.

29. **Pick Up the Pieces** by the Average White Band was a hugely successful soul and funk instrumental hit for this Scottish band. Drummer Robbie McIntosh died suddenly of drug poisoning a few months before this single and AWB album topped the charts.

30. **Have You Never Been Mellow** by Olivia Newton – John was the 2nd consecutive number one hit for the singer who was now doing well on both the

pop and country charts. After being voted by the Country Music Association as the 1974 Female Vocalist of the Year, many members were so angry that they left the CMA to form the Association of Country Entertainers.

31.   Let's Do It Again by the Staple Singers was written and produced by Curtis Mayfield for the movie of the same name starring Sidney Poitier and Bill Cosby. For the Staple Singers, it was their 2nd number one hit following 'I'll Take You There' in 1972.

32.   I'm Sorry by John Denver was a number one hit on the pop, country and Adult Contemporary charts. John Denver was at his peak in popularity in 1975 with 5 major hit singles and 2 hit albums.

33.   Get Down Tonight by K. C. & the Sunshine Band was the first of a string of pop disco hits for this Florida- based goodtime group. Many were surprised to learn that the lead singer, Casey, (who took the nickname K.C.) was white. He and Richard Finch were generally the only members of this group which numbered almost a dozen, who were not black. They also wrote and produced all of their hits and did the same the previous year for George McCrae on his number one hit 'Rock Your Baby'.

34.   Sister Golden Hair by America was produced by George Martin and featured Gerry Beckley, who also wrote the song, on lead vocals. All but their debut album titled 'America' in their first 7 albums began with the letter 'H'. This number one hit was taken from their 'Hearts' album.

35.   You're No Good by Linda Ronstadt was a remake of the 1964 Betty Everett hit. Andrew Gold, who was also the arranger of this hit, was featured on piano. This number one hit was her first top 40 hit in 5 years and the beginning of a long string of successful singles and albums.

36.Fire by the Ohio Players was their hottest hit in more ways than one topping both the pop and R & B charts and the album of the same name was certified gold 2 weeks after its release. All the members of this 7 piece band contributed to each song they recorded and 'Fire' was no exception. The cover of the album revealed a gorgeous model wearing nothing much but a fireman's helmet.

37.   I'm Not In Love by 10 C. C. was the first major hit in North America for the British group that evolved from 'Hotlegs', best known for their unusual hit 'Neanderthal Man'. Before that, Eric Stewart and Graham Gouldman were members of the 60's group the Mindbenders. 'I'm Not in Love' was a superbly-produced multi-layered hit which was innovative and original in its sound.

38.   Lyin' Eyes by the Eagles was the 2nd hit from the 'One of These Nights' album and featured Glenn Frey on lead vocals on this song about secret love. This pop country hit which was written by Glenn Frey and Don Henley won the Grammy Award for Best Pop Performance by a Group and was also nominated for Record of the Year. The single version was just under 4 minutes long while the album version was over 6 minutes.

39.   Wildfire by Michael Murphey was written back in 1968 with Larry Cansler, but didn't become a hit until it was featured on the album 'Blue Sky

Night Thunder' in 1975. Michael Martin Murphey previously went by the name Travis Lewis as a member of the duo 'Lewis and Clarke Expedition', known for their 1967 hit 'I Feel Good (I Feel Bad').

40.   Please Mr. Please by Olivia Newton – John was written by Bruce Welch and John Rostill, who were members of Cliff Richard's backing band, the Shadows. This hit was her final top 10 pop hit until her string of 3 major hit singles from 'Grease' arrived 3 years later in 1978.

41.   When Will I Be Loved by Linda Ronstadt was originally a hit for the Everly Brothers in 1960. This was one of the prime cuts from her double platinum album, 'Heart like a Wheel', produced by Peter Asher of the 60's duo Peter and Gordon. It's interesting to note that Linda Ronstadt had more recycled hits in the 70's than any other pop/rock artist with songs which included 'Heat wave', 'That'll Be The Day', 'Blue Bayou', 'It's So Easy' and 'Tracks Of My Tears' and others.

42.   Calypso by John Denver was dedicated to his friend Jacques Cousteau and his research ship bearing this name. This song was the hit 'B' side of his number one hit 'I'm Sorry', also from the 'Windsong' album.

43.   Skyhigh by Jigsaw was the highest charting hit for this quintet from England and was featured in the film 'The Man from Hong Kong' starring George Lazenby. Lead vocalist Des Dyer and keyboardist Clive Scott wrote this song, as well as Bo Donaldson and The Heywood's hit 'Who Do You Think You Are', which was popular in 1974.

44.   Jackie Blue by the Ozark Mountain Daredevils was the bigger of the 2 hits from this Southern Rock band from Springfield, Missouri. The song was sung by the group's drummer Larry Lee and was co written, with Steve Cash after they met a girl in Los Angeles who was strung out on drugs.

45.   Someone Saved My Life Tonight by Elton John was the only single from the legendary album 'Captain Fantastic and The Brown Dirt Cowboy' the first LP to debut on Billboard's album chart at number one. This song is about Elton's personal struggles at a time when he was considering marrying his girlfriend Linda Woodrow and at the same time contemplating suicide.

46.The Way I Want to Touch You by the Captain & Tennille was written by Toni Tennille as a way of expressing her love for the man who would become her husband, Daryl Dragon, known to many as 'the Captain'. This song was originally released before their first hit 'Love Will Keep Us Together' but was re-released after the huge success of what became the number one song of the entire year. Daryl Dragon got his nickname 'the Captain' from the Beach Boys' Mike Love from the cap he wore on stage touring with the Beach Boys in the early 70's.

47.   Who Loves You by the Four Seasons featuring Frankie Valli was the first top 10 hit in 8 years for this popular group from New Jersey. This disco-flavored hit was produced by former Four Season member and keyboardist Bob Gaudio, who co-wrote this hit with his wife Judy Parker. Although the group had an all new lineup with the exception of original Four Season Frankie Valli, this was their first recording on the Warner Brothers label.

48.   Magic by Pilot was produced by Alan Parsons and 2 thirds of this Scottish trio became members of the Alan Parsons Project. They took their name 'Pilot' from the initial letters of each surname, Paton, Lyall, and Tosh. Lead singer/keyboardist Bill Lyall died from AIDS related causes in 1989.

49.   Chevy Van by Sammy Johns was the only hit for this Charlotte, North Carolina singer/songwriter. Sammy Johns took advantage of the 70's van craze and wrote a song about a sweet young lady and some lovin' in his Chevy Van, when full size was the only option.

50.   At Seventeen by Janis Ian was inspired by an article in a New York Times magazine entitled 'I Learned the Truth at Eighteen'. Janis Ian changed the 18 to 17 and over 3 months wrote the thought provoking song about rejection and letdowns. This was Janis Ian's biggest hit and was popular 8 years after her social comment hit 'Society's Child' from 1967 which she wrote when she was just 14 years old.

51.   Boogie on Reggae Woman by Stevie Wonder was a more carefree, upbeat hit with some naughty lyrics and was the 2nd hit single from his 'Fulfillingness' First Finale' album. This funk hit was also produced and written by Wonder, who won 3 Grammy Awards that year including 'Album of the Year' for 'Fulfillingness' First Finale'.

52.   Some Kind Of Wonderful by Grand Funk was a remake of a 1967 soul hit by the Soul Brothers Six featuring John Ellison. This was the first of 2 major 1975 hits from their album 'All the Girls in the World Beware' produced by Jimmy Ienner.

53.   Miracles by Jefferson Starship was the first top 10 hit for this San Francisco band since 1967 when they were known as 'Jefferson Airplane' and 'White Rabbit' was a hit. 'Miracles' featured founding member Marty Balin on lead vocals on this top 5 hit from the 'Red Octopus' album. He had just rejoined the group after leaving in 1971. Key members Grace Slick and Paul Kantner continued to be part of the success under the new group name.

54.   How Long by Ace was the only hit for this British group, although lead singer Paul Carrack was a prominent member of the group 'Squeeze' in the early 80's and the lead voice of Mike and the Mechanics on their major hits including 'The Living Years' in 1989.

55.   No No Song by Ringo Starr was written by Hoyt Axton, who wrote 'Joy to the World' and 'Never Been to Spain' for 3 Dog Night. This top 10 hit for Ringo, which featured backing vocals by Harry Nilsson, was featured on his 'Goodnight Vienna' album. The 'B' side of 'No No Song' was 'Snookeroo' which featured Elton John on piano and Robbie Robertson of the Band on guitar.

56.   I'm Not Lisa by Jessi Colter was the only pop hit for this country singer who was once married to Duane Eddy and Waylon Jennings. Jessi Colter, whose real name is Miriam Johnson wrote this hit which topped the country charts and reached top 5 on the pop charts in the early summer of 1975.

57.Bad Time by Grand Funk was their 2nd major hit in 1975 following 'Some Kind Of Wonderful'. This easy going Mark Farner composition which featured an a cappela opening, became Grand Funk's final top 40 hit. 'Bad Time' was a prime cut from the album 'All The Girls In The World Beware' which featured on its cover, 4 top body builders, including their friend Arnold Schwarzenegger with the band's members faces overlaid onto their muscled bodies.

58.   Fight The Power by the Isley Brothers was a funk protest song which included the controversial lyrics '…all this bullshit going down' which didn't prevent it from reaching number one on the R & B charts and top 5 on the pop charts. Ernie Isley originally wrote the word 'nonsense', but lead singer Ronald changed it to 'bullshit'. This hit included 5 Isleys, including new recruit baby brother Marvin Isley. This single was from their number one album 'The Heat Is On'.

59.   (They Just Can't Stop It) Games People Play by the Spinners gave all 5 members a turn singing lead on this number one hit on the R & B charts. The song was released first as 'Games people Play', but underwent a title change when the staffers at the performing rights society BMI suggested royalties of the song might get mixed up with those of 'Games People Play' by Joe South, a top 10 hit in 1969.

60.   Feelings by Morris Albert was the only North American hit for this singer songwriter from Brazil. In 1975 he was nominated for the Best New Artist Grammy Award but lost to Natalie Cole.

61.   Express by B.T. Express was a pure disco hit perfect for the dance floor with repetitive lines, sax, horns a great bass line and even a string arrangement with violins. This million selling hit follow up to 'Do It (Til You're Satisfied)', was their only other major hit.

62.   Run Joey Run by David Geddes reached the top 5 with this hit in the summer of 1975. The novelty hit 'Run Joey Run' was produced and co-written by Paul Vance who is best known for his compositions 'Itsy Bitsy Teenie Weenie Yellow Polka Dot Bikini', 'Tracy' and 'Playground In My Mind.' Geddes was a 2 hit wonder who dropped out of law school once this hit began racing up the charts. His only other hit was 'The Last Game of the Season (A Blind Man in the Bleachers), also from 1975.

63.   Ballroom Blitz by the Sweet was a Chinn/Chapman composition and production for this British glam-rock band which featured Brian Connolly on lead vocals. This top 5 rockin' hit was inspired by an incident in 1973 when the band was performing at the Grand Hall in Kilmarnock in Scotland and was driven off stage by members of the crowd who got out of hand. This hit was featured on the 'Desolation Boulevard' album in North America, but not in Britain.

64.   Only Yesterday by the Carpenters was produced and co-written by Karen's brother Richard Carpenter, who was now taking a more active role in writing, producing and arranging their hits. This was the 2nd of 3 hit singles from their 'Horizon' album and popular in 1975 when lead singer Karen collapsed on stage during a performance in Las Vegas. This was the first sign that she was suffering from anorexia nervosa, an eating disorder that would eventually take her life 8 years later.

65.   **Love Won't Let Me Wait** by Major Harris was written in about 20 minutes at 3 o'clock in the morning at songwriter Bobby Eli's apartment with Gwen Barrett, under the name Vinnie Barrett. Soul singer Major Harris, who was once a member of the Delfonics, recorded this with the lights in the studio dimmed for the right atmosphere and singer Barbara Ingram did the moans to add to the sexiness of the song.

66.   **Old Days** by Chicago was written by the group's trombonist about his childhood. Peter Cetera sang lead on this uplifting nostalgic hit from their album 'Chicago 8'. Their hits were produced by James William Guercio who previously produced hits for the brass rock bands the Buckinghams and Blood, Sweat and Tears.

67.   **You Are So Beautiful** by Joe Cocker was co-written and originally recorded by Billy Preston. This hit by Joe Cocker became his biggest until the release of 'Up Where We Belong' in 1982. This top 5 1975 hit was from Cocker's album 'I Can Stand The Rain' which included musical guests Randy Newman, Ray Parker Jr. along with Jeff Porcaro and David Paich of Toto fame.

68.   **Why Can't We Be Friends** by War repeated the title over 40 times in less than 4 minutes in this repetitious, but infectious fun song with a great beat. The same year this was a hit, it was played in space when NASA beamed it to the linking of Soviet Cosmonauts and U.S astronauts. This million selling hit has also been used in about a dozen films through the years.

69.   **How Sweet It Is (To Be Loved By You)** by James Taylor was a remake of the 1965 Motown hit by Marvin Gaye. David Sanborn played sax and Carly Simon sang backup on this prime cut from his 6th album, 'Gorilla' which also included his single 'Mexico'.

70.   **Heatwave** by Linda Ronstadt was a rockin' remake of the Martha and the Vandellas' classic Motown hit from 1963. This hit was produced by Peter Asher and Andrew Gold and taken from her album' Prisoner Of Love', the follow up to 'Heart Like A Wheel'. 'Heatwave' was the 3rd of 7 consecutive hits which were remakes for this versatile singer from Tucson, Arizona.

71.   **Dance with Me** by Orleans was the first hit for this group from New York founded by John Hall. He later entered politics and became a member of the U.S House Of Representatives from New York's 19th District. In November of 2008, he was re elected.

72.   **Lonely People** by America was written by Dan Peek, who also sang lead on this hit from their 'Holiday' album, which also included 'Tin Man'. Dan Peek left the group in 1977 shortly after the release of their 'Harbor' album to pursue a Christian music career.

73.   **Mr. Jaws** by Dickie Goodman was a million selling top 10 novelty hit which featured bits of hits interwoven with spoken word, resulting in a very humorous hit. Dickie Goodman with his partner Bill Buchanan had their first big hit with this formula in 1956 with 'The Flying Saucer'. Dickie Goodman died of a self-inflicted gunshot wound in 1989.

74.   Midnight Blue by Melissa Manchester was actually written for Dionne Warwick, but she didn't respond to the demo. Melissa Manchester wrote this song with Carole Bayer Sager who co wrote hits which included 'A Groovy Kind Of Love' and 'When I Need You'. This song became Melissa Manchester's claim to fame.

75.   Walkin' In Rhythm by the Blackbyrds were formed by Donald Byrd who taught music at several Universities including Howard University in Washington where he formed this group featuring some of his best students. Donald Byrd produced this hit from their album 'Flying Start' recorded on the Fantasy record label in the Sound Factory studios in Los Angeles, California. This was their only top 10 hit.

76.   Don't Call Us, We'll Call You by Sugarloaf features a bit of the Beatles guitar riff 'I Feel Fine' after Jerry Corbetta sings 'sounds like John, Paul and George'. They took the name Sugarloaf after a mountain outside of Boulder, Colorado, where they got their first recording contract. Their first and only other hit was 'Green Eyed Lady' from 1970.

77.   Poetry Man by Phoebe Snow was the only top 10 hit from this singer with a unique voice who born in New York City and raised in New Jersey. Her debut and only major hit 'Poetry Man' earned her a 1975 Grammy Award nomination for Best New Artist which was won by Marvin Hamlisch. In 2008, Phoebe Snow performed at Howard Stern's wedding.

78.   Lady by Styx was the song that launched the career of this Chicago-based rock group. This power ballad was written by lead singer Dennis DeYoung for his wife. After their debut hit on the 'Wooden Nickel' label, they signed with A & M records where they would have all their hits that followed. Guitarist Tommy Shaw joined the group the following year in 1976.

79.   This Will Be by Natalie Cole was the first hit for the daughter of the legendary singer Nat 'King' Cole. Natalie has certainly had her personal ups and downs through the years with drug addiction, failed marriages and kidney disease. She received a kidney transplant in June of 2009 and resumed touring immediately afterwards. Her first hit 'This Will Be' was co-written and co-produced by Marvin Yancy whom she married the following year and divorced in 1980.

80.   Could It Be Magic by Barry Manilow was the 3rd hit for the singer/songwriter who sang jingles for Dr. Pepper, Pepsi and the famous 'you deserve a break today' for McDonald's before becoming a successful pop music star. 'Could It Be Magic' was inspired by Chopin's 'Prelude in C Minor'. This hit was originally included on his 1973 debut album, 'Barry Manilow 1', but didn't become a hit until 2 years later in 1975.

81.   Low Rider by War was one of the greatest cruisin' hits of the 70's and the follow up to their other 1975 hit 'Why Can't We Be Friends'. A low rider is a modified car with hydraulic lifts that allow the driver to lower each wheel and make the car bounce. This was the 5th top 10 hit for War and 6th if you count the song 'Spill the Wine' when they were fronted by Eric Burdon, formerly of the Animals.

82.   Swearin' to God by Frankie Valli was another Bob Crewe production and a disco influenced follow up to his number one ballad 'My Eyes Adored You'. 1975 was the comeback year for both Frankie Valli the solo singer, as well as the Four Seasons with Frankie. When 'Swearin' to God' left the charts, the Four Seasons began riding up the charts with 'Who Loves You'.

83.   Nights on Broadway by the Bee Gees was the follow up to their number one single 'Jive Talkin', also from the 'Main Course' album. Barry Gibb's falsetto voice was featured in this hit which led the way to a very successful career during the disco era.

84.Wasted Days & Wasted Nights by Freddy Fender was a song he originally recorded and co wrote back in 1959. His music career was stalled the following year, in 1960, when he was arrested for possession of marijuana resulting in time in prison. After the huge success of 'Before the Next Teardrop Falls', he re recorded it and it became his 2nd consecutive million selling single. The singer born Baldemar Huerta died of lung cancer in 2006 at the age of 69.

85.   One Man Woman (One Woman Man) by Paul Anka & Odia Coates was the follow up to the number one million selling 'You're Having My Baby'. Paul Anka's career spans 6 decades of singing and songwriting and in 2009, a song he co-wrote in 1983 with Michael Jackson resurfaced as 'This Is It'.

86.   Rocky by Austin Roberts was a story song with a sad ending from the singer who co-wrote and produced music for the 70's cartoons 'Scooby Doo' and 'Josie and the Pussycats'. Before his first solo hit 'Something's Wrong with Me' in 1972, Austin Roberts was a member of the group 'Arcade'. He later co –wrote several country hits including I.O.U. for Lee Greenwood.

87.   Never Can Say Goodbye by Gloria Gaynor was a disco remake of the Jackson Five hit popular in 1971.This was the title song of her debut album which featured 'Never Can Say Goodbye' in an extended mega mix with 3 other disco songs in a non stop 19 minute suite.

88.   Emma by Hot Chocolate was the first hit in North America for this British interracial rock/soul group featuring lead singer and songwriter Errol Brown. 'Emma' was a deep and dark song about a girl who could not find happiness with love and goals of becoming a movie star and would commit suicide. Mickie Most produced all of Hot Chocolate's hits during the 70's.

89.Morning Side of the Mountain by Donny & Marie Osmond was a remake of a song originally popular in 1951 by Paul Weston as well as versions by Tommy Edwards from both the early and late 50's. The year after this top 10 hit, Donny and Marie began their own musical/variety TV series which ran for 3 years.

90.   My Little Town by Simon & Garfunkel was their first hit together in 5 years. Paul Simon did not write the song about any personal experiences, but he did write it for Art's next solo album because he thought he was recording too many sweet songs and this one would be a little nasty. Art suggested Paul record it with him and it became a short reunion for the most successful pop music duo of the 60's.

91. **Rockin' Chair** by Gwen McCrae was the only major hit for this Pensacola, Florida born singer who was married to George (Rock Your Baby) McCrae who also managed her career and sang back up on this top 10 hit. George and Gwen McCrae ended their relationship the following year in 1976 after 13 years of marriage.

92. **#9 Dream** by John Lennon featured backing vocals by May Pang, his partner when he was separated from Yoko for a short time. Lennon had a fascination with the number 9, which is also featured in Revolution # 9 from the singer/songwriter born on the 9th day of October in 1940. This was the 2nd single from his 'Walls and Bridges' album which also featured the number one hit 'Whatever Gets You through the Night'.

93. **The Rockford Files** by Mike Post was the hit theme from the popular TV series which starred James Garner as Jim Rockford. Mike Post was the orchestra leader for the Andy Williams Show and the Mac Davis Show in the early 70's. Mike Post composed many TV themes including 'L.A. Law', 'Hill Street Blues', The 'A' Team', 'Remington Steele' and many others.

94. **It Only Takes a Minute** by Tavares was the first and biggest hit for this family soul group from Massachusetts. This song was written and produced by Brian Potter and Dennis Lambert who previously wrote hits which included 'One Tin Soldier', 'Don't Pull You Love' and 'Ain't No Woman like the One I've Got.

95. **I Don't like to Sleep Alone** by Paul Anka & Odia Coates was their 3rd consecutive major hit together as a duo. Sadly, Odia Coates died of breast cancer in 1991 at the age of 49.

96. **Nightingale** by Carole King featured both her young daughters, Sherry and Louise singing background on what became her final top 10 hit. This hit was from her album 'Wrap around Joy' which was completed just before her first son, Levi was born.

97. **Supernatural Thing part 1** by Ben E. King was something completely different for the former lead singer of the Drifters and singer of 'Stand by Me' as a solo performer. This was his first hit in 8 years and his first which featured a higher-pitched vocal from the man usually known for his baritone voice. Ben E. King recorded his vocal in 1 take, reading the lyrics from a piece of paper.

98. **Ain't No Way to Treat a Lady** by Helen Reddy was a song about respect written by her friend Harriet Schock. Although this song did not win after being nominated for Best Female Pop Vocal Performance in the Grammy Awards, she did win one in 1972 for her hit 'I Am Woman'. She shocked many with her acceptance speech when she said 'I want to thank everyone concerned at Capitol records, my husband and manager Jeff Wald, because he makes my success possible and God, because She makes everything possible'.

206

99.   **Brazil** by the Ritchie Family was a big disco hit which originated in the 1940's when Xavier Cugat placed it high on the charts. The Ritchie Family was not a family act, but a group named for its producer and arranger Ritchie Rome. The group consisted of various Philadelphia session singers and musicians.

100.   **Get Dancin'** by Disco Tex & the Sex-O-Lettes was a group assembled and produced by Bob Crewe, best known for co-writing and producing the hits of the Four Seasons. This one hit wonder disco studio group featured the lead voice of Sir Monti Rock the 3rd, who was the owner of a chain of hairdressing salons.

101.   **Doctor's Orders** by Carol Douglas was written by the very successful British songwriting team of Roger Cook and Roger Greenaway along with Geoff Stephens, the man who wrote and sang lead on the New Vaudeville Band's 'Winchester Cathedral'. 'Doctor's Orders' was the only hit for this Brooklyn, New York singer who was born the daughter of Minnie Newsome, a jazz performer who was the inspiration of the Cab Callaway classic 'Minnie the Moocher'.

102.   **Shame Shame Shame** by Shirley & Company was written by her friend Sylvia Robinson of Mickey and Sylvia fame. The girls knew one another from the 50's when they met on tour when Shirley Goodman recorded as 'Shirley and Lee', best known for the hit 'Let The Good Times Roll' and Sylvia had a huge hit with Mickey with 'Love Is Strange'. Shirley Goodman died in 2005.

103.   **It's a Miracle** by Barry Manilow was one of his few up tempo hits along with 'Capacabana'. Barry Manilow wrote the lyrics to this song in 1973 at his apartment just after completing 3 weeks of sold out concerts as Bette Midler's pianist. The opening line was 'you wouldn't believe where I've been'. Songwriter Marty Panzer completed the song which followed Manilow's first hit 'Mandy'.

104.   **Only Women** by Alice Cooper was a ballad about a woman in an abusive relationship and released as a single before the album 'Welcome to My Nightmare' hit the record shelves. This hit was written by Alice Cooper and Dick Wagner and was produced by Canadian Bob Ezrin who was responsible for all of this shock rocker's most successful albums during the 70's.

105.   **Get Down, Get Down (Get On The Floor)** by Joe Simon was a disco tune from the singer known for his previous hits 'The Chokin' Kind', 'Drowning In The Sea Of Love' and 'Power Of Love'. Joe Simon co-wrote and co-produced this top 10 hit with Raeford Gerald who also gave Garland Green the disco song 'Bumpin' and Stompin' at the same time. This would be Joe Simon's final top 40 hit.

106.   **What Am I Gonna Do with You** by Barry White was inspired by a line he would say to the love of his life, his wife. This was his 4th number 1 hit on the R & B charts for the singer/songwriter/producer and orchestra leader who's musical roots go back to the 50's and 60's when he wrote, played or arranged hits for others, including arranging the 1963 hit 'Harlem Shuffle' for Bob and Earl.

107.   Can't Get It out Of My Head by Electric Light Orchestra was the first North American hit for this British symphonic rock band which featured songwriter/producer Jeff Lynne on lead vocals. This prime cut from their album 'Eldorado' was reminiscent of something the Beatles could have recorded during their later years.

108.   Dynomite Part 1 by Tony Camillo's Bazuka was inspired by the phrase used by J. J. Walker in the TV series 'Good Times'. Tony Camillo was a record producer who worked with many 60's and 70's acts including Gladys Knight and the Pips with whom he co – produced 'Midnight Train to Georgia'.

109.   Long Tall Glasses (I Can Dance) by Leo Sayer was the first hit as a singer for this British performer who would have 2 consecutive number one hits in 1977 with 'You Make Me Feel Like Dancing' and 'When I Need You'. In 1974, 'The Show Must Go On', which he co wrote, became 3 Dog Night's final top 10 hit.

110.   Feel like Makin' Love by Bad Company was the biggest hit from the album 'Straight Shooter' which was recorded at Gloucestershire Castle. This hit was written by lead singer Paul Rodgers with guitarist Mick Ralphs. This was their biggest hit since their debut hit 'Can't Get Enough' in 1974.

111.   The Way We Were/Try to Remember by Gladys Knight & The Pips was a 'live' medley of a song made famous by Barbra Streisand and a mid 60's song from the off-Broadway musical 'The Fantasticks'. This was the biggest hit from their album 'I Feel a Song', which produced 4 singles.

112.   Cut The Cake by the Average White Band was the follow up to their number one hit 'Pick Up The Pieces' and only other hit to reach the top 10 for this Scottish funk band. 'Cut The Cake' was the title tune from their 3rd album which was recorded amidst much tension due to creative differences between group members and the sudden death of their original drummer Robbie McIntosh. He was replaced by drummer Steve Ferrone who was a previous member of Brian Auger's Oblivion Express.

113.   Once You Get Started by Rufus featuring Chaka Khan was written by Christopher Gavin and featured on their platinum album 'Rufusized'. Chaka Khan was born on March 3 1953 and her real name is Yvette Marie Stevens.

114.   3rd Rate Romance by the Amazing Rhythm Aces was the only pop music hit for this country-flavored Memphis group headed by singer/songwriter Howard Russell Smith. The group was brought into a studio by Knox Phillips, the eldest son of the legendary Sam Phillips of Sun records in Memphis. '3rd Rate Romance' was from their debut album 'Stacked Deck'.

115.   S.O.S. by Abba is the only song title and artist which can be read the same way in either direction, also known as a 'palindrome'. This was Abba's only charted hit in North America in 1975, but the following year they charted no less than 4 hits.

116.   Do It Any Way You Wanna by People's Choice was a pure disco dance hit produced and written by Leon Huff of Gamble-Huff fame. The title was the only lyrics in this mostly instrumental hit.

117.   Take Me in Your Arms (Rock Me A Little While) by the Doobie Brothers was written by the Motown team of Holland/Dozier/Holland and was originally a hit in the mid 60's by Kim Weston. The Doobie Brothers lead singer Tom Johnston always loved the song and eventually persuaded the band to record it. Lead singer/songwriter Tom Johnston left the Doobie Brothers shortly after this hit and was replaced by Michael McDonald who was the lead voice on the hits that would follow.

118.   Killer Queen by Queen was the first major hit for this British glam-rock group led by lead singer/pianist and songwriter Freddie Mercury. This hit was a prime cut from their album 'Sheer Heart Attack' and featured intricate 4 part harmonies and multi-tracking. This hit would be followed by their most famous masterpiece, 'Bohemian Rhapsody'.

119.   Our Day Will Come by Frankie Valli was a remake of the number one hit from 1963 by Ruby & the Romantics. This was Frankie Valli's 3rd consecutive hit in his comeback year 1975 following 'My Eyes Adored You' and 'Swearin' To God'. It also set the stage for the comeback of his group the Four Seasons with the release of both 'Who Loves You' and 'December 1963 (Oh What a Night)' in 1975, giving them their first top 10 hit since 1967.

120.   Lady Blue by Leon Russell was written for his daughter 'Blue'. The long haired and bearded Leon Russell is best known as a songwriter and a session musician who has played on hundreds of recordings since the 60's. He co-wrote hits which included 'This Masquerade', 'Superstar' and 'Delta Lady' among others. In 2010 he shared the spotlight on Elton John's album which he also contributed as a songwriter.

121.   Look in my Eyes Pretty Woman by Tony Orlando & Dawn was from their 'Prime Time' album when their prime time TV variety show, (which replaced The Sonny and Cher Show) was at its peak in popularity. This was their final single on the Bell record label where most of their hits originated.

122.   That's the Way of the World by Earth, Wind & Fire was the title song of the album which also featured their biggest hit 'Shining Star', also from 1975. The group was assembled by leader Maurice White on a vision and spiritual image that he had. Most of the members were vegetarians and all regularly meditated together to achieve a 'oneness of mind' which all were part of his creation of his dream band.

123.   Venus & Mars Rock Show by Paul McCartney & Wings was the title song from their 4th album. This was the 3rd single release and the first to fail to chart at all in Britain. It was also a disappointment in North America where it failed to reach the top 10.

124.   Eighteen with a Bullet by Pete Wingfield was the only hit as a singer for this British singer/songwriter/producer and writer. He played on numerous albums and toured extensively with major recording acts through the years. Coincidentally, 'Eighteen with a Bullet' actually placed on Billboard's Hot 100 chart at number 18 with a bullet (moving up the charts fast) in late 1975.

125.   Roll on down the Highway by Bachman-Turner Overdrive, (also known as B. T. O.) was from their most successful album, 'Not Fragile', the follow up to their number on hit 'You Ain't Seen Nothin' Yet'. 'Roll on down the Highway' was written by Randy Bachman and Fred Turner, who was featured on lead vocals on this high energy rocker.

126. Bad Luck – part 1 by Harold Melvin & the Blue Notes was more popular in dance clubs than it was on radio, although it did manage to reach the top 20 on the pop charts. Once again Teddy Pendergrass sang lead on this hit by the group which bears another name. Teddy Pendergrass died in January of 2010, while Harold Melvin passed away in 1997.

127. Sweet Surrender by John Denver was the lead single from his album 'An Evening with John Denver' which was recorded during the summer concerts at the Universal City Amphitheater in Los Angeles, California in 1974. 'Sweet Surrender' was the first of 4 notable hits written and recorded by Denver which charted in 1975.

128. Sad Sweet Dreamer by Sweet Sensation reached number one in the U.K. for this British 8 man soul group which featured 16 year old Marcel King on lead vocals. Sadly, Marcel died of a brain hemorrhage at the age of 38 in 1995. The group was discovered and signed to 'Pye' records by Tony Hatch, best known for writing most of Petula Clark's major hits including 'Downtown'.

129. (I Believe) There's Nothing Stronger than Our Love by Paul Anka & Odia Coates was their 4th consecutive duet hit together following 'You're Having My Baby', 'One Man Woman/One Woman Man', and 'I Don't like to Sleep Alone'.

130. Up in a Puff of Smoke by Polly Brown was a hit for the British singer who led the group 'Pickettywitch' known for their hit 'That Same Old Feeling'. This was the only notable hit in North America for this white soul singer from Birmingham, England.

131. Mornin' Beautiful by Tony Orlando & Dawn was the follow up to their number one hit 'He Don't Love You (Like I Love You) and the 2nd single on their new label, 'Elektra', where they would end their string of hits the following year in 1976 with 'Cupid'.

132. Harry Truman by Chicago was written by group member Robert Lamm as a tribute to a former President that he felt the American people could trust. He wrote the song after the resignation of President Richard Nixon. Harry S. Truman was the 33rd President of the United States from 1945 to 1953. This was the first single from the 'Chicago 8' album.

133. Something Better to Do by Olivia Newton-John was the first single from her album 'Clearly Love'. Songwriter/producer John Farrar, who was responsible for most of Olivia's 70 hits, describes it as a silly song and did not expect it to be released as a single. Her previous 2 1975 hits 'Have You Never Been Mellow' and 'Please Mr. Please' both reached the top 5, while this one failed to reach the top 10 on the pop charts.

134. Misty by Ray Stevens was a remake of a song Johnny Mathis made famous in 1959, although the original version was made popular by Errol Garner in 1954. This song became a major hit on the country charts and a moderate hit on the pop charts for the singer best known for his novelty hits.

135.   Rock 'N Roll (I Gave You All the Best Years of My Life) by Mac Davis was an autobiographical song from the singer/songwriter/guitarist/actor who gave Elvis Presley no less than 4 hits including 'In The Ghetto' and 'Don't Cry Daddy'. Mac Davis had his own weekly musical variety show, which ran from 1974 – 1976 when this hit reached the top 20 in early 1975.

136.   Hijack by Herbie Mann was the most popular pop and dance hit for the Jazz flautist from Brooklyn, New York. Herbie Mann, who was a pioneer in the fusion of jazz and world music, died after a long battle with prostate cancer on July 1st 2003 at the age of 73.

137.   L-O-V-E (Love) by Al Green was his first song to demonstrate the gospel influences for this soul singer who was born again after the incident that changed his life. That incident was his brush with death when his ex-girlfriend Mary Woodson scalded him with a pot of grits, then fatally shot herself.

138.   I Am Love (part 1 & 2) by the Jackson Five was their final top 40 hit for Motown and another disappointment for the group that would rarely miss the top 10. The following year the hits would start up again when they switched to the 'Epic' label and changed their name from the Jackson Five to simply 'The Jacksons'.

139.   I'm on Fire by the Dwight Twilley Band was the debut single for this Tulsa, Oklahoma act which included Phil Seymour, who shared lead vocals. 'I'm On Fire' was written by Dwight Twilley and is not to be confused with the other 1975 hit with the same title by 5000 Volts or the 1985 Bruce Springsteen song.

140.   I Want'a Do Something Freaky to You by Leon Haywood was a funk/soul hit from this soul singer/keyboardist from Houston, Texas. This hit was known for its sexy lyrics which included 'Your love is like a mountain, I'd like to slide down to your canyons, slide down, in the valley of love...' Leon Haywood was Sam Cooke's keyboardist until his death in December of 1964.

141.   The Bertha Butt Boogie by the Jimmy Caster Bunch was a humorous hit based on one of the Butt sisters introduced in the 1972 million seller 'Troglodyte'. This offbeat novelty hit surprising reached the top 20, despite the fact that it was basically a repeat of the hit it followed.

142.   I Only Have Eyes for You by Art Garfunkel was a remake of a song originally popular in the 30's and then again in 1959 by the Flamingos. Art Garfunkel performed this song on the 2nd episode of 'Saturday Night Live' and although it didn't make the top 10 in the U.S., it was a number one hit in Britain in 1975.

143.   Free Bird by Lynyrd Skynyrd became a classic rock anthem and one the group would play at the end of their concerts. The single version was just under 5 minutes, the album version was over 9 and the song generally ran over 14 minutes long when the band performed it in concert. For many years after the plane crash which claimed the life of lead singer Ronnie Van Zant in 1977, a solitary microphone with a single spotlight would be at centre stage while the band played the instrumental version.

144. **Tush** by Z. Z. Top was the first top 40 hit for this Texas rock trio who formed in 1969. Drummer Frank Beard was the only member without one. Guitarists and vocalists Billy Gibbons and Dusty Hill are as famous for there visual presentation as they are for their musicianship. They are always seen wearing sunglasses, similar black clothing (usually black leather), cowboy hats or baseball caps and chest length beards. Their rockin' good 'Tush' was from their album 'Fandango'.

145. **Black Superman (Muhammad Ali)** by Johnny Wakelin was the only North American hit for this British singer who was discovered by Pye record producer Robin Blanchflower, the man who was responsible for giving Carl Douglas his only hit 'Kung Fu Fighting'. This novelty hit was about Muhammad Ali, the greatest boxer of our time who would 'float like a butterfly' and 'sting like a bee'.

146. **Holdin' On To Yesterday** by Ambrosia was the debut hit from this Los Angeles- based pop group fronted by lead singer/songwriter David Pack. 3 years after their initial hit 'Holdin' On To Yesterday', Ambrosia had major hits with 'How Much I Feel' and in 1980 with 'Biggest Part of Me. After leaving Ambrosia, David Pack became a Grammy Award winning producer of many major record acts including Phil Collins, Aretha Franklin, Wynonna and numerous others.

147. **To The Door of the Sun (Alle Porte Del Sole)** by Al Martino was his first top 20 hit since 1965's 'Spanish Eyes'. Al Martino was one of the great American Italian crooners who was also known for his acting, in particular as singer Johnny Fontane in the Godfather. Al Martino died 6 days after his 82nd birthday on October 13th 2009.

148. **Solitaire** by the Carpenters was written by Neil Sedaka and Phil Cody and was originally featured on the 'Sedaka's Back' album. The Carpenters featured this hit on their 'Horizon' album which also included their hit singles 'Please Mr. Postman' and 'Only Yesterday'.

149. **I'll Play for You** by Seals & Crofts was the title song from their 7th studio album which included no other hit singles. Both James Seals and Dash Crofts have been members of the Baha'i Faith since 1969.

150. **The Last Farewell** by Roger Whitaker reached number 1 in 11 countries 4 years after he originally recorded it on an album in 1971. Although he has had almost a dozen hits on the easy listening radio format and many successful albums, this was his only notable hit on the top 40 pop/rock charts.

151. **What a Difference a Day Makes** by Esther Phillips was a disco remake of a song popular back in the early 30's by the Dorsey Brothers. Her first major hit arrived in 1962 with the song 'Release Me'. After several years of drug addiction, Esther Phillips died at the age of 48 as a result of kidney and liver failure in 1984.

152. **Shoeshine Boy** by Eddie Kendricks was written by Harry Booker who was once a shoeshine boy himself and co written with Linda Allen who was concerned that the song was demeaning to black people. Motown boss Berry Gordy made the decision by saying that a shoeshine boy could be anyone, black or white. This became a number one R & B hit for the former lead singer of the Temptations.

153. **Slippery When Wet** by the Commodores was a funky R & B hit written by group guitarist Thomas McClary and featured Walter Orange on lead vocals. Sax player Lionel Richie was not yet been given the chance to be the lead singer of the group, but would hit superstardom after it happened.

154. **Operator** by the Manhattan Transfer was the first hit for this New York City jazz/gospel/nostalgia vocal group discovered by Ahmet Ertegun, the founder and President of Atlantic Records. Their biggest hit arrived in 1981 with a remake of the Ad Libs hit 'The Boy from New York City'. The Manhattan Transfer was inducted into the Vocal Group Hall Of Fame in 1998.

155. **Stand by Me** by John Lennon was a remake of the 1961 Ben E. King hit which the former Beatle featured on his 'Rock and Roll' album, which included his versions of songs from the 50's and 60's. This was John Lennon's final hit before his 5 year retirement from the music industry. His next album 'Double Fantasy' in 1980 would be his final.

156. **My Boy** by Elvis Presley was originally recorded by actor Richard Harris in 1971. Elvis loved the story and decided to recorded it in Memphis in late 1973, but it didn't become a hit until the spring of 1975.The lyrics of this French composition were translated by songwriters Phil Coulter and Bill Martin who wrote many British hits including 'Puppet On A String' for Sandie Shaw and many of the hits of the Bay City Rollers including 'Saturday Night'.

157. **The Immigrant** by Neil Sedaka was inspired by John Lennon's immigration problems at the time and was the follow up single to 'Laughter in The Rain', also from his 'Sedaka's Back' album. In 2010, at age 70, Neil Sedaka was back again with the album 'The Music Of My Life'.

158. **Movin' On** by Bad Company was the 2nd hit single from their self – titled debut album which included 'Can't Get Enough'. Both hits were written by former 'Mott the Hoople' guitarist Mick Ralphs and both featured former 'Free' on lead vocals.

159. **How Long (Betcha Got A Chick on the Side)** by the Pointer Sisters was written by all 4 sisters with producer David Rubinstein. The Pointer Sisters were hot and different as they sang in nostalgic 40's style during this time. In 1976 they appeared in the movie 'Car Wash'. They dropped their nostalgic look in 1977 and in 1978 their career took off with over half a dozen top 10 hits beginning with 'Fire' written by Bruce Springsteen.

160. **Daisy Jane** by America was the follow up to their number one single 'Sister Golden Hair' from the album 'Hearts' and was also written by Gerry Beckley (who sang lead on this hit) and produced by the legendary Beatles' producer George Martin. Later that same year, they released 'History: America's

Greatest Hits' which featured an album cover designed by Phil Hartman, the actor and comedian.

161.   Blue Eyes Crying in the Rain by Willie Nelson reached number one on the country charts and top 30 on the pop charts. This was actually Willie's first hit on the pop charts as a singer, although as a songwriter he wrote 'Crazy' for Patsy Cline, 'Hello Walls for Faron Young' and 'Pretty Paper' for Roy Orbison. 'Blue Eyes Crying in the Rain' was written in 1945 by Fred Rose.

162.   Secret Love by Freddy Fender was a remake of a song Doris Day made famous in 1954. Freddy Fender's unique version was popular in his most successful year when he had 2 back to back million sellers with 'Before the Next Teardrop Falls' and 'Wasted Days and Wasted Nights'. 'Secret Love' was his only hit single from the album 'Are You Ready for Freddy?'

163.   The Last Game of the Season (A Blind Man in the Bleachers) by David Geddes was the only other hit for the singer known for his top 5 hit 'Run Joey Run', also from 1975. His real name is David Cole Idema, but he took the stage name Geddes from a street in Ann Arbor. It's interesting to note that both of his story song hits end with a death.

164.   Everytime You Touch Me (I Get High) by Charlie Rich was the final top 40 pop hit for the 'Silver Fox' although his country music chart career continued to produce major hits. In 1975 at the CMA Award, visibly intoxicated, instead of reading the name of the winner, who was John Denver, he set fire to the envelope with a cigarette lighter before announcing the award had gone to 'my friend Mr. John Denver'. Many were outraged at the behavior of Charlie Rich.

165.   You by George Harrison was from his 1975 album 'Extra Texture' and the song was originally offered to Ronnie Spector, but she never recorded it. This moderate hit featured special musical keyboard guests Gary Wright, Leon Russell and David Foster. George Harrison not only played guitar, but played the moog synthesizer on this song.

166.   Carolina in the Pines by Michael Murphey was the follow up to his million seller 'Wildfire' from the spring of 1975. This Michael Martin Murphey's 2nd hit from the album 'Blue Sky – Night Thunder' which featured music guests including the Nitty Gritty Dirt Band's John McEuen on banjo and Jeff Hanna on background vocals, as well as Tom Scott on saxophone.

167.   Hey You by Bachman-Turner Overdrive was another rocker from the Canadian group that gave us 'Takin' Care of Business' and 'You Ain't Seen Nothin' Yet'. Some believed 'Hey You', written by and featuring former Guess Who guitarist Randy Bachman on lead vocals was directed at his former band mate Burton Cummings. Their on again off again relationship was on again in the 2000's when they performed and recorded together as Bachman-Cummings.

168.   Attitude Dancing by Carly Simon featured Carole King on backing vocals on the only top 40 hit from the album 'Playing Possum'. The album cover featured a sexy photo of Carly kneeling wearing lingerie and high black

214

boots. Other musical guests featured on the album included her hubby James Taylor along with Andrew Gold, Rita Coolidge, Ringo Starr and producer Richard Perry.

169.   Part Time Love by Gladys Knight & The Pips was one of 4 moderately successful singles they released in 1975. It was also the year Gladys Knight pursued an acting career filming the movie 'Pipe Dreams'. 'Part Time Love' would be Gladys Knight and the Pips final top 20 hit of the 70's.

170.   Born to Run by Bruce Springsteen was the first hit from the New Jersey Singer/songwriter/guitarist who was often referred to as 'The Boss'. The album 'Born to Run' was both a commercial and critical success with great production similar to Phil Spector's 'Wall of Sound' yet very original and refreshing. In October of 1975, both Newsweek and Time put Springsteen on the cover of their magazine. Although this song failed to make the top 10, it is considered a true rock classic. Springsteen's greatest success came in the 80's when he sold millions of singles and albums.

More Hits of 1975

The Proud One by The Osmonds was written by the Four Seasons' Bob Gaudio and producer Bob Crewe who was responsible for composing most of their hits during the 60's.Frankie Valli had a minor hit with this song in 1966. Mike Curb produced this hit which became the Osmonds final top 40 hit of their career as a group.

Satin Soul by the Love Unlimited Orchestra was the only other top 40 hit from Barry White's 40 piece orchestra which produced the number one instrumental 'Love's Theme' in early 1974.

For The Love of You (part 1 & 2) by the Isley Brothers was the follow up to their million seller 'Fight The Power' from the summer of 1975. This song was originally written by Rudolph Isley as a poem to his wife, Elaine Jasper, sister of Isley Brothers member Chris Jasper. The brothers changed it around and it became the 2nd single released from their 'Heat is on' album.

I'm a Woman by Maria Muldaur was the only other hit for the singer best known for the 1974 hit 'Midnight at the Oasis'. 'I'm A Woman' was composed by the famous songwriting team of Leiber and Stoller, who wrote hits which included 'Jailhouse Rock', 'Stand By Me', 'Yakety Yak', 'Kansas City' and many other hits of the 50's and 60's.

Help Me Rhonda by Johnny Rivers was a remake of the number one hit by the Beach Boys from exactly 10 years earlier. Brian Wilson provided backing vocals on this remake from the singer who was known for over a dozen cover versions of hits during the 60's and 70's. Johnny Rivers also sang the theme song for 'The Midnight Special' TV show which began in 1975.

Ride 'Em Cowboy by Paul Davis was the Mississippi born singer/songwriter's first top 30 hit, although he had a minor hit in 1970 with his remake if the Jarmels' hit 'A Little Bit Of Soap'. Paul Davis died of a heart attack 1 day shy of his 60th birthday on April 22nd 2008.

Struttin' by Billy Preston was a moderate follow up to his number one hit 'Nothing from Nothing'. The 'B' side of 'Struttin' was 'You Are So Beautiful', a song Preston co-wrote which would become famous when Joe Cocker recorded it.

Emotion by Helen Reddy was originally a French tune called 'Amoreuse' and translated to English for the singer from down under to record. Although the song failed to reach the top 20 on the pop charts, it was number one on the Adult Contemporary charts. 1975 was also the year Helen Reddy began hosting the late night Friday night music show 'Midnight Special' and had a role in the film 'Airport 1975'.

Autobahn by Kraftwerk is a very abstract song featuring synthesizers from this electronic futuristic sounding band from Germany. Autobahn is a major high speed highway in Germany with no general speed limit, although the advisory limit is 130 km/h or 80 m.p.h. 'Autobahn' was Kraftwerk's only hit in North America, although the group continued to have success beyond the 70's, especially in Europe.

Just A Little Bit of You by Michael Jackson was his final single on the Motown label. 'Just A Little Bit of You' was the only hit single from the album 'Forever, Michael', released when he was 16 years old.

Your Bulldog Drinks Champagne by Jim Stafford was another offbeat hit from the singer/songwriter who's most successful year was 1974 when he charted 3 major consecutive hits beginning with 'Spiders and Snakes'. In 1975 he had his own summer variety show and in the early 80's he co-hosted 'Those Amazing Animals' on TV.

Ready by Cat Stevens was from the 'Buddha and the Chocolate Box' album and was his final single to reach the top 30 on the pop charts. Cat Stevens released 3 more studio albums during the next 2 years with limited success before converting to Islam and changing his name to Yusef Islam in late 1977.

Rockin' All Over The World by John Fogerty was the first solo hit (with the exception of the Blue Ridge Rangers) by the former front man for Creedence Clearwater Revival .This was the first single from the album simply titled 'John Fogerty' and also Fogerty's first release on the Asylum record label.

Amie by the Pure Prairie League was the debut hit for this Country-rock group from Cincinnati. Vince Gill became their lead singer beginning with their 1980 hit 'Let Me Love You Tonight' before he sought a successful solo career in Country music.

I'm on Fire by 5000 Volts was a British disco trio which featured Tina Charles on lead vocals. The intro of this hit was similar to 'Black Is Black' by Los Bravos, but much faster in pace. This hit was much more popular in Britain and Europe than it was in North America. Tina Charles enjoyed solo success the following year with the disco hit 'I Love To Love'.

Rendezvous by the Hudson Brothers was one of 2 top 40 hits for Bill, Brett and Mark from the mid- 70's. They switched labels from Casablanca to Elton

John's Rocket Records for this one and only other hit single from the Hudson Brothers.

Young Americans by David Bowie featured David Sanborn on saxophone. This was the title song from the album which changed Bowie's glam-rock image to a more soulful sound. Other guests on the album included Luther Vandross and John Lennon, who appeared on the hit 'Fame' which followed the first single released from the album 'Young Americans'.

Dancin' Fool by the Guess Who was popular the year this Canadian super group disbanded. They had several personnel changes in the early 70's and the most recent was guitarist Dominic Troiano replacing both Kurt Winter and Don McDougal in 1974. The group has had several reunions since then.

Rainy Day People by Gordon Lightfoot was a song to do with lifestyles and insecurity in relationships according to the singer/songwriter from Canada. This was from 'Cold on My Shoulder', his 11th original album and once again he composed every song on it.

Shaving Cream by Benny Bell was a novelty hit considered bordering on the rude and crude but very funny and originally recorded back in 1946, and revived in 1975. Benny Bell was a risqué singer/songwriter whose real name was Paul Wynn.

Just Too Many People by Melissa Manchester was the 2nd single from her album 'Melissa' which included her breakthrough hit 'Midnight Blue'. She studied songwriting under Paul Simon at the University School of the Arts during the early 70's. Before going solo she was a backup singer for Bette Midler.

Part of the Plan by Dan Fogelberg was produced by Joe Walsh who is also featured on lead guitar with Graham Nash on backing vocals. This prime cut from the album 'Souvenirs' was the first charted single from this singer/songwriter from Peoria, Illinois. Fogelberg charted several major soft rock hits in the early 80's. He died from prostate cancer at the age of 56 on December 16th 2007.

Pinball Wizard by Elton John was not released commercially as a single, but was a very popular hit in Canada where it charted high on the charts. This was from the movie adaptation of the Who's Rock Opera 'Tommy' which starred Elton John, Roger Daltry, Ann-Margret, Oliver Reed, Jack Nicholson, Tina Turner and many others.

Bloody Well Right by Supertramp was the debut North American hit for this progressive rock British group which was more popular in the U.K. and Canada than they were in the United States. The 'B' side of the single 'Bloody Well Right' was 'Dreamer' which was re released as a 'live' version single in 1980. Both songs were originally featured on 'The Crime of the Century' album.

Mexico by James Taylor featured backing vocals by David Crosby and Graham Nash. This was the 2nd hit from his 6th album 'Gorilla' which also featured 'How Sweet It Is (To Be Loved by You)'.

Shakey Ground by the Temptations was the final top 40 hit for this legendary

Motown group. 2 members of George Clinton's group Funkedelic were recruited for this funky hit which reached number one on the R & B charts , - the song's co-writer Eddie Hazel, on lead guitar along with bassist Billy Nelson. Dennis Edwards, who joined the Temptations in 1968, replacing David Ruffin, sang lead on this hit.

That's When the Music Takes Me by Neil Sedaka was the 3rd and final hit single from 'Sedaka's Back', one of the year's most successful albums. This was the only one which he wrote alone. His next album, 'The Hungry Years' was also a hit in 1975 and included his next single 'Bad Blood' with backing by Elton John which topped the charts a month later.

Never Let Her Go by David Gates was a solo hit for the front man and songwriter of Bread, one of the most successful soft rock groups of the early 70's. Before he led Bread to a string of hits in the 70's, David Gates was responsible for writing the hit 'Popsicles and Icicles' for the Murmaids and producing 'Baby the Rain Must Fall' by Glenn Yarborough.

Top 17 Albums of 1975

1.	Captain Fantastic & the Brown Dirt Cowboy	Elton John
2.	Physical Graffitti	Led Zeppelin
3.	One of These Nights	Eagles
4.	Chicago 9	Chicago
5.	Red Octopus	Jefferson Starship
6.	Rock of the Westies	Elton John
7.	That's The Way of the World	Earth, Wind & Fire
8.	Wish You Were Here	Pink Floyd
9.	Blood on the Tracks	Bob Dylan
10.	Heart like A Wheel	Linda Ronstadt
11.	Windsong	John Denver
12.	Have You Never Been Mellow	Olivia Newton-John
13.	Venus & Mars	Paul McCartney & Wings
14.	Still Crazy After All These Years	Paul Simon
15.	AWB	Average White Band
16.	Between The Lines	Janis Ian
17.	Fire	Ohio Players

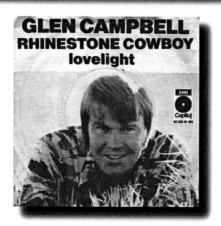

1.	Rhinestone Cowboy	Glen Campbell
2.	Before The Next Teardrop Falls	Freddy Fender
3.	Blue Eyes Crying In the Rain	Willie Nelson
4.	Always Watching You	Merle Haggard
5.	Wasted Days & Wasted Nights	Freddy Fender
6.	Daydreams about the Night Things	Ronnie Milsap
7.	Touch the Hand	Conway Twitty
8.	I'm Not Lisa	Jessi Colter
9.	She's Acting Single (And I'm Drinking Doubles)	Gary Stewart
10.	Are You Sure Hank Did It This Way	Waylon Jennings
11.	Thank God I'm A Country Boy	John Denver
12.	(Hey Won't You Play) Another Somebody...Song	B. J. Thomas
13.	Feelings	Conway Twitty & Loretta Lynn
14.	You're My Best Friend	Don Williams
15.	Lizzie & the Rainman	Tanya Tucker
16.	I'm Sorry	John Denver
17.	Hope You're Feeling Me (Like I'm Feeling You)	Charley Pride

Top 17 Disco Hits of 1975

1.	Jive Talkin'	Bee Gees
2.	Fly Robin Fly	Silver Convention
3.	That's The Way I Like It	K. C. & The Sunshine Band
4.	The Hustle	Van McCoy
5.	Lady Marmalade	Labelle
6.	Shining Star	Earth, Wind & Fire
7.	Get Down Tonight	K. C. & the Sunshine Band
8.	Express	B. T. Express
9.	Nights on Broadway	Bee Gees
10.	Never Can Say Goodbye	Gloria Gaynor
11.	Rockin' Chair	Gwen McCrae
12.	It Only Takes a Minute	Tavares
13.	Brazil	Ritchie Family
14.	Get Dancin'	Disco Tex & the Sex-O-Lettes
15.	Doctor's Orders	Carol Douglas
16.	Shame Shame Shame	Shirley & Company
17.	I Love Music	O'Jays

Top 17 One Hit Wonders of 1975

1.	Minnie Ripperton	Lovin' You
2.	Van McCoy	The Hustle
3.	Ace	How Long
4.	Jigsaw	Skyhigh
5.	Sammy Johns	Chevy Van
6.	Pilot	Magic
7.	Morris Albert	Feelings
8.	David Geddes	Run Joey Run
9.	Blackbyrds	Walkin' In Rhythm
10.	Gwen McCrae	Rockin' Chair
11.	Major Harris	Love Won't Let Me Wait
12.	Pete Wingfield	Eighteen with a Bullet
13.	Tony Camillo's Bazuka	Dynomite
14.	Polly Brown	Up In a Puff of Smoke
15.	Sweet Sensation	Sad Sweet Dreamer
16.	Johnny Wakelin	Black Superman (Muhammad Ali)
17.	5000 Volts	I'm On Fire

Top 17 Rock/Hard Rock Hits of 1975

1.	Fame	David Bowie
2.	Ballroom Blitz	Sweet
3.	Feel Like Makin' Love	Bad Company
4.	Take Me in Your Arms	Doobie Brothers
5.	Tush	Z. Z. Top
6.	Autobahn	Kraftwerk
7.	Bloody Well Right	Supertramp
8.	Roll On Down The Highway	B. T. O.
9.	Sweet Emotion	Aerosmith
10.	Movin' On	Bad Company
11.	Trampled Under Foot	Led Zeppelin
12.	Changes	David Bowie
13.	Good Lovin' Gone Bad	Bad Company
14.	Welcome To My Nightmare	Alice Cooper
15.	Hey You	B. T. O.
16.	Katmandu	Bob Seger
17.	Rock and Roll All Nite (studio version)	Kiss

17 Notable 'Lost' 45's of 1975

1.	Emma	Hot Chocolate
2.	Magic	Pilot
3.	Rocky	Austin Roberts
4.	Help Me Rhonda	Johnny Rivers
5.	Eighteen with a Bullet	Pete Wingfield
6.	The Immigrant	Neil Sedaka
7.	Shaving Cream	Benny Bell
8.	Up In a Puff of Smoke	Polly Brown
9.	Lady Blue	Leon Russell
10.	What a Difference a Day Makes	Esther Phillips
11.	Doctor's Orders	Carol Douglas
12.	Get Dancin'	Disco Tex & the Sex-O-Lettes
13.	Shame Shame Shame	Shirley & Company
14.	Dark Horse	George Harrison
15.	Rockin' All Over the World	John Fogerty
16.	The Entertainer	Billy Joel
17.	Sally G	Paul McCartney

Brandy	Feb. 11 1979	Do Ya Think I'm Sexy	Rod Stewart
Usher	Oct. 14 1978	Kiss You All Over	Exile
Eminem	Oct. 17 1972	Ben	Michael Jackson
Shakira	Feb. 2 1977	Car Wash	Rose Royce
Fergie	Mar. 27 1975	My Eyes Adored You	Frankie Valli
Pink	Sept 8 1979	My Sharona	Knack
Ben Affleck	Aug 15 1972	Alone Again Naturally	Gilbert O'Sullivan
Christina Applegate	Nov 25 1971	Theme from Shaft	Isaac Hayes
Lance Armstrong	Sept. 18 1971	Go Away Little Girl	Donny Osmond
David Arquette	Sept. 8 1972.	Brandy (You're A Fine Girl)	Looking Glass
Christian Bale	Jan. 20 1974	You're 16	Ringo Starr
Tyra Banks	Dec. 4 1973	Top Of the World	Carpenters
Drew Barrymore	Feb. 22 1975	Pick Up the Pieces	Average White Band
Lance Bass	May 4 1979	Heart Of Glass	Blondie
David Beckham	May 2 1975	(Hey Won't You Play) Another…	B. J. Thomas
Victoria Beckham	Apr. 17 1974	Bennie and the Jets	Elton John
Kate Beckinsale	July 26 1973	Bad Bad Leroy Brown	Jim Croce
Jason Biggs	May 12 1978	Night Fever	Bee Gees
Orlando Bloom	Jan. 13 1977	You Don't Have To Be A Star	M.McCoo/B.Davis Jr.
Neve Campbell	Oct. 3 1973	We're An American Band	Grand Funk
Mariah Carey	Mar. 27 1970	Bridge Over Troubled Water	Simon & Garf.
Jennifer Connelly	Dec. 12 1970	Tears Of a Clown	The Miracles
Penelope Cruz	Apr. 28 1974	T.S.O.P.	M.F.S.B.
Matt Damon	Oct. 8 1970	Ain't No Mountain High Enough	Diana Ross
Clair Danes	Apr. 12 1979	Tragedy	Bee Gees
Rosario Dawson	May 9 1979	Reunited	Peaches and Herb
Cameron Diaz	Aug 30 1972	Brandy (You're A Fine Girl)	Looking Glass
Leonardo DiCaprio	Nov. 11 1974	You Ain't Seen Nothin' Yet	B.T.O.
Snoop Dogg	Oct. 20 1972	Ben	Michael Jackson
Shannon Doherty	Apr. 12 1971	Just My Imagination	Temptations
Carmen Electra	Apr. 20 1972	First Time Ever I Saw Your Face	Roberta Flack
Colin Farrell	May 31 1976	Love Hangover	Diana Ross
Kevin Federline	Mar. 21 1978	Night Fever	Bee Gees
Nelly Fertado	Dec. 2 1978	You Don't Bring Me Flowers	Streisand/Diamond
Lara Flynn Boyle	Mar. 28 1970	Bridge Over Troubled Water	Simon & Garf.
Edward Furlong	Aug 2 1977	I Just Want To Be …Everything	Andy Gibb
Jennifer Garner	Apr. 17 1972	First Time Ever I Saw Your Face	Roberta Flack
Topher Grace	July 2 1978	Shadow Dancing	Andy Gibb
Heather Graham	Jan. 29 1970	Raindrops Keep Fallin'	B. J. Thomas
Seth Green	Feb. 2 1974	The Way We Were	Barbra Streisand
Tom Green	July 30 1971	Indian Reservation	Raiders
Josh Harnett	July 21 1978	Shadow Dancing	Andy Gibb
Ethan Hawke	Nov. 6 1970	I'll Be There	Jackson Five
Katherine Heigl	Nov 24 1978	MacArthur Park	Donna Summer

225

Katie Holmes	Dec. 18 1978	Le Freak	Chic
Kate Hudson	Apr. 19 1979	What a Fool Believes	Doobie Brothers
Enrique Iglesias	May 8 1975	He Don't Love You	Tony Orlando/Dawn
Mary J. Blige	Jan. 11 1971	My Sweet Lord	George Harrison
Melissa Joan Hart	Apr. 18 1976	Disco Lady	Johnny Taylor
Angelina Jolie	June 4 1975	Before The Next Teardrop Falls	Freddy Fender
Ashton Kutcher	Feb 7 1978	Stayin' Alive	Bee Gees
Queen Latifah	Mar. 18 1970	Bridge Over Troubled Water	Simon & Garf.
Jude Law	Dec. 29 1972	Me and Mrs. Jones	Billy Paul
Jared Leto	Dec. 26 1971	Brand New Key	Melanie
Juliette Lewis	June 21 1973	My Love	Paul McCartney
Eva Longoria	Mar. 15 1975	Black Water	Doobie Brothers
Jennifer Love Hewitt	Feb. 21 1979	Do Ya Think I'm Sexy	Rod Stewart
Tobey Maguire	June 27 1975	Love Will Keep Us Together	Capt. & Tennille
Ricky Martin	Dec. 24 1971	Family Affair	Sly & Family Stone
Rachel McAdams	Oct. 7 1976	Play That Funky Music	Wild Cherry
Jenny McCarthy	Nov 1 1972	My Ding A Ling	Chuck Berry
Ewan McGregor	Mar. 31 1971	Me & Bobby McGee	Janis Joplin
Alanis Morisette	June 1 1974	The Streak	Ray Stevens
Kate Moss	Jan. 16 1974	The Joker	Steve Miller
Jerry O'Connell	Feb. 17 1974	Love's Theme	Love Unlimited Orch.
Sandra Oh	July 20 1971	It's Too Late	Carole King
Gwyneth Paltrow	Sept. 28 1972	Baby Don't Get Hooked On Me	Mac Davis
Amanda Peet	Jan. 11 1972	Brand New Key	Melanie
Ryan Phillippe	Sept. 10 1974	You're Having My Baby	Paul Anka
Joaquin Phoenix	Oct. 28 1974	Then Came You	D.Warwick/Spinners
Jada Pinkett Smith	Sept 18 1971	Go Away Little Girl	Donny Osmond
Freddie Prinze Jr.	Mar 8 1976	Love Machine	Miracles
Ryan Reynolds	Oct. 23 1976	If You Leave Me Now	Chicago
Denise Richards	Feb. 17 1971	One Bad Apple	Osmonds
Kelly Ripa	Oct. 2 1970	Ain't No Mountain High Enough	Diana Ross
Kid Rock	Jan. 17 1971	My Sweet Lord	George Harrison
The Rock	May 2 1972	First Time Ever I Saw Your Face	Roberta Flack
Rebecca Romijn	Nov 6 1972	I Can See Clearly Now	Johnny Nash
Winona Ryder	Oct. 29 1971	Maggie May	Rod Stewart
Claudia Schiffer	Aug. 25 1970	Make It with You	Bread
Ryan Seacrest	Dec. 24 1974	Cats In the Cradle	Harry Chapin
Alicia Silverstone	Oct. 4 1976	Play That Funky Music	Wild Cherry
Tori Spelling	May 16 1973	Tie a Yellow Ribbon…Oak Tree	Tony Orlando/Dawn
Mena Suvari	Feb. 9 1979	Too Much Heaven	Bee Gees
Hilary Swank	July 30 1974	Annie's Song	John Denver
Charlize Theron	Aug. 7 1975	One of These Nights	Eagles
Rob Thomas	Feb 14 1972	Let's Stay Together	Al Green
Uma Thurman	Apr. 29 1970	ABC	Jackson Five
Liv Tyler	July 1 1977	Sir Duke	Stevie Wonder
Vince Vaughn	Mar. 28 1970	Bridge Over Troubled Water	Simon & Garf.
Rachel Weisz	Mar. 7 1971	One Bad Apple	Osmonds
Luke Wilson	Sept. 21 1971	Go Away Little Girl	Donny Osmond
Gretchen Wilson	June 26 1973	My Love	Paul McCartney
Kate Winslet	Oct. 5 1975	I'm Sorry	John Denver
Reese Witherspoon	Mar. 22 1976	Dec 1963 (Oh What A Night)	Four Seasons
Tiger Woods	Dec. 30 1975	Let's Do It Again	Staple Singers

226

♫ This 1976 Beatles hit was released as a single 10 years after it was featured on their 'Revolver' album and 6 years after they broke up.

♫ The former lead singer and songwriter for the Lovin' Spoonful had a number one hit with this TV theme.

♫ This million seller was a song about a dog, not a woman like many believed.

♫ The actress girlfriend of this superstar singer provided the whispering vocals on this number one hit.

♫ This number one hit was from the 2nd major movie of the 70's which starred Diana Ross.

♫ This one hit wonder group with a mega selling record, took their name from a box of cough drops.

FIND OUT THAT... AND MUCH MORE INSIDE... 1976

1. Tonight's The Night (Gonna Be Alright) by Rod Stewart was a sensuous song which featured the whispering voice of Swedish actress Britt Ekland, his girlfriend at the time. Rod Stewart wrote this sexually-charged hit which was also featured on his 'A Night on the Town' album.

2. Silly Love Songs by Paul McCartney & Wings was written in reaction to the critics who said McCartney's music was lightweight. This hit entered the top 10 the week McCartney began his 'Wings Over America' tour, his first concert appearance in the United States since the Beatles performed their last concert in the summer of 1966 at Candlestick park in San Francisco, California. This hit was number one for over a month.

3. Don't Go Breaking My Heart by Elton John and Kiki Dee was written by Elton John and Bernie Taupin under the pseudonym names of Carte Blanche and Ann Orson. This was Elton John's first appearance on his own Rocket Records label and one of his biggest hits of all time, topping the charts for an entire month. Kiki Dee had a solo hit on Elton's record label in 1974 with 'I've Got the Music in Me'.

4. Disco Lady by Johnny Taylor sold over 2 million copies and remained at the top of the charts for no less than a month. Producer and co-writer Don Davis originally called it 'Disco Baby', but changed it for Johnny Taylor. It was inspired by the Impression's song 'Gypsy Woman' because all the eyes were on the lady who caught their attention. Telma Hopkins of the group 'Dawn' was one of the background singers on this disco favorite.

5. Afternoon Delight by The Starland Vocal Band was the only hit for this group led by Bill Danoff and his wife Taffy. The inspiration for the song title came from the name of something on a lunch menu at a restaurant where they dined. Bill Danoff and Taffy Nivert previously co-wrote John Denver's first major hit 'Take Me Home Country Roads'. Denver later returned the favor by signing them to his 'Windsong' record label. The Starland Vocal Band won the Best New Artist Grammy Award for 1976.

6. Kiss and Say Goodbye by The Manhattans was written by group member Winfred 'Blue' Lovett with Glen Campbell in mind. What could have become a country music hit became the biggest hit for this R & B group from Jersey City, New Jersey.

7. December 1963 (Oh What A Night) by The Four Seasons was produced and co-written by Bob Gaudio and his future wife Judy Parker. The song was originally set 30 years earlier and was about the repeal of prohibition, but changed to a song about 'the first time' with a woman. Bob Gaudio credits actor Joe Pesci for introducing him to Frankie Valli and suggesting the guys form a group which found success as The Four Seasons.

8. Play That Funky Music by Wild Cherry was a multi-million selling single for this one hit wonder white funk band from Ohio. They took their name 'Wild Cherry' from a box of cough drops while visiting lead singer/songwriter Rob Parissi in the hospital.

9. 50 Ways to Leave Your Lover by Paul Simon was a humorous look at ending a relationship written after the divorce from his first wife Peggy Harper. It became the biggest hit from his album 'Still Crazy After All These Years'. Backup vocals on this number one hit were provided by Phoebe Snow, Patti Austin and Valerie Simpson with studio musician Steve Gadd playing the unique drum beat similar to a marching band.

10.   If You Leave Me Now by Chicago was written by Peter Cetera, who was also featured on lead vocals. Their biggest hit to date was taken from 'Chicago 10' and was different for the group known for its big, brassy sound. This beautiful ballad not only became a multiple week number one hit, but the winner of a couple of Grammy Awards, including Best Pop Vocal Performance by a Group or Duo.

11. A 5th of Beethoven by Walter Murphy was a disco version of Ludwig Van Beethoven's Symphony No. 5 in C minor, originally composed in 1807. This number one instrumental hit was produced by Walter Murphy who was once a Madison Avenue jingle writer and arranger for Doc Severinson and 'The Tonight Show'. This hit was also included on the soundtrack of 'Saturday Night Fever'.

12.   You Should Be Dancing by The Bee Gees was the first of 3 hit singles from their 12th studio album, 'Children of the World'. This number one disco hit featured Barry Gibb's falsetto voice and was one of many Bee Gees hits to be featured the following year on the 'Saturday Night Fever' soundtrack.

13. Disco Duck by Rick Dees and His Cast of Idiots was the biggest novelty hit of the year for this popular radio DJ who would later become the Morning host on KHJ radio in Los Angeles, California. He wrote 'Disco Duck' after hearing a guy at the gym where he worked out, do a great duck voice. He thought it would be a great idea to use it in a song and connect it with the very popular disco craze. It sold millions and went to reach number one on the pop charts.

14.   Love Hangover by Diana Ross was recorded after midnight in a studio with a strobe light, a few drinks and the right setting for a disco song that was about to hit the top of the charts. Producer Hal Davis set the mood for the recording session and Diana Ross kicked off her shoes and had some fun. There's even a part in the song where she's laughing on the track, but he decided to keep it in because he wanted to capture the spontaneity of the recording session.

15.   I Write the Songs by Barry Manilow was actually written by Beach Boy Bruce Johnston and was the Grammy Award Winning 'Song of the Year' in 1976.This was Manilow's first hit from his album 'Tryin' to Get the Feeling Again', with the title song becoming the 2nd hit single. This album also included the popular upbeat 'Bandstand Boogie', inspired by Dick Clark's American Bandstand theme.

16.   Boogie Fever by The Sylvers was the biggest hit for this family act consisting of 9 siblings. They were produced by Freddie Perren, who previously worked with the Jackson Five at Motown. The word 'Boogie' was hot at the time and Perren decided to add 'fever' to make it even hotter. He picked 18 year old Edmund to be the group's lead singer. Sadly, he died of lung cancer at age 47 in 2004 leaving behind 11 sons and daughters.

17.Convoy by C. W. McCall was a character name created for this advertising agency writer whose real name was Bill Fries. This hit written in C.B. jargon, capitalized on the popularity of the C.B. radio craze which was huge in 1976.This number one million seller was the only notable hit for C. W. McCall.

18.   Theme from S.W.A.T. by Rhythm Heritage was a number one instrumental hit and the theme for the popular prime time TV series which starred Steve Forest and Robert Urich. The tune was written by Barry DeVorzon, known for the instrumental hit 'Nadia's Theme' He was also the former lead singer of the 60's group Barry and The Tamerlanes who had a 1963 hit with 'I Wonder What She's Doing Tonight'.

19.   Welcome Back by John Sebastian was the title song of the popular TV series 'Welcome Back Kotter' starring Gabe Kaplan and introducing John Travolta. This was the first major solo hit for the lead singer and songwriter of all of the 60's hits by the Lovin Spoonful, including 'Summer In The City', 'Daydream', Do You Believe In Magic' and all the others.

20.   Love Rollercoaster by The Ohio Players was the 2nd number one hit, following 'Fire' for this red hot funk/R & B group. There was an urban legend surrounding the song at the time that the girl on the cover of their album 'Honey' was attacked or killed near the studio and her screams are heard on the song. It was just a hoax, and the woman on the album cover by the way was Ester Cordet, Playboy magazine's Playmate of the Month in October of 1974.

21.   Love Machine by The Miracles was their final top 40 hit and only number one after Smokey Robinson left the Motown group 4 years earlier. This million seller was co-written by Billy Griffin, who replaced Smokey Robinson on lead vocals. This upbeat disco hit was a prime cut from the 'City Of Angels' album produced by Freddie Perren, who co-wrote and produced many of the Jackson Five's early hits.

22.   Dream Weaver by Gary Wright was the first solo hit for the former member of the group Spooky Tooth. This million selling single was from the

231

album 'The Dream Weaver', an all-synthesiser/keyboard album which featured Gary Wright on vocals and keyboards, as well as instruments played by David Foster, who suggested to Wright to include this song on the album. This hit with the dreamy intro was later featured in the 1990 film 'Wayne's World' starring Mike Myers and Dana Carvey.

23.   **All by Myself** by Eric Carmen was the first major solo hit for the lead singer/songwriter of the Raspberries, best known for their 1972 hit 'Go All The Way'. His classical training at the Cleveland Institute of Music was prevalent on this hit based on the melody of Rachmanivoff's 'Piano Concerto no. 2'. The single version of 'All By Myself' ran just over 4 minutes, while the album version was over 7 minutes long.

24.   **Love to Love You Baby** by Donna Summer was one of the sexiest songs of the 70's and the debut hit for the lady who became known as 'The queen of disco'. This Boston singer born Adrian Donna Gaines, went on to sell over 130 million records worldwide. She wrote the lyrics to 'Love to Love You Baby' which was even more explicit and sexual on the 16 minute plus version which takes up the entire side of the album.

25. **Do You Know where you're going To (Theme from Mahogany)** by Diana Ross was from the film in which she co-starred with Billy Dee Williams. This was her 2nd major starring role in a movie following 'Lady Sings the Blues' for the former lead singer of the Supremes. This hit was written by Michael Masser and Carole King's former husband and songwriting partner, Gerry Goffin.

26.   **I'd Really Love to See You Tonight** by England Dan & John Ford Coley was the first of a string of late 70's hits for this soft rock duo. Both members of this Austin, Texas based act were formerly members of Southwest F.O.B., known for the moderately successful 1968 hit 'Smell of Incense'. England Dan Seals, who died at the age of 61 in 2009, was the younger brother of Jim Seals of Seals and Crofts fame.

27. **Get up and Boogie** by The Silver Convention was their follow up to the million selling 'Fly Robin Fly', the only other hit for this Munich, Germany based disco act. This song consisted of only 6 words, 'Get Up and Boogie, that's right'. Their hit 'Fly Robin Fly' also had only 6 different words, 'Fly Robin Fly, up, up to the sky'. This may have had to do with the fact that the singers had trouble learning English and it was easier for them to learn with fewer words.

28.   **Let Your Love Flow** by The Bellamy Brothers was the only pop hit for this country music duo from Darby, Florida. This number one pop hit was written by Larry E. Williams, a former roadie for Neil Diamond. After this hit, the Bellamy Brothers, David and Howard, became a major country music act charting about a dozen number one hits and numerous other top 10 songs. Brother David Bellamy is also known for writing the song 'Spiders and Snakes' for Jim Stafford.

29.   **Rock' 'N Me** by The Steve Miller Band paid tribute to Paul Kossoff's opening of Free's 'All Right Now' which is similar to the beginning of this number one hit. This was the 2nd of 3 major hits from their most successful album of all, 'Fly like an Eagle'.

30.   **The Rubberband Man** by The Spinners was originally written about songwriter/producer Thom Bell's son and titled 'The Fat Man', but was changed by the time the group got a hold of it. Their 6th million selling single was co-written by Thom Bell with Linda Creed, who co-composed most of the Stylistics' biggest hits, as well as Whitney Houston's 'Greatest Love of All' before her death at 26 of breast cancer.

31. **You Sexy Thing** by Hot Chocolate was written by lead singer Erroll Brown and became the biggest hit for this interracial group rock/soul group formed in London, England in 1969. All their hits were produced by Mickie Most, known for producing the hits of Donovan, Herman's Hermits, the Animals and others.

32.   **Shake Your Booty** by K. C. & The Sunshine Band became their 3rd number one hit and one Harry Casey wrote to motivate people to get up and do their thing, be their best, and don't feel insecure. He disagrees with the song being another piece of disco fluff, but a song with a message. The 'B' side of this single, 'Boogie Shoes' became popular when it was featured in the 'Saturday Night Fever' soundtrack.

33.   **You'll Never Find another Love like Mine** by Lou Rawls was his first hit in 5 years and his biggest hit of all. This million seller written and produced by Gamble and Huff was recorded by Lou Rawls the way that suits him best, 'live' to tape, as opposed to laying it down on tracks. He didn't know if the song was written from personal experience, but he did know that songwriter Kenny Gamble was going through a divorce at the time with Dee Dee Sharp, 'the Mashed Potato time' singer.

34.   **Right Back Where We Started From** by Maxine Nightingale was the biggest hit for this British R & B/Soul singer/actress. This feel good, upbeat disco hit was prominently featured in the Paul Newman film 'Slap Shot' as well as being used in the soundtrack of several other films.

35.   **Love So Right** by The Bee Gees featured Barry's falsetto voice on lead vocals. This ballad was written by all 3 Gibb brothers and was the 2nd consecutive million selling single from their 'Children of the World' album, which also included 'You Should Be Dancing'.

36.   **Lowdown** by Boz Scaggs was the first major hit for this former member of Steve Miller's band. 'Lowdown' featured 4 musicians (including David Paich and Jeff Porcaro) who would form the group Toto the following year. This million selling single was a prime cut from his most successful album, 'Silk Degrees'.

37.   **Lonely Night (Angel Face)** by The Captain & Tennille was written by Neil Sedaka, who also co-wrote their first and biggest hit 'Love Will Keep Us Together'. This was the first of 3 major hit singles in 1976 for the Captain & Tennille in the year they would also begin their own weekly show on ABC.

38.   **Wreck of the Edmund Fitzgerald** by Gordon Lightfoot was the true story of the ore vessel (named after a Milwaukee civic leader) that sank in Lake Superior on November 10th 1975. All 29 crew members perished in the sinking with no bodies being recovered. When found, it was discovered that the 'Edmund Fitzgerald' had broken in two.

39. **Let 'Em In** by Paul McCartney & Wings was taken from the album 'Wings at the Speed of Sound' released in the midst of their World tour. This follow up single to 'Silly Love Songs' makes reference to some of McCartney's friends and relatives including 'Sister Suzy', 'Brother John', 'Martin Luther' and to 'Don and Phil', because the Everly Brothers were an early influence to the former Beatle. McCartney would later write their 80's hit 'On the Wings of a Nightingale'.

40. **Moonlight Feels Right** by Starbuck was a one hit wonder from Atlanta, Georgia featuring lead singer/songwriter Bruce Blackman upfront. This goodtime hit featured a standout marimba performance by group member Bo Wagner. Lead singer Bruce Blackman was previously a main member of the group 'Eternity's Children', best known for their 1968 hit 'Mrs. Bluebird'.

41. **Fooled around and Fell in Love** by Elvin Bishop featured Mickey Thomas on lead vocals. Tulsa, Oklahoma's Elvin Bishop was the lead guitarist for the Paul Butterfield Blues Band during the late 60's. Mickey Thomas later sang lead on Starship's biggest hits 'Sara' and 'We Built This City'.

42.Bohemian Rhapsody by Queen was one of the most original sounding recordings of all time and is considered to be a true rock masterpiece. This prime cut from the 'A Night At The Opera' was written by lead singer Freddie Mercury who created this unique recording which had 3 distinct parts, an operatic segment, an a capella passage, and a heavy rock solo. This single was a major hit, especially in Britain where it remained at number one for 9 weeks.

43. **More More More** by the Andrea True Connection was the only notable hit for this disco act led by this white Nashville-born singer. Under multiple stage names, she appeared as an adult film star during the 70's. This song was sampled in the 1999 hit 'Steal My Sunshine' by the Canadian act known as 'Len'.

44. **Shannon** by Henry Gross was the only notable hit for this former member of Sha Na Na. The harmonies on this million seller are very reminiscent of the sound of the Beach Boys, which may have been influenced by the fact that he toured with them. In addition to that, this song was inspired by the death of the Irish setter of Beach Boys' Carl Wilson. Coincidentally, Henry Gross also had an Irish setter named 'Shannon'.

45. **I'll Be Good to You** by The Brothers Johnson was produced by Quincy Jones. Brother George Johnson got the inspiration for this song when he was seeing 3 young ladies at the same time and it was getting quite hectic. He decided to commit to one lady in particular, Debbie Johnson, the woman he would marry. He shared the writing credit with Brother Louis and his friend Senora Sam.

46. **Misty Blue** by Dorothy Moore was a sultry, sexy soul song from this Mississippi songstress which was originally a hit on the country charts in 1966 by Wilma Burgess and in 1967 by Eddy Arnold. The song was written by Bob Montgomery in 20 minutes and offered to Brenda Lee, who turned it down. Dorothy Moore brought her version into the top 5 on both the pop and R & B charts in the spring of 1976.

47.   **Sara Smile** by Hall & Oates was an autobiographical song written by Daryl Hall about Sara Allen. At the time he wrote this song they were living together in a small apartment in New York City. Although they are no longer together, they lived together for 28 years.

48.   **Show Me the Way** by Peter Frampton was the first hit single from 'Frampton Comes Alive', the biggest selling album of the year. This was the first of 3 hit singles from the album recorded 'live' at San Francisco's 'Winterland'. This hit was known for Peter Frampton's use of the 'talk box', an effect which connected his voice with his guitar.

49.   **Take It To The Limit** by The Eagles was the 3rd major hit single from their 'One Of These Nights' album and was the only 'A' side single which bassist Randy Meisner sang lead vocals. Meisner co-wrote this ballad with Glenn Frey and Don Henley. He left the group after the Eagles Hotel California tour in 1977 and was replaced by Timothy B. Schmidt.

50.   **Fox on the Run** by The Sweet was a song about groupies, written by all 4 members of this British glam-rock band. Previously their hits were written and produced by Chinn and Chapman, but the band wanted to remove themselves from the bubblegum music and image they were becoming identified with. This was their 14th single in Britain, but only their 3rd to chart in the top 40 in North America.

51.   **Devil Woman** by Cliff Richard was the first major hit in the United States for this British superstar who had already had great success in the U.K. and Canada during the 60's. The singer known as Cliff Richard was born Harry Rodger Webb in Lucknow, India of British parentage. In 1995, he became the first rock star to be knighted, becoming 'Sir' Cliff Richard.

52.   **More Than a Feeling** by Boston was the signature hit from 'Boston', the biggest selling debut album by an American group .Guitarist Tom Scholtz wrote this rock masterpiece over a 5 year year period. Lead singer Brad Delp committed suicide on March 9 2007 at the age of 55.

53.**Still the One** by Orleans was the most successful hit for this New York City based rock group. Lead singer and songwriter John Hall left the group the following year. He later became involved in politics and became a U.S. Congressman.

54.   **I Love Music** by The O'Jays was another million seller written and produced by Gamble and Huff for this R & B vocal group from Canton, Ohio. According to lead singer Eddie Levert, they would usually record a hit in the first 3 takes, but this one took 2 days and Kenny Gamble apparently wrote the lyrics on the spot in the studio.

55.   **Shop Around** by the Captain & Tennille was a remake of the Miracles hit originally released in 1960. After Toni Tennille heard Daryl (The Captain) playing the song on the piano one day, she suggested they redo the song from a girl's perspective. It became their 4th consecutive million seller.

56.   **Rock And Roll Music** by The Beach Boys was a remake of the Chuck Berry classic from 1957. It was the first top 10 hit for the Beach Boys since

'Good Vibrations' hit number one 10 years earlier. Mike Love was featured on lead vocals on this hit produced by Brian Wilson, who played keyboards on this prime cut from their album '15 Big Ones'. The Beatles recorded a version of this song in 1964.

57.   Only Sixteen by Dr. Hook was a remake of the Sam Cooke song from 1959. After a 3 year absence from the charts and a switch to Capitol records, the group formerly known for their novelty hits changed direction. This was the first of many hits by Dr. Hook which featured a more adult mellow sound with lead vocals from Dennis Locorriere.

58.Muskrat Love by The Captain & Tennille was originally released by the group America in 1973 with only minor results. The Captain and Tennille decided to remake this silly song about 2 muskrats and it became their most requested song in concert and their 5th and final million selling single of the 70's.

59.   Beth by Kiss was an out of character mellow song from the group known for their harder edged rock and roll. Drummer Peter Criss was featured on lead vocals on this hit which was a last minute addition to their 'Destroyer' album. It was originally released as the 'B' side of 'Detroit Rock City' as a single. Surprisingly, it became the highest charting single for the group known for its hard rock sound.

60.   Dream On by Aerosmith was originally released in 1973 with limited success. However, it was re-released 3 years later in 1976 and it became the band's first and biggest hit of the 70's. It was recorded in 1972 and released on their debut album 'Aerosmith' in January of 1973. Lead singer Steven Tyler played piano on this classic rock hit which he also wrote.

61.   Happy Days by Pratt & McClain was the theme from the popular 70's show about the 50's starring Henry Winkler and Ron Howard. This song replaced 'Rock Around The Clock' by Bill Haley & The Comets which was the original theme for the TV show 'Happy Days'. It was written by Norman Gimbel and Charles Fox, who also wrote the themes for 'Laverne & Shirley", Wonder Wonder', 'Love American Style' and 'The Love Boat' among others.

62.   Sing A Song by Earth, Wind & Fire was a prime cut from their number one double album 'Gratitude' which also included their million selling single 'Shining Star'. This popular R & B group was inducted into the Songwriters Hall Of Fame on June 17th 2010. Earlier that year, 3 of the members of Earth, Wind, & Fire, including lead singer Philip Bailey, participated in the recording of 'We Are the World 25 for Haiti'.

63.   Get Closer by Seals & Crofts featured Carolyn Willis of the group Honeycone on backing vocals. This was the title song and only hit from their 8th studio album. Jim Seals' younger brother, Dan Seals had his first hit in 1976 as 'England Dan' with John Ford Coley with 'I'd Really Love to See You Tonight'.

64.   Sorry Seems to Be the Hardest Word by Elton John was from his double album 'Blue Moves', recorded in Toronto, the city his partner David Furnish was born. This ballad was one of Elton's darker hits and was only his 2nd single on his 'Rocket Records' label.

65.   **She's Gone** by Hall & Oates originally charted in 1974 with only mediocre results, but was re-released in 1976 when it reached the top 10. John Oates wrote the lyrics for the song after he was stood up on New Years Eve by a lady he met a few days before in the middle of the night in Greenwich Village. The next day Daryl Hall sat down at the piano and wrote the music.

66.   **Love Is Alive** by Gary Wright was the follow up to 'Dream Weaver' and was also a top 5 hit by the former member of Spooky Tooth. Gary Wright also played on all of George Harrison's solo albums, as well as some of Ringo's biggest hits including 'It Don't Come Easy'. He was also the one playing piano on the opening of Nilsson's number one hit 'Without You'.

67.   **Got to Get You into My Life** by The Beatles was popular 10 years after it was featured on their 'Revolver' album. It's interesting to note that this recording was not released as a single until 6 years after the Beatles broke up. This hit featured a brass section, and was written solely by Paul McCartney, who was featured singing lead.

68.   **Sweet Thing** by Rufus featuring Chaka Khan, was written in the studio in a matter of minutes by Chaka and guitarist Tony Maiden, who had just joined the group. This million seller became their 2nd biggest hit following 'Tell Me Something Good' in 1974.

69.   **Turn the Beat Around** by Vickie Sue Robinson was a popular disco hit for this singer/actress who once appeared in the original Broadway production of the rock musical 'Hair' .This was the only notable hit for this singer who died in 2000 of cancer at the age of 45.

70.   **Summer** by War was written by all 8 members of the group, which was not unusual for this California band. This mellow summertime cruisin' hit was certainly a sound of the times with lyrics like '8 track playing all your favorite sounds' and 'rappin' on your C.B. radio in your van'. This was War's final top 10 hit.

71.   **Love Hurts** by Nazareth was a remake of a song the Everly Brothers recorded in 1960, but is best known by Roy Orbison who had a minor hit with in 1961. This was the biggest hit from this hard rock Scottish group, and was taken from their most successful album, 'Hair of the Dog'. Three years earlier they had a hit in Canada with their rock remake of Joni Mitchell's song 'This Flight Tonight' from their album 'Loud and Proud'.

72.   **Nadia's Theme** by Barry Devorzon & Perry Botkin Jr. was an instrumental hit renamed for Nadia Comaneci, the Romanian gymnast who was the star of the 1976 Summer Olympics. The tune was originally titled 'Cotton's Dream' as was the title song of the movie 'Bless the Beasts and Children' starring Billy Mumy. It was also used as the theme for the popular daytime soap 'The Young and The Restless'.

73.   **Stand Tall** by Burton Cummings was the first and biggest solo hit for the former lead singer of The Guess Who. He also wrote or co-wrote all of their biggest hits for the 10 years he fronted Canada's most successful pop/ rock group. On December 30 2009, one day shy of his 62nd birthday, Burton

Cummings was named an officer of the Order Of Canada, one of the country's highest degrees of honor.

74.You Are the Woman by Firefall was the first and biggest hit for this soft rock group from Boulder, Colorado. The group's lead singer was Rick Roberts who was once a member of the Flying Burrito Brothers with drummer Mike Clarke. Firefall began touring with Fleetwood Mac when this hit reached top 10.

75.   Breaking up Is Hard to Do by Neil Sedaka was a ballad remake of his own up tempo hit which reached number one in 1962. The idea of a slowed down version came after Lenny Welch, the singer best known for his 1963 hit 'Since I Fell For You' recorded it as a ballad in 1970 with favorable results. Neil performed it as a ballad in concert with a great response from the audience and decided to re release it.

76.   I Never Cry by Alice Cooper was a power ballad from the album 'Alice Cooper Goes to Hell' produced by Bob Ezrin. This was a concept album and sequel to his 'Welcome to My Nightmare' project written by Alice Cooper and guitar player Dick Wagner, who co-wrote many of Cooper's biggest hits.

77.   Evil Woman by Electric Light Orchestra was the first of 3 notable 1976 hits by this orchestral rock band from Birmingham, England led by Jeff Lynne, Bev Bevan and Roy Wood, 3 former members of the group 'The Move'. 'Evil Woman' was their first worldwide hit and one Jeff Lynne claims to have written the quickest of all the songs he composed for E. L. O. This hit was from the 'Face the Music' album.

78.   Magic Man by Heart was the first major hit by this rock group led by sisters Ann and Nancy Wilson. Lead singer/songwriter Ann later revealed that 'the magic man' was inspired by her relationship with her then-boyfriend and band manager Michael Fisher. This hit is known for its distinctive use of the minimoog synthesizer.

79.   Money Honey by The Bay City Rollers was the follow up to their biggest hit in North America, 'Saturday Night'. 'Money Honey', written by group members Eric Faulkner and Stuart Wood was one of 4 hit singles from their album 'Dedication' produced by Jimmy Ienner who was known for his work with 3 Dog Night, Grand Funk and the Raspberries.

80.   Let Her In by John Travolta was the first hit single for the actor who was best known for his character Vinnie Barbarino on the currently popular TV series 'Welcome Back Kotter'. The singer/actor from New Jersey would later become a superstar actor after his roles in both 'Saturday Night Fever' and 'Grease' during the late 70's.

81.   Golden Years by David Bowie was the follow up to his number one hit 'Fame'. This top 10 hit was the only hit from one of his most successful albums, 'Station To Station' recorded during a time when his cocaine addiction was at its peak. This was popular the year David Bowie starred in his first film 'The Man Who Fell to Earth'.

82.   Fool to Cry by The Rolling Stones was the lead off single from their

'Black and Blue' album which was the first featuring Ronnie Wood as the replacement for Mick Taylor. This ballad was their first top 10 hit since another ballad, 'Angie' reached number one in 1973.

83.   **Baby I Love Your Way** by Peter Frampton was the 2nd hit single from the hugely successful 'Frampton Comes Alive' album which sold well over 6 million copies. Prior to his solo career, Frampton was a prominent member in the British group Humble Pie and before that with The Herd in his teenage years. This song later became a number one hit for Will to Power in 1988 and a top 10 hit for Big Mountain in 1994.

84.   **Nights Are Forever without You** by England Dan & John Ford Coley was the 2nd consecutive hit for this soft rock duo. Their first 2 major hits were written by Parker McGee and taken from the album 'Nights Are Forever'. (England) Dan Seals later became a successful solo country singer with hits which included 'Bop' and 'Meet Me in Montana'.

85.   **A Little Bit More** by Dr. Hook was the 2nd 1976 hit for the more mature sounding group which once was known for their offbeat style and songs like 'The Cover of the Rolling Stone' when they were known as Dr. Hook and the Medicine Show'.

86.   **Junk Food Junkie** by Larry Groce was a humorous novelty hit about a guy who leads a double life by appearing to be living a healthy food lifestyle in the day, but at night is addicted to junk food. Although this was his only hit, he became known to children and their parents through the songs he recorded on 'Walt Disney Records' with the 'Children's Favorites' series.

87.   **This Masquerade** by George Benson was written by Leon Russell and was the biggest hit from 'Breezin', one of the years's best selling albums. This was the breakthrough hit for this R & B/Jazz singer/guitarist from Pittsburgh who has been performing since before he was 10 years old.

88.   **Sweet Love** by the Commodores was the first of many to feature Lionel Richie on lead vocals. Prior to this single, Walter 'Clyde' Orange was the Commodores lead singer while Richie played saxophone and sang backup vocals. This was the first of 2 ballads from 1976 to feature Lionel Richie on lead vocals with 'Just to be Close to You' being the second.

89.   **That'll Be the Day** by Linda Ronstadt was another popular remake for the talented singer from Tucson, Arizona who was making a career out of recording songs from the 50's and 60's. This Buddy Holly classic, originally popular in 1957, was from her 3rd consecutive million selling album, 'Hasten down the Wind'.

90. **Rhiannon** by Fleetwood Mac prominently features Stevie Nicks on this self-composed hit and 2nd single from their album simply titled 'Fleetwood Mac'. She has introduced this song in live performances as 'a song about a Welsh witch'. She wrote it in 1974, a few months before joining Fleetwood Mac.

91.   **Never Gonna Fall in Love Again** by Eric Carmen was the former lead singer of the Raspberries 2nd big solo hit of 1976 following 'All By Myself'.

Both songs were based on classical pieces of music with this one taken from the 3rd movement from the Second Symphony by Russian composer Sergei Rachmaninoff.

92.   The Boys Are Back in Town by Thin Lizzy was the most popular hit in North America for this rock quartet from Dublin, Ireland featuring Phil Lynott on lead vocals. This classic rocker from the 'Jailbreak' album features twin guitar leads by Scott Gorham and Brian Robertson. Front man Phil Lynott died at the age of 36 in 1986 from heart failure and pneumonia.

93.   Fernando by Abba featured Anni-Frid Lyngstad on lead vocals and was their biggest selling single of all time. The song was written for Anni-Frid and not Abba. She originally recorded it on her 1975 solo album without much success. The story song ballad reached number one in 14 countries around the world.

94.   Fanny (Be Tender with My Love) by The Bee Gees was the 3rd consecutive hit single from their comeback album 'Main Course'. The brothers Gibb stayed on course with one hit after another during their late 70's disco period. The Bee Gees have sold in excess of 200 million singles and albums worldwide.

95.   Walk Away From Love by David Ruffin was produced and arranged by Van McCoy and featured some of the top session players in the business along with 'Faith, Hope & Charity' on backup vocals. This became the biggest solo hit for the former lead singer of the Temptations during the 70's. He died of an apparent drug overdose in 1991 at the age of 50.

96.   If You Know What I Mean by Neil Diamond from the album 'Beautiful Noise' was produced by Robbie Robertson of The Band. This hit was the first and biggest hit single released from his 3rd album for Columbia records.1976 was also the year Neil Diamond appeared in the documentary film 'The Last Waltz', which was about the Band's final concert. It was directed by Martin Scorsese.

97.   Do You Feel like We Do by Peter Frampton was the 3rd consecutive 1976 hit single from the 'Frampton Comes Alive' album. This song was originally recorded in the early 70's on the album 'Frampton's Camel' with little success. When it was featured on his signature album 'Frampton Comes Alive', it was over 14 minutes long, and the single version was around half of that at 7 minutes.

98.   Heaven Must Be Missing An Angel by Tavares was a million seller for this R & B family act from Massachusetts. This hit was produced and co-written by Freddie Perren who also gave the family act The Sylvers a major hit in 1976 with 'Boogie Fever'.

99.   I Only Want to Be with You by The Bay City Rollers was a remake of a song Dusty Springfield made popular in 1964. 1976 was the biggest year of success in North America for this Scottish group, but it was also a year of change in personnel with bassist Alan Longmuir leaving and Ian Mitchell joining the tartan-clad pop idols band.

100.   Take the Money and Run by The Steve Miller Band was their first hit since 'The Joker' in early 1974. Steve Miller wrote and produced this catchy story song about 2 young bandits. This was the first of 3 big hits from the 'Fly like an Eagle' album.

101.   Times of Your Life by Paul Anka was a commercial for Kodak before it became a hit record. It was Paul Anka's idea to record the song and when he performs it in concert, there would be film of him and his family on screen showing the times of his life.

102.   Just to Be close To You by The Commodores was the song that established Lionel Richie as the lead singer and principle songwriter for this successful Motown group. Lionel Richie decided that he wanted to write the songs after he had a conversation with Motown producer Hal Davis who encouraged him to always plan for a follow-up hit.

103.   Tryin to Get the Feeling Again by Barry Manilow was the title song and 2nd single from his 3rd studio album, which was certified triple-platinum. Before he was writing and singing his own songs, he was the pianist and co-producer on Bette Midler's debut album 'The Divine Miss M' back in 1972.

104.   Say You Love Me by Fleetwood Mac from their self-titled album featured Christine McVie on lead vocals on this 3rd single which she also wrote. Her maiden name was Christine Perfect before marrying bassist John McVie in 1968, 2 years before she joined this super group.

105.   Country Boy (You Got Your Feet in L.A.) by Glen Campbell was the follow up to his most successful hit 'Rhinestone Cowboy'. 'Country Boy' was written by Lambert and Potter who produced and wrote the 1st song 'Don't Pull Your Love' in his follow up medley hit later in 1976. It was also the year he married Sarah Barg, Mac Davis' 2nd wife. Glen Campbell has been married 4 times and is the father of eight children.

106.   (Don't Fear) The Reaper by the Blue Oyster Cult was the signature hit for this hard rock group from Long Island, New York. It was from their 'Agents OF Fortune' album and was written and sung by the group's lead guitarist Donald 'Buck Dharma' Roeser. The name 'Blue Oyster Cult' came from a 60's poem written by the group's manager and producer Sandy Pearlman.

107.   Getaway by Earth, Wind & Fire was another winner from the group whose members all practiced transcendental meditation. The lyrics of this million seller were inspired by group leader Maurice White's philosophies on spirituality demonstrated by the group and on their album 'Spirit'.

108.   With Your Love by Jefferson Starship was the only hit from their album 'Spitfire', which was the follow up to 'Red Octopus'. This hit featured Marty Balin on lead vocals and was very similar to the sound and style of 'Miracles' from 1975.

109.   Rock and Roll All Nite by Kiss was an anthem song for rock's most theatrical rock group. This was a 'live' and more popular version than the one released a year before. This hit featured Gene Simmons on lead vocals and was the highlight of their breakthrough album 'Alive!'

110. **Wake up Everybody** by Harold Melvin & The Bluenotes wasn't a dance tune, but a social comment tune that you had to listen to. The message was delivered by the soulful voice of Teddy Pendergrass on this final top 40 hit by this Philadelphia soul group.

111. **You're My Best Friend** by Queen was the follow up single to their masterpiece 'Bohemian Rhapsody', also from 'A Night at the Opera' album. Bass player John Deacon, who was only 19 years old when he joined Queen, wrote this hit for his wife Veronica. Lead singer Freddie Mercury died at the age of 45 of bronchial pneumonia as a result of Aids on November 24, 1991.

112. **There's a Kind Of Hush** by The Carpenters was a remake of the top 10 hit from 1967 by Herman's Hermits. Richard Carpenter, who produced their version, later revealed that he wasn't particularly pleased with their rendition of a song which was perfectly fine by Herman's Hermits. He also said that his use of the synthesizer did not wear well with him.

113. **Takin' It to the Streets** by The Doobie Brothers was the first to feature new member Michael McDonald on lead vocals. After former lead singer Tom Johnston got ill, it led to the emergency hiring of Michael McDonald, who took over as lead singer and main songwriter resulting in a change of direction and sound for this California rock group.

114. **Livin' Thing** by the Electric Light Orchestra was the first of 3 hit singles from their platinum selling album 'A New World Record'. There have been many interpretations of this song, but according to songwriter Jeff Lynne, it was intended to be about love and the loss of love.

115. **Fly Away** by John Denver featured Olivia Newton-John on backing vocals. John Denver was not only a popular singer, but his personality branched out into TV where he hosted the Grammy Awards 5 times and guest hosted Johnny Carson's Tonight Show on numerous occasions, and eventually starring in movies.

116. **Tear the Roof off the Sucker** by Parliament was George Clinton's funk band formerly known as 'The Parliaments' in the 60's and they also recorded under the name 'Funkedelic'. This million seller was produced by George Clinton and was featured on their gold album 'Mothership Connection'.

117. **Squeeze Box** by The Who is a term used to describe an accordion, but is used as a sexual innuendo in this hit written by Pete Townsend featuring Roger Daltry on lead vocals. This was the only hit from 'The Who by Numbers' album which featured a cartoon cover drawn by group member John Entwistle.

118. **Deep Purple** by Donny & Marie Osmond was a remake of the 1963 number one hit by Nino Tempo and April Stevens, although the song itself goes back to the early 30's. This song was popular for Donny and Marie in the year they began co-hosting their own musical/variety show.

119. **Strange Magic** by Electric Light Orchestra was the 2nd hit from the 'Face the Music' album. Co-founder Roy Wood left after their first album, leaving Jeff Lynne as the group's lead singer/songwriter and producer.

120.　**Baby Face** by Wing & a Prayer Fife & Drum Corps was a disco version of a song from the 1920's. This was the only hit for this group of New York City studio musicians with 4 female singers.

121.　**I Do, I Do, I Do, I Do** by Abba topped the charts in Australia, but missed the top 10 in North America for the group that became Sweden's number one export. Abba mania was gaining momentum and they would now have an average of 3 hits per year through 1979.

122.　**Love Me** by Yvonne Elliman was a popular love ballad for this singer/actress who was born in Honolulu, Hawaii. She first gained fame when she sang the role of Mary Magdalene in the original album of 'Jesus Christ Superstar'. She also sang backup on 2 of Eric Clapton's hits of the 70's, 'I Shot the Sheriff' and 'Lay Down Sally.'

123.　**Wham Bam Shang a Lang** by Silver included John Batdorf (of Batdorf and Rodney fame) and keyboardist Brent Mydland, who later joined Grateful Dead, but died of a drug overdose in 1990 at the age of 37. This was the only hit for this soft rock/country group.

124.　**Movin'** by Brass Construction was created during a studio jam session by this 9 man band fronted by Guyana-born Randy Muller, who also co-wrote this R & B hit. Muller later organized another Brooklyn, New York based band, Skyy which featured vocals by sisters Denise, Dolores and Bonnie Dunning.

125.　**Grow Some Funk of Your Own/I feel like a Bullet (In the Gun of Robert John)** by Elton John was a double-side hit single from the 'Rock of The Westies' album. 'Grow Some Funk' was one of Elton's heavier rock songs with a prominent guitar lick by Davey Johnstone, who got a rare co-writer credit alongside John and Taupin's name. The 'B' side ballad was a song about a comparison with the shooting of Jesse James by James' outlaw-partner Robert Ford to his past failed romances.

126.　**I Want You** by Marvin Gaye was produced and co-written by Leon Ware, who worked for Motown boss Berry Gordy for many years since he was 17 years old. Gordy suggested that Marvin Gaye should be the one to record this song featuring some of the top session men in the business including Dennis Coffey and Ray Parker Jr. This hit reached number one on the R & B charts.

127.　**Love in the Shadows** by Neil Sedaka was a disco-flavored moderate hit popular at the tail end of his 1975-1976 comeback.

128.　**I'm Easy** by Keith Carradine was the Academy Award winning Best Song from the movie 'Nashville', which also starred this singer/songwriter from California. He is the son of actor John Carradine and half brother of the late David Carradine who was best known for his role in the 'Kung Fu' TV series.

129.　**The Best Disco in Town** by the Ritchie Family featured a medley of hits which included 'Reach Out, I'll Be There', 'I Love Music', 'T.S.O.P.' and other popular soul/R & B songs. This was the only other hit aside from the 1975 hit 'Brazil' for this Philadelphia disco studio group.

130. **Tangerine** by Salsoul Orchestra was a disco reworking of a song made famous in 1942 by Jimmy Dorsey. This was the biggest hit for the Salsoul Orchestra which featured up to 50 studio musicians and singers.

131. **Who'd She Coo?** by the Ohio Players was a jazz/rock/funk hit which became their final top 40 hit. Like their other hits, all their songs were written by all the members in the group, which gave everybody the right to collect royalties.

132. **Slow Ride** by Foghat was the best known hit from this British rock quartet. Lead singer/guitarist and songwriter 'Lonesome' Dave Peverett, was formerly a member of Savoy Brown. This hit was featured on their 5th album 'A Fool in the City' and also on 'Foghat Live' in 1977. The album versions ran over 8 minutes, while the single version was just under 4.

133. **Young Hearts Run Free** by Candi Staton was the most popular hit for the singer known as the first lady of southern soul. She has since changed to gospel music and no longer believes in the message in this song which encouraged young women not to get married, but to shack up. She has been married 4 times, including a commitment to soul singer Clarence Carter from 1970 to 1973.

134. **The White Knight** by Cledus Maggard and the Citizen's Band was another pop country hit that cashed in the current C. B. radio craze, like C. W. McCall did with 'Convoy' that same year. Cledus Maggard was the name advertising executive and television writer Jay Hugely chose to record a novelty hit about a semi trailer truck driver victimized by a corrupt highway patrolman's speed trap.

135. **Over My Head** by Fleetwood Mac was the first top 40 hit for this super group of the 70's. Stevie Nicks and Lindsey Buckingham joined in 1975. Keyboardist Christine McVie wrote and sang lead on this debut hit from their self-titled album. She married bassist John McVie in 1968, but divorced shortly after this song became popular.

136. **Love Ballad** by L.T.D. featured Jeffrey Osborne on lead vocals. He recorded the song at 6 o'clock in the morning after an all night recording session. Songwriter Skip Scarborough composed the song in 20 minutes and because he didn't have a title for the tune, he simply called it 'Love Ballad'.

137. **Action** by The Sweet was written by all 4 members of this British glam-rock band. This high energy hit featuring Brian Connolly on lead vocals was the follow up to 'Fox on the Run'. Brian Connolly died of liver failure in 1997 at the age of 51.

138. **Winners and Losers** by Hamilton, Joe Frank & Reynolds was the follow up to their number one hit 'Fallin' in Love'. After this hit on the 'Playboy' record label, 4 years after Tommy Reynolds left the group, they finally changed their name to 'Hamilton, Joe Frank & Dennison'. This was their final hit.

139. **Love Really Hurts without You** by Billy Ocean was the very first hit for this singer from Trinidad who was raised in England. He would have to wait

8 years before his next hit 'Carribean Queen' would arrive, but the 80's saw a string of major hits for this radio-friendly performer.

140.   Somewhere in the Night by Helen Reddy was a more popular hit in 1978 when Barry Manilow recorded this Richard Kerr/Will Jennings song. Helen Reddy's version was the 2nd single from her 'Ain't No Way to Treat a Lady' album.

141.   Shower the People by James Taylor featured his then-wife Carly Simon on harmony vocals. This hit was from his 7th album 'In the Pocket' which was his final hit with Warner before switching to the Columbia record label beginning with 1977's hits.

142.   Paloma Blanca by the George Baker Selection was one of 2 hits in North America for the Dutch music act also known for the 1970 hit 'Little Green Bag'. George Baker was the stage name for Hans Bouwens who wrote and produced this catchy melody which featured the recorder as an instrument. The title is Spanish and means 'white dove'.

143.   Baretta's Theme (Keep Your Eye on the Sparrow) by Rhythm Heritage was the theme of the popular TV series starring Robert Blake. This was the 2nd 1976 charted TV theme from this Los Angeles studio group following the number one hit 'Theme from S.W.A.T.' at the beginning of the year.

144.   Today's the Day by America was written by group member Dan Peek who decided to leave the group around the time this single came out. This George Martin produced hit was the final top 40 70's hit for America on the Warner label. They would have one more major hit in 1982 with 'You Can Do Magic' on the Capitol record label.

145.   Come on Over by Olivia Newton-John was written by Barry and Robin Gibb of the Bee Gees. The Bee Gees recorded the song on the 'Main Course' album, but never released it as a single. Olivia Newton-John loved listening to the album and decided to record her own version. It's interesting to note that both the Bee Gees and Olivia Newton-John were both born in Great Britain, but had grown up in Australia.

146.   Youngblood by Bad Company was a remake of the 1957 hit by the Coasters written by Jerry Leiber and Mike Stoller with Doc Pomus. This was the follow up to 'Feel like Makin' Love', but was their only top 40 hit from their 'Run with the Pack' album.

147.   Cupid by Tony Orlando & Dawn was the final top 40 hit for this popular act whose TV show would also end in 1976. This was a remake of the Sam Cooke song from 1961, which also became a hit for Johnny Nash in 1969 and the Spinners in 1980. The group Tony Orlando and Dawn went their separate ways the following year in 1977.

148.   Livin' for the Weekend by the O'Jays was their first single after a change in personnel when original member William Powell stopped touring because of illness. He died the following year. He was replaced by Sammy Strain who was a member of Little Anthony & The Imperials since 1964.

149. **Save Your Kisses for Me** by Brotherhood of Man was a number one hit in Britain and the winner of the Eurovision Song contest. The lineup of the group was completely different than the studio act that had a hit with 'United We Stand' in 1970. Two of the group members wrote this song along with Tony Hiller, who produced and co-wrote 'United We Stand' 6 years earlier.

150. **Last Child** by Aerosmith was the first single from their hard rock album 'Rocks' and was written by lead singer Steven Tyler with guitarist Brad Whitford who gets the spotlight when performing this in concert.

151. **Lorelei** by Styx was their first hit for A & M records and the only hit single from their 5th album 'Equinox'. This hit was co-written by lead singer/keyboardist Dennis DeYoung, who fronted this Chicago - based band on most of their hits.

152. **Union Man** by Cate Brothers was the only top 40 hit for this pop duo of twin brothers, Ernie and Earl from Fayetteville, Arkansas.

153. **Makin' Our Dreams Come True** by Cyndi Grecco was the theme from the popular TV series 'Laverne and Shirley' starring Penny Marshall and Cindy Williams. Although this was the only hit for Cyndi Grecco, the writers of this song wrote several hits and TV themes, including 'Happy Days', the show that launched this spin off.

154. **Tracks of My Tears** by Linda Ronstadt was a remake of a song originally made popular by Smokey Robison and the Miracles in 1965. It was also a top 10 hit 2 years later in 1967 by Johnny Rivers. Linda Ronstadt brought it back the 3rd time when it was released as the 2nd single from her 'Prisoner in Disguise' album.

155. **Hello Old Friend** by Eric Clapton was the most notable single from his 'No Reason to Cry' album. Eric Clapton, one of the greatest rock guitarists of all time has been a member of numerous groups through the 60's and 70's including the 'Yardbirds', 'Cream', 'Blind Faith' and 'Derek and The Dominos'.

156. **Shout It Out Loud** by Kiss was a prime cut from their 'Destroyer' album produced by Bob Ezrin, Alice Cooper's longtime producer. This high energy rockin' hit featured both Gene Simmons and Paul Stanley on lead vocals.

157. **Rock and Roll Love Letter** by the Bay City Rollers was one of 4 hits this teenybopper rock group charted in 1976 in North America. The original members consisted of brothers Alan and Derek Longmuir, Les McKeoun, Eric Faulkner and Stuart 'Woody' Wood.

158. **Good Hearted Woman** by Waylon and Willie was the Country Music Association (CMA) Song of the Year in 1976 and was originally featured on the 1972 album of the same name by Waylon Jennings. His fellow outlaw country friend Willie Nelson co-wrote and accompanied him on this popular version.

159. **This One's for You** by Barry Manilow is the title track from this singer/ pianist/songwriter who once studied at New York's Julliard School. This was 1 of 4 hit singles from this triple platinum album at a time when Barry Manilow was rarely absent from the pop charts during the late 70's.

160. **I Need to Be in Love** by the Carpenters was a much bigger hit on the Adult Contemporary charts than it was on the pop charts, where it barely made the top 30. This song, co-written by Albert Hammond, was one of Karen Carpenters' personal favorites. It was produced by Brother Richard.

161. **Love Is the Drug** by Roxy Music was the only commercially successful pop hit for this British art/rock group featuring Bryan Ferry on lead vocals and keyboards. The lyrics for this hit from the 'Siren' album were apparently written by Bryan Ferry while he was walking and kicking leaves in Hyde Park one day.

162. **Sophisticated Lady (She's A Different Lady)** by Natalie Cole was popular during the summer of 1976 when she married Marvin Yancy, her producer and co-writer. He was inspired to write a song (with Chuck Jackson and Natalie Cole) called 'Sophisticated Lady' by the music of jazz giant Duke Ellington. Although Ellington had a hit with a song titled 'Sophisticated Lady' in the 30's, this one was different and was suited to Natalie Cole, the lady who now deserved the title.

163. **One Love in My Lifetime** by Diana Ross was the 4th single from her album 'Diana Ross' which produced 2 number one singles, 'The Theme from Mahogany' and 'Love Hangover'. She would have to wait 4 more years before she would reach the top 10 again, when 'Upside Down' turned up at number one in 1980.

164. **Crazy on You** by Heart was popular in the debut year of this group from Seattle, Washington who were living in Vancouver at the time they signed with the local 'Mushroom' label and recorded their first album 'Dreamboat Annie'. The title song of this million selling debut album had 3 different versions included on the LP.

165. **A Dose of Rock and Roll** by Ringo Starr featured musical friends Peter Frampton on guitar and Dr. John on keyboards on the only top 40 single from his album 'Ringo's Rotogravure'. This was Ringo's first record release on the Atlantic' record label.

166. **Looking for Space** by John Denver was his final hit to reach top 30 on the pop charts. The singer/songwriter known for the overuse of the phrase 'far out' was not delivering the multiple million sellers like he had during the previous 5 years. John Denver once described this song as 'looking for the definition of who you are, by finding out where you are, not only physically, but mentally and emotionally'.

167. **Don't Pull Your Love/Then You Can Tell Me Goodbye** by Glen Campbell was a medley of 2 songs which he did by accident in front of his producers Dennis Lambert and Brian Potter. He started to sing the song they wrote, which was a 1971 hit for Hamilton, Joe Frank and Reynolds, and he wanted to sing it slow and just went into the line 'kiss me each morning' which was part of 'Then You Can Tell me Goodbye', which the Casinos made famous in 1967. Lambert and Potter loved the way the 2 songs sounded together that they suggested he do them as a medley.

168. **Mamma Mia** by Abba barely made the top 40 in North America but was huge in Europe. This song later became a favorite when it was featured as the title song for the Abba musical, then the movie.

169. Did You Boogie (With Your Baby) by Flash Cadillac & the Continental Kids featured Wolfman Jack coming in and out with his 'wolfmanisms'. This group appeared in the movie 'American Graffiti' as the band playing at the prom.

170. It's O.K by the Beach Boys was a return to their fun summertime sound and was featured on their album '15 Big Ones' produced by Brian Wilson. Mike Love was featured on lead vocals on this moderate hit from the summer of 1976.

More Hits of 1976

Only Love Is Real by Carole King was from her 'Thoroughbred' album, the final recording on the 'Ode' record label. Despite producer Lou Adler's best efforts and a long list of contributing musical friends who included James Taylor, David Crosby, Graham Nash, Tom Scott, J.D Souther and others, the single and album did not do as well in sales or in chart performance as expected.

Another Rainy Day in New York City by Chicago, written by Robert Lamm, was the first single released from their album 'Chicago 10'. This single was quickly replaced on the charts by 'If You Leave Me Now' which was gaining favorable response from the album before it was even released as a single.

Hurricane Pt1 by Bob Dylan was a protest song he wrote about boxer Rubin 'Hurricane' Carter who had been imprisoned for a triple murder in Patterson, New Jersey. In 1999 Norman Jewison was inspired to make a movie about the boxer titled 'Hurricane' starring Denzel Washington.

Happy Music by the Blackbyrds was the only other top 40 hit for this soul group best known for the top 10 hit 'Walkin' In Rhythm' from 1975. This group recorded on the 'Fantasy' record label where C.C.R had all their hits.

Let It Shine by Olivia Newton-John was a pop/country song written by Nashville composer Linda Hargrove. This moderately successful single was backed with her version of 'He Ain't Heavy, He's My Brother' which the Hollies made popular in early 1970. She didn't shine again with major success until 2 years later when she had 3 consecutive million selling hit singles from the musical 'Grease'.

Fallen Angel by Frankie Valli barely made the top 40 for the lead singer of The Four Seasons who made a major comeback in 1975 with 'My Eyes Adored You' and 'Swearin' to God'. This song was later prominently featured in musical play 'The Jersey Boys', the life and music of the Four Seasons.

Hit the Road Jack by the Stampeders was a remake of the number one hit by Ray Charles from 1961. A guest appearance by Wolfman Jack was the highlight of this fun revival of a classic song.

I Heard It through the Grapevine by C.C.R. was released as a single 4 years after the group broke up and originally featured on their 'Cosmo's

Factory' album in 1970. The album version ran over 11 minutes, but was edited to under 4 when released as a single in 1976.

Popsicle Toes by Michael Franks was the only pop hit by this California smooth jazz singer/ songwriter. He has released almost 2 dozen jazz albums since 1973.

The Homecoming by Hagood Hardy was originally used as a Salada Tea commercial and also used as the music for the made-for-TV pilot movie 'The Waltons' starring Richard Thomas. Hagood Hardy was a Canadian composer/ pianist/vibraphonist who was born in Indiana. He died on New Year's Day 1997 at the age of 59.

Don't think…Feel by Neil Diamond was the follow up to 'If You Know What I Mean' from the album 'Beautiful Noise' produced by Robbie Robertson. Neil Diamond co-wrote this single with Robert Maxwell.

Still Crazy After All These Years by Paul Simon was the title track of the album which won the Grammy Award for Album of the Year in 1976. It was 1 of 4 singles from his only solo album to reach number one.

Take It like a Man by Bachman Turner Overdrive features a special guest appearance by Little Richard on piano. This single featuring Fred Turner on lead vocals was from the album 'Head On', which also featured the jazzy 'Lookin' out for Number One' featuring Randy Bachman on lead vocals. Their next album 'Best of B.T.O. (So Far) was released in 1976.

Lady Bump by Penny McLean was a favorite at the discos for the solo singer who was also a member of Silver Convention, known for their hits 'Fly Robin Fly' and 'Get Up and Boogie'. Penny McLean's real name is Gertrude Wirschinger.

I Wanna Stay with You by Gallagher & Lyle was a Scottish duo who was formerly with 'McGuiness Flint', best known for the 1970 hit 'When I'm Dead and Gone'. 'I Wanna Stay with You' was only a moderately successful hit in North America, but reached the top 10 in Britain. They wrote songs for other artists including Mary Hopkin and the song 'Breakaway' for Art Garfunkel.

You Mean Everything to Me by The Real Thing was a number one hit in the U.K. for this British soul quartet. Although this Liverpool based group had several hits in Britain, their only hit in North America barely made the top 100 chart.

Anytime (I'll Be There) by Paul Anka was an easy listening follow up to his 'Times Of Your Life' hit. This Canadian born singer songwriter has also appeared on many TV shows and movies through the years including 'The Longest Day' in 1962 which featured over 40 stars including John Wayne, Richard Burton, Sean Connery, Henry Fonda and many other silver screen notables.

Hurt by Elvis Presley was the King's version of a song that has been made popular by various artists through the years including Timi Yuro's version in 1961. This was included on the album 'From Elvis Presley Boulevard, Memphis, Tennessee.

Top Albums Of 1976

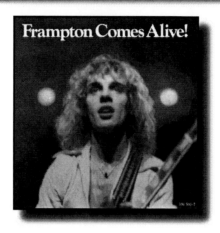

1.	Frampton Comes Alive	Peter Frampton
2.	Songs in the Key of Life	Stevie Wonder
3.	Wings at the Speed of Sound	Paul McCartney & Wings
4.	Their Greatest Hits '71 – '75	Eagles
5.	Desire	Bob Dylan
6.	Black And Blue	Elton John
7.	Presence	Led Zeppelin
8.	Gratitude	Earth, Wind & Fire
9.	Breezin'	George Benson
10.	Fleetwood Mac	Fleetwood Mac
11.	Chicago 1X	Chicago
12.	Silk Degrees	Boz Scaggs
13.	History – America's Greatest Hits	America
14.	Fly Like an Eagle	Steve Miller Band
15.	A Night at the Opera	Queen
16.	Spitfire	Jefferson Starship
17.	Thoroughbred	Carole King

Top 17 Country Hits of 1976

1. Convoy   C. W. McCall
2. Good Hearted Woman   Waylon & Willie
3. Teddy Bear   Red Sovine
4. El Paso City   Marty Robbins
5. One Piece At a Time   Johnny Cash
6. (I'm A) Stand By Your Woman Man   Ronnie Milsap
7. I Don't Want To Have To Marry You   Jim Ed Brown & Helen Cornelius
8. Good Woman Blues   Mel Tillis
9. Somebody Somewhere   Loretta Lynn
10. Thinking Of a Rendevous   Johnny Duncan
11. Sweet Dreams   Emmylou Harris
12. Somebody Somewhere   Loretta Lynn
13. You and Me   Tammy Wynette
14. Golden Ring   George Jones and Tammy Wynette
15. Cherokee Maiden   Merle Haggard
16. If you've got the Money I've Got the Time Willie Nelson
17. Among My Souvenirs   Marty Robbins

Top 17 Disco Hits of 1976

1.	Disco Lady	Johnny Taylor
2.	5th Of Beethoven	Walter Murphy
3.	You Should Be Dancing	Bee Gees
4.	Disco Duck	Rick Dees & His Cast Of Idiots
5.	Love Hangover	Diana Ross
6.	Boogie Fever	Sylvers
7.	Love Rollercoaster	Ohio Players
8.	Love Machine	Miracles
9.	Love To Love You Baby	Donna Summer
10.	Get Up and Boogie	Silver Convention
11.	Shake Your Booty	K. C. & the Sunshine Band
12.	Right Back Where We Started From	Maxine Nightingale
13.	More More More	Andrea True Connection
14.	I Love Music	O'Jays
15.	Sing a Song	Earth, Wind & Fire
16.	Turn the Beat Around	Vickie Sue Robinson
17.	Heaven Must Be Missing an Angel	Tavares

Top 17 One Hit Wonders of 1976

1.	Starland Vocal Band	Afternoon Delight
2.	Wild Cherry	Play That Funky Music
3.	Walter Murphy	5th of Beethoven
4.	Andrea True Connection	More More More
5.	Elvin Bishop	Fooled Around and Fall in Love
6.	Starbuck	Moonlight Feels Right
7.	Henry Gross	Shannon
8.	Pratt & McClain	Happy Days
9.	Vickie Sue Robinson	Turn the Beat Around
10.	Larry Groce	Junk Food Junkie
11.	Silver	Wham Bang Shang a Lang
12.	Brass Construction	Movin'
13.	Wing & A Prayer Fife and Drum Corps	Baby Face
14.	Cledus Maggard & the Citizens Band	The White Knight
15.	Cate Brothers	Union Man
16.	Cyndi Grecco	Making Our Dreams Come True
17.	Gallagher & Lyle	I Wanna Stay With You

Top 17 Rock/Hard Rock Hits of 1976

1.	Bohemian Rhapsody	Queen
2.	Dream On	Aerosmith
3.	Rock 'N Me	Steve Miller
4.	More Than a Feeling	Boston
5.	Show Me the Way	Peter Frampton
6.	The Boys Are Back In Town	Thin Lizzy
7.	Love Hurts	Nazareth
8.	Fox On the Run	Sweet
9.	Magic Man	Heart
10.	Detroit Rock City	Kiss
11.	Don't Fear the Reaper	Blue Oyster Cult
12.	Rock And Roll All Night (live)	Kiss
13.	Action	Sweet
14.	Slow Ride	Foghat
15.	Shout It out Loud	Kiss
16.	You're My Best Friend	Queen
17.	Love Is the Drug	Roxy Music

17 Notable 'Lost 45's of 1976

1.	Shannon	Henry Gross
2.	Summer	War
3.	Young Hearts Run Free	Candi Staton
4.	Love Really Hurts Without You	Billy Ocean
5.	Devil Woman	Cliff Richard
6.	Fox On the Run	Sweet
7.	Wham Bam Shang a Lang	Silver
8.	Paloma Blanca	George Baker Selection
9.	It's O. K	Beach Boys
10.	Nights Are Forever	England Dan & John Ford Coley
11.	Did You Boogie (With Your Baby)	Flash Cadillac
12.	Another Rainy Day in New York City	Chicago
13.	Strange Magic	Electric Light Orchestra
14.	Love Is the Drug	Roxy Music
15.	If You Know What I Mean	Neil Diamond
16.	Love Me	Yvonne Elliman
17.	You Mean Everything to Me	Real Thing

THE TOP 70 REMAKES OF THE 70's

Title	Remake & Year		Original 70's Artist & Year	
1. Ain't No Mountain High Enough	Diana Ross	1970	Marvin Gaye/T.Terrell	1967
2. The Locomotion	Grand Funk	1974	Little Eva	1962
3. Lucy in the Sky with Diamonds	Elton John	1975	Beatles	1967
4. You're Sixteen	Ringo Starr	1974	Johnny Burnette	1960
5. Indian Reservation	Raiders	1971	Don Fardon	1968
6. Me and Bobby McGee	Janis Joplin	1971	Roger Miller	1969
7. MacArthur Park	Donna Summer	1978	Richard Harris	1968
8. Brother Louie	Stories	1973	Hot Chocolate	1973
9. Go Away Little Girl	Donny Osmond	1971	Steve Lawrence	1963
10. Also Sprach Zarathustra (2001)	Deodato	1973	Richard Strauss	1896
11. Shop Around	Capt. & Tennille	1976	Miracles	1960
12. He Don't Love You	Tony O. & Dawn	1975	Jerry Butler	1960
13. Mandy	Barry Manilow	1975	Scott English (Brandy)	1972
14. Proud Mary	Ike & Tina T.	1971	C.C.R.	1969
15. Rockin' Robin	Michael Jackson	1972	Bobby Day	1958
16. Please Mr. Postman	Carpenters	1975	Marvelettes	1961
17. Da Do Ron Ron	Shawn Cassidy	1976	Ronettes	1963
18. You're No Good	Linda Ronstadt	1975	Betty Everett	1964
19. The Lion Sleeps Tonight	Robert John	1972	Tokens	1961
20. Puppy Love	Donny Osmond	1972	Paul Anka	1960
21. Hooked On A Feeling	Blue Swede	1974	B. J. Thomas	1969
22. Higher and Higher	Rita Coolidge	1977	Jackie Wilson	1967
23. When Will I Be Loved	Linda Ronstadt	1975	Everly Brothers	1960
24. Rock And Roll Music	Beach Boys	1976	Chuck Berry	1957
25. Paper Roses	Marie Osmond	1973	Anita Bryant	1960
26. Blue Bayou	Linda Ronstadt	1977	Roy Orbison	1963
27. On Broadway	George Benson	1978	Drifters	1963
28. Knock on Wood	Ami Stewart	1979	Eddie Floyd	1966
29. Handy Man	James Taylor	1977	Jimmy Jones	1960
30. Gypsy Woman	Brian Hyland	1970	Impressions	1961
31. Some Kind Of Wonderful	Grand Funk	1975	Soul Brothers Six	1967
32. Night They Drove Old Dixie Down	Joan Baez	1971	The Band	1969
33. Rockin' Pneumonia & Boogie….	Johnny Rivers	1972	Huey Piano Smith	1957
34. Hot Rod Lincoln	Com. Cody	1972	Johnny Bond/Cha.Ryan	1960
35. How Sweet It Is	James Taylor	1975	Marvin Gaye	1965
36. It's So Easy	Linda Ronstadt	1977	Buddy Holly	1958
37. Get Ready	Rare Earth	1970	Temptations	1966
38. Hello It's Me	Todd Rundgren	1973	Nazz	1969
39. I'm Leaving It Up To You	Donny & Marie	1974	Dale & Grace	1963
40. Yo Yo	Osmonds	1971	Billy Joe Royal	1967
41. Amazing Grace	Royal Scots	1972	John Newton	1779
42. Mockingbird	Carly & James	1974	Charlie & Inez Foxx	1963

256

43. The Wonder of You	Elvis Presley	1970	Ray Peterson	1959
44. Everlasting Love	Carl Carlton	1974	Robert Knight	1967
45. Hello Stranger	Yvonne Elliman	1977	Barbara Lewis	1963
46. Spanish Harlem	Aretha Franklin	1971	Ben E. King	1961
47. Danny's Song	Anne Murray	1973	Loggins & Messina	1971
48. The Twelfth Of Never	Donny Osmond	1973	Johnny Mathis	1957
49. Heatwave	Linda Ronstadt	1975	Martha & the Vandellas	1963
50. Love Hurts	Nazareth	1976	Roy Orbison	1961
51. Only 16	Dr. Hook	1976	Sam Cooke	1959
52. Breaking Up Is Hard To Do	Neil Sedaka	1976	Neil Sedaka	1962
53. Ooh Baby Baby	Linda Ronstadt	1979	Miracles	1965
54. House of the Rising Sun	Frigid Pink	1970	Animals	1964
55. Daddy's Home	Jerm. Jackson	1973	Shep & the Limelites	1961
56. Never Can Say Goodbye	Gloria Gaynor	1975	Jackson Five	1971
57. Another Saturday Night	Cat Stevens	1974	Sam Cooke	1963
58. You're My World	Helen Reddy	1977	Cilla Black	1964
59. That'll Be the Day	Linda Ronstadt	1976	Buddy Holly	1957
60. Soul Man	Blues Brothers	1979	Sam & Dave	1967
61. I Know I'm Losing You	Rare Earth	1970	Temptations	1966
62. Too Young	Donny Osmond	1972	Nat 'King' Cole	1951
63. Bridge Over Troubled Water	Aretha Franklin	1971	Simon & Garfunkel	1970
64. The Letter	Joe Cocker	1970	Box Tops	1967
65. Little Bitty Pretty One	Jackson Five	1972	Thurston Harris	1957
66. You Won't See Me	Anne Murray	1974	Beatles	1965
67. I Only Want To Be With You	Bay City Rollers	1976	Dusty Springfield	1964
68. Cherish	David Cassidy	1971	Association	1966
69. Morning Side of the Mountain	Donny & Marie	1975	Tommy Edwards	1959
70. Jambalaya	Blue Ridge Ran.	1973	Hank Williams	1952

♫ Bruce Springsteen wrote this number one hit for this British band who last topped the charts in 1964.

♫ Earth, Wind and Fire backed this girl group on one of the decade's biggest hits.

♫ This number one hit was recorded by an actor who was currently starring in one of the top rated TV Shows.

♫ She may have been a one hit wonder, but her dad charted more than 3 dozen top 40 hits.

♫ This number one Stevie Wonder hit was a tribute to a legendary jazz man.

♫ This teen idol topped the charts with a song the Crystals had a hit with in 1963.

FIND OUT THAT...AND MUCH MORE INSIDE...1977!

1.   **You Light up My Life** by Debby Boone was the number one song of the year. Debby Boone also won the Grammy Award for 'Best New Artist' of 1977. It's interesting to note that both Debby and her father Pat Boone were both 20 years old when they each had their first hit. This title song of the movie which starred Didi Conn, was written and produced by Joe Brooks, an advertising executive turned songwriter.

2.   **How Deep Is Your Love** by the Bee Gees was their first single from the 'Saturday Night Fever' soundtrack which included half a dozen recordings by the Gibb brothers. This song was originally intended for Yvonne Elliman, who recorded another song written by the Bee Gees, 'If I Can't Have You'. The 'Saturday Night Fever' double album was the biggest selling soundtrack album of the 70's and the one that best represented the disco era.

3.   **I Just Want to Be Your Everything** by Andy Gibb was written by his Bee Gee brother Barry. This was the first of a string of hits for 19 year old Andy who would have 5 consecutive million sellers beginning with this hit. Barry Gibb wrote this song in Manager Robert Stigwood's Bermuda home one afternoon.

4.   **Best of My Love** by The Emotions was produced and co-written by Maurice White of Earth, Wind and Fire, who provided backup instrumentation on this multi million seller which spent over a month at number one. The Emotions were a female trio of sisters from Chicago. They returned the favor a couple of years later when they sang backup on Earth, Wind and Fire's million selling 'Boogie Wonderland'.

5.   **Love Theme from 'A Star Is Born' (Evergreen)** by Barbra Streisand was not her first number one hit, but it was the first hit she wrote. Her boyfriend Jon Peters, who produced the film with Streisand, convinced her that she could write a song if she really wanted to. She did, and with lyricist Paul Williams she composed the music for this Academy and Grammy Award winning song from the film in which she starred with Kris Kristofferson.

6.   **Sir Duke** by Stevie Wonder was a tribute to Duke Ellington, the Jazz great who passed away in 1974. The song also makes reference to some of

his other musical heroes, Count Basie, Glenn Miller, Louis Armstrong and Ella Fitzgerald. This was the 2nd consecutive number one hit from his album 'Songs in the Key of Life'. Surprisingly, one of the most popular songs on the album 'Isn't She Lovely' was never released as a single.

7. **Star Wars Theme/Cantina Band** by Meco was written by London Symphony Orchestra conductor and composer John Williams. Meco Menardo, a record producer who lived in New York City saw the George Lucas movie many times, including on opening night. He loved the music and decided to give it a disco treatment and included the music played by the Cantina band in the bar on Tattooine. He hired 75 musicians to play on this tune which went to number one.

8. **Dancing Queen** by Abba was a massive hit which reached number one in 13 countries for this Swedish super group. This follow up single to 'Fernando' was also recorded at the same time in August of 1975.This upbeat Abba hit features shared lead vocals by Agnetha Faltskog and Anni-Frid Lyngstad.

9. **Torn Between Two Lovers** by Mary MacGregor was co-written and co-produced by Peter Yarrow of Peter, Paul and Mary fame. The inspiration of the song began when his wife told him how she was moved by the 'Dr. Zhivago' novel of a man loving 2 women at the same time. Yarrow decided to turn it around and write the song from the female perspective. This was Mary MacGregor's only major hit.

10. **Rich Girl** by Hall & Oates was originally a song about an ex-boyfriend of Daryl Hall's girlfriend, Sara Allen, but they changed it to a girl for the song. This was their first official number one hit. This was their last hit to reach the top 10 in the 70's, but in the early 80's, they would chart a dozen more top 10 hits including 5 number ones.

11. **Hotel California** by the Eagles was the title song from the album which is considered to be the best from this Country/Rock band from Los Angeles, California. Don Henley sings lead on this hit which he co wrote with Glenn Frey and Don Felder who constructed the song's basic elements including the 12 string introduction and the solos at the end. The Eagles won 'Record of the Year' at The Grammy Awards for this song in 1977.

12. **Car Wash** by Rose Royce was written and produced by Norman Whitfield who did the same for many of Motown's biggest hits of the 60's and early 70's. This number one hit was the title song of the movie which starred Richard Pryer, The Pointer Sisters, George Carlin and other notables.

13. **You Don't Have to Be a Star** by Marilyn McCoo & Billy Davis Jr. was a number one hit for the married couple from the 5th Dimension who were now together as a duo. Originally they were planning solo careers after they left the 5th Dimension, but Billy decided that their first project should be an album of duets. Their success on the pop charts led to a summer variety show in 1977. Marilyn then hosted the 2nd season of the music TV series 'Solid Gold'.

14. **When I Need You** by Leo Sayer became his 2nd consecutive number one hit and the biggest of his career. The song was written by Carole Bayer Sager, (who wrote 'A Groovy Kind Of Love' when she was still a teenager) with Albert

Hammond, who had a big hit of his own 5 years earlier with 'It Never Rains In Southern California', as well as co-writing 'The Air That I Breathe' for the Hollies and 'Little Arrows for Leapy Lee. This was the 2nd of 3 hit singles from the 'Endless Flight' album.

15.   Don't Leave Me This Way by Thelma Houston was originally recorded by Harold Melvin & The Blue Notes with Teddy Pendergrass on lead vocals in 1975 without much success. This million seller was written by Kenny Gamble, Leon Huff and Cary Gilbert and was the winner of the 1978 Grammy Award for Best Female R & B Vocal performance. Thelma Houston later performed this song on American Idol on April 22, 2009.

16.   Blinded by the Light by Manfred Mann's Earth Band was written by Bruce Springsteen and originally featured on his debut album 'Greetings from Asbury Park'. The lead singer on this hit is Chris Thompson whose line 'rewed up like a deuce' comes out more like 'wrapped up like a douche'. The original Springsteen lyric is neither of the above, instead 'cut loose like a deuce'. Group leader and keyboardist Manfred Mann also had a number one hit in 1964 with 'Do Wah Diddy Diddy'.

17.   You Make Me Feel like Dancing by Leo Sayer was this British singer/ songwriter's first number one hit and first of 3 hits from his 'Endless Flight' album produced by Richard Perry. Before becoming a pop star, Leo Sayer had a short career as a commercial artist and spent time as a street busker in London. This hit won the Grammy Award for Best R & B Song in 1978.

18.   Got to Give It Up by Marvin Gaye was a funk tune with a chant that was completely different for this Motown singer/producer and writer. He was originally going to give the song the title 'Dancing Lady' after being inspired by Johnny Taylor's 'Disco Lady'. This hit was recorded 'live' at the London Palladium and was Marvin Gaye's final hit for Motown, a company he was part of for 20 years.

19.   Southern Nights by Glen Campbell was written by Allen Toussaint, the New Orleans producer/songwriter who composed many big hits in the past including 'Mother-In-Law' for Ernie K. Doe and 'Working in a Coal Mine' for Lee Dorsey to name just two. This number one hit became Glen Campbell's final top 10 hit.

20.   Undercover Angel by Alan O'Day was the only hit for this Hollywood born singer, although he did write major hits for others including 'Angie Baby' for Helen Reddy and 'Rock And Roll Heaven' for the Righteous Brothers. His own recording of his composition 'Undercover Angel' had sexual undertones with a spacey sound and an unusual echo effect, resulting in a number one smash.

21.   Dreams by Fleetwood Mac was the biggest hit single of all time for this British/American super group of the 70's. This was the 2nd of 4 major hits from 'Rumours', one of the topping selling albums of the decade and one that was recorded when personal breakups within the group were happening. Keyboard player Christine McVie was separating from her husband, bass player John McVie, singer Stevie Nicks was ending an 8 year relationship with guitarist Lindsey Buckingham and drummer Mick Fleetwood was going through divorce proceedings with his wife.

22. Gonna Fly Now (Theme from Rocky) by Bill Conti was almost an instrumental had it not been for the 30 words Carol Connors wrote for this million selling movie hit. Back in the 50's she was one of the members of The Teddy Bears under her real name Annette Kleinbard on the hit 'To Know Him Is to Love Him'. Bill Conti was also the conductor at many Academy Award Shows and has written many TV show and movie themes, with this one starring Sylvester Stallone being the big one.

23. New Kid in Town by The Eagles was the first single from their legendary 'Hotel California' album. This ballad was written by Glenn Frey, Don Henley and non Eagle J. D Souther. This number one hit featured Glenn Frey on lead vocals with main harmony vocals by Don Henley. After this album, original member Randy Meissner left the group and was replaced by Timothy B. Schmidt, the new kid in the group.

24. Don't Give up on Us by David Soul was written and produced by Tony MacAuley, the British composer who co wrote many hits including 'Build Me up Buttercup', 'Love Grows (Where My Rosemary Goes), 'Smile A Little Smile for Me' and many others. David Soul was starring in the prime time TV series 'Starsky and Hutch' as Detective Ken Hutchinson when this hit went to number one. It became his only major hit.

25. I Wish by Stevie Wonder was a song he wrote on a Saturday afternoon on the day of a Motown picnic in the summer of '76. He had such a good time that he was inspired to go to the studio right afterward and put this song together. This was the first hit single from his long awaited double album 'Songs in the Key of Life'. Stevie Wonder not only produced the album, but wrote or co-wrote all of the songs.

26. Looks Like We Made It by Barry Manilow was a million selling number one hit written by Richard Kerr and Will Jennings. Although the song appears at first to be optimistic, it is about a guy and his ex-lover finding happiness, though not with each other. This was Barry Manilow's 3rd and final official number one hit single.

27. Da Do Ron Ron by Shawn Cassidy was a remake of the Crystal's 1963 top 10 hit. This was the first of 3 consecutive million selling singles for the Hardy Boys teen idol. He was married to actress and Playboy playmate Ann Pennington from 1979 to 1991 and to actress Susan Diol from 1995 to 2003.

28. I'm Your Boogie Man by K.C & The Sunshine Band was the 4th number one hit for this disco/R &B band from Florida. Lead singer and songwriter Casey (K.C.) originally titled this song 'I'm a Son Of A Gun (Look What You've Done) instead of 'I'm Your Boogie Man (That's What I Am) but decided to change it from about being about a relationship gone bad to an ode to a disc jockey.

29. Fly like an Eagle by the Steve Miller Band almost soared to number one, but stalled just short of where his previous single 'Rock 'N' Me' landed. This was the 3rd and final hit from the 4 million selling, 'Fly like an Eagle' album which also included 'Take the Money and Run' and 'Rock 'n Me'. Steve Miller got his first guitar lesson from the legendary Les Paul, a friend of his dad's.

30. Don't It Make My Brown Eyes Blue by Crystal Gayle was the biggest pop hit for the younger sister of country singer Loretta Lynn. This hit won the lady with the longest hair in show business a Grammy Award for Best Female Country Vocal Performance in 1978. This hit was written by Richard Leigh and produced by Allen Reynolds, who later produced the albums of country superstar Garth Brooks. Reynolds also wrote the 1966 Vogues' hit 'Five O'clock World'.

31. Boogie Nights by Heatwave was a multi million seller for this disco/jazz group from Germany. The song was written by the group's keyboardist Rod Temperton who decided to retire from touring with the group in 1978. He continued to write for the group, but had even greater fame writing a couple of major hits for Michael Jackson including 'Thriller' and 'Rock with You'.

32. Nobody Does It Better by Carly Simon was written by Carole Bayer Sager and Marvin Hamlisch for the James Bond movie 'The Spy Who Loved Me' starring Roger Moore. It was the first theme song from a James Bond movie which was titled differently from the film. It was nominated for an Academy Award for 'Song of the Year', but lost to 'You Light up My Life'.

33. (Your Love Is Lifting Me) Higher & Higher by Rita Coolidge was a remake of the Jackie Wilson hit from 1967. This hit from the album 'Anytime…Anywhere' became her biggest hit. She was married to Kris Kristofferson from 1973 to 1980.

34. Keep It Comin' Love by K. C. & the Sunshine Band was inspired by Casey looking out over the crowd while on tour and thinking about all the people in love out there. This was their 5th major hit of the late 70's. They would have one more number one with the out of character ballad 'Please Don't Go' in 1979, before hanging up their boogie shoes on the pop and R & B charts.

35. Blue Bayou by Linda Ronstadt was a remake of the song Roy Orbison charted in 1963. Ronstadt's version became a bigger hit and was of one the prime cuts from her platinum selling album 'Simple Dreams' which also included 'It's So Easy' and 'Poor Poor Pitiful Me'.

36. That's Rock And Roll by Shawn Cassidy was written by Eric Carmen. Teen idol Shawn Cassidy was starring with Parker Stevenson in the Hardy Boys TV series when this hit reached number one. While his half brother David Cassidy was a teen idol and TV star in the early 70's, Shawn Cassidy covered that territory in the late 70's.

37. I'm in You by Peter Frampton featured Mick Jagger on background vocals and Stevie Wonder on synthesizer on this title song of the album which followed his enormously successful 'Frampton Comes Alive'. His follow up single was Stevie Wonder's 'Signed, Sealed, Delivered, I'm Yours', also featured on this album.

38. I Like Dreamin' by Kenny Nolan was the biggest hit for this Los Angeles based singer songwriter who co-wrote with Bob Crewe 3 major hits from 1976, 'Lady Marmalade', 'My Eyes Adored You' and 'Get Dancin'. His only other top 40 hit as a singer was his follow up to 'I like Dreaming', which was 'Love's Grown Deep', also from 1977.

39. Don't Stop by Fleetwood Mac was written by Christine McVie about her separation from bass player John McVie after 8 years of marriage. This song was also later used as the theme for Bill Clinton's Presidential campaign. This hit was the 2nd of 4 major hits from their 'Rumours' album.

40. **Dazz** by Brick was a combination of jazz-disco for this group of guys straight out of college. They took the group name 'Brick' when they were in the backyard of one of the members when the father was building a swimming pool and thought of Brick. This hit reached top 5 on the pop charts and stayed at number one on the R & B charts for a full month.

41. **Couldn't Get It Right** by Climax Blues Band was the first and biggest hit for this British blues/rock band from Stafford, England. Both Colin Cooper and Derek Holt sang lead in unison with one lower than the other, giving the song a unique sound. They had one other major hit in 1981 with 'I Love You'. Colin Cooper died of cancer at age 69 in 2008.

42. **Easy** by the Commodores was a ballad with country and western roots written by the group's lead singer Lionel Richie. This was the Commodores hit which crossed over to pop radio in a very successful way for the group previously known primarily as a 'funk' band. This was the first of 2 major hits from their self-titled album.

43. **Handy Man** by James Taylor was a ballad produced by Peter Asher of a song which was previously an upbeat hit in 1960 by Jimmy Jones. The song was co-written by Otis Blackwell, the man responsible for 'Great Balls Of Fire' and some of Elvis Presley's biggest hits including 'Don't Be Cruel', 'All Shook Up' and 'Return to Sender'. This was James Taylor's final hit to reach the top 10.

44. **Night Moves** by Bob Seger was the first official top 10 hit for this Detroit rocker. This hit was recorded in Toronto and produced by Jack Richardson, who did the same for the Guess Who. The setting of the song is summertime 1962 with teenage lust and a '60 Chevy.

45. **(Every Time I Turn Around) Back in Love Again** by L.T.D. featured Jeffrey Osborne on lead vocals on this million seller from 1977. L.T.D. stands for 'Love, Togetherness and Devotion. Jeffrey Osborne left this 10 man funk band from North Carolina for a solo career which led to hits which included 'On the Wings of Love' and 'Love Power' with Dionne Warwick.

46. **It's Ecstasy When You Lay down next To Me** by Barry White was his final top 10 hit and one of the few that he did not write. This Barry White produced hit was written by session backup singer/songwriters Nelson Pigford and Ekundayo Paris. Although Barry White changed their song to suit his style, they were thrilled to have their song reach top 5 on the pop charts and number one on the R & B charts.

47. **Baby What a Big Surprise** by Chicago was written by Peter Cetera, who is also featured on lead vocals on their final top 10 hit of the 70's. This hit was also the last to feature group member Terry Kath, who died of an accidental self-inflicted gunshot a few months later in January 1978. It was also their last hit produced by James William Guercio, the producer of all of their hits up to that point.

48.   Lucille by Kenny Rogers was his first hit in 7 years and his first major country hit as a solo artist after leaving his group the First Edition. This story song was inspired by co-writer Hal Bynum's real life events as his marriage was in trouble. This song launched Kenny Rogers' career as a country music superstar.

49.   My Heart Belongs to You by Barbra Streisand was originally considered for the soundtrack of 'A Star Is Born', but was not included on that project. The song was written by Alan Gordon who co-wrote some of the Turtles' biggest hits including 'Happy Together' and for 3 Dog Night he composed 'Celebrate'. This hit featured top session players Jeff Porcaro, Larry Carlton, David Foster and a 40 plus orchestra which cut this track between 7pm and 4 in the morning.

50.   Float On by The Floaters was the only notable hit for this Detroit soul group discovered by James Mitchell of the Detroit Emeralds. This number one hit on the R & B charts was written by James Mitchell, along with Arnold Ingram who played piano and Marvin Willis who played drums. One of the session musicians featured on this hit was Dennis Coffey with his unique sounding guitar.

51.   Feels like the First Time by Foreigner was written by Mick Jones and was the debut hit for this British/American group who formed in New York City in 1976. Some of the key members came from other bands with Mick Jones from Spooky Tooth and Ian McDonald from King Crimson. Lou Gramm was the lead singer on Foreigner's biggest hits.

52.   D o You Wanna Make Love by Peter McCann was the only hit as a singer for this ABC Music staff writer from Connecticut. Although this was his only million seller as a singer, his composition 'Right Time Of The Night' became the first major hit for Jennifer Warnes. What's even more interesting is the fact that his only 2 notable songwriting hits were popular at the same time in the spring of 1977.

53.   The Things We Do for Love by 10 C. C. was a million seller for this British art rock group after 2 of the 4 members, Kevin Godley and Lol Creme left to form 'Godley and Creme'. Remaining members Eric Stewart and Graham Gouldman decided to add new members and continue with 10 c.c. Eric Stewart composed the lyrics of the song after walking through the rain and snow in Manchester to find a phone to call the girl he would later marry.

54.   Strawberry Letter 23 by The Brothers Johnson was another million seller produced by Quincy Jones for the siblings from Los Angeles. This song was written by Shuggie Otis, who wrote the song for a girlfriend who used strawberry scented paper when she wrote letters to him. Studio musician Lee Ritnour was the one playing the funky guitar solo on this summer '77 hit.

55.   Enjoy Yourself by The Jacksons was the first hit without the '5' on the group's name and their first hit on the 'Epic' record label after leaving Motown. This multi-million selling top 10 single was very different in its sound, probably since it was written and produced by the legendary Gamble and Huff, known for their Philadelphia soul sound. This was the first Jacksons' hit to feature Randy Jackson, who replaced Jermaine, who stayed with Motown.

56.   Hot line by The Sylvers was another million seller for the Memphis family act of 10 brothers and sisters that gave us 'Boogie Fever' in 1976. The bubblegum hit 'Hotline' was also produced and co-written by Freddie Perren, who also gave the Jackson Five, Peaches and Herb. Gloria Gaynor and Yvonne Elliman some of their biggest hits.

57.   It's So Easy by Linda Ronstadt was a remake of the Buddy Holly song from 1958 which did not even chart in the top 40.Linda Ronstadt's version reached the top 5 and was popular simultaneously with her remake of the Roy Orbison classic 'Blue Bayou'. Both hits were featured on her 5th consecutive million selling album, 'Simple Dreams'.

58.   Brick House by The Commodores was their final major hit of the 70's to feature Walter Orange on lead vocals. The lyrics of the song were inspired by the wife of group member William King, whose wife Shirley Hanna-King came up with the now famous term 'Brick house'. The term came from the slang for a voluptuous woman who is 'built like a brick shit house'.

59.   I Feel Love by Donna Summer was a techno pop disco song which reached the top 10 and sold a million copies for the Queen of the Disco'. This hit sounded very futuristic with the synthesizer and electronic instrumentation produced by Giorgio Moroder and Pete Belotte. They also wrote the song from the album 'I Remember Yesterday' with Donna Summer.

60.   I've Got Love on My Mind by Natalie Cole was on the charts when she announced that she was pregnant and disclosed that she had married her producer and co-writer Marvin Yancy in July of 1976. This love ballad won her the Best Female Vocalist American Music Award in 1977.

61.   Angel in Your Arms by Hot was a one hit wonder hit for 3 girls with different ethnic backgrounds. Gwen Owens is black, Cathy Carson is white and Juanita Curiel is Mexican. They recorded this catchy chorus with catty but coy lyrics at Muscle Shoals Studios in Alabama.

62.   Cold as Ice by Foreigner was the 2nd single from their self-titled debut album. This energetic rocker was written by Mick Jones and lead singer Lou Gramm. Coincidentally, this was the 2nd popular album during the 70's to be titled 'Foreigner', with the first being Cat Stevens' album from 1973.

63.   Heaven on the 7th Floor by Paul Nicholas was his only hit as a pop singer, although he did much more as an actor. In the late 70's alone, he appeared in the movie 'Tommy' and in the film 'Sgt. Pepper's Lonely Heart's Club Band' in 1978. This British performer has also starred in many stage shows through the years.

64.   Whatcha Gonna Do by Pablo Cruise was the first and biggest hit for this San Francisco based pop/rock quartet. This group formed in 1973 with 3 former members of the band 'Stoneground' and 1 member, Bud Cockrell of the group 'It's A Beautiful Day'. Cockrell left Pablo Cruise in 1977 and was replaced by Bruce Day from Santana.

65.   We're All Alone by Rita Coolidge was written by Boz Scaggs and was featured on his 'Silk Degrees' album in 1976. Jerry Moss, the co-owner (with Herb Alpert) of her record label, A & M Records suggested she record the song because he believed it could be big. It became a million seller and followed her previous 1977 hit 'Higher & Higher' into the top 10.

66. Right Time of the Night by Jennifer Warnes was written by Peter McCann who had his only hit with 'Do You Wanna Make Love' which was on the charts simultaneously with this top 10 hit.This was the first hit for Jennifer Warnes, who would later have 2 number one duet hits in the 80's with 'Up Where We Belong' with Joe Cocker and '(I've Had) The Time Of My Life' with Bill Medley.

67. Telephone Line by the Electric Light Orchestra or E. L. O. as they are often referred was the 3rd and most popular of the 3 singles from their 'New World Record' album produced by lead singer and songwriter Jeff Lynne. This hit became the band's first million selling single. This song was the theme of the 1977 film 'Joyride' starring Desi Arnaz Jr. and Melanie Griffith.

68. Margaritaville by Jimmy Buffet is the signature hit for this singer/songwriter/ guitarist who has a following of fans known as 'parrotheads'. He got the idea for the song when he came to Key West, watching tourists, and then came up with the title while sitting at a bar in Austin, Texas drinking a frozen Margaritta. He owns the Margaritaville Cafe restaurant chain.

69. So in to You by Atlanta Rhythm Section was the first major hit from this group which evolved from the 60's group 'The Classics 1V' and Roy Orbison's band 'The Candymen'. Atlanta Rhythm Section members J.R.Cobb and Buddy Buie formerly with the Classics 1V , also wrote their best known hits including 'Spooky', 'Stormy' and 'Traces'.

70. Year of the Cat by Al Stewart was produced by Alan Parsons and recorded at Abbey Road Studios in London. This was the biggest hit for this Glasgow, Scotland born singer/songwriter/guitarist. The album 'Year of the Cat' also included his similar sounding follow up hit 'On the Border'.

71. After the Lovin' by Engelbert Humperdinck was offered originally to Tom Jones, but he turned it down. It became Engelbert's first top 10 hit since 'Release Me' 10 years earlier in 1967.This hit produced by Charlie Calello and Joel Diamond was Humperdinck's first hit on the 'Epic' record label.

72. Just a Song before I Go by Crosby, Stills & Nash, without Neil Young, was their first major hit in 7 years. It took Graham Nash 15 minutes to write this song about leaving loved ones behind before going out on tour. This reunion produced the album CSN, which almost made it to number one, but Fleetwood Mac's 'Rumours' would not let go of the top spot.

73. Jet Airliner by the Steve Miller Band was the 1st and biggest of the 3 hit singles from his 10th album, 'Book of Dreams'. This 3 times platinum album features a heavy use of synthesizer played by Miller. This group's big break came in 1967 when they played at the Monterey Pop Festival, which led to a recording deal with Capitol Records.

74. Lonely Boy by Andrew Gold features backing vocals by Linda Ronstadt whom he co-produced and worked with as a backing musician on many of her albums. Although this song seems to be autobiographical with similarities between the boy, Andrew Gold, has denied this, despite great similarities between the lyrics and his own life. The lyric, "He was born on a summer day in 1951", matches Andrew Gold's August 1951 birthday, and "In the summer of '53 his mother brought him a sister" matches his sister's birthday.

75. You Make Lovin' Fun by Fleetwood Mac was the 4th of 4 major hit singles from the 'Rumours' album. This hit was written by Christine McVie, who also sings lead on this prime cut from one of the biggest selling albums of all time.

76. You and Me by Alice Cooper was another ballad for the shock rocker from Detroit. This song was the only hit from his album 'Lace and Whiskey' which featured guest musicians Al Kooper on piano, Jim Gordon on drums and Tony Levin on bass.

77. Weekend in New England by Barry Manilow was written by Randy Edelman on an old Steinway upright in New Jersey in the house where he grew up and composed the lyrics on a plane while traveling. Arista President Clive Davis told Edelman that if he changed the arrangement, he would submit it to Manilow, This ballad became another top 10 hit for the singer/songwriter/pianist/producer who would chart an average of 3 hit singles a year during the late 70's.

78. Smoke from a Distant Fire by Sanford- Townsend Band was the only hit for this Los Angeles band led by Ed Sanford and Johnny Townsend. This catchy, hook-laden hit was recorded at the famous Muscle Shoals Studio in Alabama. Ed Sanford later worked as a back up for Michael McDonald and co-wrote his hit 'I Keep Forgettin'.

79. Walk this Way by Aerosmith peaked on the charts the year lead singer Steven Tyler's daughter Liv was born. She later became a successful actress. This hit was written by Steven Tyler and guitarist Joe Perry and was featured on their album 'Toys in the Attic' which was released 2 years earlier in 1975.

80. Lost Without Your Love by Bread was a revival for the soft rock group which disbanded in 1973.This was the final hit for Bread, although lead singer/songwriter David Gates went solo and had a hit the following year with 'Goodbye Girl', the title song of the Neil Simon movie starring Richard Dreyfuss and Marsha Mason.

81. Go Your Own Way by Fleetwood Mac was the first of 4 major hit singles from their most successful album 'Rumours'. This hit was written by Lindsay Buckingham with regard to his bandmate Stevie Nicks with whom he had just ended a romantic relationship. Fleetwood Mac were inducted into the Rock and Roll Hall of Fame in 1998.

82. Swayin' To the Music (Slow Dancing) by Johnny Rivers was the final top 10 hit for the singer/songwriter/guitarist/producer known for his many hits of the 60's. This soothing and relaxing ballad even included the sound of crickets to give it that summer night feeling.He was born John Ramistella but named Johnny Rivers by legendary DJ Alan Freed.

83. Carry on Wayward Son by Kansas was the first major hit for this progressive rock group which featured Steve Walsh on lead vocals. Back then he was quite the performer and known for doing hand stands on his keyboards. Guitarist and keyboardist Kerry Livgren wrote or co-wrote all of the songs from this album 'Leftoverture'

84. Lido Shuffle by Boz Scaggs was the follow up to 'Lowdown' and both were featured on his most successful album, 'Silk Degrees'. This hit was co-written with David Paich, the son of jazz composer/arranger/musician Marty Paich. Boz Scaggs was born William Royce Scaggs in Ohio and raised in Texas.

85. You Made Me Believe in Magic by the Bay City Rollers was the last major hit in North America for this tartan-clad Scottish band. This mid tempo disco-flavored tune featured strings and horns and was from the album 'It's A Game'.

86. Tryin' to Love Two by William Bell was the only major hit for this singer songwriter who was studying to be a doctor until he was sidetracked and invited to do a session for a new label called 'Stax'. Although he had a few minor to moderate hits with Stax in the 60's, he had his first major hit on the Mercury label with this song recorded at Allen Toussaint's studio in New Orleans.

87. Life in the Fast Lane by the Eagles was the 3rd consecutive hit single from the 'Hotel California' album. The main riff of this rock song was something that guitarist Joe Walsh came up with while warming up during rehearsal. Don Henley sang lead on this hit which he wrote with Glenn Frey and Joe Walsh.

88. I Wanna Get Next To You by Rose Royce was a ballad written and produced by Norman Whitfield, formerly with Motown during the 60's and early 70's. This was their follow up to the number one 'Car Wash' and was also included in the movie's soundtrack. Rose Royce were a Los Angeles based soul group consisting of almost 10 members and featuring Rose Norwalt on lead vocals.

89. Maybe I'm Amazed by Paul McCartney & Wings was a 'live' version of the song from McCartney's first solo album in 1970. This is one of McCartney's personal favorites and one he dedicated to his wife Linda when he wrote it in 1969 when the Beatles were near their break up. This version was included on the 'Wings over America' album released in 1976.

90. On and On by Stephen Bishop was a title he came up with while walking to the neighborhood store. He tucked it away on a piece of paper and put it in his wallet until one day he looked out the window of his apartment at the beautiful, tropical garden of his 85 year old landlady. He thought of a tropical paradise and an escape to Jamaica and this feel good song was completed in one day.

91. Barracuda by Heart was a harder edged rock song for the group from Seattle, Washington led by the Wilson sisters, Nancy and lead vocalist Ann. This was the only hit single from their album 'Little Queen', their follow up to their debut album 'Dreamboat Annie'.

92. Just Remember I Love You by Firefall featured backup vocals by Timothy B. Schmidt, who joined the Eagles in 1977. Next to their debut hit 'You Are the Woman', this was Firefall's biggest hit. Founding member Rick Roberts wrote and sang lead on this top 10 hit.

93. Star Wars (Main Theme) by The London Symphony Orchestra with John Williams was from the original soundtrack of George Lucas' blockbuster film. John Williams not only composed this movie hit, but numerous others through the years including the themes for 'Jaws', 'Jurassic Park', 'E.'T', and 'Harry Potter'.

94. We Just Disagree by Dave Mason was the biggest solo hit for the former member of the group Traffic. He played and performed with many legendary musicians including George Harrison, Eric Clapton, Michael Jackson, The Rolling Stones, Jimi Hendrix and many others.

95. You Can't Turn Me Off (In The Middle of Turning Me on) by High Energy were discovered by Gwen Gordy, the sister of Motown boss Berry Gordy, who groomed them and got them signed to her brothers label. The 4 girls, including 2 sisters from Pasadena, California could not repeat the success of their first and only hit.

96. Ain't Gonna Bump with No Fat Woman by Joe Tex was a fun disco million seller which became the final hit for the soul singer from Texas. Joe Tex, who had hits in the 60's with 'Hold What You've Got' and 'Skinny Legs and All' and in 1972 with 'I Gotcha', died on August 13th 1982 of a heart attack at his home, just 5 days after his 49th birthday.

97. Livin' Thing by E. L. O. was the first of 3 hit singles from the 'New World Record' album. Lead singer, producer and writer Jeff Lynne claims this song is simply about love and the loss of love. The album was recorded at Musicland Studios in Munich, Germany.

98. Boogie Child by The Bee Gees was their 3rd hit single from their 'Children of the World' album which featured a guest appearance by Steve Stills on percussion. Their previous 2 singles from this album, 'You Should Be Dancing' and 'Love So Right' each reached the top 10 and became million sellers, which 'Boogie Child' failed to do. The album was recorded at both Criteria Studios in Florida and 'Le Studio' in Canada.

99. Somebody to Love by Queen was the lead off single from 'A Day at the Races' album and used multi-tracking voices to make it sound like a 100 voice gospel choir. This complex song about soul searching, desperation and faith was written by lead singer Freddie Mercury.

100. Knowing Me, Knowing You by Abba was the follow up to 'Dancing Queen' and was also included on their album 'Arrival'. This song featured Anni-Frid Lyngstad on lead vocals and was the first of 4 Abba songs about 'breakups' with the others being 'The Winner Takes It All', 'One of Us' and 'When All Is Said and Done'. Both Abba couples would divorce, Bjorn and Agnetha in 1979 and Benny and Frida in 1981.

101. The King Is Gone by Ronnie McDowell was released almost immediately after the shocking news that Elvis Presley had died. This Tennessee born singer/ songwriter's voice had a striking resemblance to that of the King of Rock and Roll. It was his voice that was used on the soundtrack of the 1979 made-for-TV movie 'Elvis' which starred Kurt Russell in the lead role.

102. Isn't It Time by the Babys was the debut top 40 hit for this British rock group which featured John Waite on lead vocals. Michael Corby plays the distinctive piano introduction on this top 20 power ballad. Lead singer John Waite later joined the group Bad English and then went solo and had a number one hit with 'Missing You'.

103. Give A Little Bit by Supertramp, featuring Roger Hodgson on lead vocals, was the only hit single from their progressive album 'Even in the Quietest Moments'. Although Hodgson wrote the song solely, it is also credited to group member Rick Davies because they made a pact where both names would appear on their compositions, similar to what Lennon and McCartney did for the Beatles recordings.

104. Jeans On by David Dundas was originally a commercial in Britain for Brutus Jeans. This singer/actor's claim to fame happened almost 10 years earlier when he had an intimate scene with actress Judy Geeson in the 1968 film 'Prudence and The Pill' which starred Deborah Kerr and David Niven. David Dundas wrote the fun-loving 'Jeans On' with Roger Greenaway who co-wrote, 'You've Got Your Troubles, 'Green Grass', My Baby Loves Lovin' and several other hits from the 60's and 70's.

105. Hello Stranger by Yvonne Elliman was a very close copy of the original version from 1963 by Barbara Lewis, who also wrote this love ballad. Yvonne Elliman, who was born in Honolulu, Hawaii got her first big break when she appeared as Mary Magdalene in Jesus Christ Superstar' and had a hit with 'I Don't Know How To Love Him', which Helen Reddy also made popular.

106. Heard It in a Love Song by The Marshall Tucker Band was the biggest hit for this southern rock band from North Carolina. There was no member in the band by the name of Marshall Tucker. That name came from the piano tuner owner of the band's rehearsal hall. Two of the members of this 6 man band, Toy and Tommy Caldwell are now deceased. Tommy died in a car accident at age 30 in 1980 and Toy died of respiratory failure in 1993 at the age of 45.

107. Swingtown by The Steve Miller Band was the 3rd and perhaps the catchiest sounding single from the very successful 'Book of Dreams' album. Steve Miller produced this album, wrote or co-wrote most of the songs, and is featured on lead vocals, guitar, synthesizer and sitar. In October of 2009, Norton Buffalo, who was a member of the band for over 30 years, died at the age of 58.

108. Help Is on Its Way by The Little River Band was the first top 20 hit for this Australian pop/rock group featuring lead singer Glenn Shorrock. This was from their North American breakthrough album 'Diamantina Cocktail', which also included their follow up single 'Happy Anniversary'. 'Help Is on Its Way' reached number one in Australia.

109. Can't Stop Dancin' by The Captain & Tennille was surprisingly written by funnyman Ray Stevens, who was best known for his novelty hits during the 60's and 70's. This hit was a change of pace for this popular 70's duo because of its driving beat, big production and backing singers.

110. Hard Luck Woman by Kiss was the first single from the 'Rock and Roll Over' album and was one Paul Stanley wrote with Rod Stewart in mind. When Stewart showed no interest in singing it, Kiss drummer Peter Criss, who sang lead in the preceding hit 'Beth', was given the lead vocal task.

111. Black Betty by Ram Jam was a funky and rockin' remake of a song written by the legendary blues/folk musician Leadbelly (Huddie William Ledbetter) who was popular during the 30's and 40's. Ram Jam's lead singer and guitarist Bill Bartlett was previously a member of the Lemon Pipers, who were best known for their 1968 number one hit 'Green Tambourine'. This was Ram Jam's only hit.

112. Say You'll Stay until Tomorrow by Tom Jones was his final top 20 North American hit on the pop charts and his first hit on the country charts. This hit was written by well known British songwriters Roger Greenaway and Barry Mason.

Roger Greenaway co-wrote the hits of the Fortunes as well as 'Green Grass' 'My Baby Loves Lovin' for the White Plains. Barry Mason co-wrote 'Delilah', 'The Last Waltz', 'Love Grows (Where My Rosemary Goes) and many other notable hits from the 60's and 70's.

113. Way Down by Elvis Presley was the final single released while the King was still alive. This hit was on the charts at the time of his shocking death on August 16, 1977. It was the 2nd single from the 'Moody Blue' album which was released in July of 1977. The deeper-than-deep voice prominent on the end of this song is that of J.D. Summer, one of the members of his backup vocal group the Stamps. The 'B' side of this single was 'Pledging My Love' which was the final hit for Johnny Ace in early 1955.

114. Your Love by Marilyn McCoo & Billy Davis Jr. was the follow up to their number one hit 'You Don't Have to Be a Star (To Be In My Show)' from the beginning of 1977. This was a moderate hit and only other top 40 entry on the pop charts for the former members of the 5th Dimension.

115. Calling Mr. Love by Kiss was written by Gene Simmons and inspired by a Three Stooges short which included the announcement over the hospital intercom 'Calling Dr. Howard, Dr. Fine, Dr. Howard'. This was the 2nd single from the 'Rock and Roll Over' album.

116. It Was Almost like a Song by Ronnie Milsap was the first hit on the pop charts for this blind since birth country singer from Robbinsville, North Carolina. This hit reached number one on the country charts and was co written by Hal David, who was Burt Bacharach's songwriting partner on dozens of major hits during the 60's and 70's.

117. You're My World by Helen Reddy was a remake of the Cilla Black hit from 1964. This hit produced by Kim Fowley was from the album 'Ear Candy' and was Helen Reddy's final top 40 hit. In 1977 she also starred in the movie 'Pete's Dragon' with Mickey Rooney and Shelley Winters.

118. Telephone Man by Meri Wilson was a sassy novelty hit written by this one hit wonder raised in Marietta, Georgia. This song filled with inviting innuendos, was inspired by a telephone man she once dated. After her 2 minutes of fame, she became a chorale director at a high school in Atlanta.

119. Don't Worry Baby by B. J. Thomas was a remake of the Beach Boys hit from 1964. After 2 decades and over a dozen notable hits, this became his final top 40 hit before switching his direction to gospel and country music.

120. How Much Love by Leo Sayer was his 3rd consecutive hit of 1977 following his back-to-back number ones 'You Make Me Feel like Dancing' and 'When I Need You'. Like the previous 2 hits, this was also from his 'Endless Flight' album which included musical guests Ray Parker Jr., Nigel Olson, Larry Carlton, Jeff Porcaro, Lee Ritenour and other notables.

121. Signed, Sealed, Delivered, I'm Yours by Peter Frampton was a remake of Stevie Wonder's top 10 hit from 1970. This hit was the 2nd single from the album 'I'm In You' and was recorded at Electric Lady Studios in New York City's

Greenwich Village, a recording studio originally built by Jimi Hendrix in 1970, the year he died.

122. High School Dance by the Sylvers was the final hit for this bubblegum soul/pop music family act known for their million sellers 'Boogie Fever' and 'Hot Line'. Later in 1977, the group decided not to re-team with producer/writer Freddie Perren and their career failed to chart any further hits.

123. Do Ya Wanna Get Funky with Me by Peter Brown was the debut hit for this disco/funk singer/songwriter/producer from Illinois. This was the first of 3 hit singles from his first album 'A Fantasy Love Affair' which also included his 1978 top 10 hit 'Dance with Me'.

124. Your Smiling Face by James Taylor was an upbeat hit popular the year he switched from Warner to Columbia records. This hit from the album 'JT' was the follow up to the Grammy Award winning 'Handy Man'. Notable guests featured on the album included Linda Ronstadt, Graham Nash, David Sanborn, Peter Asher and his wife Carly Simon.

125. Dusic by Brick was the follow up to their million seller 'Dazz' from earlier in the year. This was the only other top 40 hit for this disco-jazz group that formed in Atlanta, Georgia in 1972.

126. My Way by Elvis Presley was a 'live' recording from the CBS TV special and album 'Elvis in Concert'. This hit was on the pop charts in November of 1977, 3 months after his death. The song was co-written by Paul Anka and recorded by Frank Sinatra in 1969

127. Send in the Clowns by Judy Collins was a re-release of the song she charted 2 years earlier in 1975 from her album 'Judith'. This Stephen Sondheim song was from his 1973 musical 'A Little Night Music' and has been recorded by numerous music artists through the years. Sondheim claims that the 'clowns' in the title do not refer to circus clowns. Instead they symbolize 'fools' and in hindsight the song should have been called 'Send in the Fools'.

128. Love's Grown Deep by Kenny Nolan was the follow up to his biggest hit 'I like Dreamin' from earlier in 1977. This Los Angeles-based balladeer was named Billboard's New Pop Singles Artist of 1977'. This was his final notable hit.

129. It's Sad to Belong by England Dan & John Ford Coley was written by Randy Goodrum, who also wrote late 70's hits 'Bluer than Blue' for Michael Johnson and 'You Needed Me' for Anne Murray. This top 30 hit by this soft rock duo was very similar to the style of their 2 major hits in their debut year, 1976, with 'I'd Really Love to See You Tonight' and 'Nights are forever without You'.

130. Crackerbox Palace by George Harrison is named for the Los Angeles mansion owned by Lord Buckley, a legendary comedian whom he admired for many years. This was the 2nd single from his '33 and a 3rd' album, which included musical guests Billy Preston, Gary Wright, Tom Scott and David Foster. Harrison appeared on Saturday Night Live on November 20th, 1976 with Paul Simon to coincide with the album's release and the two performed an acoustic set together.

131. Surfin' U. S.A. by Leif Garrett was a remake of the Beach Boys hit from 1963 and was the first hit for this Hollywood-born teen idol singer/actor. Since his 70's-exclusive hit career, he's been known more for his drug abuse and legal troubles, than he is for his acting and music career.

132. Sam by Olivia Newton-John was a ballad recorded in Nashville which producer John Farrar co-wrote with 2 other songwriters, Hank Marvin and Don Black. Black was best known for writing the lyrics to the number one hits 'To Sir with Love' by Lulu and 'Ben' for Michael Jackson. Her next big success was 3 consecutive million selling singles from the movie 'Grease' which she co-starred with John Travolta.

133. Ain't Nothin' like the Real Thing by Donny & Marie Osmond, produced by Mike Curb, was a remake of the 1968 Motown hit which Marvin Gaye and Tammi Terrell popularized. Donny and Marie had their own prime time weekly variety TV show when this hit was in the top 30.

134. Slow Dancin' Don't Turn Me On by the Addrisi Brothers was a hit 5 years after their catchy composition 'We've Got to Get It on Again' was popular. Before that, Don and Dick Addrisi were best known for writing the million seller 'Never My Love' for the Association. They worked together until Don died of cancer in 1984.

135. Dancin' Man by Q was the only hit for this pop quartet from Beaver Falls, Pennsylvania led by Robert Peckman and Don Garvin, formerly of the group Jaggerz, known for their 1970 hit 'The Rapper'. This upbeat danceable hit was by a group with the shortest name ever to reach the top 40, with the exception of 'M', who hit number one in 1979 with 'Pop Muzik'.

136. She Did It by Eric Carmen was on the charts at the same time another song he wrote, 'That's Rock and Roll' by Shawn Cassidy was number one. This self-composed hit was from the album 'Boats Against The Current' and featured several musical guests including Andrew Gold, Bruce Johnston of the Beach Boys, Burton Cummings and Jeff Porcaro of Toto.

137. Saturday Nite by Earth, Wind & Fire was written by Maurice White, Al McKay and lead singer Phillip Bailey. This was the 2nd single from the 'Spirit' album which was nominated for an American Music Award for favorite soul/R & B album. The band's elaborate stage show, complete with magic and more, was directed by Doug Henning and a young David Copperfield.

138. Save It for a Rainy Day by Stephen Bishop featured Eric Clapton on guitar and Chaka Kahn on background vocals. This was the first hit for this California singer/songwriter/guitarist who was the folk singer in the film 'National Lampoon's Animal House' who had his guitar smashed by John Belushi.

139. The First Cut Is the Deepest by Rod Stewart was the follow up to his biggest hit of all, 'Tonight's The Night' and was also from the album 'A Night on the Town'. This song was written by Cat Stevens and was the only cut on the album recorded at the famous Muscle Shoals Studio in Alabama. Notable musicians featured on this album include Steve Cropper, Donald 'Duck' Dunn, Al Jackson and David Foster.

140. Long Time by Boston was the 2nd of 3 hits from their self-titled massive selling debut album. On the album, 'Boston', this song runs almost 8 minutes as 'Foreplay/Long Time', featuring a 2 and a half minute instrumental introduction to the main song 'Long Time'. The band from the biggest city in Massachusetts is centered on producer/songwriter/guitarist and keyboardist Tom Scholz. Brad Delp was the band's lead singer.

141. Luchenbach, Texas (Back to the Basics of Love) by Waylon Jennings was number one on the country charts for a month and a half in the spring of 1977. Willie Nelson made a guest appearance at the end of this hit which makes reference to 'Blue Eyes Crying in the Rain', which Willie recorded in 1975. Waylon Jennings died in his sleep on February 13, 2002 as a result of complications with diabetes.

142. Mainstreet by Bob Seger was the 2nd and only other hit from the 'Night Moves' album which was recorded at studios in Toronto, Detroit and at Muscle Shoals in Sheffield, Alabama. This hit featured guitar work by Jimmy Johnson from the Muscle Shoals Rhythm Section.

143. Whodunit by Tavares was a number hit on the R & B charts co written by Keni St. Lewis who was a big fan of detective stories. Charlie Chan, Sherlock Holmes, McCloud, Dirty Harry and Baretta all get honorable mentions in this hit from this family act from Massachusetts. This hit was produced and also co written by Freddie Perren.

144. Jungle Love by the Steve Miller Band was the 2nd of 3 hit singles from his triple platinum album 'Book of Dreams'. This hit began with a very spacey sound and the album prominently featured synthesizer throughout, played by Steve Miller, who also produced. This was the follow up to the 'Fly like an Eagle' album, which also included 3 hit singles.

145. Daybreak by Barry Manilow was a 'live' version of the tune from his album 'This One's For You'. This was his 3rd hit single of 1977 following 'Weekend In New England' and 'Looks Like We Made It' and was the only one that did not reach the top 10, The first of four Barry Manilow TV Specials aired in 1977 with huge audience numbers and winner of an Emmy Award.

146. Gone Too Far by England Dan & John Ford Coley was from their album 'Dowdy Ferry Road' and was written by Coley, who was a classically trained pianist. England Dan Seals' brother, Jim Seals of Seals and Crofts fame played guitar and provided backing vocals on this album.

147. Shake Your Rump to the Funk by The Barkays , was popular 10 years after most of the original band members were killed in a plane crash with Otis Redding. The 2 remaining members of the band reformed the band and had a top 40 hit with this funk song from their album 'Too Hot to Stop' .The title song of the album was later used in the opening of the 2007 movie 'Superbad'.

148. Here Comes Those Tears Again by Jackson Browne was his first top 40 hit since his debut hit 'Doctor My Eyes' 5 years earlier. The singer/songwriter/ guitarist/pianist born in Heidelberg, Germany moved to Los Angeles when he was 3 years old. John Hall, the lead singer of Orleans, provided a guitar solo on this hit and Bonnie Raitt sang harmony vocal.

149. Disco Lucy (I Love Lucy Theme) by Wilton Place Street Band was a disco version of the theme from the iconic TV comedy from the 50's starring Lucille Ball. This one hit wonder group of studio musicians were assembled, arranged and produced by Trevor Lawrence and the band was named after where he resided in Los Angeles.

150. Do Ya by Electric Light Orchestra was a re-recording of their very first North American hit single from 1972 which they released as 'The Move'. This Jeff Lynne-penned hit was the 2nd of 3 hit singles from their album 'New World Record'.

151. Christine Sixteen by Kiss was written and sung by Gene Simmons from the album 'Love Gun'. The song was about an older man with a crush on a 16 year old named Christine and was quite controversial because of the lyrics and subject matter. In 1977 a Gallup Poll named Kiss as the most popular band in the United States.

152. Edge Of the Universe by The Bee Gees was a 'live' version of the song they released as the 'B' side of their 1975 hit 'Nights On Broadway' as a studio version. They would follow this hit with superstardom success with 'How Deep Is Your Love', the 1st of 3 consecutive number one hits from the 'Saturday Night Fever' movie soundtrack.

153. The Greatest Love of All by George Benson was from the movie 'The Greatest' starring Muhammad Ali and was the original version of the song Whitney Houston brought to number one 9 years later.

154. Living Next Door To Alice by Smokie was a top 30 hit for this British group which featured Chris Norman on lead vocals. Two years later he had a million selling hit with Suzi Quatro with the song 'Stumblin' In'. Both hits were written by Nicky Chinn and Mike Chapman who also gave the British glam-rock band The Sweet some of their biggest hits.

155. This Song by George Harrison was about his plagiarism suit between his song 'My Sweet Lord' and the Chiffon's 'He's So Fine'. This was the first single off his album '33 & a 3rd' which was his age when he started to record the album and not the record speed which is associated with the number. This was George Harrison's first release on his own 'Dark Horse' record label.

156. Free by Deniece Williams was the first solo hit for the former member of Stevie Wonder's back up vocal group, 'Wonderlove' along with Minnie Ripperton and Syreeta Wright. The following year Deniece Williams would reach number one alongside Johnny Mathis with the duet 'Too Much, Too Little, Too Late'.

157. Ariel by Dean Friedman was an offbeat, fun and catchy song from this one hit wonder from New Jersey. Although he had only pop hit, this multi-talented singer/ songwriter/musician is also an author, video game designer and has written, performed and produced theme music for various TV shows.

158. Gloria by Enchantment was a love ballad by this soul quintet which formed in Detroit during their high school years. This was their first and biggest hit and the only one they recorded on the United Artists record label.

159. She's Not There by Santana was a remake of the Zombies hit from 1964 written by Rod Argent. This top 30 hit was included on their studio and 'live' double album 'Moonflower'. Carlos' Santana's group had many personnel changes through the years including the addition of percussionist Raul Rekow in 1977.

160. Daytime Friends by Kenny Rogers was the follow up to his first country crossover hit 'Lucille'. In 1977 when 'Daytime Friends and Nighttime Lovers' was a hit, he married Marianne Gordon of TV's 'Hee Haw'. At last report he is still married to his 5th wife, Wanda Miller.

161. Uptown Festival part 1 by Shalamar was formed by Don Cornelius, the producer and host of TV's 'Soul Train'. This hit featured a medley of several Motown hits of the 60's including 'I Can't Help Myself', Uptight (Everything's Alright), It's The Same Old Song' and other soul favorites.

162. Cat Scratch Fever by Ted Nugent was the signature solo hit for this Detroit born rocker and former leader of the Amboy Dukes. He is probably just as well known for his hard rock musicianship as he is for his conservative political and unrestricted gun ownership views and other social issues.

163. I Believe You by Dorothy Moore was the only other pop hit from the Jackson, Mississippi born singer who had a major hit with 'Misty Blue' in the summer of 1976. This song was written by the Addrisi Brothers, who also wrote 'Never My Love' for the Association in 1967.

164. Whispering/Cherchez La Femme/Se Ci Bon by Dr. Buzzard's Original 'Savannah' Band was a New York City 30's style disco group. 'Whispering' was a remake of a hit by Paul Whiteman from 1920 while C'est Si Bon was a hit for various artists through the years including Eartha Kitt in 1953.

165. Bite your lip (Get Up and Dance) by Elton John was a moderate hit for the 70's superstar who was rarely absent from the top 10. This was Elton's final hit of the 70's co-written by Bernie Taupin, his longtime songwriting partner. They each collaborated with other songwriters beginning in late 1977, but reunited professionally in the early 80's.

166. My Fair Share by Seals & Crofts was the theme from the movie 'One on One' starring Robby Benson. All songs from the movie were written by Paul Williams and Charles Fox and performed by Seals and Crofts.

167. Show You the Way to Go by The Jacksons was their follow up to 'Enjoy Yourself', their first hit on the Epic record label. Lead vocals on this hit, written by Gamble and Huff, were shared by Jackie, Marlon and Michael Jackson. Although this single barely made the top 30, it became a number one hit for the Jacksons in Britain.

168. Moody Blue by Elvis Presley was popular while he was still alive in the year he died. This song was written by Mark James, who also wrote 1969's 'Suspicious Minds', his final number one hit. Elvis died 6 months after this song was top 40 on the pop charts and number one on the country charts. The 'B' side of this single was 'She Thinks I Still Care' which was a number one country hit for George Jones in 1962.

169. **Hard Rock Café** by Carole King was the final top 40 hit of the 70's for the Brooklyn-born singer who was best known as a prolific songwriter and pianist. This single was from the album 'Simple Things', her first for Capitol records. Both Carole's daughters Louise and Sherry Goffin sang background vocals on this album.

170. **Back Together Again** by Hall & Oates was the follow up to their number one 1977 hit 'Rich Girl', also from their album 'Bigger than the Both of Us'. This song was written solely by John Oates.

More Hits of 1977

N.Y. You Got Me Dancing by Andrea True Connection was the only other top 40 hit for the singer of the 1976 million seller 'More More More'. This was another disco-friendly dance floor song for the singer who moved to New York City from Nashville in 1968.

The Killing of Georgie by Rod Stewart was based on a real life acquaintance of the raspy-voiced singer, who was a homosexual murdered in New York City. This song was written by Rod Stewart and was the 3rd hit single from his 'A Night on the Town' album.

So You Win Again by Hot Chocolate was a moderate hit for the group in North America, but a number one hit in the U.K. for this British group previously known for their hits 'You Sexy Thing' and 'Emma'. This was their final hit on the 'Big Tree' label and their first not written or co-written by lead singer Errol Brown. This song was written by Argent guitarist Russ Ballard.

Slide by Slave was the only hit for this 9 man funk band from Dayton, Ohio. They got their name during a rehearsal when one of the members, Floyd Miller, walked in with a t-shirt that read 'slave'. This hit slid into the number one spot on the R & B charts.

Calling Occupants of Interplanetary Craft by the Carpenters was something completely different for this soft pop duo known for their love ballads. This big production by the Carpenters featured numerous musicians and was a featured cut on their 'Passage' album, produced by Richard Carpenter. The single version was slightly over 4 minutes long, while the album version checked in at over 7 minutes. This was a cover of the Klaatu song from less than a year later.

My Sweet Lady by John Denver was a moderate hit for this pop/folk singer in 1977 and was previously the 'B' side of his number one hit 'Thank God I'm A Country Boy' in 1975. 'My Sweet Lady' was also a hit 2 years earlier by singer/ actor Cliff DeYoung.

Cherry Baby by Starz was the most popular hit for this rock quintet which was fronted by Michael Lee Smith. 2 of the members of the band came from The Looking Glass, known for the hit 'Brandy (You're A Fine Girl)' after their breakup. They recorded for Capitol records and this was the only hit of their 6 singles in the late 70's which charted in the top 40, despite a cult following.

Peace of Mind by Boston was the 3rd and final hit single from their self-titled debut album which also included the hits 'More Than a Feeling' and 'Long Time'. 'Peace of Mind' is a social comment song about the growing materialism of the Baby Boomer generation as they enter the workforce.

Sunflower by Glen Campbell was written by Neil Diamond, but never released on a single or album by him. This moderate hit was produced by Gary Klein, who co-produced Barbra Streisand's 'My Heart Belongs to You' which was on the charts at exactly the same time in the summer of 1977.

In the Mood by Henhouse Five Plus Two was actually funnyman Ray Stevens doing chicken sounds to the tune Glenn Miller made famous in 1939.

On the Border by Al Stewart was the follow up to his signature hit 'Year of the Cat' also included on the album recorded at Abbey Road studios. This Glasgow, Scotland born singer/songwriter/guitarist would emerge the following year with the very successful 'Time Passages'.

Dreamboat Annie by Heart was 1 of 3 hit singles from their popular debut album of the same name. There were 3 different versions of this song on the album.

Yesterday's Hero by The Bay City Rollers was included on their 'Dedication' album. 'Yesterday's Hero' was an appropriate title for the Scottish teenybopper band that created 'Rollermania' in the late 70's. This song was written by Harry Vanda and George Young, formerly with the Easybeats and writers of hits including 'Love Is in the Air'.

Seaside Woman by Suzy & the Red Stripes was actually Paul and Linda McCartney in disguise. This fun song was written by Linda McCartney during a visit to Jamaica in 1971. It was recorded by Wings during the 'Red Rose Speedway' sessions in 1972, but never released.

I'm Scared by Burton Cummings was the follow up to the lead singer of the Guess Who's first big solo hit 'Stand Tall'. Although his solo hit career was limited in the United States, he continued to chart many more hits in Canada during the 70's and 80's.In his hometown of Winnipeg, Manitoba stands 'The Burton Cummings Theatre'.

Sub Rosa Subway/Calling Occupants by Klaatu was a Canadian group who some believed were the Beatles in disguise since the band's identity was a mystery and there were some similarities in the sound. This was a double-sided hit single which included 'Calling Occupants' which the Carpenters covered in 1977. They took the name 'Klaatu' from the extraterrestrial character played by Michael Rennie in the film 'The Day the Earth Stood Still'.

C.B. Savage by Rod Hart was a one hit wonder novelty hit with a gay-themed take on the C.B. craze of the late 70's.

(Remember the Days Of The) Old Schoolyard by Cat Stevens was the final top 40 hit for this folk/pop singer/songwriter who converted to Muslim and took the name Yusef Islam. This lyrically nostalgic hit from the album 'Izitso' was recorded with British singer Elkie Brooks.

1.	Rumours	Fleetwood Mac
2.	Hotel California	The Eagles
3.	A Star Is Born	Barbra Streisand/Kris Kristofferson
4.	Simple Dreams	Linda Ronstadt
5.	Wings over America	Wings
6.	Barry Manilow 'Live'	Barry Manilow
7.	I'm In You	Peter Frampton
8.	A Day at the Races	Queen
9.	Book of Dreams	Steve Miller
10.	Aja	Steely Dan
11.	Boston	Boston
12.	A New World Record	E. L. O.
13.	The Best of the Doobies	Doobie Brothers
14.	Leftoverture	Kansas
15.	Foot Loose and Fancy Free	Rod Stewart
16.	Superman	Barbra Streisand
17.	Live	Commodores

1.	Luchenbach, Texas (Back to the Basics)	Waylon Jennings
2.	Here You Come Again	Dolly Parton
3.	Don't It Make My Brown Eyes Blue	Crystal Gayle
4.	Heaven's Just a Sin Away	The Kendalls
5.	It Was Almost Like a Song	Ronnie Milsap
6.	Lucille	Kenny Rogers
7.	Near You	George Jones & Tammy Wynette
8.	Southern Nights	Glen Campbell
9.	The Wurlitzer Prize (I Don't Want To Get Over U)	Waylon Jennings
10.	Rollin' With the Flow	Charlie Rich
11.	Daytime Friends	Kenny Rogers
12.	Way Down	Elvis Presley
13.	Say You'll Stay until Tomorrow	Tom Jones
14.	I Can't Believe She Gives It All to Me	Conway Twitty
15.	I'm Just a Country Boy	Don Williams
16.	I've Already Loved You In my Mind	Conway Twitty

Top 17 Disco Hits of 1977

1.	How Deep Is Your Love	Bee Gees
2.	Best of My Love	Emotions
3.	Sir Duke	Stevie Wonder
4.	Dancing Queen	Abba
5.	Car Wash	Rose Royce
6.	Don't Leave Me This Way	Thelma Houston
7.	Got To Give It Up	Marvin Gaye
8.	I'm Your Boogie Man	K.C. & the Sunshine Band
9.	Keep It Comin' Love	K. C. & the Sunshine Band
10.	Dazz	Brick
11.	Back In Love Again	L. T. D.
12.	Brick House	Commodores
13.	I Feel Love	Donna Summer
14.	Heaven on the 7th Floor	Paul Nicholas
15.	Enjoy Yourself	The Jacksons
16.	Ain't Gonna Bump With No Fat Woman	Joe Tex
17.	Disco Lucy	Wilton Place Street Band

Top 17 One Hit Wonders of 1977

1.	Debby Boone	You Light Up My Life
2.	Meco	Star Wars Theme
3.	Mary MacGregor	Torn Between Two Lovers
4.	Thelma Houston	Don't Leave Me This Way
5.	Alan O'Day	Undercover Angel
6.	David Soul	Don't Give Up on Us
7.	Floaters	Float On
8.	Peter McCann	Do You Wanna Make Love
9.	Hot	Angel in Your Arms
10.	Paul Nicholas	Heavon on the 7th Floor
11.	Sanford – Townsend Band	Smoke from a Distant Fire
12.	High Energy	You Can't Turn Me Off
13.	David Dundas	Jeans On
14.	Ram Jam	Black Betty
15.	Bill Conti	Gonna Fly Now (Theme from Rocky)
16.	Meri Wilson	Telephone Man
17.	William Bell	Tryin' To Love Two

Top 17 Rock/Hard Rock hits of 1977

blinded by the light
**MANFRED MANN'S
EARTH BAND**

1.	Blinded By The Night	Manfred Mann's Earth Band
2.	Feels Like the First Time	Foreigner
3.	Cold as Ice	Foreigner
4.	Walk This Way	Aerosmith
5.	Carry On Wayward Son	Kansas
6.	Life in the Fast Lane	Eagles
7.	Barracuda	Heart
8.	Hard Luck Woman	Kiss
9.	Swingtown	Steve Miller Band
10.	Calling Mr. Love	Kiss
11.	Long Time	Boston
12.	Christine Sixteen	Kiss
13.	Cat Scratch Fever	Ted Nugent
14.	Jungle Love	Steve Miller
15.	I Just Want To Make Love To You (Live)	Foghat
16.	Back In the Saddle	Aerosmith
17.	Do Ya	E. L. O.

1.	Smoke From A Distant Fire	Sanford-Townsend Band
2.	Telephone Line	E. L. O.
3.	Ariel	Dean Friedman
4.	Isn't It Time	Babys
5.	Tryin' To Love Two	William Bell
6.	Jeans On	David Dundas
7.	Crackerbox Palace	George Harrison
8.	Dancin' Man	Q
9.	Jungle Love	Steve Miller Band
10.	Calling Occupants (Of Interplanetary Craft)	Klaatu
11.	She Did It	Eric Carmen
12.	(Remember the Days Of The) Old Schoolyard	Cat Stevens
13.	Love's Grown Deep	Kenny Nolan
14.	Don't Worry Baby	B. J. Thomas
15.	Seaside Woman	Suzy & the Red Stripes
16.	Heard It in a Love Song	Marshall Tucker Band
17.	On The Border	Al Stewart

Top 17 Hits from the Summer 0f 1970

1.	Close To You	The Carpenters
2.	Mama Told Me (Not To Come)	3 Dog Night
3.	Make It With You	Bread
4.	The Long and Winding Road	The Beatles
5.	War	Edwin Starr
6.	Band of Gold	Freda Payne
7.	The Love You Save	Jackson Five
8.	Signed, Sealed, Delivered, I'm Yours	Stevie Wonder
9.	In The Summertime	Mungo Jerry
10.	Ball of Confusion	Temptations
11.	Get Ready	Rare Earth
12.	Ride Captain Ride	Blues Image
13.	Up Around the Bend	C. C. R.
14.	Hitchin' a Ride	Vanity Fare
15.	Lay Down (Candles in the Rain)	Melanie
16.	Tighter, Tighter	Alive and Kicking
17.	O –O – H Child	Five Stairsteps

Top 17 Hits from the Summer Of 1971

1.	It's Too Late	Carole King
2.	How Can You Mend a Broken Heart	Bee Gees
3.	You've Got a Friend	James Taylor
4.	Indian Reservation	Raiders
5.	Mr. Big Stuff	Jean Knight
6.	Take Me Home Country Roads	John Denver
7.	Rainy Days and Mondays	Carpenters
8.	Treat Her Like A Lady	Cornelius Bros. & Sister Rose
9.	Signs	Five Man Electrical Band
10.	Don't Pull Your Love	Hamilton, Joe Frank & Reynolds
11.	It Don't Come Easy	Ringo Starr
12.	Draggin' the Line	Tommy James
13.	Mercy Mercy Me	Marvin Gaye
14.	Sweet Hitch Hiker	C. C. R.
15.	Bridge Over Troubled Water	Aretha Franklin
16.	Beginnings	Chicago
17.	When You're Hot You're Hot	Jerry Reed

Top 17 Hits from the Summer Of 1972

1.	Alone Again Naturally	Gilbert O'Sullivan
2.	Lean On Me	Bill Withers
3.	Brandy (You're A Fine Girl)	Looking Glass
4.	The Candy Man	Sammy Davis Jr.
5.	I'll Take You There	Staple Singers
6.	Song Sung Blue	Neil Diamond
7.	Too Late To Turn Back Now	Cornelius Bros. & Sister Rose
8.	Outa Space	Billy Preston
9.	If Loving You Is Wrong I Don't Want To Be Right	Luther Ingram
10.	Saturday in the Park	Chicago
11.	Daddy Don't You Walk So Fast	Wayne Newton
12.	Nice To Be With You	Jim Gold & the Gallery
13.	Hold Your Head Up	Argent
14.	Where Is the Love	Roberta Flack & Donny Hathaway
15.	Troglodyte (Caveman)	Jimmy Caster Bunch
16.	School's Out	Alice Cooper
17.	Rocket Man	Elton John

Top 17 Hits from the Summer OF 1973

1.	My Love	Paul McCartney
2.	Bad Bad Leroy Brown	Jim Croce
3.	Will It Go Round in Circles	Billy Preston

4.	Brother Louie	The Stories
5.	The Morning After	Maureen McGovern
6.	Frankenstein	Edgar Winter Group
7.	Touch Me in the Morning	Diana Ross
8.	Kodachrome	Paul Simon
9.	Shambala	3 Dog Night
10.	Let's Get It On	Marvin Gaye
11.	Say, Has Anybody Seen … Gypsy Rose	Tony Orlando & Dawn
12.	I'm Gonna Love You Just A …More Baby	Barry White
13.	Smoke on the Water	Deep Purple
14.	Pillow Talk	Sylvia
15.	Monster Mash	Bobby 'Boris' Pickett
16.	Loves Me like A Rock	Paul Simon
17.	My Maria	B. W. Stevenson

Top 17 Hits from the Summer Of 1974

1.	Billy, Don't Be a Hero	Bo Donaldson & Heywoods
2.	Rock Your Baby	George McCrae
3.	You're Having My Baby	Paul Anka & Odia Coates
4.	Rock the Boat	Hues Corporation
5.	Annie's Song	John Denver
6.	Rock Me Gently	Andy Kim
7.	The Night Chicago Died	Paperlace
8.	Band on the Run	Paul McCartney & Wings
9.	I Shot the Sheriff	Eric Clapton
10.	Feel Like Makin' Love	Roberta Flack
11.	You Make Me Feel Brand New	Stylistics
12.	Don't Let the Sun Go Down On Me	Elton John
13.	Rock and Roll Heaven	Righteous Brothers
14.	Rikki Don't Lose That Number	Steely Dan
15.	Tell Me Something Good	Rufus
16.	If You Love Me (Let Me Know)	Olivia Newton-John
17.	Please Come To Boston	Dave Loggins

Top 17 Hits from the Summer of 1975

1. Love Will Keep Us Together — Captain & Tennille
2. Jive Talkin' — Bee Gees
3. One of These Nights — Eagles
4. Listen to What the Man Said — Paul McCartney & Wings
5. The Hustle — Van McCoy
6. Fallin' In Love — Hamilton, Joe Frank & Reynolds
7. Sister Golden Hair — America
8. Thank God I'm A Country Boy — John Denver
9. Get Down Tonight — K.C. & the Sunshine Band
10. I'm Not in Love — 10 C. C.
11. Please Mr. Please — Olivia Newton – John
12. When Will I Be Loved — Linda Ronstadt
13. Wildfire — Michael Murphey
14. I'm Not Lisa — Jessi Colter
15. How Sweet It Is (To Be Loved By You) — James Taylor
16. Bad Time — Grand Funk
17. Old Days — Chicago

Top 17 Hits from the Summer of 1976

1. Don't Go Breaking My Heart — Elton John & Kiki Dee
2. Afternoon Delight — Starland Vocal Band
3. Kiss and Say Goodbye — Manhattans

4.	Love Is Alive	Gary Wright
5.	Get Up and Boogie	Silver Convention
6.	Let 'Em In	Paul McCartney & Wings
7.	Misty Blue	Dorothy Moore
8.	Moonlight Feels Right	Starbuck
9.	I'll Be Good to You	Brothers Johnson
10.	More More More	Andrea True Connection
11.	Shop Around	Captain & Tennille
12.	Rock and Roll Music	Beach Boys
13.	Shannon	Henry Gross
14.	Happy Days	Pratt & McLain
15.	Get Closer	Seals & Crofts
16.	Summer	War
17.	Go To Get You into My Life	The Beatles

Top 17 Hits from the Summer of 1977

1.	I Just Want To Be Your Everything	Andy Gibb
2.	Best of My Love	Emotions
3.	Undercover Angel	Alan O'Day
4.	Dreams	Fleetwood Mac
5.	Got To Give It Up	Marvin Gaye
6.	Da Do Ron Ron	Shawn Cassidy
7.	Gonna Fly Now (Theme from Rocky)	Bill Conti
8.	Looks Like We Made It	Barry Manilow
9.	I'm In You	Peter Frampton
10.	Do You Wanna Make Love	Peter McCann
11.	Easy	Commodores
12.	My Heart Belongs To You	Barbra Streisand
13.	Lucille	Kenny Rogers
14.	Angel in Your Arms	Hot
15.	Whatcha Gonna Do	Pablo Cruise
16.	Lonely Boy	Andrew Gold
17.	Margaritaville	Jimmy Buffet

Top 17 Hits from the Summer of 1978

1.	Shadow Dancing	Andy Gibb
2.	Grease	Frankie Valli
3.	Kiss You All Over	Exile
4.	Three Times a Lady	Commodores
5.	You're The One That I Want	John Travolta & Olivia Newton-John
6.	Miss You	Rolling Stones
7.	Too Much, Too Little, Too Late	Johnny Mathis & Deniece Williams
8.	Baker Street	Gerry Rafferty
9.	Take a Chance on Me	Abba
10.	Last Dance	Donna Summer
11.	It's A Heartache	Bonnie Tyler
12.	Used Ta Be My Girl	O'Jays
13.	Still the Same	Bob Seger
14.	Feels So Good	Chuck Mangione
15.	Summer Nights	John Travolta & Olivia Newton-John
16.	Love Will Find A Way	Pablo Cruise
17.	You Belong To Me	Carly Simon

Top 17 Hits from the Summer of 1979

1. My Sharona   The Knack
2. Bad Girls   Donna Summer
3. Ring My Bell   Anita Ward
4. Hot Stuff   Donna Summer
5. Good Times   Chic
6. We Are Family   Sister Sledge
7. Love You Inside Out   Bee Gees
8. Just When I Needed You Most   Randy Vanwarmer
9. The Main Event/Fight   Barbra Streisand
10. Chuck E's In Love   Rickie Lee Jones
11. Gold   John Stewart
12. Makin' It   David Naughton
13. The Logical Song   Supertramp
14. She Believes In Me   Kenny Rogers
15. Boogie Wonderland   Earth, Wind & Fire with Emotions
16. When You're In Love With A Beautiful Woman   Dr. Hook
17. I Want You to Want Me   Cheap Trick

♫ Aside from all the major hits the Bee Gees achieved as a group in 1978, they also contributed to no less than 8 hits by other artists that year.

♫ This number one hit by the lead singer of the Four Seasons was written for the movie of the same name by one of the Bee Gees.

♫ The queen of disco remade this epic song originally performed by an actor in 1968.

♫ This solo singer was previously the voice of 'Stuck In The Middle With You' in 1973 by Stealer's Wheel.

♫ These two individual music superstars came together for this million selling single by accident.

♫ Although Saturday Night Fever was the top soundtrack album of the year, this film was close at second with 4 major hit singles.

FIND OUT THAT...AND MUCH MORE INSIDE ... 1978!

1. Night Fever by The Bee Gees was their biggest hit of all time and one that remained at the top of the pop charts for 2 months. This was their 3rd consecutive number one hit from the 'Saturday Night Fever' soundtrack. In March of 1978 when this hit was number one, the Bee Gees were responsible for performing and/or writing all top 5 hits on Billboard's top 10 with 'Stayin' Alive', 'Emotion', which they wrote for Samantha Sang, '(Love Is) Thicker Than Water', which Barry had co-written for brother Andy and 'If I Can't Have You', which the brothers Gibb wrote for Yvonne Elliman.

2. Shadow Dancing by Andy Gibb was a song he wrote with all 3 Bee Gee brothers in Los Angeles one night while his brothers were filming the movie 'Sgt. Pepper's Lonely Hearts Club Band'. This became his 3rd consecutive number one hit. Contributing on the album were Eagles' Joe Walsh and Don Felder and the same string musicians used on the 'Hotel California' album played on the 'Shadow Dancing' single.

3. Stayin' Alive by The Bee Gees is the song playing in the opening scene of the film 'Saturday Night Fever' as John Travolta is strutting down the sidewalk in New York City. This is the hit most identified with the soundtrack that went on to sell more than 25 million copies, becoming the best selling album of the 70's.

4. Le Freak by Chic was a multi million selling disco hit for the New York City group featuring lead singers Norman Jean Knight and Luci Martin. This hit was written and produced by Nile Rodgers and Bernard Edwards, who were also guitarists for the band. Rodgers started out as a guitarist with a 'Sesame Street' touring band. He later produced and/or wrote/co wrote 'Upside Down' for Diana Ross, 'Rapper's Delight' by the Sugarhill Gang, 'Let's Dance' by David Bowie, 'We Are Family' by Sister Sledge and other notable hits.

5. Kiss You All Over by Exile was written by Mike Chapman and Nicky Chinn, the popular British songwriters/producers who wrote the biggest hits of the Sweet, Suzi Quatro and others. This sensuous, soft rock hit with a hypnotic beat stayed at the top of the charts for a full month. This band from Lexington, Kentucky, switched to a career in country music in the 80's and charted numerous hits, including almost a dozen number one hits.

6. Boogie Oogie Oogie by A Taste of Honey was a multi-million seller for this disco group from Los Angeles who took their name from the song of the same name. Vocalists Janice Marie Johnson and Hazel Payne also played guitars while singing lead. This group won the Best New Artist Grammy Award in 1978. In 1981 they resurfaced as a duo and had a million seller with their remake of the song 'Sukiyaki'.

7. MacArthur Park by Donna Summer was a disco version of a song actor Richard Harris had a hit with 10 years earlier in 1968. The song was written by Jim Webb, who composed many of the 5th Dimension's hits including 'Up, Up and Away' and a string of Glen Campbell hits including 'Galveston'. The queen of the disco served it up her way and presented it in less than 4 minutes on the single and over 7 minutes on the album.

8. Baby Come Back by Player was written by 2 of the group's members after both had broken up with their respective girlfriends. This number one hit was produced by Dennis Lambert and Brian Potter and written by lead singer John Charles Crowley with Peter Beckett. Bassist Ronn Moss later became an actor, appearing as Ridge Forrester in over 2,000 episodes of 'The Bold and The Beautiful' since 1987.

9. Grease by Frankie Valli was written by Barry Gibb of the Bee Gees specifically for the film of the same name. The film was based on the Broadway play set in the late 50's and was a huge box office success, starring John Travolta, (the same year he hit it big with 'Saturday Night Fever') and Olivia Newton- John. They also had 2 million selling hit singles together from the film.

10. Three Times a Lady by the Commodores was written by Lionel Richie after he heard the speech by his father at his parent's 37th wedding anniversary party. It was the first single from their 'Natural High' album and first to reach number one on the pop charts.

11. (Love Is) Thicker than Water by Andy Gibb was the 2nd consecutive number one hit for the youngest member of the Gibb brothers, who was 19 at the time he recorded this song. He co wrote this song with brother Barry in Bermuda. Exactly 10 years after this hit topped the charts, Andy Gibb died a few days after his 30th birthday as a result of an inflammatory heart virus.

12. You Don't Bring Me Flowers by Neil Diamond & Barbra Streisand was originally recorded separately as album cuts by each artist, but a DJ in Kentucky spliced the two recordings together and played it on the radio. The response was phenomenal. Producer Bob Gaudio then suggested the 2 Brooklyn superstars record it together as a duet. It went all the way to number one.

13. With A Little Luck by Paul McCartney & Wings was written in Scotland by the former Beatle at the time his wife Linda was pregnant and he decided to put the band on hold. 'With A Little Luck', from the album 'London Town', was released on St. Patrick's Day and was recorded just before Wings' members Jimmy McCulloch and drummer Joe English left the band.

14. Miss You by the Rolling Stones was the first and biggest hit from their 'Some Girls' album which sold several million copies. The eye-catching cover originally featured pictures of Lucille Ball, Farrah Fawcett and Judy Garland, but was changed due to legal issues. 'Miss You' was a bluesy, punk and disco hit and the first single to top the charts for the Stones since 'Angie' in 1973.

15.Hot Child in the City by Nick Gilder was a number one hit for the former lead singer of Sweeney Todd, known for their major Canadian hit 'Roxy Roller'. He moved from London, England to Vancouver, British Columbia, Canada when he was 10 years old. This hit was co-written by Nick Gilder and produced by Mike Chapman, who also produced 'Kiss You all Over' by Exile, which this song replaced at number one.

16.If I Can't Have You by Yvonne Elliman was written by all 3 members of the Bee Gees and became the 4th number one single from the 'Saturday Night Fever' soundtrack. The Bee Gees originally wrote 'How Deep Is Your Love' for Yvonne Elliman, but their manager Robert Stigwood insisted that they record it themselves.

17.You're the One That I Want by John Travolta & Olivia Newton-John was the first number one hit from the movie soundtrack of 'Grease'. This song was written specifically for the film by John Farrar, who wrote and produced most of Olivia Newton-John's major hits of the 70's.John Travolta was in New York shooting 'Saturday Night Fever' when the call was made for plans to pair the two together onscreen, - Olivia's major debut on the big screen.

18.Too Much, Too Little, Too Late by Johnny Mathis & Deniece Williams was one of the biggest hits of the year, and the first top 10 hit for Mathis since 1963. The original choice for this number one million selling duet was Minnie Ripperton, but when she was unavailable, Deniece Williams agreed to record with Johnny Mathis. Both female singers previously sang with Stevie Wonder as part of the group 'Wonderlove'.

19.You Needed Me by Anne Murray was popular after she returned to show business after a 2 year hiatus after the birth of her first child. This number one hit was written by Randy Goodrum, who also wrote Michael Johnson's 1978 hit 'Bluer than Blue'.

20.Baker Street by Gerry Rafferty was the first solo hit for the singer known for singing lead on Stealer's Wheel classic 'Stuck in the Middle with You'. 'Baker Street' from the album 'City To City', was named after the famous London Street, and featured a prominent saxophone and guitar solo backing the unique voice of this Scottish singer/songwriter.

21.The Closer I Get to You by Roberta Flack & Donny Hathaway was the 2nd major duet they recorded together following 'Where Is the Love' in 1972. Donny Hathaway committed suicide less than a year after this soul ballad was recorded.

22.Double Vision by Foreigner was a million seller from the group that took its name from the fact that its members came from both sides of the Atlantic Ocean with 3 from London, England and the other 3 from New York. Their hit 'Hot Blooded' was still on the charts when this Mick Jones and Lou Gramm composition was hot on the tracks of heading for the top 5.

23.Just the Way You Are by Billy Joel was written for his first wife Elizabeth whom he divorced 4 years later in 1982. He got the idea for the song when he was in the middle of a meeting and immediately excused himself to go home and write this song that came into his head. It became his first top 10 hit single and won the Grammy Award for both 'Record of the Year' and 'Song of the Year' in 1978.

24.Short People by Randy Newman was a humorous statement, but some took this song about the vertically-challenged quite seriously and were quite upset that he would record such a song. This hit featured backing vocals by J.D Souther and the Eagles' Glenn Frey and Timothy B. Schmit. Randy Newman not only wrote the number one hit 'Mama Told Me (Not To Come)' by 3 Dog Night, but went on to compose film scores for dozens of films including all 3 'Toy Story' movies, 'Monster's Inc,' 'Cars', and 'Parenthood'.

25.Lay Down Sally by Eric Clapton was the first hit from his 'Slow Hand' album. This pop country hit was co-written by back up singer Marcy Levy, who previously toured with Bob Seger. The follow up single from this album was 'Wonderful Tonight', which also featured Levy on backing vocals, along with Yvonne Elliman.

26.Can't Smile without You by Barry Manilow was originally recorded on albums by both the Carpenters and Engelbert Humperdinck without much success. Arista President Clive Davis suggested Barry Manilow consider recording it, although he was less than happy with the song. He eventually gave in and it became one of his biggest hits and one of the most popular in concerts.

27.How Much I Feel by Ambrosia was a prime cut from the album 'Life Beyond L.A.' and was the first top 10 hit for this Los Angeles based soft rock group fronted by lead singer/songwriter David Pack. In 1980, they had 2 more soft rock hits with 'Biggest Part of Me' and 'You're The Only Woman'.

28.Emotion by Samantha Sang featured Barry Gibb on backing vocals on the song he wrote with Bee Gee brother Robin. Australian Samantha Sang, whose real name was Cheryl Gray, sang on the radio when she was 8 and met Barry Gibb when she was 16. This million seller was her only notable hit and was popular when the Bee Gees ruled the radio airwaves and charts.

29.Sometimes When We Touch by Dan Hill was co-written with Barry Mann who created many hits with his wife Cynthia Weil including 'You've Lost That Loving Feeling', 'On Broadway', 'Kicks' and dozens of others. Dan Hill is a Canadian singer/songwriter from Toronto who had many hits with ballads including 'Can't We Try', a duet he recorded with Vonda Shepard in 1987.

30.Last Dance by Donna Summer was the Academy Award winning 'Best Original Song' awarded in early 1979 from the 1978 song and movie 'Thank God It's Friday'. Donna Summer appeared in the film as Nicole Sims, an aspiring disco singer, along with a young Jeff Goldblum and a soon-to-be-discovered Debra Winger.

31.Hopelessly Devoted to You by Olivia Newton-John was a million selling ballad from the 'Grease' movie soundtrack written by her longtime songwriter/ producer John Farrar specifically for the film. This song was nominated for an Academy Award in the 'Best Original Song' category, but lost to Donna Summer's Last Dance' from the film 'Thank God Its Friday'.

32.Hot Blooded by Foreigner is considered to be the group's signature song and was the first single released from their 2nd album 'Double Vision', the title song of the 2nd single. This album was produced by Keith Olsen.

33.Take a Chance on Me by Abba was one of the biggest hits from this super group from Sweden. The working title of this song was 'Billy Boy' and it was one of the first Abba compositions which did not include Stig Anderson, who was busy managing the group fulltime.

34.Here You Come Again by Dolly Parton was written by the popular songwriting team Barry Mann and Cynthia Weil. This became Dolly Parton's first million selling pop crossover hit. It earned Dolly the Best Female Country Vocal at the Grammy Awards in 1979.

35.It's a Heartache by Bonnie Tyler was the first hit for this raspy-voiced singer from Wales. Mike Gibbons of Badfinger played drums on this pop/country hit which sold a million copies in early 1978. 5 years later she released the biggest hit of her career with 'Total Eclipse of the Heart', written by Jim Steinman, who wrote Meatloaf's biggest hits.

36.Reminiscing by The Little River Band was the biggest hit of all for this group from down under. This hit was written by guitarist Graham Goble with lead vocals by Glenn Shorrock and is a song about a couple looking back on the past with references of music by Glenn Miller. This was the first of 2 major hits from the 'Sleeper Catcher' album, which also included their top 10 hit 'Lady'.

37.We Are the Champions/We Will Rock You by Queen was 2 separate songs which both became well known at major sports events. 'We Are the Champions' was written by Freddie Mercury. 'We Will Rock You' was written by Brian May, and aside from his guitar solo, the song is a cappella accompanied by clapping and stomping as a rhythmic beat. Both songs are from the album 'News of the World'.

38.You're In My Heart (The Final Acclaim) by Rod Stewart was the first and biggest hit from his 'Footloose & Fancy Free' album released in late 1977. Rod Stewart wrote this song which includes a mention of his 2 favorite football teams in the lyrics 'Celtic, United'. The inner sleeve to the album also pictures artwork with the names 'Glasgow Celtic and Manchester United' coming out of the car stereo.

39.Used to Be My Girl by the O'Jays was a nostalgic R & B hit reminiscent of the sound of the doo wop groups of the 50's and 60's. This Gamble and Huff composition and production was the final major hit and million seller for this soul group from Ohio.

40.I Just Wanna Stop by Gino Vannelli was the biggest hit for this singer/ songwriter from Montreal, Quebec, Canada. Montreal gets an honorable mention in this love ballad which reached number one in Canada and gave Vannelli a nomination for a Grammy Award. He won many Juno Awards in Canada (the equivalent of a Grammy in the U.S.) including Best New Artist in 1974.

41.Still the Same by Bob Seger was the first of 4 hit singles from his 10th album, 'Stranger in Town'. Although he formed the Silver Bullet Band in 1976, this was the first Bob Seger hit to include the band name on the single. The album was recorded at studios in Miami, Florida, Detroit, Michigan and Sheffield, Alabama at the famous Muscle Shoals.

42.Feels So Good by Chuck Mangione was a huge instrumental hit written and produced by the master of the flugelhorn. He once described this odd instrument saying 'it looks like a trumpet in the 6th month of pregnancy'. Chuck Mangione was born in Rochester, New York and on February 12th 2009 2 of his band members were killed not far from there when a commercial aircraft crashed near Buffalo, New York killing all 49 on board.

43.I Love the Nightlife by Alicia Bridges was one of the most popular songs on the disco dance floors in the summer of 1978 for this one hit wonder singer/songwriter from Lawndale, North Carolina. She continues to record music and for many years has been a radio DJ/Producer.

44.Summer Nights by John Travolta & Olivia Newton-John was one of 4 million selling singles from the 'Grease' movie soundtrack. Of the 4 major hits from the film, this was the only original song from the Broadway Musical which debuted in 1971.The film also included performances by the 50's nostalgia group Sha Na Na.

45.Don't Look Back by Boston was the title song from their 2nd album. The original title was 'Arrival', but when it was discovered that it would be the title of Abba's new album, it was changed to 'Don't Look Back'. This was their last major hit until 1986 when they resurfaced with the number one hit 'Amanda'.

46.Whenever I Call You Friend by Kenny Loggins, featured Stevie Nicks on harmony vocal. This was the first of many solo hits for this popular singer/songwriter/guitarist after his career as half of the popular duo 'Loggins and Messina' ended. His most success came in the 80's, especially with his movie hits 'Footloose', 'I'm Alright' and 'Danger Zone'.

47.An Everlasting Love by Andy Gibb was the 3rd of 4 1978 hits for the Bee Gees younger brother. This hit was written solely by his brother Barry, who wrote or co wrote all of his major hits. In 1978, while Andy was performing a concert in Miami, Florida, his brothers, the Bee Gees, made a surprise appearance and it became the first time all four Gibbs appeared on stage together.

48.Slip Slidin' Away by Paul Simon featured backup vocals by the Oak Ridge Boys and was one of 2 songs from his album 'Greatest Hits, Etc'. This smooth ballad was originally considered for his album 'Still Crazy After All These Years'.

49.I Go Crazy by Paul Davis was on Billboard's Hot 100 chart for 40 weeks, a record for the longest run on the chart up to that time. Although he had previous hits, this pop ballad was his first official top 10 hit. This was a prime cut from the album 'Singer of Songs, Teller of Tales'.

50.You Belong to Me by Carly Simon was co written by Michael McDonald and featured backing vocals by her husband, James Taylor. This was the lead off single from her 'Boys in the Trees' album which also included her duet remake of the Everly Brothers hit 'Devoted to You' with James.

51.Love Will Find a Way by Pablo Cruise was one of two major hits this San

Francisco pop/rock quartet achieved during the late 70's. Dave Jenkins co-wrote and sang lead on this summer of '78 hit from their 4th album, 'Worlds Away'. Before this album was released, Bud Cockrell left the band and was replaced by Bruce Day, formerly with Santana. Steve and Mike Porcaro of Toto played on this album.

52. **Hey Deanie** by Shawn Cassidy was his 2nd consecutive major hit written by Eric Carmen. This was the 3rd and final million selling single for the teen idol and star of the Hardy Boys TV series which ran from 1977 – 1979. His next single was a remake of the Lovin' Spoonful's 'Do You Believe in Magic' but it failed to reach the top 30.

53. **Love Is in the Air** by John Paul Young was the most successful hit in North America for this singer/songwriter/pianist from Glasgow, Scotland. This hit was written and produced by Harry Vanda and George Young, who were previously founding members of the Easybeats. George Young was also known for his production with AC/DC which featured his younger brothers Malcolm and Angus Young.

54. **The Groove Line** by Heatwave was the 3rd and final hit for this Multi-national disco group formed in Germany by brothers Johnnie and Keith Wilder. Their hits were written by keyboardist Rod Temperton who left the group in 1978 to concentrate on songwriting. He later wrote some of the biggest hits for others, including Michael Jackson's 'Thriller' and Patti Austin's 'Baby Come To Me'.

55. **Time Passages** by Al Stewart was an easy listening hit produced by Alan Parsons. It became the successful follow up to his album and single 'Year of the Cat'. 'Time Passages' spent 10 weeks at number one on Billboard's Adult Contemporary chart.

56. **Imaginary Lover** by Atlanta Rhythm Section was a major hit for this 70's pop/ jazz group from Georgia. Around the time this hit was popular, they performed at the White House because President Jimmy Carter knew them from his days when he was the Governor of Georgia. Original drummer and songwriter Robert Nix left the band shortly after recording this hit.

57. **Jack and Jill** by Raydio, featuring Ray Parker Jr., was the first of many hits for this newly-formed band headed by one of California's top session guitarists. This hit was a psychedelic soul hit inspired by the children's nursery rhyme. The lead singer, Ray Parker Jr, would later score a number one solo hit in with the title song of the movie 'Ghostbusters' in 1984.

58. **On Broadway** by George Benson was a jazzed up 'live' remake of the Drifters hit from 1963. This version charted even better than the original and won a Grammy Award for 'Best R & B Vocal Performance' in 1978. This was the biggest hit from his 'Weekend in L.A.' album and in 1979 this song was used in the opening of the film 'All That Jazz'.

59. **Sentimental Lady** by Bob Welch featured Christine McVie and Lindsey Buckingham on backing vocals. He was a member of Fleetwood Mac from 1971 to 1974, before they became a major act. This was the first of 3 notable late 70's solo hits for this Los Angeles-born singer/guitarist.

60.Copacabana (At the Copa) by Barry Manilow was originally considered to be a novelty track from the album 'Even Now', but the response was so great that it was released as a single and sold millions. Barry Manilow claims to have written the music for this upbeat song in less than 15 minutes to the lyrics composed by Bruce Sussman and Jack Feldman. It later inspired a made-for-TV movie starring Barry Manilow.

61.Dance with Me by Peter Brown featured Betty Wright on backing vocals on what became the biggest hit for this R & B singer/songwriter/keyboardist/producer. This was a huge hit at the discos for this multi talented music artist who was known for recording some of his songs in his home.

62.Count on Me by Jefferson Starship was the first of 2 hit singles from the 'Earth' album recorded at Wally Heider Studios in San Francisco. Marty Balin sang lead on this top 10 hit which also featured Grace Slick and Paul Kantner.

63.Come Sail Away by Styx featured the distinctive voice of Dennis DeYoung, who also played the synthesizer on this top 10 hit which he also wrote. This was the biggest hit from their triple-platinum album 'Grand Illusion'.

64.Beast Of Burden by the Rolling Stones was their 2nd major hit from the multi-million selling 'Some Girls' album. A beast of burden is an animal that is semi-domesticated, like or horse or an oxen that labors for the benefit of man. This hit was popular the year Mick Jagger divorced Bianca, and was seen frequently at Studio 54 with model Jerry Hall, whom he married in 1990.

65.Love Is Like Oxygen by the Sweet was the final hit in North America for this British glam-rock band best known for their hits 'Ballroom Blitz', 'Fox On The Run' and 'Little Willy'. After recording the album 'Level Headed', lead singer Brian Connolly left the group for a solo career. He died in 1997 at the age of 51 as a result of complications from chronic alcoholism and drummer Mick Tucker died of leukemia in 2002 at the age of 54.

66.Magnet and Steel by Walter Egan featured backing vocals by Fleetwood Mac's Stevie Nicks and Lindsey Buckingham. This was the only top 40 hit for this singer/songwriter from Jamaica, New York, although he wrote the 1979 hit 'Hot Summer Nights' for the group 'Night'.

67.(Our Love) Don't Throw It All Away by Andy Gibb was the 4th major hit of 1978 for the youngest brother of the Bee Gees. This hit was written by his brother Barry Gibb with Blue Weaver, formerly of the British groups Amen Corner and The Straubs. The Bee Gees included their own version of this song in 1979 on their album 'Bee Gees Greatest'.

68.Shame by Evelyn "Champagne' King was the only major 10 hit for this Bronx, New York born singer who turned 18 when this hit reached the top 10 in the summer of '78.She was discovered while working with her mother as a cleaning lady at Philadelphia International Records.

69.Got to Get You into My Life by Earth, Wind & Fire was the highest charting hit from the recordings released from the movie soundtrack to 'Sgt. Pepper's Heart Club Band' which starred the Bees Gees, Peter Frampton and many others. Earth,

Wind and Fire also appeared in the film in which they resurrected this Beatles hit from 1966 which was originally featured on their 'Revolver' album.

70.Thunder Island by Jay Ferguson was the biggest solo hit for the former member of the groups 'Spirit' and 'Jo Jo Gunne'. This catchy goodtime hit was his most notable solo effort; however he later became a movie and TV show composer, best known as the creator of the theme for the U.S. version of 'The Office' starring Steve Carell.

71.Get Off by Foxy was the first and biggest hit for this Miami, Florida-based dance band that was once kicked off the stage by a club owner and his bouncers when they performed this song. That was before this sassy song became a major hit on the charts and on radio in the summer of '78. One of the members of the band was Richie Puente, who was the son of the famous late bandleader Tito Puente. The younger Puente died in 2004 at the age of 51.

72.Our Love by Natalie Cole was co-written by her husband Marvin Yancy, who also played piano on this million selling ballad. Unfortunately due to Natalie's drug problems, they separated and divorced shortly after and he later died of a heart attack at the age of 34.

73.Two out Of 3 Ain't Bad by Meatloaf was a power ballad from the legendary album 'Bat Out Of Hell', written by Jim Steinman and produced by Todd Rundgren. This was the first major hit for the singer/actor born Marvin Lee Aday, who was previously known for his role as Eddie in the cult film 'Rocky Horror Picture Show'.

74.We'll Never Have To Say Goodbye Again by England Dan & John Ford Coley was the 5th top 30 hit for the soft pop duo who made their debut 2 years earlier with 'I'd Really Love To See You Tonight'. Dan Seals, the brother of Jim Seals of Seals and Crofts fame, got the nickname 'England Dan' when he was a kid because he loved the music of the Beatles and would sometimes put on an English accent. Seals died March 29th 2009 at age 61.

75.You Never Done It Like That by the Captain & Tennille was the 3rd major hit for this duo co written by Neil Sedaka. This was their final hit on the A & M label, before Neil Bogart signed them to his Casablanca label in 1979 when they would have 1 final number one hit with 'Do That to Me One More Time'.

76.Baby Hold On by Eddie Money was the first hit for this New York Police Officer-turned singer. His real name is Edward Mahoney and he was discovered and managed by rock promoter Bill Graham. Eddie Money was sued for using the lyrics 'Que Sera Sera, whatever will be will be' in this top 10 hit.

77.Running on Empty by Jackson Browne was recorded at a concert at Merriweather Post Pavillion in Columbia, Maryland in the summer of '77. He wrote and produced this song about the rigors of a musician's life on the road and its life effects. Jackson Browne's personal life saw tragedy when his wife Phyllis committed suicide in 1976, a year after they were married.

78.This Time I'm in It for Love by Player was the only other top 10 hit for this pop/rock group from Los Angeles who scored a number one hit earlier in the year with 'Baby Come Back'. They took their name 'Player' when they saw the word on

TV when the players from the show were listed. They just took off the's' and went with the singular name.

79.Disco Inferno by the Trammps gained fame when this song was featured on the 'Saturday Night Fever' soundtrack and is also known as 'burn baby burn' to many listeners. The album version ran almost 11 minutes. This was the biggest hit for this Philadelphia disco group.

80.Ready to Take a Chance Again by Barry Manilow was written by Charles Fox and Norman Gimble and was originally featured in the film 'Foul Play' starring Chevy Chase and Goldie Hawn. The song was nominated for an Academy Award in the 'Best Original Song' category, but lost to 'Last Dance' by Donna Summer from the film 'Thank God It's Friday'.

81.Peg by Steely Dan featured Michael McDonald on backing vocals and Donald Fagen on lead vocals. This was the first of 3 hits from their first platinum album 'Aja', which was recorded at about half a dozen different studios and featured dozens of top session musicians. In 2003, Rolling Stone magazine ranked this as number 145 on the listed of '500 Greatest Albums of All Time'.

82.Strange Way by Firefall was the final of the 3 notable late 70's hits for this soft rock group from Boulder, Colorado. This hit was written by lead singer Rick Roberts and was featured on their album 'Elan'.

83.Bluer than Blue by Michael Johnson was written by Randy Goodrum, who also wrote Anne Murray's biggest hit 'You Needed Me', also from 1978. This 70's balladeer became a successful country singer in the 80's.

84.Hollywood Nights by Bob Seger was the 2nd of 4 hits from his 'Stranger in Town' album. This fast-paced hit may be about Hollywood, but this Detroit rocker continues to live in Michigan. He was inducted into the Rock and Roll Hall of Fame in 2004.

85.How You Gonna See Me Now by Alice Cooper was co-written with Bernie Taupin, longtime Elton John collaborator and was produced by David Foster. This was Alice Cooper's 4th consecutive hit ballad and his only hit single from the album 'From The Inside', a concept album inspired by his stay at a New York sanitarium due to alcoholism.

86.Fool (If You Think Its Over) by Chris Rea was a hit he wrote for his sister and was included on his debut album 'Whatever Happened to Benny Santini' produced by Gus Dudgeon. This British singer/songwriter known for his husky voice was not happy with the album which was his only success in the United States, despite his popularity in the U.K. where he charted over 20 singles.

87.Life's Been Good by Joe Walsh was popular when he was still an active member of the Eagles. This offbeat hit was featured in the soundtrack of the movie 'FM' and also included on his album 'But Seriously, Folks' which featured backup by all other members of the Eagles, as well as Jay Ferguson, formerly of Spirit.

88.The Name Of The Game by Abba was the first single from their 5th studio album simply titled 'Album'. This was the last Abba hit which their manager Stig

Anderson would contribute by co writing the lyrics, because he was too busy running the record label , 'Polar' and managing this superstar group. Abba was inducted into the Rock and Roll Hall Of Fame on March 15, 2010.

89.Right down the Line by Gerry Rafferty was the 2nd consecutive hit from the 'City To City' album for this singer/songwriter/guitarist from Paisley, Scotland. The album dethroned 'Saturday Night Fever' to become number one in July of 1978. Gerry Rafferty's success though, may have been limited due to the fact that he had no desire to ever tour North America.

90.Turn To Stone by Electric Light Orchestra was the first of 3 hit singles from their popular double album 'Out Of The Blue' which leader Jeff Lynne wrote in under a month He was in a creative mood after isolating himself in a rented chalet in the Swiss Alps. This symphonic rock album was recorded at Musicland Studios in Munich, Germany.

91.Runaway by Jefferson Starship was the follow up to their hit 'Count on Me', also from the 'Earth' album and also featuring Marty Balin on lead vocals. Former lead singer Grace Slick left the group in 1978, shortly after this hit, but returned in 1981 and remained with the band during their 'Starship' years in the mid to late 80's.

92.Because the Night by the Patti Smith Group was co-written with Bruce Springsteen and was included on her album 'Easter', produced by Jimmy Iovine. The singer referred to as the 'Godmother of Punk' was inducted into the Rock and Roll Hall Of Fame in 2007.

93.My Angel Baby by Toby Beau was the only hit for this Texas band discovered by Sean Delaney, a one-time producer for the rock group 'Kiss'. Although this was their only hit, lead singer Balde Silva revived and reformed the band in the late 90's and has been performing mostly on cruise ships ever since.

94.Who Are You by the Who was released just a few weeks before drummer Keith Moon died suddenly of an overdose of pills at the flat he rented from Harry Nilsson, just hours after he was Paul McCartney's guest at a film preview of the 'Buddy Holly Story'. Buddy Holly was born September 7th; Keith Moon died on September 7th 42 years later at the age of 32. The hit 'Who Are You' was written by guitarist Pete Townsend who was prominently featured the synthesizer.

95.What's Your Name by Lynyrd Skynyrd was from the album 'Street Survivors' which was released just 3 days before core members Ronnie Van Zant and Steve Gaines were killed in a plane crash. The original cover sleeve for 'Street Survivors' featured a photograph of the band, particularly Steve Gaines, engulfed in flames. Out of respect for the deceased, MCA Records withdrew the original cover and replaced it with a similar image of the band against a simple black background. This hit reached the top 20 on the pop charts 3 months after the crash, in January of 1978.

96.Theme from 'Close Encounters of the Third Kind' by John Williams was from the Steven Spielberg film which starred Richard Dreyfuss. This composer/pianist/conducter has written many of the most famous film scores in Hollywood history, including almost all of Spielberg's movies.

97. Falling by Leblanc & Carr was the only hit for this duo from Florida, although both have been successful as studio musicians. Lenny Leblanc played on many hits for others, but in the late 80's, he began recording Christian-themed music and opened his own recording studio in Muscle Shoals, Alabama. Pete Carr remained busy as a studio musician for others including Rod Stewart, Bob Seger and Paul Simon.

98. Ebony Eyes by Bob Welch was the 2nd hit from his 'French Kiss' album which included musical contributions from Mick Fleetwood, Christine McVie and Lindsey Buckingham, members of Fleetwood Mac, with whom he was a member from 1971 to 1974.

99. Alive Again by Chicago was a first in many ways for this brass rock band from the windy city. This was from the album 'Hot Streets', their first produced by Phil Ramone, after the group parted ways with James William Guercio who produced all of their recordings up to this point. It was also the first to feature guitarist Donnie Dacus, who replaced Terry Kath after his accidental death. This energetic hit was written by James Pankow and featured Peter Cetera on lead vocals.

100. Runaround Sue by Leif Garrett was a remake of the hit Dion brought to number one in 1961. Before his teen idol years, he was a child actor in several films including all 3 'Walking Tall' movies in which he played the son of the character Sheriff Buford Pusser.

101. You and I by Rick James was the first major hit for this Buffalo, New York born funk rock singer who started his career as a member of the group 'The Mynah Birds' in Toronto with Neil Young back in he 60's. This was an up tempo love song which he wrote about his wife. Rick James died at the age of 56 on August 6th, 2004.

102. Goodbye Girl by David Gates was the biggest solo hit for the former front man for the soft rock group Bread. This was the title song from the Neil Simon movie starring Marsha Mason and Richard Dreyfuss. His follow up to this hit, 'Took the Last Train' was his final appearance in the top 30 on the pop charts.

103. Flash Light by Parliament was a million selling progressive funk rock hit for this unique-sounding group led by singer/songwriter/producer George Clinton. This hit was co-written by bassist William 'Bootsy' Collins who created the distinctive bass line on the recording.

104. Don't Let Me Be Misunderstood by Santa Esmeralda was a disco remake of the classic 1965 hit by the British group The Animals. Lead singer Leroy Gomez was also an accomplished sax man who played on various other recordings including Elton John's 'Goodbye Yellow Brick Road' album.

105. Serpintine Fire by Earth, Wind & Fire was number one on the R & B charts for almost 2 months. This was a prime cut from the album 'All'n All', recorded at Hollywood Sound, which leader Maurice White claims is the group's pop breakthrough.

106. Straight On by Heart was the first hit single from their 4th studio album 'Dog and Butterfly' which also included the title track as their next single release. It's interesting that side 1 on the album was the 'Dog' side featuring rockin' songs while the 'Butterfly' side was all ballads. This hit was written by Ann and Nancy Wilson and songwriter Sue Ennis, who co-composed many of their songs.

107. **Happy Anniversary** by The Little River Band was the 2nd hit from their 'Dementia Cocktail' album and was written by new member David Briggs. The group took their name from an Australian road sign for the Victorian township of Little River. They were the first Australian rock group to have major success in North America.

108. **Oh Darling** by Robin Gibb was a remake of the Beatles hit from their 'Abbey Road' album as delivered by the Bee Gee twin of the late Maurice Gibb. This was Robin's biggest solo hit and was from the soundtrack of the movie 'Sgt. Pepper's Lonely Heart's Club Band' starring the Bee Gees, Peter Frampton, Earth, Wind & Fire, Steve Martin, George Burns and many others.

109. **Wonderful Tonight** by Eric Clapton was a song he wrote for his wife Patti Boyd, George Harrison's ex. This hit from the 'Slow Hand' album featured backing vocals by Yvonne Elliman and Marcy Levy. Eric Clapton was one of the featured musicians in the 1978 film 'The Last Waltz' directed by Martin Scorsese about The Band's final concert.

110. **Desiree** by Neil Diamond was produced by Bob Gaudio of the Four Seasons. The song is about a man's first sexual experience with a woman twice his age and was the first hit from the album 'I'm Glad You're Here With Me Tonight'.

111. **I'm Not Gonna Let You Bother Me Tonight** by the Atlanta Rhythm Section was a moderate hit for the Georgia group which evolved from the Classics 4. All of the hits of the ARS were produced and co-written by Buddy Buie, who did the same in the 60's for the Classics 4 on their hits 'Spooky', 'Stormy', 'Traces' and 'Everyday With You Girl'.

112. **Back in the U.S.A.** by Linda Ronstadt was a remake of the Chuck Berry classic and the title song from her 3rd consecutive number one album. In 1978, Rolling Stone magazine declared her 'by far America's best known female rock singer'.

113. **She's Always a Woman** by Billy Joel was the 4th of 4 notable hits from his breakthrough album 'The Stranger', his 5th studio album. This love ballad was written by Billy Joel and produced by Phil Ramone. Billy Joel was inducted into the Rock and Roll Hall OF Fame in 1999.

114. **Sweet Talkin' Woman** by Electric Light Orchestra was the 2nd hit single from the double album 'Out Of The Blue'. The original title of this single was 'Deadend Street', but it was changed during the recording so it would not be confused with the title of the 1966 Kinks hit of the same name. This studio album was E. L. O. 's most successful of all their releases and the production by lead singer/songwriter Jeff Lynne was superb.

115. **Every Kinda People** by Robert Palmer was the first top 40 hit for this British born rock singer. This Caribbean-flavored hit was written by Andy Fraser of the group 'Free' of 'All Right Now' fame. This was from Robert Palmer's self-produced 4th solo album, 'Double Fun'.

116. **Movin' Out (Anthony's Song)** by Billy Joel was the 2nd of 4 hit singles from 'The Stranger' album. It was a social comment song written by Billy Joel about people working longer hours just to keep up with the Joneses to get bigger and better material things in life.

117. **(What A) Wonderful World** by Art Garfunkel with James Taylor & Paul Simon was a mellow remake of the Sam Cooke hit from 1960 which was co-written by Herb Alpert. The tempo of the song was similar to the style James Taylor used when he remade 'Handy Man' the previous year. This 3-part harmony song was only featured on Art Garfunkel's album, 'Watermark'.

118. **Always and Forever** by Heatwave was a million selling ballad which followed their debut hit 'Boogie Nights' from 1977. Johnnie Wilder who was featured on lead vocals on this hit, was in a car accident the following year, which left him a paraplegic. He died in 2006 at the age of 56.

119. **King Tut** by Steve Martin was a novelty hit from the 'wild and crazy' guy who was a stand up comedian turned movie star. 1978 was the year he also starred in 'Sgt. Pepper's Lonely Heart's Club Band', the first of many movies for this funnyman.

120. **Sweet Life** by Paul Davis was another heartwarming love ballad from the singer/songwriter who achieved great success earlier in the year with 'I Go Crazy'. Paul Davis survived a shooting in Nashville in the summer of 1986. He was born in Meridian, Mississippi and he died of a heart attack on April 22 2008, 1 day after his 60th birthday and 1 day after the death of soul singer Al Wilson, who was also born in the same town.

121. **I Can't Stand the Rain** by Eruption was a Jamaican-born, London, England based disco funk band that were discovered after they won in the British 'Soul Search' competition. Their only hit was a remake of the 1973 Ann Peebles hit.

122. **Talking in Your Sleep** by Crystal Gayle was her 3rd consecutive number one hit on the country charts. She was the youngest of 8 children, and the only one born in a hospital. In 1978 Crystal Gayle was awarded 'Female Vocalist of The Year' by the Country Music Association Awards. Aside from her vocal talent, she is known for her almost floor- length hair.

123. **Change Of Heart** by Eric Carmen was the title song from his 3rd solo album which also included his remake of the Four Tops' 'Baby I Need Your Lovin'' and his own composition 'Hey Deanie' which Shawn Cassidy had a million seller with in 1978. Special musical guests on the album included Burton Cummings on piano, Nigel Olsson on drums, Bruce Johnston of the Beach Boys on backup vocals and Toto's Jeff and Mike Porcaro.

124. **Deacon Blues** by Steely Dan was the 2nd hit single from their album 'Aja'. This mostly studio group featured front men Walter Becker and Donald Fagen, who composed their hits with Fagen featured on lead vocals and keyboards and Becker on bass and vocals. Among the guest musicians featured on this hit were Larry Carlton and Lee Ritenour on guitars.

125. **Dance (Disco Heat)** by Sylvester was the first and biggest hit for this gay drag singer from Los Angeles. This disco hit was produced by Harvey Fuqua who was one of the first songwriter/producers for Motown records and was the founding member of the Moonglows. Singer Sylvester died of Aids-related complications in 1988 at the age of 41.

126.   Stay/Load Out by Jackson Browne was the 2nd hit from his album 'Running on Empty' and both were recorded at a concert in the summer of '77 at the Merriweather Post Pavilion in Columbia, Maryland. This hit was 2 songs in one with 'The Load Out' being a song about the daily routine of a road crew on a concert tour and the song 'Stay' is a remake of the Maurice Williams and The Zodiacs hit from 1960. Rosemary Butler is featured on backing vocals with David Lindley providing the falsetto vocal, steel guitar and violin.

127.   Werewolves of London by Warren Zevon was produced by Jackson Browne and featured Mick Fleetwood on drums and John McVie on bass guitar. This was the Chicago born singer/songwriter/pianist's most popular solo hit and was taken from the album 'Excitable Boy'. He died of cancer at the age of 56 on September 7th, 2003.

128.   You're the Love by Seals & Crofts was from the album 'Takin' It Easy' and was the last top 30 hit for this popular 70's duo. This hit was co written by Louie Shelton, who produced all of their hits during their heyday.

129.   Two Doors Down by Dolly Parton was a number one hit on the country charts and the follow up to her million seller 'Here You Come Again', also from 1978.Dolly Parton wrote this song from a woman's perspective who has just broken up with her boyfriend and is debating on attending a party two doors down from her apartment. Dolly Parton was born in Sevierville, Tennessee, the 4th of 12 children.

130.   Even Now by Barry Manilow was the title song from the album of the same name which produced 4 hit singles. This song was one of Manilow's personal favorites and one he wrote the music for in Florida on Golden Beach, collaborating with lyricist Marty Panzer. He recorded the album at A & M Studios in Hollywood, California.

131.   The Way You Do the Things You Do by Rita Coolidge was a remake of the Temptations very first hit from 1964. This hit was her follow up to her back-to-back million selling singles 'Higher and Higher' and 'We're All Alone'. She met and married Kris Kristofferson in 1973 after meeting while filming 'Pat Garrett & Billy the Kid'. They divorced in 1980.

132.   I Was Only Joking by Rod Stewart was the 3rd hit single from his album 'Footloose & Fancy Free' which featured musical guests David Foster, Steve Cropper, Carmine Appice and Nicky Hopkins. This song was about Rod Stewart's love life and his lack of commitment for a serious relationship.

133.   Macho Man by The Village People was the breakthrough hit for this New York City disco group which featured members dressed as a cop, an Indian Chief, a cowboy, a construction worker, a military man and a biker. This upbeat party song was the first of 3 consecutive million selling singles.

134.   Two Tickets to Paradise by Eddie Money was the follow up to his debut hit 'Baby Hold On' from earlier 1978. He was inspired to write this song after hearing that his girlfriend's mother wanted her to marry a doctor or a lawyer, not a musician. This was his plea to take her away.

135.   Long Long Way from Home by Foreigner was a moderate hit between major hit singles 'Cold as Ice' and 'Hot Blooded'. This single, which features a mellotron, was the 3rd hit from their debut album 'Foreigner' and was written by Mick Jones, Lou Gramm and former King Crimson member Ian McDonald.

136.   I'm Every Woman by Chaka Khan was written by Ashford and Simpson and produced by Arif Mardin, who was responsible for many of Aretha Franklin's biggest hits. This song about women's independence and strength reached number one on the R & B charts, where it remained on top for almost a month. Whitney Houston revived it in 1993.

137.   It's a Laugh by Hall and Oates was one of their mid chart hits in the period of 1978 to 1980 when they had a dry spell. That all changed when they had several major hits, including 5 number ones in the early 80's. This hit was from the album 'Along the Red Ledge' produced by David Foster.

138.   Native New Yorker by Odyssey was the only top 40 hit for this New York disco trio featuring sisters Lillian and Louise Lopez from the Virgin Islands and Tony Reynolds from Manilla. The song was written by Sandy Linzer and Denny Randell who wrote several hits for the Four Seasons including 'Working My Way Back to You', 'Opus 17' and 'Let's Hang On'.

139.   Love Theme from 'Eyes of Laura Mars' by Barbra Streisand was from the movie which starred Faye Dunaway and Tommy Lee Jones. This film was co-produced by her then-boyfriend Jon Peters and is the only film to feature a theme song by Barbra Streisand in which she does not appear.

140.   Don't Want to Live without You by Pablo Cruise was the follow up single of 'Love Will Find A Way', also from their 4th studio album 'Worlds Away'. This was also written by lead singer Dave Jenkins and keyboardist/singer Cory Lerios. The song 'I Go to Rio', co written by Peter Allen, is also included on this album.

141.   Stuff Like That by Quincy Jones was the first top 30 hit as an artist for this legendary producer. This song was written by half a dozen writers including Ashford and Simpson. In 1978, he was also producing the Brothers Johnson and working on the soundtrack to the movie 'The Wiz' starring Michael Jackson and Diana Ross. Quincy Jones was married to Peggy Lipton of TV's Mod Squad fame from 1974 to 1989.

142.   Come Together by Aerosmith was a remake of the Beatles song originally featured on their 1969 album 'Abbey Road'. Aerosmith's version was from the movie soundtrack to 'Sgt. Pepper's Lonely Hearts Club Band and would be their final top 40 hit in almost 10 years.

143.   Follow You Follow Me by Genesis was the first North American hit by this progressive British band which formed almost 10 years earlier in 1967. In 1975, when Peter Gabriel left the group, Phil Collins replaced him as lead singer. This hit was from the album '...And Then There Were Three' which referred to the group that was now a trio with Phil Collins, Mike

Rutherford and Tony Banks who all composed 'Follow You, Follow Me'.

144.   **Only the Good Die Young** by Billy Joel was the 3rd of 4 hit singles from his album 'The Stranger' and one that was banned on some radio stations because of its content. It was considered controversial because of the lyrics describing a boy who tries to convince a Catholic girl, who is a virgin, to have sex with him. After it was banned in some areas, the album sold even better.

145.   **Theme song from 'Which Way is Up'** by Stargard was the only top 30 hit for this disco trio. This was the title song of the film which starred Richard Pryer. In 1978, they appeared in the film Sgt. Pepper's Lonely Hearts Club Band as 'The Diamonds', not to be confused with the 50's group of the same name.

146.   **Lady Love** by Lou Rawls was an easy listening hit for the singer with the voice as smooth as silk. Before becoming a star on his own, the former high school classmate of Sam Cooke sang back up on the 1962 hit 'Bring It on Home to Me'. Lou Rawls had his first top 40 hit in 1966 with 'Love Is a Hurtin' Thing'. He died of cancer January 6, 2006 at the age of 72.

147.   **Blue Collar Man (Long Nights)** by Styx was written by Tommy Shaw, who is featured on lead vocals and guitar on this lead off single from the 'Pieces Of Eight' album. Dennis DeYoung once described the album as not giving up on your dreams just for the pursuit of money and material things.

148.   **Thank God It's Friday** by Love and Kisses was a one hit wonder disco studio group. This was the title song of the film which featured a soundtrack which included hits by Donna Summer, The Commodores, Diana Ross, Thelma Houston and other disco hit makers of the day.

149.   **FM** by Steely Dan was the title song of the movie about a number one radio station in Los Angeles and the music they play, with a cast that included Martin Mull, Michael Brandon and Eileen Brennan. The soundtrack featured hits of the day by Bob Seger, Steve Miller, Foreigner, The Eagles, Billy Joel and many more. Steely Dan had 3 hit singles in 1978 from their 'Aja' album which did not include the song 'FM'.

150.   **The Way I Feel Tonight** by the Bay City Rollers was the final top 40 hit in North America for this late 70's Scottish teen idol group. Founding member Alan Longmuir rejoined the group in 1978 after being replaced by Ian Mitchell at the peak of their popularity in 1976.

151.   **Thank You for Being a Friend** by Andrew Gold was a hit the year after his biggest hit 'Lonely Boy' reached the top 10. Although he had only 2 hits, he was a very successful session musician and producer for other notable artists including Linda Ronstadt, Art Garfunkel and James Taylor. This song later became the theme for the TV series 'The Golden Girls' starring Betty White and Bea Arthur.

152.   **Hot Legs** by Rod Stewart was the 2nd of 3 hit singles from his 'Footloose & Fancy Free' album. Like the single that followed, this song was written by Rod Stewart and Gary Grainger. In the U.K. it was a top 5 hit backed with 'I Was Only Joking', while in the U.S. it barely made the top 30 on the pop charts.

153.   **I Will Still Love You** by Stonebolt was a popular love ballad for this rock group from Vancouver, British Columbia, home of the 2010 Winter Olympics. Although the group had hits with rock songs, this was their only notable hit outside of Canada.

154.   Part Time Love by Elton John was popular at a time when the superstar performer decided to take a break from performing and from his longtime lyricist Bernie Taupin, whom he had the most success with. This song was co written with Gary Osborne and was featured on the album 'A Single Man'.

155.   Before My Heart Finds Out by Gene Cotton was the most successful pop hit for this singer/songwriter from Columbus, Ohio who moved to Tennessee in the late 70's. He devoted much of his time helping under privileged children with a program known as 'Kids on Stage'.

156.   If Ever I See You Again by Roberta Flack was written and produced by Joe Brooks, who was the man who wrote 'You Light up My Life', the biggest hit of 1977 as recorded by Debby Boone. Joe Brooks also decided to star in the movie which also starred Shelley Hack, who joined Charlie's Angels' the following year. This was Roberta Flack's final hit of the 70's.

157.   The Power of Gold by Dan Fogelberg & Tim Weisberg, featured Don Henley on harmony vocals. This was the only hit from the album 'Twin Sons of Different Mothers'. Dan Fogelberg's most successful period was during the early 80's when he charted 9 top 30 hits between 1980 and 1984. He died of cancer December 16th 2007 at the age of 56.

158.   Ffun by Con Funk Shun was a goodtime, upbeat funk song complete with horns, a flute, guitars, keyboards and a great beat from this California band. The song was written by lead singer Michael Cooper who formed the nucleus of this band in the late 60's while in high school.

159.   Too Hot Ta Trot by the Commodores was a rush release written by all 6 members of the band for the film 'Thank God It's Friday'. Drummer Walter 'Clyde' Orange sang lead on this hit while the rest of the group sang the title. The critics hated the movie, but the soundtrack was well-received.

160.   You by Rita Coolidge was the final 70's hit for this Tennessee born singer with Scottish and Cherokee Native American ancestry. Before meeting her husband Kris Kristofferson, she was romantically involved with Steve Stills and Graham Nash when Crosby, Stills, Nash and Young were still together. While this upbeat song was a moderate hit, a duet album with her husband titled 'Natural Act' was released.

161.   Close the Door by Teddy Pendergrass was his most successful solo hit after leaving as lead singer of Harold Melvin and The Blue Notes. This million seller was written and produced by Gamble and Huff for the singer who became a sex symbol of soul. Sadly, he died January 13th 2010 at the age of 59.

162.   Just What I Needed by the Cars was the very first top 40 hit for this rock group from Boston and was from their self-titled debut album, 'The Cars'. It was bass guitarist Benjamin Orr who was featured on lead vocals on this hit, not guitarist Ric Ocasek , their usual lead singer. Benjamin Orr, who also sang lead on their biggest hit 'Drive' from 1984, died of cancer in October 2000 at the age of 53.

312

163.   **One Nation under a Groove** by Funkedelic was another George Clinton creation while he was also active in his other group 'Parliament' who also had a major hit in 1978 with 'Flashlight'. He had 2 groups and at the time would be seen arm in arm with 2 girlfriends. This hit reached number one on the R & B charts where it stayed on top for over a month.

164.   **Boogie Shoes** by K.C. & the Sunshine Band was originally the 'B' side to their number one hit 'Shake Your Booty', but was re released as a single when it was included in the 'Saturday Night Fever' soundtrack.

165.   **Almost like Being in Love** by Michael Johnson was the follow up to his major hit 'Bluer than Blue'. This song was a remake of a 1947 song written by Frederick Lowe and Alan Jay Lerner from the musical 'Brigadoon'.

166.   **Theme from Close Encounters of the Third Kind** by Meco was his version of the tune John Williams composed for the Steven Spielberg Sci-Fi film which starred Richard Dreyfuss. Meco had a number one hit the previous year with his disco version of the 'Star Wars' theme.

167.   **My Best Friend's Girl** by the Cars was the 2nd hit single from their debut album, 'The Cars' and featured guitarist Ric Ocasek on lead vocals. This hit with a memorable beat was written by Ocasek and produced by Roy Thomas Baker, best known for producing some of the best known work by Queen, including 'Bohemian Rhapsody'.

168.   **5,7,0,5,** by City Boy was the only North American hit for this British rock group produced by Robert John 'Mutt' Lange. Lol Mason was the lead singer of this pop/rock sextet.

169.   **Can We Still Be Friends** by Todd Rundgren was said to be written after his breakup with Bebe Buell, a former 'Playboy Playmate of The Year' whom he dated for a period of time. This unique –sounding hit was written and produced by this talented multi-instrumentalist and was included on his 'Hermit of Mink Hollow' album. It has also been featured in the films 'Dumb and Dumber' and 'Vanilla Sky'.

170.   **Heartless** by Heart was their only hit from the 'Magazine' album and due to a legal battle with their record company 'Mushroom Records', the album was re recorded a year after its initial release in April of 1977. This was their last single release on that label.

More Hits of 1978

Paradise by the Dashboard Light by Meatloaf became the most popular cut from the iconic album 'Bat out Of Hell' and was a duet with singer Ellen Foley. This epic recording was created by Jim Steinman, (who also played keyboards) and produced by Todd Rundgren, (who also played guitar and sang backup) with a special appearance by play-by-play New York Yankees' announcer Phil Rizzuto.

Mull of Kintyre by Paul McCartney & Wings was a huge hit in Britain and only a minor hit in the United States. The song was written by Paul and Wing member Denny Laine as a tribute to the place in Scotland where McCartney owned a home and recording studio. This hit featured bagpipes from the local Campeltown

Pipe Band. This single was a double sided hit with the upbeat rock song 'Girl's School' sharing the spotlight.

Rivers of Babylon by Boney M was a song inspired by the Biblical Hymn Psalm 137 and was featured on the album 'Nightflight to Venus'. Boney M was a disco band formed in Germany by producer Frank Farian.

Rasputin by Boney M was a popular disco and party song based on the 'Mad Monk', Grigori Rasputin. The group's creator and producer Frank Farian sang lead on this standout song.

Songbird by Barbra Streisand was more successful on the easy listening charts as it was on the pop charts, and was popular at the same time as 'The Theme from 'Eyes of Laura Mars'. Her album 'Songbird' included the original version of 'You Don't Bring Me Flowers' which she brought to number one with Neil Diamond later that year.

More Than a Woman by Tavares was a popular song from the 'Saturday Night Fever' soundtrack album which also included the Bee Gees original version. This was the family act's final hit of the 70's.

Poor Poor Pitiful Me by Linda Ronstadt was written by Warren Zevon and was popular the same year his signature hit 'Werewolves of London' was on the charts. This hit was included on Ronstadt's 'Simple Dreams' album.

I've Had Enough by Paul McCartney & Wings was a moderate hit from the 'London Town' album, recorded on board the boat 'Fair Carol' in the Virgin Islands. The 'B' side was the 2nd and final Wings recording to feature group member Denny Laine on lead vocals.

Took The Last Train by David Gates was the final top 40 hit by the singer/songwriter/producer who led Bread to a long string of hits beginning with 'Make It With You' in 1970.

Oh What A Night For Dancing by Barry White was the final top 40 hit for the sensuous soul singer of the 70's, until the release of 'The Secret Garden' with Quincy Jones in 1990. In 1979 he left the 20th Century Fox, the label that charted all of his 70's hits, to launch his own label.

Josie by Steely Dan was the 3rd and final hit single from their critically acclaimed album 'Aja'. Some of the studio musicians joining Steely Dan's Walter Becker and Donald Fagen on this hit include Timothy B. Schmidt, Larry Carlton, Tom Scott, Lee Ritenour and Jim Keltner on drums. This was Steely Dan's final hit of the 70's.

Point Of No Return by Kansas was sandwiched between their only 2 million selling singles, 'Carry on Wayward Son' and 'Dust in the Wind' and was the title song from their 5th album. Lead singer/songwriter Steve Walsh left the group briefly during the recording of this album because he was not happy with the direction of the band.

Almost Summer by Celebration with Mike Love was a side project from the Beach Boys lead singer with a song he wrote with Brian Wilson and Al Jardine. This moderate hit was the title song of the film of the same name which starred Bruno Kirby and Tim Mathison.

I'm Gonna Take Care Of Everything by Rubicon was the only hit for this American band, although horn player Jerry Martini was a member of Sly and the Family Stone for 10 years and Jack Blades and Brad Gillis went on to form the group 'Night Ranger'.

Tumbling Dice by Linda Ronstadt was a remake of the Rolling Stones hit from 1972. She was persuaded to record the song by Mick Jagger backstage at a concert he attended of hers in 1976 saying that she sang too many ballads. That same year she made a guest appearance onstage when the Stones performed in her hometown of Tucson, Arizona when she performed 'Tumbling Dice' with the bad boys of rock 'n roll.

Cheesburger in Paradise by Jimmy Buffet was one of 2 of his most famous songs which became the name of his restaurant chains with 'Margaritaville' being the other. This was from his 9th album, 'The Son of a Son of a Sailor'.

The Circle Is Small by Gordon Lightfoot was originally written and recorded on one of his albums 10 years earlier in 1968. This version was from his 13th original album 'Endless Wire'.

Mr. Blue Sky by Electric Light Orchestra was a great production from their album with the spaceship on the cover, 'Out Of The Blue', a double studio album. Although this hit did not perform as well as expected on the charts, it was one of Jeff Lynnes' most ambitious recordings, with great instrumentation and vocals with the unique 'vocoded' voice singing the title.

Let's All Chant by the Michael Zager Band was the only hit for this New Jersey disco band, although the leader later became a successful producer and writer. Michael Zager not only produced artists including the Spinners, Whitney Houston, Gladys Knight and several others, but he has composed the music for hundreds of commercials through the years.

You Really Got Me by Van Halen was a remake of the Kinks classic from 1964. This was the debut hit from the hard rock group from California featuring brothers Eddie and Alex Van Halen, David Lee Roth and bassist Michael Anthony. This hit was from the album 'Runnin' with the Devil', produced by Ted Templeman.

The Dream Never Dies by the Cooper Brothers were a Canadian Southern Rock band from Ottawa, Ontario led by brothers Dick and Brian. This hit recorded on the Capricorn record label, had a memorable a cappella introduction and was their most notable hit.

Raise A Little Hell by Trooper was the biggest hit in the United States for this Canadian rock group from Vancouver, British Columbia. They had a long string of hits during the 70's in Canada, all featuring Ra McGuire on lead vocals. In February of 2010 the band performed at the Vancouver Winter Olympics' Victory ceremonies.

Arms of Mary by Chilliwack was one of the few non original compositions for this Canadian rock band from British Columbia led by singer/songwriter Bill Henderson. 'Arms of Mary' was a cover of the song written and originally recorded by The Sutherland Brothers. Chilliwack evolved from the 60's group 'The Collectors'.

TOP 17 ALBUMS OF 1978

1.	Saturday Night Fever	Soundtrack
2.	Grease	Soundtrack
3.	52nd Street	Billy Joel
4.	Some Girls	Rolling Stones
5.	Don't Look Back	Boston
6.	City To City	Gerry Rafferty
7.	Living In the U. S. A.	Linda Ronstadt
8.	'Live' and More	Donna Summer
9.	Natural High	The Commodores
10.	Double Vision	Foreigner
11.	Stranger in Town	Bob Seger
12.	All 'N One	Earth, Wind & Fire
13.	Out Of the Blue	E.L.O.
14.	Darkness on the Edge of Town	Bruce Springsteen
15.	Who Are You	Who
16.	Footloose and Fancy Free	Rod Stewart
17.	Sgt. Pepper's Lonely Heart's Club Band	Movie Soundtrack

TOP 17 COUNTRY HITS OF 1978

1.	Mammas Don't Let Your Sons Grow ...Cowboys	Waylon & Willie
2.	Sleeping Single in a Double Bed	Barbara Mandrell
3.	The Gambler	Kenny Rogers
4.	I've Always Been Crazy	Waylon Jennings
5.	Out of My Head & Back in My Bed	Loretta Lynn
6.	Heartbreaker	Dolly Parton
7.	Only One Love in My Life	Ronnie Milsap
8.	Take This Job and Shove It	Johnny Paycheck
9.	Do You Know You Are My Sunshine	Statler Brothers
10.	Talking In Your Sleep	Crystal Gayle
11.	Don't Break the Heart That Loves You	Margo Smith
12.	Someone Loves You Honey	Charley Pride
13.	Georgia on My Mind	Willie Nelson
14.	What a Difference you've Made in My Life	Ronnie Milsap
15.	Sweet Desire	The Kendalls
16.	Blue Skies	Willie Nelson
17.	I'll Be True To You	Oak Ridge Boys

TOP 17 DISCO HITS OF 1978

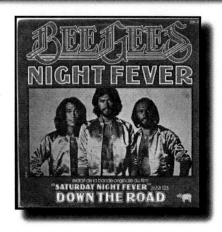

1. Night Fever   Bee Gees
2. Stayin' Alive   Bee Gees
3. Le Freak   Chic
4. Boogie Oogie Oogie   A Taste Of Honey
5. If I Can't Have You   Yvonne Elliman
6. Last Dance   Donna Summer
7. I Love the Nightlife   Alicia Bridges
8. Dance Dance Dance   Chic
9. Dance With Me   Peter Brown
10. Shame   Evelyn 'Champagne' King
11. Get Off   Foxy
12. Flashlight   Parliament
13. Disco Inferno   Trammps
14. Don't Let Me Be Misunderstood   Santa Esmeralda
15. I Can't Stand …   Eruption
16. Dance (Disco Heat)   Sylvester

TOP 17 ONE HIT WONDERS OF 1978

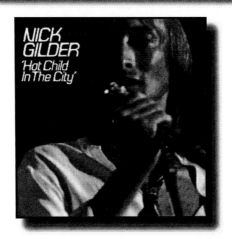

1.	Nick Gilder	Hot Child in the City
2.	Samantha Sang	Emotion
3.	Alicia Bridges	I Love the Nightlife
4.	Walter Egan	Magnet and Steel
5.	John Paul Young	Love Is In the Air
6.	Toby Beau	My Angel Baby
7.	Leblanc and Carr	Falling
8.	Santa Esmeralda	Don't Let Me Be Misunderstood
9.	Foxy	Get Off
10.	Eruption	I Can't Stand the Rain
11.	Odyssey	Native New Yorker
12.	City Boy	5,7,0,5
13.	Rubicon	I'm Gonna Take Care of Everything
14.	Cheryl Ladd	Think It Over
15.	Love and Kisses	Thanks God It's Friday
16.	Sylvester	Dance (Disco Heat)
17.	Con Funk Shun	Ffun

TOP 17 ROCK/HARD ROCK HITS OF 1978

1.	Miss You	Rolling Stones
2.	Double Vision	Foreigner
3.	We Are the Champions/We Will Rock You	Queen
4.	Hot Blooded	Foreigner
5.	Don't Look Back	Boston
6.	Come Sail Away	Styx
7.	Paradise by the Dashboard Light	Meatloaf
8.	Beast of Burdon	Rolling Stones
9.	Life's Been Good	Joe Walsh
10.	Hollywood Nights	Bob Seger
11.	Who Are You	Who
12.	Straight On	Heart
13.	Come Together	Aerosmith
14.	You Really Got Me	Van Halen
15.	Rocket Ride	Kiss
16.	You Make Me Crazy	Sammy Hagar

1.	Rivers Of Babylon	Boney M
2.	Fool (If You Think It's Over)	Chris Rea
3.	My Angel Baby	Toby Beau
4.	Thunder Island	Jay Ferguson
5.	Alive Again	Chicago
6.	Jack and Jill	Raydio
7.	Mr. Blue Sky	E.L.O.
8.	Ebony Eyes	Bob Welch
9.	Turn To Stone	E.L.O.
10.	Falling	Leblanc and Carr
11.	Magnet and Steel	Walter Egan
12.	Sweet Life	Paul Davis
13.	Sweet Talkin' Woman	E.L.O.
14.	Desiree	Neil Diamond
15.	Can We Still Be Friends	Todd Rundgren
16.	Took the Last Train	David Gates
17.	Change Of Heart	Eric Carmen

70's Dead Music Stars...Had They Lived, How Old Would These Music Artists be Today? *(As of the end of 2011)*

70's Music Artist	Birthdate	Age had they lived
John Bonham (Led Zeppelin drummer)	5/31/48	63
Sonny Bono	2/16/35	76
James Brown	5/3/28	83
Karen Carpenter	3/2/50	61
Harry Chapin	12/7/42	69
Ray Charles	9/23/30	81
Jim Croce	1/10/43	68
John Denver	12/31/43	68
John Entwistle (Who bassist)	10/9/44	67
Tom Evans (Badfinger)	6/5/47	64
Freddy Fender	6/4/37	74
Dan Fogelberg	8/13/51	60
Marvin Gaye	4/2/39	72
Andy Gibb	3/5/58	53
Maurice Gibb	12/22/49	62
Pete Ham (Badfinger)	4/27/47	64
George Harrison	2/24/43	68
Bobby Hatfield (Righteous Bros.)	8/10/40	71
Donny Hathaway	10/1/45	66
Isaac Hayes	8/20/42	69
Michael Jackson	8/29/58	53
Waylon Jennings	6/15/37	74
Eddie Kendricks (Temptations)	12/17/39	72
John Lennon	10/9/40	71
Phil Lynott (Thin Lizzy lead singer)	8/20/51	60
Curtis Mayfield	6/3/42	69
Freddie Mercury	9/5/46	65
Van McCoy	1/6/44	67
Keith Moon	8/23/47	64
Jim Morrison	12/8/43	68
Rick Nelson	5/8/40	71
Nilsson	6/15/41	70
Robert Palmer	1/19/49	62
Teddy Pendergrass	3/26/50	61
Wilson Pickett	3/18/41	70
Elvis Presley	1/8/35	76
Billy Preston	9/9/46	65
Eddie Rabbit	11/27/44	67
Lou Rawls	12/1/35	76
Charlie Rich	12/14/32	79
Minnie Ripperton	11/8/47	64
David Ruffin (Temptations)	1/18/41	70
Edwin Starr	1/21/42	69
Joe Tex	8/8/33	78
Ronnie Van Zant	1/15/48	63
Barry White	9/12/44	67
Carl Wilson	12/21/46	65
Dennis Wilson	12/4/44	67
Frank Zappa	12/21/40	71
Warren Zevon	1/24/47	64

♬ The artist who had a number one hit with this instrumental was the co owner of a major record label back then.

♬ This Gold record featuring Stevie Nicks was a hit for a former member of the Kingston Trio who wrote one of the Monkees' biggest hits.

♬ This number one Grammy Award winning hit by the Doobie Brothers was co written by Kenny Loggins.

♬ This disco hit by a one hit wonder was originally popular in 1966 by soul singer Eddie Floyd.

♬ Chicago's Peter Cetera backed Billy Joel on vocals on this number one hit from his '52nd Street' album.

♬ One of the most unique and fun tunes of the year was by a one hit wonder with one letter as a name.

FIND OUT THAT...AND MUCH MORE INSIDE...1979!

1.   **My Sharona** by The Knack was written in one afternoon by lead singer Doug Fieger, although the very recognizable guitar riff was created by guitarist Berton Averre years before he joined the group. The Beatles were a major influence on this rock band from Los Angeles and it was Mike Chapman, one of the hottest producers in Britain, who helped make it the top song of the year. Lead singer Doug Fieger died on Valentines Day in 2010 as a result of cancer at the age of 57.

2.   **Bad Girls** by Donna Summer was the 2nd consecutive multi million selling number one hit from the double album of the same name. This hit was written by 4 composers, including Donna Summer and her fiancé Bruce Sudano of the backing group 'Brooklyn Dreams' who was a former member of 'Alive and Kickin', known for their 1970 hit 'Tighter, Tighter'. This upbeat hit known for its 'toot toot' 'beep beep' chant, was a hot hit at the discos and radios everywhere in 1979.

3.   **Do Ya Think I'm Sexy** by Rod Stewart was a multi-million selling disco hit which he co wrote with drummer Carmine Appice, formerly of the group Vanilla Fudge. George Hamilton's ex-wife, Alana found Rod to be sexy, because she married him when this hit was hot. Rod Stewart donated the proceeds of this single to the United Nations Children's Fund and performed it at the Music for UNICEF concert that same year.

4.   **Reunited** by Peaches and Herb was a multi million selling love ballad by the sweetheart duo who returned in 1979 after a string of love hits during the late 60's. This hit was written by Dino Fekaris and Freddie Perren and featured Linda Green as 'Peaches'. The original 'Peaches from the 60's, Francine Barker left in 1968. She died at the age of 62 in 2005.

5.   **I Will Survive** by Gloria Gaynor was originally the 'B' side of 'Substitute' on the single, but discos and radio stations played the flip side instead and it went all the way to number one. This hit about woman's defiant declaration of independence became her signature hit. The song was written and produced by Dino Fekaris and Freddie Perren, who also gave Peaches and Herb the number one hit 'Reunited' in 1979.

6.   **Hot Stuff** by Donna Summer would also describe the queen of disco in

1979, having 5 million selling singles including 3 number ones. Casablanca owner Neil Bogart suggested she pass 'Hot Stuff' on to his just-signed singer Cher, but Donna insisted on recording it herself. She was also referred to as 'the first lady of lust', which she got tired of quickly.

7. **Escape (Pina Colada Song)** by Rupert Holmes was the last number one hit of the 70's.This story song was written by this British songwriter who previously wrote another song with a surprise twist, 'Timothy' by the Buoys, a song about cannibalism after being trapped in a mine. This song was more lighthearted and dealt with a relationship between 2 people who thought they knew each other, but didn't. Holmes later became a successful author of plays, stories and novels.

8. **Too Much Heaven** by The Bee Gees was the first of 3 consecutive number one hits from the 'Spirits Having Flown' album. The brothers Gibb generously donated proceeds of this ballad, complete with strings and voice layering, to the Music for UNICEF. They also performed it on the TV telecast 'A Gift of Song' concert.

9. **Babe** by Styx was written by lead singer Dennis DeYoung for his wife's birthday because he had been traveling a lot and was feeling depressed and guilty about the separation. This ballad became their biggest hit of all time topping the charts in the last month of the last year of the 70's.

10. **Tragedy** by The Bee Gees featured a falsetto-voiced Barry Gibb on lead vocals on this up tempo hit from the 'Spirits Have Flown' album. This hit was the 5th of 6th consecutive number one hits for the brothers Gibb, who also wrote and co-produced it. In 1979, The Bee Gees embarked on their most extensive tour ever, covering over 40 dates, including an invitation to the White House where President Carter congratulated them on their efforts with UNICEF.

11. **Rise** by Herb Alpert was the biggest solo hit by the leader of the most successful instrumental group from the 60's, The Tijuana Brass. This number one instrumental hit became very popular after it was featured in some episodes of the daytime soap 'General Hospital'. 'Rise' rose to number one replacing Michael Jackson's 'Don't Stop 'Till You Get Enough'. Herb Alpert was the 'A' in 'A & M' records which he co- owned with Jerry Moss.

12. **No More Tears (Enough Is Enough)** by Barbra Streisand and Donna Summer featured two of the most popular divas of the day who were united for one very successful number one hit co-written by Paul Jabara, who also composed the Oscar-winning 'Last Dance' for Donna Summer. This was from Streisand's concept album 'Wet' which included all songs pertaining to that theme including 'Kiss Me in the Rain', 'Splish Splash', and 'Niagara' among others.

13. **Ring my Bell** by Anita Ward was originally written by songwriter Frederick Knight for 11 year old singer Stacey Lattisaw, but she signed with someone else. He then rewrote the lyrics with a more sexual and suggestive feel and Anita Ward heated up the charts with it, taking it all the way to number one, where it sold millions. It became Anita Ward's only major hit.

14. **Pop Muzik** by M was one of 1979's most ear-catching and unique sounding hits, with its techno pop sound and fun lyrics. One hit wonder 'M' was British songwriter/producer Robin Scott who wanted to summarize the last 25 years of pop music in one fun number one hit.

15. **What a Fool Believes** by The Doobie Brothers was written by lead singer Michael McDonald along with Kenny Loggins. Ted Templeman produced this number one hit which won Grammy Awards for both 'Record of the Year' and 'Song of the Year'. This was the first and biggest hit of the 3 singles from their 'Minute By Minute' album.

16. **Sad Eyes** by Robert John was a ballad by this falsetto-voiced singer/songwriter from Brooklyn, New York who had a million seller earlier in the 70's with his remake of the Tokens' 'The Lion Sleeps Tonight'. Robert John first recorded in the late 50's when was just 12 years old and has released several hits before he finally topped the charts with this hit which he also wrote.

17. **Don't Stop It 'Til You Get Enough** by Michael Jackson was produced by Quincy Jones and became the first single released from the multi million selling 'Off The Wall' album, his first solo album on the 'Epic' records label. This was Michael Jackson's first number one solo hit since 'Ben' in 1972. He just came up with the melody and wrote this song while walking around the house before recording the song on his 24 track studio and presenting it to Quincy Jones.

18. **Heart of Glass** by Blondie was a song lead singer Deborah Harry and her lover/band mate Chris Stein wrote and recorded 4 years earlier as 'Once I Had a Love', in a slower reggae style. This disco/new wave number one hit was much more successful than Deborah Harry expected and Andy Warhol threw a party for the song's success at Studio 54, where the video was shot.

19. **Still** by The Commodores was the 2nd major ballad of 1979 written by lead singer Lionel Richie. Like the song 'Sail On', this song was also written about a marriage break up of 2 friends who decided that marriage was not the thing for them, and they were better off as simply friends. Lionel Richie split from the Commodores in 1982, a year after he began a successful solo career.

20. **Good Times** by Chic was the 2nd number one hit for the 'Le Freak' disco group and one which ran over 8 minutes on their album 'Risque', produced and written by Nile Rodgers and Bernard Edwards. This was not only their 4th and final million seller in a 2 year span, but it was their final hit to reach top 40 on the pop charts.

21. **Knock on Wood** by Amii Stewart was a number one disco remake of a 1966 soul hit by Eddie Floyd. This one hit wonder singer was also an actress, and although she was born 'Amy' Stewart, she changed the spelling of her first name to 'Amii' because there was already an Amy Stewart registered with 'Actor's Equity'.

22. **Heartache Tonight** by the Eagles was written by Bob Seger, J.D. Souther and group members Don Henley and Glenn Frey. This was the first of 3 hit singles from 'The Long Run' album, which was almost released as a double album, but was cut down to a single disc. This was the first Eagles album not to feature founding member Randy Meisner, who was replaced by Timothy B. Schmidt. Glenn Frey provided lead vocals on this Grammy Award winning 'Best Rock Performance by A Duo or Group' hit.

23. **Love You Inside Out** by The Bee Gees was the 3rd consecutive number one hit from 'Spirits Having Flown' and their 6th consecutive number one hit. This was the final number one hit of their career, but Barry Gibb went on to produce/write major hits with and without the Bee Gees for Barbra Streisand, Dionne Warwick and Kenny Rogers.

24.   Y. M. C. A. by The Village People was the signature song for this New York City disco group made up of a cast of characters created by producer Jacques Morali. This multi-million seller became a dance of its own with people spelling out Y.M.C.A. with their arms at dances and parties for many years after disco music died. Creator Morali died as a result of AIDS in 1991 at the age of 44.

25.   We Are Family by Sister Sledge became the signature hit for this family of 4 sisters from Philadelphia. Their record company didn't care much for this song and decided to release 'He's The Greatest Dancer' as their first single. When 'We Are Family' was released, it became a million seller and yet another successful hit for the songwriting and production team of Nile Rodgers and Bernard Edwards who did the same for the group 'Chic'.

26.   Fire by The Pointer Sisters was written by Bruce Springsteen and originally written for one of his childhood idols, Elvis Presley. The Boss never managed to have The King record the song, but when the Pointer Sisters did, it became their first million seller, and one of the 'hottest' hits of '79.

27.   After The Love Has Gone by Earth, Wind & Fire was a ballad written by David Foster, Jay Graydon and Bill Champlin. Two of the songwriters were reunited in the early 80's when Bill Champlin became a member of Chicago and David Foster became their producer. This hit from the album 'I Am' was produced by Earth, Wind & Fire's leader, Maurice White.

28.   Dim All the Lights by Donna Summer was the 3rd major hit from the 'Bad Girls' album produced by Giorgio Moroder and Peter Belotte. The queen of disco solely wrote this song which begins as a ballad and picks up speed after her sustained note about 1 minute into this dance floor favorite.

29.   My Life by Billy Joel featured backing vocals by Peter Cetera and was the first of 3 major hit singles from the best selling album '52nd Street'. This hit was also used as the theme for the early 80's TV series 'Bosom Buddies', starring Tom Hanks.

30.   The Devil Went Down To Georgia by Charlie Daniels Band was a fast paced fiddle-filled pop country hit which raced up the charts to number one on the country charts and top 5 on the pop charts in the summer of '79. In 1980, this song was featured in the film 'Urban Cowboy' in which he also appeared. Singer/songwriter/guitarist and fiddler Charlie Daniels was finally inducted into the Grand Ole Opry in 2008.

31.   The Main Event/Fight by Barbra Streisand was from the boxing film 'The Main Event' starring Streisand and Ryan O'Neal. This song was co-written by Paul Jabara, who also did the same on her number one hit with Donna Summer 'No More Tears' (Enough Is Enough) also from 1979.

32.   In the Navy by The Village People was the 2nd biggest hit following 'Y.M.C.A.' for the New York City disco group. This was another sing-a-long song from their peak year of popularity. Lead singer Victor Willis left the group in late

1979 and this became their final major hit. The following year they appeared in the film 'Can't Stop the Music', directed by actress Nancy Walker.

33. **A Little Bit More** by Olivia Newton-John was her first hit of 1979, hot on the heels of 3 consecutive million sellers from the 'Grease' soundtrack. She changed her image to a leather-clad look which is displayed on the cover of her album 'Totally Hot' which produced this hit single.

34. **Music Box Dancer** by Frank Mills was a major instrumental hit for this Toronto born pianist who was inspired to write this tune one day when his young daughter came to him with a broken music box to mend. There was a little dancer who popped up and spun around on a pedestal. Her arm was broken off. After he looked at it, he decided to name the tune 'Music Box Dancer'.

35. **Heaven Knows** by Donna Summer and Brooklyn Dreams was the first of 5 major 1979 hits for the queen of the disco. In 1979 she became engaged to Bruce Sudano of the group Brooklyn Dreams and they married the following year in 1980. She is joined on this hit by the lead singer of that group, Joe 'Bean' Esposito.

36. **Don't Bring Me Down** by E.L.O. was the 2nd single and the biggest hit from their 'Discovery' album which contained 4 hit singles. This was the first E.L.O. hit not to feature a signature string section, yet it became their biggest hit ever. The song was dedicated to the Nasa Skylab space station, which re-entered the Earth's atmosphere over the Indian Ocean and Western Australia on July 11 1979.

37. **Send One Your Love** by Stevie Wonder was from 'The Secret Life of Plants' soundtrack from the documentary film based on the book of the same name by Peter Tompkins and Christopher Bird. The album was mostly instrumental with all tunes written or co-written by Stevie Wonder. The album cover contained some Braille and when unsealed and opened, it smelled like a flower.

38. **Stumblin' In** by Suzi Quatro & Chris Norman was written by British songwriter/producers Mike Chapman and Nicky Chinn. This was from the album 'If You Knew Suzi…" and was the biggest hit in North America for this singer born in Detroit who moved to Britain when she was discovered by producer Mickie Most at the age of 21. Norman was the lead singer of the group 'Smokie'.

39. **Sultans of Swing** by Dire Straits was one of the most unique and innovative hits of 1979. This debut hit for this British rock group led by singer/ songwriter/guitarist Mark Knopfler caught everyone's attention when it graced the radio airwaves for almost 6 minutes per play. It was from their self-titled debut album produced by Muff Winwood, Steve's older brother and one time member of the Spencer Davis Group.

40. **Just When I Needed You Most** by Randy Van Warmer was written when he was heart broken after a girl he met left him when he was 18 years old. The Lovin' Spoonful's John Sebastian plays the autoharp on this love song. Sadly, in 2004, one hit wonder Randy Van Warmer died at the age of 48 of leukemia. In line with one of his greatest loves, his cremated remains were sent into space in 2007.

41. **Sail On** by The Commodores was a ballad lead singer Lionel Richie wrote after his boyhood buddy's marriage breakup. The song was a result of an all night talk the two of them had about the traumatic life experience. 'Sail On' was the first of 2 major hits the Commodores charted in 1979, with the follow up 'Still' being the other.

42.   Shake Your Groove Thing by Peaches & Herb was a comeback hit from the sweetheart duo of the 60's who had not had a hit in almost a dozen years. This million selling disco hit led the way to their biggest hit of all, 'Reunited' which was hot on its heels. Although there have been several different women in the role of 'Peaches', Herb Fame has been constant since the 60's.

43.   She Believes in Me by Kenny Rogers was a powerful ballad by one of 1979's most successful recording stars. This was the follow up single to 'The Gambler' and both were featured on the album of the same name. In 2010, the TV Special 'Kenny Rogers: The First 50 Years' aired with special guests who included Dolly Parton and Lionel Richie.

44.   Goodnight Tonight by Paul McCartney & Wings was recorded at the 'Back to the Egg' sessions, but was not included on the album. This disco-inspired song was quite different with its flamenco guitar break and the fact that the band dressed in 1930's costumes for the video and the cover.

45.   Makin' It by David Naughton was from the TV sitcom of the same name, as well as the movie 'Meatballs' starring Bill Murray. David Naughton was also an actor who starred in 'An American Werewolf in London' and in the popular 'I'm A Pepper, You're A Pepper' TV commercials for Dr. Pepper.

46.   I'll Never Love This Way Again by Dionne Warwick was produced by Barry Manilow and written by Richard Kerr and Will Jennings, who wrote some of his biggest hits. This was a comeback hit for Dionne Warwick, since it was 5 years since her last hit, 'Then Came You' with the Spinners and 9 years since her last solo hit, 'I'll Never Fall In Love Again'.

47.   Hold the Line by Toto was the debut hit for this group formerly known as session musicians on the hits of other recording artists including Boz Scaggs, Steely Dan, Cher and many others. This song was written by Toto's keyboardist vocalist David Paich who also wrote hits for others including 'Lady Love Me (One More Time) by George Benson and 'Got to Be Real' by Cheryl Lynn.

48.   Gold by John Stewart featured Stevie Nicks on backing vocals and Lindsey Buckingham on guitar. This was the biggest solo hit for the former member of the Kingston Trio who wrote the Monkees' number one hit 'Daydream Believer'. John Stewart died in early 2008 at the age of 69.

49.   Lead Me On by Maxine Nightingale was one of only 2 major hits for this British singer with 'Right Back Where We Started From' from 1976 being the other. When she was only 17, she joined the British production of 'Hair' and also performed in productions of 'Jesus Christ Superstar' and 'God spell'.

50.   Sharing the Night Together by Dr. Hook was the first of 2 very similar million sellers for this band in 1979. After switching from Columbia to Capitol records and dropping 'the Medicine Show' from their name, they began a career of soft rock hits with songs like 'A Little Bit More', 'Only Sixteen', 'Sexy Eyes' and others which featured Dennis Locorriere on lead vocals.

51.   Logical Song by Supertramp was the first and biggest hit single from their biggest selling album 'Breakfast in America'. This was their most recognizable song and one that featured Roger Hodgson on lead vocals. The song is a story about lost innocence and idealism and features sax, castanets, synthesizer, electric piano, Hammond organ and other great instruments.

52.   When you're in Love with a Beautiful Woman by Dr. Hook was the 2nd million selling single of 1979 for this New Jersey band whose style and image was completely different when they were fronted by Ray Sawyer. Dennis Locorriere was the lead singer on their adult contemporary hits including this one recorded at Muscle Shoals in Alabama.

53.   Boogie Wonderland by Earth, Wind & Fire and the Emotions was the 2nd major hit featuring these 2 groups together. EWF backed the Emotions on their mega hit 'Best of My Love' and they returned the favor by singing backup on this energetic million seller from their 'I Am' album.

54.   Every One's a Winner by Hot Chocolate was the final major hit for this British group featuring Errol Brown on lead vocals. This hit was similar in style to 'You Sexy Thing', their biggest hit. This group also wrote and originally recorded 'Brother Louie' which became a number one hit for the Stories in the summer of 1973.

55.   Lonesome Loser by The Little River Band was the first single and first cut from the album 'First Under The Wire'. In 1979, bass guitarist George McArdle left the band for bible study and became a minister. This Australian rock group had over a dozen top 40 hits from the late 70's to the early 80's.

56.   Shake Your Body (Down To the Ground) by The Jacksons, was popular the year the Jacksons received a Star on the Hollywood Walk of Fame. Michael and Brother Randy Jackson wrote this double platinum hit single from the 'Destiny' album, which became their biggest since leaving Motown 4 years earlier.

57.   I Want You to Want Me by Cheap Trick was the first major hit for the band that was once referred to by the Japanese press as 'The American Beatles'. This hit was recorded 'live' at their show at the Budokan concert hall in Japan. This song was originally featured on their 1977 album 'In Color', but it was the 'live' version 2 years later that became their signature hit. The guitarist with the baseball cap, Rick Neilsen wrote this hit which featured Robin Zander on lead vocals.

58.   I Want Your Love by Chic was another million selling single by this New York City disco band produced by Nile Rodgers and Bernard Edwards, who also wrote their material. This song was originally intended for Sister Sledge whom they wrote the hit 'We Are Family', also in 1979. 'I Want Your Love' was the follow up to their mega hit 'Le Freak', also from the album 'C'est Chic'.

59.   You Decorated My Life by Kenny Rogers was his 4th consecutive major hit of 1979, the year he charted more hits on the pop charts than any other year in his successful career. This love ballad, similar to 'She Believes in Me', was the first hit from his album simply titled 'Kenny'. The next single was 'Coward of the County' which became another made-for-TV movie in which he starred.

60.   You're Only Lonely by J.D. Souther featured backup vocals by Jackson Browne. Although he wasn't a member of the band, J.D.Souther co wrote some of the Eagles' biggest hits including 'New Kid in Town', 'Heartache Tonight' and 'Best of My Love'.

61.   **Ooh Baby Baby** by Linda Ronstadt was a remake of the Smokey Robinson & The Miracles' hit from 1965. Her top 10 version from the album 'Living in the U.S.A.' featured a sax solo by David Sanborn.

62.   **September** by Earth, Wind & Fire was influenced by the doo- wop harmonies and was the first of 3 million selling singles in 1979 for this R & B/ Jazz/funk band from Los Angeles. Up until now, it was unusual for their songs to be composed by writers outside of the band, but group leader/producer Maurice White brought in Al McKay and Alee Willis to assist on this upbeat hit.

63.   **Lotta Love** by Nicolette Larson was written by her good friend Neil Young whom she met through Linda Ronstadt. He was looking for a back up singer and she stepped in and helped fill the void on his 'Comes a Time' album. 'Lotta Love' was produced by Ted Templeman, who also gave the Doobie Brothers and Van Halen their sound. Nicolette Larson died in late 1997 at the age of 45.

64.   **Take Me Home** by Cher was her first top 10 hit since 'Dark Lady' 5 years earlier. This was from the album of the same name which featured scantily-clad Cher in a Viking outfit. This album was co-produced by Ron Dante, who not only produced Barry Manilow's album, but was the lead singer on the Archies' 1969 number 1 hit 'Sugar Sugar'. This single was Cher's first hit on the Casablanca record label which she remained with for only 1 year.

65.   **Mama Can't Buy You love** by Elton John was produced by Philadelphia's Thom Bell and written by Leroy Bell and Casey James, who were also known as the popular duo 'Bell and James'. This hit was something completely different for Elton John, who up until now worked almost exclusively with lyricist Bernie Taupin and producer Gus Dudgeon.

66.   **Shine A Little Love** by E.L.O. was the first track from their 'Discovery' album, which group member Richard Tandy nicknamed 'Disco Very' because of the strong influence of the disco music scene which was at its peak in 1979. The album was the first to reach number one in the U.K. for this British orchestral rock band led by singer/songwriter/producer Jeff Lynne.

67.   **Tusk** by Fleetwood Mac was a very abstract hit by one of the most successful bands of the 70's. This hit featured the U.S.C. Trojan Marching Band and was recorded 'live' at Dodger Stadium. Lindsey Buckingham wrote and sang lead on this title song from their double album.

68.   **He's the Greatest Dancer** by Sister Sledge was the first hit from Debra, Joan, Kim, and Cathy Sledge from Philadelphia. This hit was produced and written by Bernard Edwards and Nile Rodgers and was originally intended for their group 'Chic'. This was from the album 'We Are Family' which included their next and biggest single of all, also popular in 1979.

69.   **Promises** by Eric Clapton from the album 'Backless' reached top 10 in North America, but barely made the top 40 in the U.K. He couldn't keep his promise to perform at the Rock and Roll Hall Of Fame 25 Anniversary Concert in 2010 because of gallstone surgery.

70.   You Can't Change That by Raydio was the 2nd and last hit by the group before 'Ray Parker Jr,' was added to the front of the name. This top 10 hit featured Ray Parker, who was one of the top session guitar players in the business, before forming his own band. He played on dozens of hits including those by Stevie Wonder, Aretha Franklin, The Carpenters and many others.

71.   What You Won't Do for Love by Bobby Caldwell was the only top 40 solo hit for this New York City born singer/songwriter multi-instrumentalist who previously played percussion for both hard rock acts Johnny and Edgar Winter. The singer of this love ballad also wrote hits for others including the number one hit 'The Next Time I Fall' by Peter Cetera and Amy Grant.

72.   Somewhere In The night by Barry Manilow was his 4th hit single from his triple-platinum album 'Even Now'. This hit was previously recorded by Helen Reddy, Kim Carnes and Yvonne Elliman, but it was Manilow who had the biggest hit with it in early 1979. It was the year that ABC aired his very successful 3rd Barry Manilow Special with John Denver as his guest.

73.   You Take My Breath Away by Rex Smith was from the made-for-TV movie 'Sooner Or Later' which launched the career of this teen idol. Although his hit recording career was brief, he appeared in movies, TV shows and starred in Broadway productions including 'Pirates of Penzance with Linda Ronstadt, which was also a movie in 1983.

74.   Ships by Barry Manilow was the only top 10 hit from his 'One Voice' album which also included his remake of the 1942 hit by Harry James, 'I Don't Want To Walk Without You'. In 1979, Barry Manilow produced Dionne Warwick's comeback album 'Dionne', which included the hits 'Ill Never Love This Way Again' and 'Déjà vu'.

75.   Take the Long Way Home by Supertramp was the 3rd of 3 major hit singles from their 'Breakfast in America' album which was more popular in Canada than it was in America. This great production featured Roger Hodgson on lead vocals and piano and guitar, with co writer Rick Davies on synthesizers, Hammond organ and harmonica. Rounding out the quintet is John Helliwell on soprano sax, Dougie Thomson on bass guitar and Bob Siebenberg on drums.

76.   Lady by The Little River Band was the first of 3 top 10 hits in 1979 for this Australian rock band which featured Glenn Shorrock on lead vocals. This hit from their platinum album 'Sleeper Catcher' was the follow up to their biggest hit, 'Reminiscing'.

77.   Love Is the Answer by England Dan & John Ford Coley was written by Todd Rundgren and was the final major hit for this soft pop duo. This hit had a different sound than their usual hits because of the gospel section and classical base. After the duo's break up, (England) Dan Seals became a successful pop country singer.

78.   I Was Made for Lovin' You by Kiss was a disco-flavored hit written by Paul Stanley along with Desmond Child and Vini Poncia who produced this hit from the 'Dynasty' album. Paul Stanley sings lead on this million selling Kiss hit which was their biggest since 'Beth' in 1976.

79. **Don't Cry Out Loud** by Melissa Manchester was written by Peter Allen and was nominated for a Grammy Award in the Best Pop Female Vocal Performance. She performed 2 songs at the 1979 Academy Awards. This singer from the Bronx studied songwriting under Paul Simon at The University School of The Arts.

80. **I Was Made for Dancin'** by Leif Garrett was the biggest hit for this teen idol singer and actor. In 1979 he started dating actress Nicollette Sheridan when she 15 years old and 2 days before his 18th birthday, he crashed his car while drunk. It left his best friend a paraplegic. Leif Garrett has had many problems with drugs and arrests since his teen idol years.

81. **Good Girls Don't** by The Knack was the follow up to the mega hit 'My Sharona' and both songs were included on their debut album 'Get the Knack' produced by Mike Chapman. Lead singer Doug Fieger wrote this suggestive hit from their debut album which was recorded in 2 weeks at a cost of under $20,000. It went on to sell several million copies worldwide.

82. **Heaven Must Have Sent You** by Bonnie Pointer was her biggest solo hit after leaving the Pointer Sisters the year before. Sister June Pointer also had left the sister act by 1978. June died of lung cancer in 2006 at the age of 52. 'Heaven Must Have Sent You' was a remake of a minor hit by the Detroit R & B group The Elgins in 1966.

83. **Love Takes Time** by Orleans was the final hit for this rock group from New York City led by John Hall, who left the group in 1977.Group members the Hoppen Brothers, Lance and Lawrence continued with Wells Kelly and signed a new deal contract with Infinity records.

84. **Got to Be Real** by Cheryl Lynn was co written with David Foster and Toto keyboardist David Paich. She was discovered performing on 'The Gong Show', hosted by Chuck Barris. Although this was her only hit, she continued to perform on stage and as a session singer for others.

85. **Disco Nights (Rock a Freak)** by G.Q. was a number one hit on the R & B charts for this 2 hit wonder soul group from the Bronx. This disco hit evolved by the band when they were known as the Melody Makers and an earlier version of the song was titled 'Soul on the Side' in the early 70's, all with the original writer and band member Emmanuel Rahiem LeBlanc.

86. **Deeper than the Night** by Olivia Newton-John was from her album 'Totally Hot' which also described her new sexier image which changed from her girl-next-door look, to her spandex-clad appearance. This song was co written by Tom Snow who composed hits which included 'Let's Hear It for the Boy', 'He's so Shy' and others.

87. **Cruel to Be Kind** by Nick Lowe was the biggest hit on the pop charts for this British singer/songwriter who later produced albums including Elvis Costello, Graham Parker and others. He wrote this song with former Brinsley Schwarz member Ian Gomm. When 'Cruel to Be Kind' was riding up the charts, Nick Lowe married Carlene Carter, daughter of country singer Carl Smith and June Carter Cash and stepdaughter of Johnny Cash.

88. **I Just Fall in Love Again** by Anne Murray was originally recorded by the

Carpenters on an album in 1977. Anne Murray brought this first hit from her album 'New Kind Of Feeling' to number one on both the country and easy listening charts.

89. Dirty White Boy by Foreigner was the first and biggest single from their 'Head Games' album. British guitarist/songwriter founding member Mick Jones recruited American singer/guitarist Lou Gramm for the band in 1976. Lou Gramm was born Louis Grammatico.

90. Broken Hearted Me by Anne Murray was one of 3 major hits she charted in 1979, all of which went to number one on the country charts. At the time she recorded this song; Anne Murray was pregnant and had chronic sinusitis, making the session quite difficult for her. This song was written by Randy Goodrum, who also gave her the ballad 'You Needed Me'.

91. Rock 'N Roll Fantasy by Bad Company was written by lead singer Paul Rodgers, who was previously the front man for the group Free on 'All Right Now'. This million selling single was from the album 'Desolation Angels' and is considered to be among their very best.

92. Ain't No Stoppin' Us Now by McFadden & Whitehead was written on the spot as they were recording at Philadelphia International studios where the O'Jays recorded their song 'Backstabbers' 7 years earlier. This song was played at the 2008 Democratic National convention on the night Illinois senator Barack Obama accepted the Democratic Party nomination for President of the United States.

93. New York Groove by Ace Frehley was the most popular solo hit for the lead guitarist of 70's super group Kiss. He was 'the spaceman' in this costumed, theatrical rock group. This hit was written by Russ Ballard, formerly of the group 'Argent' and songwriter of hits which include 'Liar' for 3 Dog Night and 'You Can Do Magic' by America.

94. Shake It by Ian Matthews was formerly with Matthews Southern Comfort, best known for their mellow hit version of 'Woodstock' in 1971. His real name is Ian McDonald, not to be confused with the musician connected with King Crimson and Foreigner. Ian Matthews was also a member of the group 'Fairport Convention' before going solo.

95. Suspicions by Eddie Rabbit was his follow up to his first pop hit, 'Every Which Way But Loose' and was the first and only hit from his 'Loveline' album. He started the 70's decade with Elvis Presley having a hit with his composition, 'Kentucky Rain'. Eddie Rabbit died of lung cancer at the age of 56 back in 1998.

96. We've Got Tonite by Bob Seger was the 3rd consecutive hit from the 'Stranger in Town' album. This piano-based ballad written by Bob Seger was later revived by Kenny Rogers and Sheena Easton in 1983 when it charted even higher than the original.

97. Everytime I Think of You by The Babys featured John Waite on lead vocals. 5 years later he had a number one solo hit with 'Missing You' and 10 years later he became lead singer of the band 'Bad English'. 'Everytime I See Your Face' was the biggest hit from their 3rd album 'Head First'.

98. Bad Case of Loving You by Robert Palmer is also known to many as

'Doctor, Doctor' and was a feel good, high energy hit from the album 'No Secrets' which he recorded in the Bahamas. This top 20 hit was written by Moon Martin, who had his only hit the same year with 'Rolene'.

99.   Soul Man by The Blues Brothers was a remake of the classic Sam & Dave hit from 1967 by 2 of the most popular characters from Saturday Night Live, Jim Belushi and Dan Ackroyd. This hit was included in their 'Briefcase Full Of Blues' album which was followed by The Blues Brothers movie which featured appearances by many notable music artists including Ray Charles, Aretha Franklin, Cab Callaway, James Brown and many others.

100.   Let's Go by The Cars was written by Ric Ocasek with bassist Benjamn Orr on lead vocals. This was the first single from their popular 'Candy-O' album which featured a sexy cover painted by artist Alberto Vargas who was known for his provocative pinups in Playboy and Esquire magazines from the 1940's and 60's.

101.   Minute by Minute by The Doobie Brothers was the title song of their 8th studio album and was the follow up single to their number one hit 'What a Fool Believes'. This Doobie Brothers album was the last to feature Jeff 'Skunk' Baxter, who joined the band in 1974 after leaving Steely Dan.

102.   Big Shot by Billy Joel was the 2nd single from the very successful '52nd Street' album which included accompaniment by Chicago's Peter Cetera and Donnie Dacus, as well as musician Dave Crusin. In 2003, Rolling Stone magazine ranked '52nd Street' as number 352 on their list of 500 Greatest Albums of all Time.

103.   No Tell Lover by Chicago featured Peter Cetera and Donnie Dacus on lead vocals. Donnie Dacus replaced Terry Kath, who died suddenly in 1978, but he was replaced later in 1979 by Bill Champlin. This was from the 'Hot Streets' album and was the only Chicago album of new material that did not have a numbered title.

104.   Head Games by Foreigner was the title cut from the album which featured a cover which showed a worried young woman in a men's washroom. This hit was popular in the year bass guitarist Rick Wills was replaced by Ed Gagliardi. This hit was written by group members Lou Gramm and Mick Jones.

105.   Goodbye Stranger by Supertramp was the 2nd of 3 major hits from their most successful album, 'Breakfast in America'. This hit features Rick Davies on lead vocals and electric piano while guitarist Roger Hodgson sings background vocals. Davies and Hodgson were the nucleus of this British rock quintet and wrote most of their hits together.

106.   Driver's Seat by Sniff 'n' the Tears was the only hit for this British rock group led by lead singer/songwriter/guitarist Paul Roberts. According to Paul Roberts, 'Driver's Seat' isn't about driving, but rather 'fragmented, conflicting thoughts and emotions that might follow the break-up of a relationship'. He has also been known as an accomplished artist for many years as a painter.

107.   Come to Me by France Joli was the only major hit from this 16 year old singer from Montreal, Quebec. In her big year in the spotlight she appeared on the 'Midnight Special', 'The Merv Griffin Show, 'The Mike Douglas Show' and a guest shot on one of Bob Hope's Specials. This disco hit was written and produced by fellow Quebec recording artist Tony Green.

108.   I Can't Stand It No More by Peter Frampton was the former Humble Pie guitarist's final top 40 hit. This was the only hit single from his 6ᵗʰ studio album 'Where Should I Be' which featured special guests Steve Cropper, Donald 'Duck' Dunn and the Tower Of Power horn section. This was Frampton's first release since his near fatal car accident in June of 1978 in the Bahamas, which left him with broken bones, a concussion and muscle damage.

109.   Old Time Rock and Roll by Bob Seger was the 4ᵗʰ single from the 'Stranger in Town' album and although it barely made the top 30 on the charts at the time, it became a classic for the Detroit rocker. This nostalgic look back at a previous generation was also identified with being featured in the Tom Cruise movie 'Risky Business'.

110.   Livin' It Up (Friday Night) by Bell and James was popular the same year they wrote and produced 'Mama Can't Buy Me Love' by Elton John. Leroy Bell was the nephew of songwriter/producer Thom Bell, who got them signed to Philadelphia's Gamble and Huff as songwriters. 1979 was the best year for this R & B duo from Florida who had only one notable hit.

111.   Born to Be Alive by Patrick Hernandez was the only hit for this singer/songwriter from Paris. An unknown Madonna was a back up singer for Hernandez for a brief time and was once quoted as saying to him 'Success is yours today, but it will be mine tomorrow'. This hit sold millions worldwide and was a staple at the discos.

112.   Half The Way by Crystal Gayle was the 3ʳᵈ and final crossover hit solo hit for this long haired country singer who was born Brenda Gail Webb. Her next and only other pop hit was her 1982 duet 'You and I' with Eddie Rabbit.

113.   Dance the Night Away by Van Halen was the first major hit for this California hard rock band which featured David Lee Roth on lead vocals. This song was written at the recording sessions for the album 'Van Halen 2'. Guitarist Eddie Van Halen married actress Valerie Bertinelli in 1981.

114.   Lovin', Touchin', Squeezin' by Journey was the debut hit for this San Francisco rock band. Drummer Aynsley Dunbar departed from the band in 1979 due to the direction lead singer Steve Perry was taking the band. He was replaced by Steve Smith on drums. Band members Gregg Rolie and Neal Schon came to the group from Santana.

115.   Blow Away by George Harrison was written on a rainy day and became the title song of his 1979 album. He recorded this album in 1978, a happy time for Harrison because he married Olivia and fathered his son Dhani. His next hit would be in 1981 with 'All Those Years Ago', a tribute to John Lennon after he was murdered in December of 1980.

116.   The Gambler by Kenny Rogers was the title song from this very popular album which featured guest singers and musicians The Jordanaires, Pete Drake on steel guitar, Tony Joe White on guitar, Bill Medley on background vocals to name just a few. This single was one of 5 consecutive number one hits on the country charts and later became the story of a made-for-TV movie starring Kenny Rogers.

336

117. Blue Morning, Blue Day by Foreigner was the 3rd single from the 'Double Vision' album and was written by Lou Gramm and Mick Jones. Additional background vocals on this album were supplied by Ian Lloyd, the voice of the Stories on the number one hit 'Brother Louie'.

118. If You Remember Me by Chris Thompson was popular when he was a prominent member of the group 'Night' just after leaving Manfred Mann's Earth Band, where he sang lead on their biggest hit 'Blinded by the Night'. This love ballad was the theme from the movie 'The Champ' starring Jon Voight, Faye Dunaway and Ricky Schroder.

119. Crazy Love by Poco was the biggest hit from their most successful album, 'Legend' which featured a horse drawing on the cover created by a then-unknown Phil Hartman, who later became famous as an actor/comedian. Rusty Young wrote and sang lead with Paul Cotton on this soft rock hit.

120. Hold On by Ian Gomm was the only solo hit for the former member of the British band Brinsley Schwarz. This distinctive sounding hit was popular the year he co wrote former fellow band mate Nick Lowe's biggest hit 'Cruel to Be Kind'.

121. Spooky by Atlanta Rhythm Section was a remake of the Classics 4 hit from 1967, which was interesting since most of the members of this band evolved from that 60's group. It's also interesting to note that 2 hits from the 60's by the Classics 4 were revived in 1979 with 'Stormy' by Santana being the other.

122. Renegade by Styx was a story song written by Tommy Shaw from the album 'Pieces Of Eight'. The band broke up when Dennis DeYoung and Tommy Shaw went solo in 1984, but resurfaced years later with Canadian Larry Gowan replacing Dennis DeYoung as keyboardist and vocalist.

123. Days Gone Down by Gerry Rafferty was the first single from his 'Night Owl' album and another song easily identified as a hit from the Scottish singer with a unique voice. Although he has kept a low profile since his late 70's days in the spotlight, he contributed to the 1983 Scottish film 'Local Hero'. In 2009, 30 years after this hit, he released an album titled 'Life Goes On'. His life ended in 2011.

124. Hot Summer Nights by Night was written by Walter Egan who recorded the song in 1978. This group featured lead singers Stevie Lange and Chris Thompson, who had a solo hit in 1979 with 'If You Remember Me'.1979 was the only year on the pop charts for this band from Los Angeles, California. They broke up in 1983.

125. Different Worlds by Maureen McGovern was the theme from the TV show 'Angie' starring Donna Pescow. This TV hit was written by Norman Gimbel and Charles Fox, who also wrote the themes for 'Happy Days' and 'Laverne & Shirley' as well as major hits like 'Killing Me Softly With His Song' and 'I Got A Name'. Maureen McGovern had several movie theme songs including 'The Morning After' from The Poseidon Adventure' and 'Can You Read My Mind' from 'Superman'.

126. Dancin' Shoes by Nigel Olsson was the most successful solo hit for the former drummer for Elton John. He's also known for his stage appearance of wearing headphones and gloves while drumming.

127. Does Your Mama Know by Abba was their only hit to feature Bjorn Ulvaeus on lead vocals. Abba's hits normally featured Agnetha and Anni-Frid on lead vocals. This hit from the album 'Voulez-Vous' was popular the year that their fans were shocked to hear that Agnetha and Ulvaeus were getting divorced.

128. Love Ballad by George Benson was the only hit single from his double album 'Livin' inside Your Love'. Jazzman George remade some soul classics on this album including 'Love Is a Hurtin' Thing', 'Soulful Strut', and 'Hey Girl'. He would follow this hit with 1980's 'Give Me the Night' produced by Quincy Jones.

129. Precious Love by Bob Welch was the final hit for the former Fleetwood Mac member who also scored with the late 70's solo hits 'Sentimental Lady' and 'Ebony Eyes'. Like his album 'French Kiss', this album also featured his former band members Christine McVie, Mick Fleetwood and Stevie Nicks.

130. I Want You Tonight by Pablo Cruise was the only single released from their album 'Part of the Game'. Lead singer and bassist Dave Jenkins co wrote all of the songs on the album which leaned towards a more disco sound to take full advantage of its popularity.

131. Do It or Die by The Atlanta Rhythm Section reached the top 20 like the single that followed, 'Spooky', both of which were featured on the album 'Underdog'. This Southern rock band also released a live album in 1979 which became the final year for their hits on the Polydor label.

132. The Boss by Diana Ross was the title song of the album which reunited the former Supreme with Ashford and Simpson who wrote her first 2 solo hits, 'Reach Out and Touch (Somebody's Hand)' and 'Ain't No Mountain High Enough', her first solo number one. The album was also produced by Nickolas Ashford and Valerie Simpson, who also provided backup vocals.

133. I Got My Mind made Up by Instant Funk was produced by 60's singer Bunny Sigler, who got the band signed to a recording contract on the 'Salsoul' label. This million selling number one hit on the R & B charts was their only hit, although they were the backup band on many other recordings by others including Lou Rawls, O'Jays and Evelyn 'Champagne' King.

134. The Night Won't Last Forever by Michael Johnson was the 3rd and final late 70's hit for this folk singer/songwriter best known for his hit 'Bluer than Blue'. Over a dozen albums were released after 'Dialogue', which included 'The Night Won't Last Forever', but none could repeat his late 70's success. In 2007 he underwent successful quadruple bypass heart surgery.

135. Getting Closer by Paul McCartney & Wings was a rock song written and co-produced by the former Beatle and was the 2nd hit from the 'Back to the Egg' album. This was McCartney's first album for Columbia records.

136. Heart of the Night by Poco was the follow up to 'Crazy Love' and was also featured on their popular 'Legend' album. Former members of this soft rock 70's group included Richie Furay, Jim Messina, Randy Meisner and Timothy B. Schmidt. This hit was written by Paul Cotton who shared lead vocals with group founder Rusty Young.

137. I Know a Heartache When I See One by Jennifer Warnes was also popular on the country charts. It was a hit the same year that she recorded the song 'It Goes Like It Goes' from the movie 'Norma Rae', starring Sally Field, which went on to win the Academy Award for Best Original Song in 1979.

138. Forever in Blue Jeans by Neil Diamond was taken from his album 'You Don't Bring Me Flowers' from 1978. This mid temp hit was written by Neil Diamond and his guitarist Richard Bennett and produced by Bob Gaudio, former Four Seasons' keyboardist and songwriter.

139. Is She Really Going out with Him by Joe Jackson was the first hit for this new wave British singer/songwriter/pianist. This hit was from his debut album 'Look Sharp' and was later used in the 1998 romantic comedy movie 'There's Something About Mary' starring Ben Stiller and Cameron Diaz.

140. I Do Love You by G.Q. was the follow up to their only other hit 'Disco Nights' from earlier in the same year. This soul ballad was a remake of the Billy Stewart song which he charted back in 1965.

141. Get Used to It by Roger Voudouris was a one hit wonder singer/songwriter/guitarist from Sacramento, California. This catchy sounding hit was from his album 'Radio Dream', which he lived exclusively in 1979 in North America. He had a cult following in Japan and was regarded as a sex symbol in Australia. He died at the age of 49 in 2003 as a result of liver disease.

142. Get It Right Next Time by Gerry Rafferty was the 2nd single from his 'Night Owl' album and the final hit in North America to reach the top 40 for the former voice of 'Stuck In The Middle With You' as a member of Stealer's Wheel.

143. Don't Hold Back by Chanson was a one hit wonder disco studio band featuring James Jamerson Jr. on lead vocals. He was the son of bass player James Jamerson Sr who played on numerous Motown hits as a member of what became known as the Funk Brothers. He died in 1983 at the age of 47.

144. Morning Dance by Spyro Gyra was the brainchild of Jay Beckenstein, writer/co-producer and saxophone player for this Jazz/pop band from Buffalo, New York. Although this was their only notable pop hit, they had great success in the field of jazz releasing over 25 albums and actively touring throughout the years since this hit was popular.

145. One Way or Another by Blondie was the 2nd hit from the album 'Parallel Lines'. Before becoming a music star, lead singer Deborah Harry was a Playboy Bunny waitress in the late 60's. The catchy and upbeat 'One Way or Another', written by Deborah Harry and bassist Nigel Harrison, has been used in many movies through the years including 'Coyote Ugly' and 'Donnie Brasco'.

146. Hot Number by Foxy was the follow up to their only other hit 'Get Off' from 1978 by this Miami-based Latino/disco group. This band was managed by Brian Avnet, who later became singer Josh Groban's manager.

147. Honesty by Billy Joel was the 3rd single released from his Grammy Award winning album of the year '52nd Street'. 3 years later, it became the first compact disc released by Sony. 'Honesty' was a ballad written by Billy Joel and produced by Phil Ramone.

148. What Cha Gonna Do with My Lovin' by Stephanie Mills was the first hit for this singer/actress from Brooklyn, New York. 4 years before this hit, she starred as Dorothy in the movie 'The Wiz', alongside Michael Jackson, whom she became romantically involved with for a short time.

149. I Don't Know If Its Right by Evelyn 'Champagne' King was still a teenager when this follow up to her biggest hit 'Shame' sold a million records. This Bronx, New York born singer came from a family with a showbiz background; her father sang backup for groups at New York's Apollo Theater and her uncle played the part of 'Sportin' Life' in 'Porgy & Bess'.

150. Ain't Love A Bitch by Rod Stewart, co written with guitarist Gary Grainger, was the follow up to his multi million seller 'Do Ya Think I'm Sexy', also from the 'Blondes Have More Fun' album. It was also available as a 'picture disc' with the entire front cover embedded on the vinyl record.

151. Maybe I'm a Fool by Eddie Money was the only top 40 hit from his second album 'Life for the Taking'. After a 3 year dry spell, this former New York City cop resurfaced on the charts with half a dozen more hits in the 80's. Eddie Money is married with 5 children.

152. Where Were You When I Was Falling in Love by Lobo was the first top 40 hit in 4 years and final hit of the 70's-exclusive career for the singer born Roland Kent Lavoie. Although he wrote most of his hits, this one was written by a trio of staff songwriters for a company in Nashville and produced by Bob Montgomery.

153. People of the South Wind by Kansas refers to the meaning of the Siouan word 'Kansa' the Indian tribe for which the state of Kansas was named. This was from their 6th studio album, 'Monolith'.

154. Please Don't Leave by Lauren Wood featured Michael McDonald on harmony vocals on this one hit wonder singer/songwriter/keyboardist's hit from late 1979. Her only other notable release, 'Fallin'' from the 'Pretty Woman' soundtrack, failed to reach the top 40.

155. Shadows in the Moonlight by Anne Murray was the 2nd hit from her 13th studio album 'New Kind Of Feeling' produced by Jim Ed Norman. Canada's sweetheart was having one pop/country crossover hit after another during this time period. This mid tempo hit featured a guitar solo by Bob Mann and a saxophone segment near the end by Don Thompson.

156. Gotta Serve Somebody by Bob Dylan was a gospel rock song that won this legendary singer/songwriter a Grammy Award for Best Rock Vocal Performance. This became Bob Dylan's final hit to reach top 40 on the pop charts. It was produced by Jerry Wexler and Barry Beckett and recorded at the famed Muscle Shoals Studios in Alabama.

157. Bicycle Race/Fat Bottomed Girls by Queen was a double-sided hit single from their 'Jazz' album, which was their first to be recorded outside of the U.K. for tax purposes. It was recorded at Mountain Studios, Montreux in Switzerland. 'Bicycle Race' was written by lead singer Freddie Mercury and 'Fat Bottomed Girls' was written by guitarist Brian May.

158. Baby I'm Burnin' by Dolly Parton was a disco hit for this superstar country artist. Dolly Parton wrote this hit from the 'Heartbreaker' album which featured a number one country hit 'I Really Got the Feeling' as its 'B' side.

159. Rainbow Connection by Kermit (Jim Henson) was from the Muppet Movie which included cameos by many notable stars including Bob Hope, Mel Brooks, Elliot Gould, Edgar Bergen, Dom Deluise and many others. This hit featuring Jim Henson as 'Kermit the Frog' and was co-written by Paul Williams.

160. Take Me to the River by Talking Heads was the first top 40 hit for this New York City based new wave quartet which featured David Byrne on lead vocals. This song was a remake of a song Al Green co wrote and recorded in 1974.

161. Dependin' On You by The Doobie Brothers was the 3rd single from the 'Minute By Minute' album featuring Michael McDonald on lead vocals. Nicolette Larson sang back up on 'Dependin' On You' which was written by Michael McDonald and Patrick Simmons.

162. Superman by Herbie Mann was the 2nd biggest pop music hit, following 1975's 'HiJack' for this legendary jazz flutist born Herbert Jay Soloman. He played his first gig at the catskills when he was 15 years old and performed his last at the New Orleans Jazz Festival at the age of 73 in 2003. He died less than 2 months later after a long battle with prostate cancer.

163. Home and Dry by Gerry Rafferty was the first of 3 hits for this Scottish singer/songwriter/guitarist in 1979 and the 3rd and final single from his 'City' To City' album which included his signature hit 'Baker Street'. He accomplished 5 top 30 hits from 1978 to 1979, but absolutely none after that.

164. Up on the Roof by James Taylor was a remake of the Drifter hits from 1963 written by Carole King and Gerry Goffin. When this was new in the spring of 1979, James Taylor performed it when he was the musical guest on Saturday Night Live. This was from his 10th album, 'Flag' and featured his wife Carly Simon on backing vocals.

165. Instant Replay by Dan Hartman was the first solo hit for the former member of the Edgar Winter Group who also wrote their hit 'Free Ride'. He died of a brain tumor in 1994 at the age of 43.

166. Highway Song by Blackfoot was the first and most notable hit for this band from Jacksonville, Florida. This group featured 2 former members of Lynyrd Skynyrd, including Blackfoot lead singer Rick Medlocke. This rock band toured heavily in 1979 and opened for the Who that year.

167. Damned If I Do by Alan Parsons Project was the first top 30 hit by this British progressive rock band which featured Eric Woolfson on lead vocals. The 2 founding members met at Abbey Road where Alan Parsons was a recording engineer on the Beatles 'Abbey Road' and 'Let It Be' albums. Eric Woolfson died of cancer in December of 2009 at age 64.

168. Dreaming by Blondie was the 3rd consecutive hit from their debut year on the pop charts. Lead singer Debbie Harry was the lead voice of this New York City techno-pop sextet formed in 1975. This was the only hit single from the 'Eat to the

Beat' album and was written by Deborah Harry and her partner Chris Stein. Ellie Greenwich supplied back up vocals on this moderate hit.

169. Roxanne by The Police was a song written about a prostitute in Paris and was the very first hit for this British trio. This was from their debut album 'Outlandos D'Amour', which included 10 songs all written or co-written by lead singer Sting, whose real name is Gordon Sumner.

170. Song on the Radio by Al Stewart was the 4th and final hit of the late 70's produced by Alan Parsons. This singer/songwriter/guitarist born in Glasgow, Scotland moved to Los Angeles, California in the late 70's.

More Hits of 1979

Weekend by Wet Willie was the 3rd and final hit for this 70's band from Mobile, Alabama led by brothers Jack and Jimmy Hall. This hit was from the album 'Which One Is Willie?' which was inspired by a question asked about this Southern Rock band.

Arrow Through Me by Wings was a softer R & B influenced hit which was something different from the former Beatle and was the 3rd single from the 'Back To The Egg' album. Some of this album was recorded at McCartney's farm in Scotland.

So Good, So Right by Brenda Russell was the first notable hit for this singer from Brooklyn, New York who moved to Canada when she was 12 years old. She wrote and did session work for many notable singers and in 1988 had a major hit with a song she co-wrote, Piano in the Dark'. In 2005, she wrote the score of the Oprah Winfrey produced Broadway show 'The Color Purple'.

Rolene by Moon Martin was the only top 40 hit for this singer/songwriter/guitarist from Oklahoma, although he wrote Robert Palmer's 1979 hit 'Bad Case of Loving You'. He got the nickname 'Moon' because so many of his songs had that word in the lyrics.

(If Loving You Is Wrong) I Don't Want to Be Right by Barbara Mandrell was a remake of the 1972 soul hit by Luther Ingram. This was this country singer's biggest hit on the pop charts.

Every Which Way but Loose by Eddie Rabbit was the very first hit on the pop charts for this country singer/songwriter/guitarist from Brooklyn, New York, raised in East Orange, New Jersey.
This was the title song of the movie which starred Clint Eastwood with an orangutan.

Stormy by Santana was a remake of the Classics 4 hit from 1968 and was from the 'Inner Secrets' album. This was the beginning of a new sound for Santana, moving away from the fusion, Latin jazz and blues sound to a more rock-oriented presentation.

Bustin' Loose by Chuck Brown & the Soul Searchers originated back in 1976 and after all the great reaction they got when they performed it at clubs, they decided to record it. This funky rhythm hit was a 1 month number 1 hit on the R &

B charts and a moderate hit on the pop charts.

Ain't That a Shame by Cheap Trick was a remake of the Fats Domino classic from the 50's. This was recorded 'live' at the Budokan concert in Japan and was the follow up to their million seller 'I Want You To Want Me'.

Girl of My Dreams by Bram Tchaikovsky was a rock quartet from Lincolnshire, England led by Peter Bramall. The sound of this song is reminiscent of Springsteen's 'Born to Run' with a touch of Moody Blues. This was Bram Tchaikovsky's only top 40 hit.

Video Killed The Radio Star by The Buggles was the very first video played on MTV when it was launched on August 1 1981. This British duo consisted of Geoff Downs and Trevor Horn who both joined the group 'Yes' the following year in 1980.

Highway To Hell by AC/DC was the debut hit for this hard rock Australian band featuring lead singer Bon Scott and brothers Angus and Malcolm Young. The album of the same name was produced by Robert 'Mutt' Lange and was the last to feature Bon Scott, who died the following year at age 33 from an over-consumption of alcohol.

Message in a Bottle by the Police was one of the breakthrough hits for this British rock and new wave trio which featured Sting on lead vocals. This was their first number one hit in the U.K. and was very popular hit in Canada as well. This was from their album 'Regatta De Blanc' which was self-produced by the 3 band members which included Stewart Copeland and Andy Summers.

Four Strong Winds by Neil Young was a remake of the classic 60's Canadian song written by Ian Tyson and recorded by Ian and Sylvia. This hit was from the album 'Comes a Time' which was recorded in 5 different studios over a two year period. His friend Nicolette Larson provided harmony vocals and also had a hit with the song 'Lotta Love' which was included on this album.

Kiss in the Dark by Pink Lady was the only hit for this female disco duo from Japan who hosted their own TV variety show in the summer of 1979. They learned how to sing this disco song phonetically in English.

Hold on by Triumph was the first hit in the United States for this Hard rock trio from Toronto. The band consisted of Rik Emmet on lead vocals and guitar, Gil Moore on drums and Mike Levine on keyboards and bass. This hit was from their 3rd album, 'Just a Game'.

1.	The Long Run	The Eagles
2.	In Through the Out Door	Led Zeppelin
3.	Spirits Having Flown	Bee Gees
4.	Breakfast in America	Supertramp
5.	Bad Girls	Donna Summer
6.	Get the Knack	The Knack
7.	Minute By Minute	Doobie Brothers
8.	Blondes Have More Fun	Rod Stewart
9.	Barbra Streisand's Greatest Hits Vol. 2	Barbra Streisand
10.	Briefcase Full Of Blues	Blues Brothers
11.	You Don't Bring Me Flowers	Neil Diamond
12.	2 Hot	Peaches and Herb
13.	Dire Straits	Dire Straits
14.	Candy-O	Cars
15.	Cruisin'	Village People
16.	Desolation Angels	Bad Company
17.	Midnight Magic	Commodores

TOP 17 COUNTRY HITS OF 1979

#	Song	Artist
1.	Amanda	Waylon Jennings
2.	Every Which Way But Loose	Eddie Rabbit
3.	If I Said You Had A Beautiful Body…	Bellamy Brothers
4.	I Just Fall In Love Again	Anne Murray
5.	Happy Birthday Darlin'	Conway Twitty
6.	Golden Tears	Dave and Sugar
7.	She Believes In Me	Kenny Rogers
8.	Last Cheater's Waltz	T. G. Sheppard
9.	You Decorated My Life	Kenny Rogers
10.	Come With Me	Waylon Jennings
11.	All the Gold in California	Larry Gatlin & Gatlin Brothers
12.	You're The Only One	Dolly Parton
13.	Why Have You Left the One You Left For Me	Crystal Gayle
14.	The Devil Went Down To Georgia	Charlie Daniels Band
15.	Shadows in the Moonlight	Anne Murray
16.	Suspicions	Eddie Rabbit
17.	(If Loving You Is Wrong) I Don't Want…Right	Barbara Mandrell

TOP 17 DISCO HITS OF 1979

1.	Bad Girls	Donna Summer
2.	I Will Survive	Gloria Gaynor
3.	Hot Stuff	Donna Summer
4.	Ring My Bell	Anita Bell
5.	Don't Stop It 'Til You Get Enough	Michael Jackson
6.	Good Times	Chic
7.	Knock On Wood	Amii Stewart
8.	Y. M. C. A.	Village People
9.	We Are Family	Sister Sledge
10.	In The Navy	Village People
11.	Shake Your Groove Thing	Peaches and Herb
12.	Makin' It	David Naughton
13.	Boogie Wonderland	Earth, Wind and Fire
14.	I Want Your Love	Chic
15.	He's The Greatest Dancer	Sister Sledge
16.	Got To Be Real	Cheryl Lynn
17.	Disco Nights	G. Q.

TOP 17 ONE HIT WONDERS OF 1979

1.	M	Pop Muzik
2.	Anita Ward	Ring My Bell
3.	Amii Stewart	Knock On Wood
4.	Randy Van Warmer	Just When I Needed You Most
5.	David Naughton	Makin' It
6.	Bobby Caldwell	What You Won't Do For Love
7.	Cheryl Lynn	Got To Be Real
8.	Ian Matthews	Shake It
9.	Sniff 'n The Tears	Driver's Seat
10.	Patrick Hernandez	Born To Be Alive
11.	Ian Gomm	Hold On
12.	Instant Funk	I Got My Mind Made Up
13.	Roger Voudouris	Get Used To It
14.	Lauren Wood	Please Don't Leave
15.	Bram Tchaikovsky	Girl of My Dreams
16.	Buggles	Video Killed the Radio Star
17.	Pink Lady	Kiss in the Dark

TOP 17 ROCK/HARD ROCK HITS OF 1979

1.	My Sharona	The Knack
2.	Heartache Tonight	The Eagles
3.	Sultans of Swing	Dire Straits
4.	Don't Bring Me Down	E. L. O.
5.	I Want You to Want Me	Cheap Trick
6.	Highway to Hell	AC/DC
7.	Shine A Little Love	E. L. O.
8.	Take the Long Way Home	Supertramp
9.	Good Girls Don't	The Knack
10.	Dirty White Boy	Foreigner
11.	Rock And Roll Fantasy	Bad Company
12.	Bad Case of Loving You	Robert Palmer
13.	Let's Go	Cars
14.	Head Games	Foreigner
15.	Driver's Seat	Sniff 'N the Tears
16.	Lovin, Touchin' and Squeezin'	Journey
17.	Bicycle Race/Fat Bottomed Girls	Queen

1. Video Killed the Radio Star — Buggles
2. Born To Be Alive — Patrick Hernandez
3. Blow Away — George Harrison
4. If You Remember Me — Chris Thompson
5. Get It Right Next Time — Gerry Rafferty
6. Driver's Seat — Sniff 'N the Tears
7. Where Were You When I Was Falling In Love — Lobo
8. Weekend — Wet Willie
9. Up On the Roof — James Taylor
10. Hold On — Ian Gomm
11. Precious Love — Bob Welch
12. No Tell Lover — Chicago
13. Get Used To It — Roger Voudouris
14. Cruel To Be Kind — Nick Lowe
15. Love Is the Answer — England Dan & John Ford Coley
16. Every One's A Winner — Hot Chocolate
17. Promises — Eric Clapton

STAIRWAY TO HEAVEN

"Stairway to Heaven" by Led Zeppelin is one of the most well-known and popular rock songs never to have been released as a single. It is often rated among the greatest songs of all time. It was included in the untitled 4th studio album usually referred to as Led Zeppelin 4, released in late 1971, and peaking in popularity in 1972. This song, which runs almost 8 minutes, was written by guitarist Jimmy Page and lead vocalist Robert Plant in an old English mansion without electricity, in front of a roaring log fireplace. Jimmy Page was strumming the chords of his guitar while Robert Plant had pencil in hand writing 90% of the lyrics on the spot. The song is composed of several sections, starting as a slow acoustic-based folk song with a 6 string guitar and recorders, followed by a middle section which has electric instrumentation followed near the end by a faster, hard rock final section. Bass player John Paul Jones opted for playing wooden recorders, flute and keyboards, while John Bonham's drums did not kick in until halfway through this masterpiece.

The song is also known for its alleged hidden messages when played backwards. One example of such hidden messages that was prominently cited, apparently occurs during the middle section of the song ("If there's a bustle in your hedgerow, don't be alarmed now...") when played backwards, was purported to contain the Satanic references "Here's to my sweet Satan" and "I sing because I live with Satan."

The only thing known for sure is that Led Zeppelin's 'Stairway to Heaven' is a timeless classic and is one of the greatest musical gems of the 70's.

About the author

Ted Yates is an on air radio broadcaster with over 35 years behind the microphone. Most of his radio years have also been spent programming the music and writing radio features and specials, as well as creating music countdowns. Ted is an expert on the hits of the 60's and 70's and his love for the decade began when they were new hits during his childhood years.

Ted has interviewed over a hundred well known music celebrities of the 60's and 70's including Tommy James, Neil Sedaka, Paul Anka, Bobby Vinton, Peter Noone of Herman's Hermits, Andy Kim, Mark Volman of The Turtles, Bruce Johnston of The Beach Boys, Del Shannon, Johnny Mathis, Gary Lewis, Bobby Vee, Martha Reeves and many more!

It was during the 70's, in 1973 that he began his career in radio, broadcasting at a station just outside of Toronto doing the 7 to midnight show 6 nights a week. During the 70's he worked at radio stations in Southern Ontario in Ajax, Orillia, Peterborough and St. Catharines. He is currently a radio broadcaster at Oldies 1150 CKOC in Hamilton, Ontario, Canada.

Ted's hobby is music, music and music and now he wants to once again share his vast knowledge with you in one incredible book about the hits of the 70's and the fascinating facts you'll find both interesting and sometimes surprising!

Ted is also the author of timeless 2010 book 'The 60's The Hits and The Trivia', also available at fine bookstores and well known websites everywhere.

Photo courtesy Ron Vansomeren

The 60s - The Hits and the Trivia
Ted Yates

The 60's - The Hits and Trivia is a quick, concise and factual trip back to a fun and exciting decade and is a 'must' for every music lover of the 60's. Rediscover the hits you may have forgotten that you want to remember again. You'll find out little known and sometimes surprising facts about almost 2000 hits of the 60's. it's your one-stop 60's music book.

The accompanying CD contains interviews by Ted Yates with some of the biggest names of that decade, including Del Shannon, Bo Diddley, Paul Anka, Peter Noone (Herman's Hermits), Otis Williams (the only surviving member of the Temptations), Burton Cummings of the Guess Who, Denny Doherty of the Mamas and the Papas, Bobby Vee and Vinton, and more.

ISBN 978-1-926592-18-3
At all good book stores and on-line!